Remembering refugees

MANCHESTER
1824

Manchester University Press

In memory of Mark Reece

Remembering refugees

Then and now

Tony Kushner

Manchester University Press
Manchester and New York
distributed exclusively in the USA by Palgrave

The right of Tony Kushner to be identified as the author of this work has been asserted by him in accordance with the Copyright, Designs and Patents Act 1988.

Published by Manchester University Press
Oxford Road, Manchester M13 9NR, UK
and Room 400, 175 Fifth Avenue, New York, NY 10010, USA
www.manchesteruniversitypress.co.uk

Distributed exclusively in the USA by
Palgrave, 175 Fifth Avenue, New York,
NY 10010, USA

Distributed exclusively in Canada by
UBC Press, University of British Columbia, 2029 West Mall,
Vancouver, BC, Canada V6T 1Z2

British Library Cataloguing-in-Publication Data
A catalogue record for this book is available from the British Library

Library of Congress Cataloging-in-Publication Data applied for

ISBN   0 7190 6882 7   *hardback*
EAN   9780 7190 6882 9

ISBN   0 7190 6883 5   *paperback*
EAN   9780 7190 6883 6

First published 2006

15 14 13 12 11 10 09 08 07 06   10 9 8 7 6 5 4 3 2 1

Edited and typeset
by Frances Hackeson Freelance Publishing Services, Brinscall, Lancs
Printed in Great Britain
by CPI, Bath

Contents

Preface and acknowledgements

Remembering Refugees: Then and Now reflects the evolution of my historical research over several decades. Refugees, from being one of many areas of interest, have become a primary focus, as reflected in my co-authored book with Katharine Knox, *Refugees in an Age of Genocide* (1999). Researching and writing that book, it was apparent that while a few refugee groups in Britain had subsequently been positively remembered, indeed celebrated, many more had been utterly forgotten. Parallel to a growing interest in refugees has been an increasing fascination with the development of historical memory, especially historiography and the heritage industry and how the past has been instrumentalised in the present. Such academic interests have coincided with the growing politicisation of refugee issues at global and local levels and the rise, from the late twentieth century, of what I term asylum-seeker phobia. When approached by the University of Manchester to give the 2002 Sherman Lectures at the Centre for Jewish Studies it seemed intellectually as well as socially and politically appropriate to devote them to the theme of 'Refugees – then and now'. Since giving these lectures the hostility towards refugees and asylum seekers has further intensified. I hope that in its small way this book will help provide some perspective and calm in an area that is increasingly subject to hysteria and prejudice. Its aim is to stimulate a degree of self-reflexivity in relation to the refugee, especially amongst those who, at a professional and popular level, represent the past.

Many thanks are in order. First, to the Centre for Jewish Studies at the University of Manchester for inviting me to give the Sherman Lectures and for providing such warm hospitality in my city of birth. In particular, I would like to acknowledge Bernard Jackson and Philip Alexander, the Centre's co-directors, and Daniel Langton and Bill Williams, good friends who share my commitment to the refugee, past and present. Second, to colleagues inside and outside the University of Southampton where I gave my inaugural lecture in 2003 and who provided me with such a positive response. Thanks especially with regard to this inaugural lecture to Colin Holmes for his introduction and Bill Brooks for his vote of thanks. Both have played a key role in my career: Colin Holmes for encouraging me to develop my expertise in immigrant and minority histories, including that of refugees, and Bill Brooks for his past and ongoing support for the University of Southampton's Parkes Institute for the Study of Jewish/non-Jewish relations. Third, to Alison Welsby at Manchester University Press for her encouragement over this project and to MUP's anonymous readers for their positive responses and constructive criticism. Fourth, to those good friends who have so generously read draft material; Greg Walker, Colin Richmond and Brian Klug. I owe much to these three not just for their helpful suggestions, but also through the stimulation that their own work and approaches, in different areas, has provided. I have benefited greatly also from discussing specific aspects of this book with a range of colleagues, including Liza Schuster, John Solomos, Louise London, Alan Dein, Barbara Rosenbaum and Sue Vice as well as those involved with the support of refugees on a day-to-day basis. Fifth, to my colleagues who have been part of the AHRC Parkes Research Centre for the Study of Jewish/non-Jewish relations. This book is part of the 'Race, Ethnicity and Memory' project within it. The AHRC Parkes Research Centre has been a challenging, if rewarding, experience and I would like to pay tribute to Jo Reilly and then Steve Taverner who were its administrators and made the whole project run smoothly. Amidst the blood, sweat and tears there has been fun and stimulation. Sixth, to the archivists, librarians and museum workers who have provided advice and expertise for this project including Chris Woolgar, Karen Robson and Jenny Ruthven at Special Collections, University of Southampton; Dorothy Sheridan and Joy Eldridge at the Mass-Observation archive, University of Sussex and to the Trustees of Mass-Observation for permission to use their material; and to those at the National Archives, Kew; the British Library; Southampton City Archives and Local History Library; Manchester Central Reference Library Local Studies; Bury Art Gallery and Museum; Cheadle Library; Manchester Jewish Museum; Museum of London; London Metropolitan Archives; British Library; Rothschild Archive; the Refugee Council; Imperial War Museum; National Labour Museum; and Museum of London.

Finally, as ever, to family, friends and Cavaliers for their support during the creation of this book. The epic victory of the Cavaliers over Wessex Archaelogy at Hurstbourne Priors, August 2005, was part of a truly memorable summer of cricket. In the final stages of completion of the manuscript I was contacted by distant relatives who provided information about my father's family left behind in eastern Europe. Only one survived the Holocaust, Saul Kushner, himself the only survivor of the massacre of the Jews of Vasilishki in 1942. An attempt is being made to commemorate the murdered Jews of this *shtetl*, now located in Belarus. Much has been made of the failure of post-war eastern Europe to recognise the Holocaust. It will take an equal effort for those in the west to acknowledge its past role, especially after 1918 and the worst days of European Jewry, in excluding and stigmatising those such as the family and friends of Saul Kushner. This book is intended to be part of the process of facing up to the past – critically, inclusively and openly.

Southampton

Introduction

The primary concern of this book is to explore the memory work associated with 'the refugee'. It is only secondarily a history of refugee movements and settlements. The particular slant of *Remembering Refugees: Then and Now* requires some explanation and justification as the historical treatment of refugees, including responses to them, is still in its infancy; there are still huge gaps in our knowledge and understanding. Yet rather than stand as an indulgent exercise given the dearth of historical writing on the subject, this study explores why this lacuna has developed. As will emerge in the first chapter, the lack of attention given to refugees by historians has deep causes, reflecting particularly the limitations imposed by narrowly-defined national frameworks. It also reflects the emphasis placed by many in the historical profession on continuity of presence rather than temporariness, flux and statelessness – the conditions that in many ways typify the experiences of refugees. Writing refugees 'back' into history is thus not easily remediable. Nevertheless, recognising the structural rather than the accidental causes of this absence is a first step in countering the invisibility of refugees in critical as well as celebratory engagements with the past.

It is essential to acknowledge from the start that the experience of refugees and representations of them have often had very little in common. This study excavates the formation and re-formation of 'local' and 'global' identities recognising that while the 'local' and 'global' are often constructed as being polar opposites this need not be the case. The refugee, one of the ultimate symbols of placelessness, can be excluded as not 'one of us' or, alternatively, included if the 'local' is inscribed with universal meaning and associations. Refugees themselves, often, by necessity and circumstances, marginal figures, rarely can shape the dominant images others hold of them – especially as their representations are fashioned more by myth than reality. Yet refugee voices will still feature prominently in the chapters that follow. As Liisa Malkki has warned that 'in universalizing particular displaced people into "refugees" – in abstracting

their predicaments from specific political, historical, cultural contexts –
humanitarian practices tend to silence refugees'. She adds that

> if humanism can only constitute itself on the bodies of dehistoricized,
> archetypical refugees and other similarly styled victims ... then citizenship
> in this human community itself remains curiously, indecently, outside of
> history.[1]

In this book, making refugees visible in the past and present will not be
at the expense of rendering them mute.

In his pioneer work, *On Collective Memory*, Maurice Halbwachs argued that

> What makes recent memories hang together is not that they are continu-
> ous in time: it is rather that they are part of a totality of thoughts common
> to a group, the group of people with whom we have a relation at the
> moment ... To recall them it is hence sufficient that we place ourselves in
> the perspective of this group, that we adopt its interests and follow the
> slant of its reflections.[2]

Subsequently some scholars have objected to Halbwachs' term, pointing
out that memory is intrinsic only to the psychology and identity of the
individual.[3] Within this study, the individual and his/her life story is often
the point of focus, but the analysis will be on how such identities are
constructed in relation to (either positively, negatively or, most frequently,
ambivalently) the 'local', 'national' and 'global' – they are not, in short,
formed in isolation from the world around them.[4]

Refugees themselves have faced the dilemmas of self-definition within
these place orientated constructs. While the legal and social restrictions
they have experienced have often limited their freedom to do so, for those
refugees lucky enough to have access to public media and forms of cultural expression, the internal tensions have led to remarkable articulations of collective identities. A classic example includes the creation in
Britain during the 1930s of what has been termed 'international Englishness' by a group of Jewish refugee film makers, led by Alexander Korda.
In making historical dramas such as *The Private Life of Henry VIII* (1933),
Greg Walker has suggested that while it

> might be that the past is a foreign country ... for Korda, whose sense of
> the present was always that of an outsider, stressing its familiarity was the
> more attractive prospect ... His interest in the internationalism of the na-
> tional, of the ready translatability of all stereotypes between national cul-
> tures, was part of a refashioning of the past which was also a refashioning
> of the self.[5]

In contrast, Korda's fellow Hungarian, George Mikes, provided a critique of Englishness in his satire, *How to be an Alien* (1946). It extended

to the work of Korda and others when Mikes quipped, not without foundation, that 'A little foreign blood is very advantageous, almost essential, to become a really great British film producer'. No doubt with the historical license liberally employed by Korda in mind, Mikes teased that a 'slight change in the character of a person is highly recommendable, and I advise the filming of *Peter Pan* as a thriller, and the *Concise Oxford Dictionary* as a comic opera'.[6] In apparent contradistinction to Korda's chameleon tendencies, Mikes took pride in his Hungarianness, flattered to be told after eight years in Britain that 'You really speak a most excellent accent without the slightest English'.[7] Yet it was Korda who continued to surround himself throughout his life with a Hungarian (Jewish) coterie and it was Mikes, and Gerard Hoffnung after him, both refugees, who played on the English language to parody the British to themselves.[8] The point to be emphasised here is that local, national and global identities are made and re-made and are not in any way innate and static. The same is equally true of the labels associated with 'refugees'.

Liza Schuster has argued that the hostility directed towards asylum seekers in the late twentieth and early twenty-first centuries is part of a process in 'the role of the state in the construction both of racism and of nations'. Asylum seekers are singled out, she suggests, 'as legitimate targets for hostility'. Of crucial importance, however, as Schuster continues, is that asylum seekers are constructed 'not solely as a legal category' (that is those awaiting a decision on their applications to be recognised as a refugee):

> 'Asylum-seeker' is now a term that is used unambiguously, and immediately conjures up cheat, liar, criminal, sponger – someone deserving of hostility by virtue not of any misdemeanour, but simply because he or she is an asylum-seeker – a figure that has by now become a caricature, a stereotype, in the way that 'Blacks', 'Jews' and 'Gypsies' have been and still are.[9]

Similarly, in the third edition of his *Folk Devils and Moral Panics* (2002), Stanley Cohen outlines recent manifestations of how 'deviant groups' have been constructed in society and the media since he originally wrote his seminal text about the hysteria created by the 'Mods and Rockers' during the 1960s. Cohen outlines seven recent 'moral panics' in Britain, ranging from child murderers through to welfare cheats and single mothers.[10] The last in Cohen's list are 'refugees and asylum seekers' but there is, as he suggests, something 'crucially different' in this case from his other six examples. First, Cohen outlines how in the case of refugees/asylum seekers 'although there have been intermittent panics about specific newsworthy episodes, the overall narrative is a single, virtually uninterrupted message of hostility and rejection'. There are exceptions to this negativity, as will be explored throughout *Remembering Refugees*. Yet rather than query the picture described by Cohen of 'a constant background screen, interspersed with vivid little tableaux', these exceptions will be shown largely to emphasise it further. The second difference identified by Cohen relates to how reactions to asylum seekers 'are more overtly political than any others – not just because the problem is caused by global political changes, but because the reactions have a long history in British political culture'. In fact, it extends way beyond the political sphere. Stanley Cohen suggests that 'successive British governments have not only led and legitimated public hostility, but spoken with a voice indistiguishable from the tabloid press'.[11]

It is the explosive mixture of governmental, state, media and public animosity that makes asylum-seeker phobia so dangerous today. Even within the 'long history' referred to by Cohen, there is something unprecedented in the contemporary animus against asylum seekers, as the final chapter and conclusion of *Remembering Refugees* will explore. The situation, if anything, has deteriorated since Cohen wrote in 2002. For example, a poll carried out in February 2003 revealed that 65 per cent believed that the 'current system for handling asylum seekers … increased the threat of terrorism in Britain' and a similar percentage of Conservative supporters agreed that they were 'a major reason why public services such as health and education are overburdened'. The same poll revealed that the number of asylum seekers was the issue causing 'the most serious problem in Britain at present'. As many as 39 per cent placed the entry of asylum seekers as their highest concern and a further 50 per cent (i.e. together nearly nine out of ten) believed it was a 'serious problem'.[12] Opinion polls have a limitation in this area through their lack of depth, suggestibility and yes/no crudity. Nevertheless, the final chapter, by analysing the autobiographical responses of the social anthropological body, Mass-Observation, confirms the depth of feeling, if providing a more complex and nuanced reading of the public mood. What is not at doubt at a national level is the attention given to 'asylum' in British party politics, the 'issue' becoming a key battleground in the 2005 general election. Indeed, 'asylum' has achieved, it is possible to argue, the highest political prominence of an immigration-related theme since the agitation that led to the Aliens Act one hundred years earlier. Nevertheless, if the intensity of the current campaign is exceptional, the socially and legally constructed labelling process, as outlined by Schuster, has itself a long history.

The 'aliens debate' at the start of the twentieth century proved to be seminal in British immigration control. Superficially it concerned increased movement into Britain (largely of east European Jews) but at a deeper level was nothing to do with the impact these 'aliens' made. Concern about the 'question of England', and especially the fitness of its people to compete internationally both militarily and commercially, tied in with debates about national efficiency, eugenics, free or fair trade and differing party political appeals to a mass electorate, were just some of the wider issues that underpinned the more specific question about the control of alien entry.[13] Within the debate itself, however, inside and outside parliament, the justification for controls depended ethically on categorising the east European Jews not as deserving refugees but as unwanted and undesirable aliens. The Liberal opponents of control emphasised the Tsarist oppression and persecution that these Jews had fled. They attempted to take the moral high ground further and accused the Conservative restrictionists themselves of being motivated by antisemitic hostility. The Conservative Prime Minister, Arthur Balfour, rejected such claims and instead, articulating his own ethical narrative, emphasised 'the undoubted evils which had fallen upon portions of the country from an alien immigration which was largely Jewish'. Rather than being motivated by prejudice, Balfour, providing a template that has been subsequently followed by leaders of many political hues, claimed that control was needed to avoid such hostility at home. Balfour's contribution to the debate, however, has even greater contemporary resonance: his justification for restriction was allied to the claim that liberties were being taken with Britain's generosity. There was 'reason to fear', he argued, that

> this country might be, at however great a distance, in danger of following the evil example set by other countries; and human nature being what it was, it was almost impossible to guard against so great an evil unless they took reasonable precautions to prevent what was called 'the right of asylum' from being abused.[14]

There were thus those worthy and unworthy of asylum, just as the Victorians separated out the deserving and undeserving poor in distributing relief along 'scientific' grounds. To prove that east European Jews were undeserving, the legitimacy of their right to asylum had to be queried. They were, therefore, as the *Daily Mail* argued, 'so-called refugees' – a menace rather than souls deserving sympathy and therefore hospitality.[15] In the twenty-first century the terminology has changed, but the meanings ascribed to them very little – there are, it is alleged, especially by the right-wing populist tabloids, some genuine refugees, but they are eclipsed by a much greater number of 'bogus' or 'abusive' asylum seekers.[16]

In the First World War, the arrival of a quarter of a million Belgians revealed that the title 'refugee' still had positive connotations in British society, culture and politics. They were initially welcomed as pitiful and defenceless victims of German aggression and brutality. Yet later in the

war the Belgians were both socially and legally treated as 'aliens', subject
to popular attack and then removal by the state. Thus even the same
group within a short period of time could be re-defined to suit changing
circumstances.[17] Through aliens legislation in 1914 and 1919, the 'asylum clause' of the 1905 Aliens Act was removed and those trying to
restore it were told firmly that this was impossible due to 'the changed
and changing conditions both here and abroad ... In other words, the
question of alien immigration is now indissolubly bound up with other
broad questions of national domestic policy.'[18] Jews escaping from pogroms, poverty and civil war in the Ukraine, who most probably would
have been viewed as 'genuine refugees' before 1914 were, during the
1920s, treated as racially undesirable aliens. They were unwanted
transmigrants who should be settled elsewhere or returned 'home'. That
the Ukrainians and others ended up stranded in England for many years
was regarded by the state as a bureaucratic nuisance, rather than a humanitarian tragedy.[19] Subsequently, as will emerge in chapter 2, they have
been forgotten – they had literally no place in Britain at the time and
thereafter no place in its collective memory.

During the 1930s Britain eventually allowed entry (largely temporary)
to 80,000 Jewish refugees. Subsequently, alongside the Huguenots, they
have become the most famous and celebrated group of refugees in British
history and heritage. At the time, as will be illustrated in chapters 3 and
4 of this study, their reception and treatment was mixed. Hostility, at
particular moments, was intense, so much so that in early 1938 the Jewish Refugee Committee changed its title to the German Jewish Aid Committee because the word 'refugee' had developed negative connotations.[20]
Generally, however, it was rare for the term 'refugee' *itself* to have anything other than positive associations and in the Second World War another battle of nomenclature developed concerning those who had escaped the Third Reich.

In September 1939, the Home Secretary, John Anderson, told the House
of Commons that there was a 'general desire to avoid treating as enemies
those who are friendly to the country that has offered them asylum'.[21]
Nevertheless, there were many who *did* distrust the refugees, through
their Jewishness, Germanness, or foreignness in general. In the spring
and early summer military crisis months of 1940, those hostile in the
state, government, media and public got their way. The refugees were
transformed into 'enemy aliens' and a policy of mass internment and
deportation was implemented.[22] After the invasion panic died down and
some of the more blatant abuses were exposed, most of the internees
were released, subsequently attempting to re-style themselves as 'His
Majesty's Most Loyal Enemy Aliens'.[23] Nevertheless, their status as

'genuine' refugees was inevitably queried by the internment episode and the continuing legal status of being 'enemy aliens'. Indeed, the Home Office's later moral justification of mass internment, written as part of a wider internal history of its Alien Branch in 1950, revealed the ongoing struggle over the politics of labelling. It was based on the premise of emphasising the alien (and thereby negative) qualities of those who came during the 1930s and undermining their refugee status (and thereby their deservingness).

Writing of the situation in 1940, the Home Office historian complained that 'The friends of the aliens were far too prone to speak as though every refugee was *ipso facto* a crusader of saintly and heroic character whose sole object in coming here was to devote his life and energies to campaigning against the enemy.' Instead, he portrayed 'a good many of them' as purely self-interested, a status which did not give 'them any claim to the gratitude of the British people'. They had, he added, 'no desire to make any kind of sacrifice, even for the noblest of causes, if they could avoid it', before concluding that a

> certain number of aliens ... could only be classed as refugees because they had been forced to leave their own country by reason of their race, religion, or political activities were in fact shown by their character or history to be extremely undesirable and even dangerous residents.[24]

Mass internment, in the official Home Office view, was thus only right and proper.

After the Second World War, when 'Europe had never seen so many [up to 30 million] refugees',[25] yet another process of re-labelling occurred. Those refugees languishing in camps were now termed 'displaced persons'. As Bernard Wasserstein astutely comments, 'The British and American governments, who found themselves primarily responsible for dealing with the problem, hesitated to use the word "refugee" since that might imply acceptance that the person in question could not return to his home country.'[26] The same process has occurred in the last decades of the twentieth century and beyond as western states attempt to minimise their obligations under the 1951 United Nations Convention Relating to the Status of Refugees (known widely as the Geneva Convention). It has been a period when 'an unprecedented but accelerating process of relabelling refugees and the humanitarian principles which underpin refugee assistance has taken place ... New labels are being used, not only to recognize the complexity of forced migration, but more as instruments of control, restrictionism and disengagement.'[27]

The slippage from 'refugee' to 'undesirable alien', 'transmigrant', 'enemy alien', 'displaced person', and 'asylum seeker' shows how such terminology from the late Victorian era onwards has not been just legally, but also socially constructed, and often negatively so. There is, however, a parallel if less powerful history of romanticising the status of 'refugee', one that has been articulated most recently by certain postmodern writers. For them, according to Phil Cohen, 'Exile becomes no longer a sign of bondage or self-alienation, but of freedom from constraint. The migrant is considered an orphan from the storms of modernity, but one whose salvation lies in boldly proclaiming that fact.' Cohen points as an example to the work of Juan Goytisolo who describes himself as a writer 'not claimed by anybody, alien and opposed to all groupings and ideologies, defined as a Castilian in Catalonia, a French speaker in Spain, a Spaniard in France, a Latin in North America, an infidel in Morocco, and a Moor everywhere as a result of my wanderings'. Goytisolo then connects himself to those forcibly displaced in what Cohen labels a deceit of 'postmodern geography of exile', one that ignores 'that the real marginal and dispossessed are immobilized in low-paid jobs, incarcerated in hostels and detention centres, continually stopped and searched by police, and many are sick and homeless'.[28] Similarly bell hooks has criticised anthropological theorist James Clifford's 'playful' celebration of travel by suggesting that it is 'not a word that can be easily evoked to talk about the Middle Passage, the Trail of Tears, the landing of Chinese immigrants at Ellis Island, the forced relocation of Japanese-Americans, the plight of the homeless'.[29] At a more popular level and away from the musings of postmodernist writers and cultural theorists, is the portrayal of Merhan Karimi Nasseiri, an Iranian refugee. Nasseiri, finding himself in Paris without the necessary papers to leave, got stuck in the bureaucratic 'Kafkaesque' nightmare of European immigration control. Remarkably, he has been stateless in Charles de Gaulle airport since 1988. Nasseiri's story has been utilised in a Steven Spielberg film, *The Terminal Man* (2004). Inevitably the story is distorted and depoliticised (the hero refuses to be treated as a refugee and only wants to return 'home') and, as a Hollywood epic, it has a happy ending. In reality, Nasseiri is a victim of the re-labelling process that denies him the status of refugee and, after literally decades, he has been left mad, disturbed and utterly confused about his identity, styling himself a British aristocrat, Sir Alfred Mehran.[30] The German Jewish writer, Joseph Roth, wrote in the 1920s that 'papers! half a Jew's life is consumed by the futile battle with papers'.[31] The same could be written of the hundreds of thousands of asylum seekers in the West today of whom Nasseiri is perhaps the most famous. In contrast to Spielberg's representation, there is little glamour to be found in a world of bureaucracy and endless queuing, rejection and temporariness.

Refugees, in short, have huge additional burdens imposed on them as being on the one hand portrayed and treated as 'undeserving' and 'abusive' and, on the other, being the subject of unrealistic expectations through 'utopian representation'.[32] *Remembering Refugees* will explore further the processes by which refugees have been constructed and re-constructed, labelled and re-labelled. It will be possible to have the sufficient depth to do so by focusing on particular times and places, specificities that require explanation before this study moves on to its detailed analysis and commentary.

The major focus is on the British experience. Britain is far from alone in having had a long tradition of refugee settlement. Many other countries could have been chosen in this respect, although the absence of a historiography in this particular national example makes this study especially necessary and desirable. Moreover, Britain is an especially interesting case study because of its fundamentally ambivalent relationship to refugees. It has both embraced a historical commitment to the 'right to asylum' and distanced itself from the reality of what, in the words of a civil servant, this 'well-sounding but vague' axiom has meant in practice.[33] More precisely in terms of geography, it will concentrate on several areas from the north and south of England. These places – largely in and around Manchester, London and Southampton – have significant connections, associations and absence of associations with refugees. That, however, is not why they were chosen for analysis. The argument is that other places could have been (relatively) as easily selected. They also would have revealed, through a detailed micro-history and anthropology, the processes of selective memory and amnesia that have been integral to the construction of local identities. The approach of this study is that of Walter Benjamin's *Das Passengen-Work* (or 'Arcades' project) and his forensic archaeology of the nineteenth-century streets of Paris. As Benjamin wrote:

> The first stage in this undertaking will be to carry over the principle of montage into history. That is, to assemble large-scale constructions out of the smallest and most precisely cut components. Indeed, to discover in the analysis of the small individual moment the crystal of the total event.[34]

Focusing on the local is thus not necessarily parochial or restrictive. As historical geographer, Doreen Massey, suggests, 'places, in fact, are always constructed out of articulations of social relations (trading connections, the unequal links of colonialism, thoughts of home) which are not only internal to that locale but which link them to elsewhere'. As she emphasises, 'Their "local uniqueness" is always already a product of wider contacts; the local is always already a product in part of "global" forces.'[35] Equally, its analysis will be drawn from a wide range of source materials: more 'traditional' historical evidence such as printed documents, letters, diaries, oral and written testimonies, governmental papers, newspapers and so on, but also buildings, monuments and memorials, museums, fictional writing, and the landscape (both urban and rural) itself.

The second theme that runs through this book is temporal. The past explored here covers close to half a millennia – from early modern through to the twenty-first century. Nevertheless, the key refugee movement in relation to memory work in Britain, it argues, has become that of the refugees from Nazism. In this respect, they have partly replaced or supplemented the earlier iconic status of the Huguenots. It is necessary to emphasise that this study does *not* argue for the privileging of the experiences of those who escaped from the Third Reich, a development that is already happening in the limited historiography of refugee movements to Britain. Indeed, the hope is that in a modest way this study will challenge the historical profession and heritage world to bring other refugee movements out of obscurity or condescension, that is 'to visualize the invisible'.[36] Equally, it does not suggest that the refugees from Nazism were in some way more legitimate, more deserving than other, later, asylum seekers even though this has been how they have been increasingly regarded, especially as engagement with the Holocaust has heightened. Such an approach would also be fundamentally ahistorical – chapter 3 explores how contemporaries in Britain struggled to come to terms with these refugees. It utilises the archive of the social anthropological organisation, Mass-Observation, and how through directives and diaries, ordinary people in Britain wrote about the refugees with (frequently intermingled) layers of sympathy, empathy, friendship, love, exasperation, suspicion, fear, antipathy and sometimes even hatred. Chapter 4, a case study within a case study, examines the memory work associated with the *Kindertransport*, now the most famous and commemorated group of refugees coming to Britain, increasingly memorialised nationally and internationally. By charting the memory work associated with the *Kindertransport* chronologically, however, it will again highlight contemporary ambivalence, which was followed after 1945 by several decades of silence, indifference and obscurity before the recent (largely) celebratory approach has emerged.

The justification for this focus is partly to explore why there has been such an intensity of recent memory work associated with refugees from Nazism, and especially those that came as children. It is equally concerned, however, with the *politicisation* of such memory work and how it has been used both for (and against) more recent arrivals. The final chapter uses a case study of Roma asylum seekers from the continent of Europe and how, in contrast to them, past refugees, especially those from the 1930s, have been constructed as genuine and beneficial to Britain. It unravels this instrumentalisation of the past within political discourse at Westminster and Whitehall, the media and the public (again utilising the archive of Mass-Observation).

Finally, some comments are in order about the style of the chapters that follow. The five chapters first evolved in the Sherman Lectures given at the University of Manchester in 2002, the first one of which was developed further in my inaugural lecture (also the Parkes Lecture) at the University of Southampton in 2003. This first lecture has now been expanded and become chapters 1 and 2 of *Remembering Refugees*, focusing on historiography and heritage work respectively, a necessary distinction as the 'past' looms ever larger in contemporary society and culture. The remaining three chapters are loosely based on the other three 2002 Sherman Lectures, extended and formalised. Nevertheless, some elements of these lectures that dealt with the autobiographical have been maintained, not out of any sense of self-indulgence, but because a major theme of this study is that through a life-story approach we can see how refugees are encountered. In 2000, Mass-Observation carried out a detailed study on 'Coming to Britain'. Many of those responding initially denied that they had any connection to refugees but then, through more detailed consideration, wrote how at certain points their lives, or those of their family, had indeed been shaped by refugees (or, indeed, that they had some refugee origins themselves). A similar process has occurred in my professional life. Encountering the History Department at the University of Southampton in 1986, which has been my academic home subsequently, I was struck by its apparent 'Englishness'. It emerged on closer inspection that of my colleagues, two were refugees from Nazism, another was of Yugoslav origin and born in exile in France, and another the child of Czech social democrats who came to Britain after 1945.[37] Adding myself, close to one third were from refugee backgrounds. Similarly, the late Tim Reuter, who transformed the History Department in the 1990s and to whom my inaugural lecture was dedicated, was a man of impeccable 'English' reserve.[38] In fact, he was the son of a child refugee (his grandfather, Ernst Reuter, was a leading socialist in Berlin).[39] It will become apparent that this twoness, of refugees being everywhere and nowhere, is a tension running throughout this study of British history, heritage and politics.

I teach now in a building which used to house a school, Taunton's College, of which the most famous 'old boy' was Benny Hill. Its gym (where Benny, or Alfred as he then was, made his comic stage debut), now the major lecture theatre of the University's School of Humanities, was briefly and obscurely an internment camp for refugees in 1940. There is a serious point to be made here. As Doreen Massey suggests, 'The identity of places is very much bound up with the *histories* which are told of them, *how* those histories are told, and which memory turns out to be dominant.'[40] So far, the history of refugees in Britain has been marginalised or pathologised. The autobiographical is one route through which the marginality of the refugee in the construction of the past can at least begin to be challenged.

The conclusion of this study addresses the issue of ethics, and its absence or distortion, in debates about asylum. It argues that a historical perspective undermines many of the reasons given *not* to help refugees. It also, following the final chapter, explores what has recently been described as 'the moral state we're in' – how the most vulnerable in society are treated not with dignity and respect but with disdain and often hatred.[41] *Remembering Refugees* is thus a plea to bring back the refugee into our understanding of the past and present. It is also a call to recognise that the right to asylum is not just a basic human right for the oppressed but also a touchstone for the non-persecuted, revealing the fundamental nature of who we are.

Notes

1 Liisa Malkki, 'Speechless Emissaries: Refugees, Humanitarianism, and Dehistoricization', *Cultural Anthropology* vol. 11 no. 3 (August 1996), pp. 378, 398.

2 Maurice Halbwachs, *On Collective Memory* edited and translated by Lewis Coser (Chicago: University of Chicago Press, 1992), p. 52.

3 For critical comment see Noa Gedi and Yigal Elam, 'Collective Memory – What is it?', *History & Memory* vol. 8 no. 1 (spring/summer 1996), pp. 30–50.

4 I share the perspective of Robert Eaglestone, *The Holocaust and the Postmodern* (Oxford: Oxford University Press, 2004), p. 77 that 'Collective memory is not "a misleading new name" for "myth" [the critique of Gedi and Elam]; it is not some spurious entity like Jung's "Collective unconscious" but constantly acted out and embodied in collective practices, material and otherwise.'

5 Greg Walker, *The Private Life of Henry VIII* (London: I.B. Tauris, 2003), p. 40, a theme developed further in idem, 'The Roots of Alexander Korda: Myths of Identity and the International Film', *Patterns of Prejudice* vol. 37 no. 1 (March 2003), pp. 3–25.

6 George Mikes, *How to be an Alien* (London: Andre Deutsch, 1946), pp. 66, 71.

7 Ibid., p. 41.

8 Annetta Hoffnung, *Gerard Hoffnung: His Biography* (London: Gordon Fraser, 1988).

9 Liza Schuster, 'Common Sense or Racism? The Treatment of Asylum-seekers

in Europe', *Patterns of Prejudice* vol. 37 no. 3 (2003), p. 244.

10 Stanley Cohen, *Folk Devils and Moral Panics* (London: Routledge, 2002, 3rd edition [orig. 1972]), introduction to the third edition.

11 Ibid., p. xix.

12 Poll details in *The Times*, 12 February 2003.

13 David Feldman, *Englishmen and Jews: Social Relations and Political Culture 1840–1914* (New Haven: Yale University Press, 1994), part 3.

14 In *Hansard* (HC) vol. 149 col. 155 (10 July 1905).

15 *Daily Mail*, 3 February 1900.

16 Ronald Kaye, 'Redefining the Refugee: The UK Media Portrayal of Asylum Seekers', in Khalid Koser and Helma Lutz (eds), *The New Migration in Europe: Social Constructions and Social Realities* (Basingstoke: Macmillan, 1998), pp. 163–82.

17 Tony Kushner, 'Local Heroes: Belgian Refugees in Britain During the First World War', *Immigrants & Minorities* vol. 18 no. 1 (March 1999), pp. 1–28.

18 J.R. Clynes to D'Avigdor Goldsmid, 26 February 1930, in Board of Deputies of British Jews archive, E3/80, London Metropolitan Archives.

19 Tony Kushner and Katharine Knox, *Refugees in an Age of Genocide: Global, National and Local Perspectives During the Twentieth Century* (London, Frank Cass, 1999), chapter 3.

20 German Jewish Aid Committee Executive minutes, 5 January 1938, Central British Fund archives, 174/263, London Metropolitan Archives.

21 In *Hansard* (HC) vol. 354 col. 367 (4 September 1939).

22 See David Cesarani and Tony Kushner (eds), *The Internment of Aliens in Twentieth Century Britain* (London: Frank Cass, 1993).

23 The phrase is by Klaus Hinrichsen in a Bewick Film documentary, 1991.

24 Mr Eaglestone's 'History of the Aliens Branch', 1950, in National Archives, HO 213/1772.

25 Michael Marrus, *The Unwanted: European Refugees in the Twentieth Century* (Oxford: Oxford University Press, 1985), p. 297.

26 Bernard Wasserstein, *Vanishing Diaspora: The Jews in Europe since 1945* (London: Hamish Hamilton, 1996), p. 8.

27 Roger Zetter, 'Refugees and Refugee Studies – A Valedictory Editorial', *Journal of Refugee Studies* vol. 13 no. 4 (2000), p. 353.

28 Phil Cohen, 'Rethinking the Diasporama', *Patterns of Prejudice* vol. 33 no. 1 (1999), pp. 17–19.

29 bell hooks, 'Representing Whiteness', in Lawrence Grossberg, Cary Nelson and Paula Treicher (eds), *Cultural Studies* (New York: Routledge, 1992), p. 343.

30 Steven Spielberg, *The Terminal Man* (2004); Paul Berczeller, 'The Man who Lost his Past', *Guardian*, 6 September 2004; Sir Alfred Mehran, *The Terminal Man* (London: Corgi, 2004).

31 Joseph Roth, *The Wandering Jews* (London: Granta, 2001), p. 68.

32 Cohen, 'Rethinking the Diasporama', p. 10.

33 The phrase is that of Eaglestone in his Home Office history. See National Archives, HO 213/1772.

34 Walter Benjamin, *The Arcades Project* translated by Kevin Eiland and Kevin McLaughlin (Cambridge, MA: Harvard University Press, 1999), p. 461. More generally on his approach in this work see Richard Sieburth, 'Benjamin the Scrivener', in Gary Smith (ed.), *Benjamin: Philosophy, Aesthetics, History* (Chicago: University of Chicago Press, 1989), pp. 13–37.
35 Doreen Massey, 'Places and Their Pasts', *History Workshop Journal* no. 39 (spring 1995), p. 183.
36 Alan Rice, 'Exploring Inside the Invisible: An Interview with Lubaina Himid', *Wasafari* no. 40 (Winter 2003), p. 24.
37 For one of these, a leading modern British and German historian, see Edgar Feuchtwanger, 'Recovering from Culture Shock', in Peter Alter (ed.), *Out of the Third Reich: Refugee Historians in Post-war Britain* (London: I.B. Tauris, 1998), pp. 43–54.
38 In her obituary, Henrietta Lyser refers to 'a certain shyness and reserve ... [that] remained with him all his life'. In *German History* vol. 21 no. 1 (January 2003), pp. 82–5, esp. p. 82.
39 In contrast to Leyser's obituary, that by Jinty Nelson in the *Guardian*, October 2002, does not refer to his refugee origins. It is significant, perhaps, that Leyser's husband, Karl, the supervisor of Tim Reuter, was a refugee from Nazism.
40 Massey, 'Places and their Pasts', p. 186.
41 Julia Neuberger, *The Moral State We're In: A Manifesto for a 21st Century Society* (London: HarperCollins, 2005).

1

Refugees: the forgotten of history, the abused of politics

Introduction

In his last public speech, Rabbi Hugo Gryn predicted that future historians 'will call the twentieth century not only the century of great wars,
but also the century of the refugee. Almost nobody at the end of the
century is where they were at the beginning of it. It has been an extraordinary period of movement and upheavals.'[1] Similarly John Berger states
that 'Ours is the century of enforced travel … the century of disappear-
ances. The century of seeing others, who were close to them, disappear
over the horizon.'[2] With these words, first from a Holocaust survivor
from the Carpathian town of Berehovo, who came to Britain at the end
of the war before embarking on a career that took him to India and the
USA before returning to this country, and second from an art historian,
journalist, novelist and critic who was born in Britain but lives in France,
Katharine Knox and myself opened *Refugees in an Age of Genocide*.[3]
These are powerful statements from committed internationalists whose
evocativeness and universalism was reinforced by the image used in the
cover illustration – a photograph by Howard Davies of a Bosnian Mus-
lim refugee returning to his village after living in London for four years
and discovering that his home had been destroyed. Davies specialises in
photographs of refugees from all parts of the world that reveal under
their collective loss an individuality and humanity. He does so without
romanticising or sentimentalising their plight, offering 'an insight into
the hardships which refugees face, not only in the countries from which
they flee, but also in the countries where they hoped to find safety'.[4]
Cultural anthropologist Liisa Malkki has commented that visual representations can silence the voice of refugees and capture them only as a
'blur of humanity'.[5] Davies's photographs show that this need not be the
case.

By the end of the twentieth century the number of refugees worldwide, including those internally displaced, had reached close to 30 million.

Surely few would query the sentiments expressed by Gryn or Berger or would challenge the centrality of refugee or, more accurately, anti-refugee politics in almost all European countries and beyond? As British Prime Minister, Tony Blair, stated in May 2002 before the major European Union summit in Seville, asylum was 'one of the most pressing issues of our time'. But equally few are willing to accept beyond a surface emotional reaction what it has meant in reality to confront the last bloody century – indeed Blair did not have in mind Hugo Gryn's perspective but the reverse: in the politician's words 'how we make sure that the external borders of Europe are made secure'.[6]

Judging by the number of television programmes (and now channels), books (including novels), magazines and heritage centres devoted to the subject, it seems that today we cannot get enough of history, making feasible the claim that it is 'the new rock 'n' roll'.[7] One area, however, that is noticeable by its absence, or as will be shown in this opening chapter, by its *partial* absence, is the history of refugees. Indeed, Hugo Gryn may not quite have realised how far he was asking the historical profession to move in recognising the significance of the refugee in the modern world. Taking Britain, where the word 'refugee' was coined in relation to the French Huguenot arrivals in the late seventeenth and eighteenth centuries,[8] *Refugees in an Age of Genocide* was the first attempt at an inclusive account of their reception and experiences in the modern era. Broadening out to the whole of Europe, the dominant area in determining the international treatment, legal definition and rights of refugees for the greater part of the twentieth century, we find less than a handful of major studies. First, Sir John Hope Simpson wrote in 1939 for the Royal Institute of International Affairs and was understandably very much geared towards the contemporary (Jewish) refugee crisis.[9] One then has to wait around fifty years for Michael Marrus's classic work, *The Unwanted* (1985), which covers European refugees in the first half of the twentieth century and Gerard Noiriel's more general work, *La Tyrannie du National: le droit d'asile en Europe, 1793–1993* (1991).[10] To put this in a localised perspective, there is only one major study of the Belgian refugee movement, the largest perhaps in the whole gamut of British history, totalling some quarter of a million people (not including, of course, the fictional sleuth, Hercule Poirot).[11]

Almost every area of Britain had its local Belgian refugee committee looking after the new arrivals, adding up to at least two and a half thousand in England and Wales alone.[12] To Agatha Christie in wartime Devon the new arrivals provided the inspiration for her new detective hero. In her autobiography she highlighted the dilemmas of finding a suitable figure, especially one who would be a contrast to the most famous fictional detective, Sherlock Holmes:

> A schoolboy? Rather difficult. A scientist? What did I know of scientists? Then I remembered our Belgian refugees. We had quite a colony of Belgian refugees living in the parish of Tor.[13]

It is significant that Christie chose a Belgian, rather than say an East European Jewish refugee as her hero figure. Christie's Jews were, at best, cast in ambivalent light, existing either side of respectability in the twilight world. Poirot, in spite of, or even because of his eccentric and painfully fastidious nature ('a speck of dust would have caused him more pain than a bullet wound')[14] was always sympathetically drawn by Christie. In contrast, at the start of her novel, *The Mystery of the Blue Train* (1928), Christie gratuitously introduces Boris Ivanovitch/Monsieur Krassnine, the son of a Polish Jew, living in Paris:

> A little man with a face like a rat. A man, one would say, who could never play a conspicuous part, or rise to prominence in any sphere. And yet, in leaping to such a conclusion, an onlooker would have been wrong. For this man, negligible and inconspicuous as he seemed, played a prominent part in the destiny of the world. In an Empire where rats ruled, he was the king of the rats.[15]

As will be shown, valorising refugees has been a selective process in the twentieth century – Christie herself when considering her choice of a Belgian detective reflected that 'There were all types of refugees'. The Belgians, to her, were deserving and grateful.[16] Yet even the favoured Belgians were largely forgotten in the historiography – if not in individual memory – of the First World War. This amnesia extends even into the first attempts to historicise refugee movements. Hope Simpson, in defining the scope of his 1939 refugee survey, excluded 'purely temporary movements, such as the exile of the Belgians and Serbians during the Great War'.[17] Contrast this absence of historical attention with the near obsession with racist and fascist groups in British history. In the case of the British Union of Fascists and its leader, Sir Oswald Mosley, for example, the number of studies, academic and popular, is now close to one hundred with no indication of the demand being satiated.[18]

The nature of history

This chapter aims to tease out the apparent paradox between the scale and impact of twentieth-century refugee crises and the failure to place the movement of refugees and responses to them in history. It argues that this absence in history and within the memory process more generally is neither accidental nor without significance. It is not just an oversight

that can, therefore, be easily be rectified. Instead it reflects a larger malaise in society as a whole: the general inability and unwillingness to confront the awkward questions posed by the existence of refugees and our
relationship to them. In his book *Frontiers of Identity: The British and
Others* (1994), Robin Cohen concludes that 'As the asylum seeker, stranger
or alien is silhouetted and identified, the British are ... delineating one or
other aspect of themselves. Their national identity is thereby continually
defined and redefined. The processes of exclusion and rejection uncover
and reveal and become constitutive of the national identity itself.'[19] If
Cohen is correct, and the increasing obsession with asylum seekers in
contemporary politics and culture in the decade and beyond after his
book was published suggests he is, we can see two results of this self-
other relationship.[20] In terms of *now*, there is a powerful tendency in
modern Britain to define national identity by what one is not; that is the
unstable figure of the bogus or abusive asylum seeker who is rootless,
criminal, subversive and diseased.[21] In terms of *then*, British history is
widely perceived and represented through the attributes of permanence,
stability, longevity, honesty, rigour and healthiness. Thus the mass circulation right-wing tabloid, the *Daily Mail*, responded to the BBC's 'Great
Britons' competition by bemoaning the choice of the top one hundred
figures as a 'distortion of a proud history'. 'New Labour', apparently,
was to blame: 'the most disturbing symbol of this loss of national identity is the fact that we have lost control of our own borders'.[22]

It is the strength of belief in a narrowly constructed idea of an 'authentic' national past that explains why the passing of the Queen Mother in
2002, whose life neatly covered the whole of the twentieth century, caused
so much collective feeling. Here was British tradition personified. The
alien outsider has little place in such popular mythologising of the past –
even if the Queen Mother was exceptional in being the first British-born
partner of a serving monarch in centuries. 'How long have your family
lived in England?', the Queen Mother asked a Jewish friend, Brian Klug,
dancing with him at a student ball in London during the early 1970s.
'Not as long as yours, ma'am', he replied. In reality, the Saxe-Coburg-
Gothas, more recently known as the Windsors, had more in common
with the Klug family's immigrant background than either dance partner
was willing to acknowledge.[23]

But it would be too simplistic to say that refugees per se are missing
from narratives of British history and the construction of the country's
collective memory. Certain groups have been given honourable mention
if not always centre stage in the dominant Simon Schama-esque story of
Kings, Queens and leading politicians.[24] Huguenots, after the revocation
of the Edict of Nantes in 1685, and then Jews escaping Tsarist and Hitlerite

persecution represent an honourable but very elite club of what are perceived as *genuine* refugees. These are portrayed as individuals and groups who were welcomed into Britain from their wicked foreign oppressors and who, in return, have contributed generously to the economic and cultural benefit of the nation. Neither the welcome nor certainly the contribution is wholly imaginary. What is critical here, however, is the importance that is attached to the belief in the decent and fair treatment of genuine refugees – it is essential to notions of Britishness and the belief in an innate tolerance, a mythology shared across the political spectrum. Belief in this myth creates a gulf between the nations that persecute their minorities and the nation that welcomes those that can escape from their less civilised, unjust counterparts. Karl Marx, for example, and some of his revolutionary friends, were thus allowed into mid-Victorian Britain not because of any sympathy for what they stood for, but because adherance to the concepts of liberty and toleration distanced the country from the 'diseased' continent of Europe which had created such figures in the first place. The Prime Minister, Arthur Balfour, made this point clearly in the parliamentary aliens debate in 1905:

> We supposed ourselves, and with considerable reason, to be the best governed country in Europe. We were aware that there were a great many countries in Europe where tyranny prevailed and where it produced, as a natural consequence, conspiracies and in many cases armed rebellion; and we prided ourselves upon giving asylum to the protagonists in a cause which we regarded as, with some exceptions, the cause of freedom.[25]

Balfour was far less sympathetic to the circumstances of the East European Jews who his government was attempting to keep out. In addition, he ignored the less flattering reality that earlier refugees were often treated with xenophobic disdain in Britain. As Bernard Porter eloquently argues, in the 1850s 'The refugees in England … were in a curious situation. Most of them were unloved by most Englishmen, who made them feel very little welcome, but tolerated their presence in deference to what purported to be a great and selfless humanitarian principle: the doctrine of asylum.'[26]

The Huguenots, the Jews escaping Tsar and Fuhrer, and more recently, on the edge of acceptance, the Ugandan Asians, have one crucial factor in common. They are safely in the past. Even if some are still alive and in this country, no more will join them. Theirs are thus 'neat' contained narratives constructed with a happy ending of success and integration into Britain. The complexity that in all these cases initial hostility, including from the state, pushed many, often forcibly, into seeking their livelihoods elsewhere, is conveniently forgotten. There is similar amnesia over the dilemmas faced by many in confronting their past persecution, continuing marginality and conditional acceptance in the place of exile.[27] The experiences of these groups of refugees have been carefully shaped; critical history becomes a luxury in such a process. Moreover, incorporating other refugee movements in the past that cannot be so easily manipulated means that they have to be ignored or made invisible through dispersal and detention, especially contemporary asylum seekers. Indeed, the past 'genuine' refugees can be used as a stick to hit the modern-day alleged abusers of the system.[28]

In the early 1990s Britain attempted to shirk any responsibilities towards refugees as Yugoslavia fell apart in genocidal fury. It did so by supporting the creation of 'safe havens' which, as the Bosnian Muslims found in a series of massacres, were appallingly neither. Robin Cohen suggests that such strategies were used 'to keep asylum-seekers as far away from British shores as possible'. Meanwhile, in rhetoric, he adds, 'Britain's "honourable tradition" of giving refuge [was] simultaneously used as a convenient fig leaf to mask the exclusionist policy'.[29] Since Cohen wrote in the early 1990s, the tendency to stress the 'honourable tradition' has intensified in equal proportion to the growth of anti-asylum seeker sentiment. It has become almost formulaic and automatic. Labour's White Paper, *Fairer, Faster and Firmer* (1998), the basis of the Asylum and Immigration Act of 1999, while strong on detail in terms of the faster and firmer, only offered the past as an example of the fairer. In its words, 'The UK has a long standing tradition of giving shelter to those fleeing persecution in other parts of the world, and refugees in turn have contributed much to our society and culture'.[30]

Such lip-service to past generosity cuts across party boundaries. Conservative leader Michael Howard began the 2005 election campaign with a commitment to firm immigration control as well as acknowledging that 'Britain has always offered a home to genuine refugees and to families who want to work hard. I know – my family was one.'[31] History, however, is often far too messy for such political opportunism. It emerged that Howard's father, who came from Romania to Britain in 1939, had lied on his naturalisation form and that it was possible that his grandfather had entered the country illegally in the same decade. Howard was left bewildered by this information but such details of family history simply expose that the division between 'genuine refugee' and 'illegal immigrant', past and present, are constructed socially and culturally and then made manifest in law.[32] In 1904, the London Committee of Deputies of British Jews complained that for Russian Jews attempting to leave Tsarist Russia, 'Police Certificates of character [because of the corruption of that regime] … are a farce'.[33] Describing the plight of transmigrants in Berlin during the 1920s, the writer Joseph Roth recognised that 'The struggle for papers, the struggle against papers, is something an Eastern [European] Jew gets freely of only if he uses criminal methods to take on society ... He gets to Germany on false papers, or with with none at all'.[34] The legal documentation of refugees and asylum seekers for the rest of the twentieth century and beyond has had and continues to have similar status. To judge the genuineness of refugees by their paperwork is to ignore totally the worlds they have left behind and the demands of receiving societies trying to keep them out. The 'lessons of history' that politicians and commentators wish to impart do not, in reality, make comfortable reading for those wanting to find moral justification through the past for contemporary restrictionism.

Louise London, a former immigration lawyer, is the author of *Whitehall and the Jews* (2000), a magisterial history of British immigration control procedures during and immediately after the Nazi era.[35] After watching a television squabble over asylum featuring the then Home Office minister Barbara Roche with the then shadow Home Secretary, Anne Widdecombe, London wrote that her 'curiosity was not so much about *whether* Roche would mention our proud tradition of asylum as about exactly *how* her version would be worded. Gabbling in her haste to squeeze it into her soundbite, Roche said, "this country has a proud tradition of taking in refugees over many centuries"'. Louise London adds that 'Suddenly it occurred to me to wonder what adjective Roche would propose ... to describe Britain's history of *not* taking in refugees: would that be proud too? Or would it be the opposite? Shamefaced? Hidden? Denied? Suppressed?'[36]

To summarise so far: the myth of fairness operating within the dominant discourse of Britishness demands recognition of *some* refugee movements in the construction of the country's past – including their arrival and reception in and contribution to Britain. Nevertheless, the even more powerful myth of ethnic homogeneity which stresses the absence of past immigration and diversity beyond the Norman invasion ensures that the number of these isolated cases has to be kept to a minimum. As the Conservative, R.A. Butler, then Chancellor of the Exchequer, argued in the House of Commons when opposing the mass and permanent settlement of Hungarian refugees after the failed Hungarian uprising in 1956, 'The United Kingdom was not an immigration country'.[37] Even to suggest that it was, argued Guyanese writer, Michael Gilkes, as late as 1988, 'might give offence'.[38] The absolute numbers with the Huguenots, the Jewish refugees of the 1930s and the Ugandan Asians were, in hindsight, relatively small and they were escaping malevolent foreign dictators – leaders who at the time and subsequently have been regarded as evil personified – whether Louis XIV, Adolf Hitler or Idi Amin. They could therefore be seen as historical quirks, exceptions that proved the rule of non-post conquest settlement. Read any textbook on modern British history and the material on refugees, if combined, usually would at most fill a paragraph.[39] And for textbooks read national and local museums and other forms of the heritage industry. Heritage will be explored in detail in the following chapter but an indication of its limitations is provided at a micro-historical level. The only mention in a public space I have come across, for example, in the county of Hampshire is in the 'Huguenot Garden' in Southampton in what was once a predominantly French-speaking part of the city. Its plaque, the narrative of which will be interrogated shortly, reads

> This small garden of French species of plants was created in 1985 by Southampton City Council. It commemorates the arrival and integration of French Huguenot Refugees to the City 300 years earlier to escape the persecution which followed the revocation of the Edict of Nantes by Louis XIV.

Remembering and forgetting

Hampshire is the local case study part of the global–national–local axis in which *Refugees in an Age of Genocide* rests. It is not, alas, as one kindly American reviewer believed, one of the key points of settlement of refugees in Britain, but his confusion in this matter is revealing.[40] The book, limited to twenty odd refugee movements in the twentieth century, required an enormous amount of patient detective work of both archival sources and oral testimony as well as a close reading of the landscape. Hampshire has indeed some unique pieces of refugee history. It has been a result of a mixture of geography (the importance of its ports and the legacy of its army, navy and airforce presence in the form of camps in which refugees were often placed. Lee-on-the-Solent would have been the latest example, had it not been for the success of anti-asylum seeker campaigners, a remarkable localised moral panic that will be investigated in the following chapter).[41] It has also been the result of sheer chance. While Hampshire has been important, it is not especially unusual and other places, aside from the obvious such as the East End of London, could reveal an equally rich history of refugee presence, and equally important, to echo Louise London's concern, an *absence* of refugees at critical moments.

On this last point of emptiness, it should be noted that historians of groups previously marginalised such as women and ethnic minorities have been very successful in recent decades at showing how they were, in fact, active in the British past in spite of attempts to ignore their presence.

Titles such as Sheila Rowbotham's *Hidden from History: 300 Years of Women's Oppression and the Fight Against It* or Peter Fryer's *Staying Power: The History of Black People in Britain* are classic examples of such recovery work, both with an overtly politicised agenda. Rowbotham wrote in 1973 that she was 'turning up the top soil in the hope that others will dig deeper. I know that already the women's movement has made many of us ask different questions of the past.' Similarly, Fryer's book was a response to the suggestion that 'traces of black life have been removed from the British past to ensure that blacks are not part of the British future'. *Staying Power*, he concluded, was 'offered as a modest contribution to setting the record straight'.[42]

But such specialists have been less good at explaining the silence resulting not from the bias/biased use of sources but the enforced and absolute absence coming out of discrimination, exclusion and expulsion. As Colin Holmes, the modern pioneer of the historical study of immigrants and minorities in Britain, has pointed out, 'Refugees who sought shelter on account of racial, religious or political persecution have been [particularly] neglected'.[43] Returning to Hampshire, it is significant that the only refugee group referred to, and then in passing, are the Huguenots. It is mainly in the form of recognition of one family, the Portals, who established a paper mill in the countryside which was used by the Bank of England to produce its first banknotes – patriotism and economic utility combining neatly here – and also in the Huguenot garden in what is now the heart of Southampton's heritage area. It is significant that in relation to the latter, the plaque highlights not only the arrival but also the *integration* of the Huguenots, a word that almost automatically accompanies the arrival of the Huguenots in later accounts. Thus Hampshire Record Office takes pride in highlighting its archives relating to the Huguenots and how these refugees 'became integrated into British life, sometimes prospering greatly, as was the case for several prominent Hampshire families such as the Portals and the Garniers'.[44] Many other groups in the region were unable to integrate not out of a lack of desire, but because either the time and facilities were not available for them to do so, or, more blatantly, through their forced removal by the state.

Atlantic Hotel, for example, was built not as its recent re-developers have stressed, for those travelling first class on the luxury liners leaving Southampton such as the *Titanic*.[45] In fact it was closer to an immigrant doss-house, a cheap place to stay for transmigrants, mainly East European Jews, before travelling steerage to the new world. It was opened initially as an Emigrants Home by Mrs Eliot Yorke, a Rothschild daughter.[46] Tens, maybe hundreds of thousands of East European Jews passed through Southampton en route to the new world as the port began to

rival Liverpool in the lucrative business of transmigrancy. Their treatment was often rough – one of the companies brought the refugees to
Southampton in sealed railway compartments, ensuring that they did
not settle in Britain before their departure for other lands.[47] The lowly
origins of Atlantic Hotel from the 1890s to 1914 and its overcrowded
and unhygienic dormitories of unwashed men, women and children have
been literally covered up today by a communal kingsize rubbish bin of
what are now upmarket flats in the increasingly desirable and expensive
dock area of the city.[48]

In the capital itself, the Huguenots' exceptional status as ideal citizens
in the making is exploited in the property market. The developers of
Atlantic Hotel decided to tout for business by emphasising what proves
to be a rather tenuous link to the *Titanic*; the original owner, Mrs Doling,
and *not* her residents, was on board the ship. Its refugee connection is
forgotten although, ironically, Mrs Doling was on the *Titanic* hoping to
expand her transmigrant business.[49] In contrast, those responsible for
building expensive apartments in Spitalfields in the last few years relish
in calling it the 'Silk quarter', highlighting the tradition of excellence and
quality that the Huguenots brought to the area: more, apparently, than
an address, but actually 'the essence of living'.[50] It was, of course, exactly
the same area that became the heart of the Jewish East End in the century
from 1850 to 1950: somehow 'schmatter tenements' does not quite have
the same upmarket ring to it.[51] If the charge of a racialised heritage hierarchy sounds far-fetched it was made explicit in Spitalfields during the
1980s, a key decade in the area's conservation. Patrick Wright in his *A
Journey through the Ruins* (1991) outlines the distress caused to 'new
Georgian' sensitivities when the local Bengalis took chain-saws to the
old galleries in the former Huguenot church (later a synagogue and now
a mosque) on the corner of Brick Lane and Fournier Street. Wright suggests that the frustrations at such activities can be detected through the
writing of Gavin Stamp, architectural critic of the right-wing weekly,
The Spectator. Stamp 'described the Huguenots as successful immigrants
who had been "indistinguishable from the English by colour and race"
and did nothing to "offend national sensibilities".'[52] Wright, by using the
word 'frustrations' softens the nature of such racialisation and the processes by which who is deemed to belong, and not belong, to the locality
are made. As *The Spectator*'s byline made explicit, 'Gavin Stamp compares present immigrants unfavourably with the Huguenots'. Stamp's
particular animus was against Islam which 'is alien not only to English
but to Western Christian culture'. In contrast, amongst the virtuous in
Stamp's world view, were post-war Poles and Ukrainians whose loyalty
to Britain, as with the Huguenots, had 'never been in doubt'.[53]

It is true that the Soup Kitchen for the Jewish Poor round the corner from the 'Silk quarter' and the Huguenot church has been transformed, with wonderful irony, into exclusive apartments. The frontage of the soup kitchen in Spitalfields, however, only survives because Bill Fishman, and a handful of other activists, were strenuous in their efforts to preserve some physical remains of the Jewish East End (and the East End as a whole) for future generations. As Fishman stated as early as 1979:

> a crime has been committed against the past. In the race for functional conformity, and from the pressing needs for rehousing the people, the little streets and their ancient communities have fallen before the demolishers.[54]

The Soup Kitchen's façade received listed status but the interior, a century after it was first opened, now represents another world with features such as 'modern monastic' kitchens and a bath with the 'feel of some very exotic, chi-chi Balinese hotel'.[55] Alas it is testament to the indifference, perhaps even the antipathy, of London Jewry to its East End roots, and, until recently, the apathy of the non-Jewish heritage world, that so little of the once vibrant Jewish East End, once home to well over one hundred thousand Jews, now survives in marked contrast to its equivalent, the Lower East Side of Manhattan. As Beth Wenger has suggested, 'The Lower East Side as a neighborhood and a site of memory was never lost, waiting in the wings to be resurrected, but ran more continuously as a thread through American Jewish culture.'[56] For British Jewry, lacking the American myth of being, in John F. Kennedy's words, 'a nation of immigrants', major places of primary settlement such as London's East End, Manchester's Cheetham Hill, the Glasgow Gorbals or Leeds' Leylands, were there to be abandoned in place and in memory, rather than being part of a re-usable past.[57]

Closer to my original home, a similar process of neglect evidenced in the East End has occurred in Manchester. Bill Williams and his remarkable team created the Manchester Jewish Museum in 1984. The elite Spanish and Portuguese synagogue was transformed into an evocative display of Manchester Jewish history, outlining in particular the experiences of many ordinary immigrants who would never have wanted to set foot (or been allowed to set foot) in such a grand religious building. Yet if the preservation and transformation of the synagogue was a tremendous and award-winning success, it is necessary also to remember that the first choice of a museum building, its near neighbour, the Great Synagogue, an even grander structure, was demolished in 1986. Such is the place of its physical heritage on the part of much of Manchester Jewry. As one journalist on the local *Jewish Gazette* put it in 1978, 'Manchester Jewry needed a museum like it needed a ham sandwich'.[58]

Two decades on, the Museum continues to put on excellent exhibitions

and plays a major role in multi-faith education at all levels. That it continues to struggle financially is an indication of the continuing legacy of
the antipathy expressed when its idea was first mooted: as one corre-
spondent to the *Jewish Gazette* argued in 1979:

> You ask Mr Levi or Cohen in Hale or Whitefield and he will very conve-
> niently forget his back-to-back in Strangeways. Not surprising then that
> the masses who have spent the past decades running away from their hard
> lives, without bathrooms, without shoes are not waiting with bated breath
> for Mr Williams to inspire the community to remember its past. Sorry, but
> there never was a chance.[59]

Revealing this 'distancing' process nearly two decades earlier, but in critical
vein, another Mancunian, the humorist Barney Rosemarine, expressed
his irritation with his fellow first generation Jews who 'pretend not to
understand Yiddish expressions'. Perceptively Rosemarine outlined the
'reason for this – or should I say an excuse? There are folk who in their
desire to show themselves as being contained with "British" culture ...
seem to fie the fact that at one time they were associated with conditions
which had some link with the language being sometimes used'.[60] The
arrivals of tens of thousands of New Commonwealth migrants in the
1950s and 1960s for many was thus a relief: attention, some hoped,
would be taken away from Jews as a visible minority group. It also acted
as a further stimulus to disguise immigrant origins, especially given the
animosity faced by the newcomers.[61]

Memory, politics and comparative migration

The fear of being linked to the new arrivals as fellow immigrants was not
paranoia. T.W.E. Roche was a senior immigration official who in 1969
published *The Key in the Lock: A History of Immigration Control in
England from 1066 to the Present Day*. This is Roche writing of the
Indians coming into Britain after the Second World War:

> here were people with whom the majority of the population had come
> into contact only as soldiers, students or politicians turning up in our
> midst with a way of life wholly different from our own, bewildered, gre-
> garious, defensive, like those Russian Jews about whom our grandfathers'
> generation had complained so bitterly seventy years before.

Roche concluded that 'If the West Indian "invasion" had come as a surprise, that from the Indian sub-Continent which followed in its wake
was a veritable shock'.[62] His book was published the year after the second Commonwealth Immigration Act was passed in record time, designed deliberately and blatantly to keep Kenyan Asians out of Britain.[63]

Roche's comments about another refugee group, however, in contrast to those about the strange Indians and Russian Jews, are worthy of note: 'There is no doubt that of all the refugee waves which have washed ashore on these islands, one of the most beneficial and widely welcomed by the native population was the Huguenots, with their intelligence, steadfastness, culture and love of liberty'.[64]

The example of the Huguenots was thrown at the East European Jews at the start of the twentieth century by anti-alien politicians such as William Evans Gordon, Conservative MP for Whitechapel. The supposed assimilatory capacity of the Huguenots was contrasted to the alleged clannishness of the East European Jews. Indeed, Evans Gordon was at pains to draw a 'vital distinction' between the 'Huguenots and other persecuted Protestants' and the turn of the century Jewish immigrants who 'unlike any other alien colony in the land, forms a solid and permanently distinct block – a race apart, as it were, in an enduring island of extraneous thought and custom'.[65] Praising some immigrant or refugee groups, critically from the past, while simultaneously attacking others, those in the present, was also a way of avoiding, or attempting to avoid, accusations of prejudice and racism. W.H. Wilkins in one of the first major published polemics in the debate, *The Alien Invasion* (1892) was at pains to stress that he was not against 'foreign immigration as a whole, but only that part of it which exercises an injurious effect upon our own people'. As ever, the Huguenots were his prized example of a beneficial immigrant group:

> They had not much money, perhaps, but they brought with them something more precious than mere wealth, – the brain, the bone, the muscle, and the manufacturing talent of France. They introduced into England arts and manufactures hitherto unknown, and they added to the lustre of their adopted country by contributing to the science and the literature of the day. They were in fact the *fine fleur* of the French nation.

In contrast, argued Wilkins, the East European Jews brought nothing but crime, disease and overcrowding, but he felt it 'necessary to make clear that one is animated by no sentiments of racial or religious animosity ... Nothing would harm the [anti-alien] movement more than to create a *Judenhetze* in England, the home of religious liberty'.[66]

The memory of the Huguenots was, however, contested and was also used *against* the control of aliens in the 1900s. In 1950, the Home Office commissioned one its civil servants, a Mr Eaglestone, to write a history of its 'Aliens Branch'. Eaglestone acknowledged that 'The reception of the Huguenot refugees after the Revocation of the Edict of Nantes and the benefits which had resulted from it figured largely in the case against restriction.' Some half a century on, however, he was anxious to put the matter straight. The use of this precedent 'entirely ignored the essential fact that the conditions of 1685 were entirely different from those of 1905'. Ignoring the heated contemporary debates raised by the Huguenot presence, Eaglestone provided an official version of history:

> At the earlier date England was a thinly populated and mainly agricultural country with abundant scope for the introduction of new trades and manufactures; the number of the immigrants though large was not unlimited, and the main flow of emigration ceased in a few years; the quality of the incoming refugees was very high, and in ideas, way of life, and religious beliefs they harmonised thoroughly with large classes of the native population and were easily and quickly assimilated.[67]

It was clear that Eaglestone had very little knowledge of the Huguenot refugee movement and his summary of their presence was, in reality, simply a rehearsal, as with Gavin Stamp a generation later, for providing an alternative reading of the later 'aliens' arriving in Britain. Indeed, that the East European Jews were the Huguenots' 'others' was confirmed as Eaglestone's narrative continued:

> In 1905 England was densely populated and highly industrialised; the number of potential immigrants was for practical purposes unlimited, and the movement continually increased because each family settled here tended to send for relatives to follow …

It was not simply a matter of context and scale that differentiated the Jews from the Huguenots. It was also a matter of quality:

> [T]he immigrants were mostly of a lower grade of civilisation and standard of living than the native English and brought few new trades of any value, so that they swamped the labour market and increased existing difficulties of housing and unemployment …

and, argued Eaglestone, of nature:

> [T]he requirements of their religion cut them off from the English population – and the more in proportion as they were strictly observed – and operated to keep the separation permanent and prevent assimilation after the difference of language had ceased to be a bar.[68]

With these parallel but Manichaean accounts, it was hardly necessary for Eaglestone to 'sum up' his message to his fellow civil servants. Nevertheless, he was happy to do so: 'the fact that 80,000 French Huguenots were admitted in 1685 with good results did not show that five or six million Russian and Polish Jews would be welcome in the 20th century'.[69] Re-running these debates fifty years on was not, however, purely for reasons of historical satisfaction. If the restrictionists were at least partially successful in getting their way in 1905 (and more so thereafter), the battle over Huguenot memory was revived in the renewed debate about refugee entry during the Nazi era, the context within which Eaglestone's account is to be located.

In arguing the positive case for the 'economics of the refugee problem', campaigners supporting more generous measures towards those escaping Nazism wanted contemporaries to learn what they called 'the lesson of history'. Its message was spelt out clearly by leading non-conformist, Dorothy Buxton: 'The history of our country during the last four centuries shows that our present suspicious and reluctant attitude towards refugees represents a deplorable drop in our standards.' She provided a very different reading of history than was to be shortly constructed by Eaglestone. Buxton, by explicitly comparing responses to Jewish refugees in the 1930s to those towards Huguenots, attempted to install perspective. She also issued a warning of what might be lost if the government gave way to anti-alien antipathy:

> From 80,000 to 120,000 persons ... took refuge in the United Kingdom as a result of the Revocation of the Edict of Nantes. 80,000 would represent 1.6 per cent of the population of that time. A corresponding proportion of the total population now would be represented by 800,000 refugees.
>
> It is true that there were not wanting sectional interests at the period of influx of Huguenots (and many others), who protested against the foreigners in exactly the same terms as those with which we are now familiar, but the general public was not seriously swayed by them. If sectional interests had been as well organised as they are now our ports would have been closed to the Huguenots, as they are to-day to all but a tiny minority of the victims of persecution.

Buxton concluded that 'The lesson of history as to the amazing benefits we have derived from immigrants cannot be disputed.'[70] Anti-alien campaigners, however, refused to accept her logic. Lord Lymington, a right-wing believer in a 'back-to-the-land' policy, asked, with regard to refugees, whether 'England [is] to be a dumping ground for foreign rubbish now and always?' Responding directly to the work of Buxton and others, he added that

> Much has been made of our acceptance of the Huguenot refugees, and the great benefit which they brought with them, but the point is that the Huguenots were craftsmen and these refugees of today are not; for every valuable technician who comes to this country there are ten thousand who [know] no trade but usury pouring into this over-populated little island.[71]

It might be argued that Buxton represented the majority of (liberal-minded) British people in the 1930s and Lymington only the antisemitic extreme minority. Yet the fact remains that while, as Louise London argues, 80,000 Jewish refugees were given (largely temporary) refuge in Britain before the Second World War, these represented only a small fraction of the '500,000 to 600,000 family and individual case files in the archives of Britain's main Jewish organisation dealing with the refugees'.[72] In short, Buxton and her pro-refugee allies were only partially successful in communicating their 'lesson of history'. That it was not accepted at state level is revealed in the Home Office's own narrative of migration which, post–1945, still maintained the necessity and morality of pre-war controls. Indeed, Eaglestone's critique of the character of East European Jews extended to their co-religionists fleeing Nazism. He refused to accept that Britain had any meaningful tradition of granting asylum or of continuous refugee presence. Instead, Eaglestone argued that in its 'modern conditions, [Great Britain] cannot be a country of settlement – that is it cannot provide a permanent home for any large mass of refugees'. At best, or worst, it might 'be a country of immediate refuge', that is, of temporary transit.[73]

The number of Jewish and other refugees admitted during the 1930s corresponds closely to the absolute number of Huguenots allowed into Britain after 1685. Nevertheless, it did not come near to reaching, as Buxton hoped, the proportion, per capita, of the earlier movement which would have enabled all those applying for refuge during the 1930s to have found safety.[74] Eaglestone, writing in 1950, wrote the official Home Office view of why this, ultimately, was just and right: 'When a ship goes down one lifeboat can only take a certain amount of survivors, and when it is full, the crew must, however regretfully, refuse to rescue any more.'[75] The 'lifeboat' metaphor is one frequently evoked by those in many different contexts seeking to justify refugee restrictionism on moral grounds. The ethics of refugee entry and exclusion will be explored at a general level in the Conclusion. Here the attention will focus on the restrictionists use/abuse of past precedents of refugee movements in Britain.

There were certain ironies in the historical 'evidence' utilised by anti-alien campaigners in the 1900s and 1930s and in Eaglestone's later official defence of them. First, contemporaries attacked the Huguenots for *not* assimilating and for continuing to use French – many of the men, it was reported as late as the mid-eighteenth century, did not know any English at all.[76] In 1710 in *A Letter to the French Refugees concerning their Behaviour to the Government*, their persistence in speaking French and living together led to the accusation that the Huguenots 'were a separate body in the nation'.[77] Nor did such antipathy disappear quickly. In 1753, at the time of the Jew Bill controversy, the slogan 'No Jews, No Wooden Shoes' was a rhyme neatly encapsulating opposition to two immigrant and minority groups.[78]

Second, by the 1960s, more up-to-date anti-alienists, most notoriously

Enoch Powell, were using the example of the integration of East European Jews before the First World War to offer what they saw as a stark
contrast to the essentially un-English, new Commonwealth migrants. At
Eastbourne in November 1968 Powell infamously stated that

> Sometimes people point to the increasing proportion of immigrant off-
> spring born in this country as if the fact contained within itself the ulti-
> mate solution. The truth is the opposite. The West Indian or Asian does
> not, by being born in England, become an Englishman. In law he becomes
> a United Kingdom citizen by birth; in fact he is a West Indian or an Asian
> still.[79]

In two major television interviews in 1969, first with David Frost and
then with Trevor Huddleston, Bishop of Stepney, Powell was pressed to
make a comparison between new Commonwealth migrants and the influx of East European Jews into Britain at the turn of the century. Asked
to defend his comments about a coloured 'alien wedge', for example,
Huddleston quizzed Powell about what was different to earlier immigrants: 'we have got a good many of them in this country who have been
absorbed perfectly well. We have still a very large Jewish community
(thank God) in this country, which has been absorbed perfectly well.
Why is there, then, this sudden trauma?' Powell gave his standard response: 'I think you've failed to see the essential importance of numbers
and time. That factor has been utterly different in these other cases, unless one goes back to the Scandinavian invasions in the tenth century.'[80]
In the earlier interview, Frost had made an explicit reference to the debate of the 1900s, reproducing contemporary comments about an alien
takeover that almost exactly replicated those of Powell's over sixty years
later. In response, Powell, if grudgingly, accepted that subsequently Jews
and non-Jews in Britain had 'learnt to live together', while still praising
the Aliens Act for restricting numbers.[81] Powell was unwilling to denounce
earlier manifestations of anti-alienism. Nevertheless, he also refused to
accept that the later integration of East European Jews and other immigrants and their descendants in any way challenged his views that those
of colour coming into Britain since the Second World War would change
'the character of the country ... beyond recognition ... in a way which its
people neither chose nor expected nor desired'.[82]

  Few in mainstream British politics during the 1960s were willing to
use the emotive and provocative language of Powell. Yet the view of the
newly-emerging Labour politician, Roy Hattersley, that '[racial] integration without [immigration] limitation is impossible',[83] summarised the
position of the two major parties. It led to increasingly restrictive legislation which culminated in the 1971 Immigration Act.[84] Hattersley went
even further and, predicting the intervention of right-wing Conservative,

Norman Tebbitt, a quarter of a century later, suggested 'a test which tries to analyse which immigrants, as well as having jobs or special skills, are most likely to be assimilated into our national life'. Hattersley's emphasis was on Pakistani immigrants, 'whose willingness and ability to be integrated is a good deal less than those from other parts of the Commonwealth'. Their inability to speak English, argued Hattersley, created 'in our major towns problems a good deal more severe than West Indian immigrants'.[85]

Such differentiation of 'good'/'bad' immigrants or refugees had, as we have seen, a long pedigree. Sir John Pedder was a senior civil servant dealing with alien matters from the 1900s through to the early 1930s. He was, in the phrase of bureaucratic historian, Jill Pellew, a 'career official' who, through working on alien legislation in 1904 and 1905, became the Home Office's first 'expert' on the subject. The 1905 Aliens Act 'brought promotion for Pedder who became principal clerk of a small, new department'. After the First World War, Pedder had advanced further within the Home Office. The 1919 Aliens Restriction Act was almost totally exclusionary. Very few immigrants and refugees were allowed entry. Instead, the attention of the Home Office was focused on whether to grant naturalisation to aliens who had come to Britain in an earlier period. In 1924, showing the continuity of an earlier animus against those from eastern Europe, Pedder justified and made explicit the racialised basis of British government naturalisation policy:

> It rests on experience that different races display very different qualities and capabilities for identifying themselves with this country ... Latin, Teuton and Scandinavian races... with a certain kinship with British races ... are easily assimilated. On the other hand, Slavs, Jews and other races from Central and Eastern parts of Europe stand in a quite different position. They do not want to be assimilated.[86]

Similarly, in the 1930s, government officials and refugee bodies demanded the selection of the 'right type of refugee' as against those presenting themselves who were 'so filthily dirty'. This prejudice, aimed particularly against East European Jews, continued even after the Second World War when such people, survivors of the Holocaust now languishing in displaced persons camps, were largely rejected as desirable immigrants to Britain because they were seen as economically unsuitable workers, politically subversive and socially and culturally unassimilable. At the same time, however, tens of thousands of non-Jews were recruited from these camps to fill gaps in the British labour market.[87] What makes the entry of members of Michael Howard's family to Britain in the 1930s and 1940s so intriguing is that they represented, to government officials, the 'wrong type' of immigrant – i.e. *ostjuden* from Romania. Romanian and other East European Jews during the Nazi era were equally, if not more in need of refuge than the more 'desirable' German Jews. It appears that the irregularities in the Howard family paperwork are to be explained by the Howards' (previously the Hechts') attempt to overcome the huge procedural barriers erected by the British government against the entry of East European Jews.

In the 1960s, the sober contribution to the debate of Michael Foot, future leader of the Labour Party, that it was a 'justifiable proposition that every wave of immigration we have had into this country has benefited this country', was largely ignored. Foot, echoing Dorothy Buxton thirty years earlier, urged his fellow politicians 'to put the question of immigration into historical perspective'.[88] In fact, the past *was* instrumentalised in the attempt to restrict new Commonwealth migration as much as that against alien entry; the problem was that 'history' was simply not being utilised in the progressive manner that Foot or Buxton had desired. Hostile contemporaries either separated out those trying to settle in Britain as desirable/undesirable or differentiated between those in the past who were deserving against those in the present who were not.

The third irony in the instrumentalisation of the Huguenots takes us back to the French refugee community in Southampton and also to the contributions of the then Labour Home Secretary, David Blunkett, to debates about community relations after the so-called northern riots in Oldham, Burnley and Bradford in 2001. Blunkett, rather than focusing fully on the forces of racial violence and exclusion faced by many Muslims in Britain, as well as the cultural denigration of their faith, chose to place emphasis on their alleged lack of integration. Ordering them, like his Conservative predecessors of the 1980s and 1990s, and Hattersley a generation earlier, to 'be British', Blunkett specifically attacked Muslims for not speaking English, even within the privacy of their own homes and families, because he regarded it as divisive.[89] While he was later keen to correct the impression that he had 'never said, or implied, that lack of fluency in English was in any way directly responsible for the disturbances in Bradford, Burnley and Oldham in the summer of 2001', David Blunkett was still keen to highlight that

> speaking English enables parents to converse with their children in English, as well as their historic mother tongue, at home and to participate in wider modern culture. It helps overcome the schizophrenia which bedevils generational relationships.[90]

In this respect, an alternative historic perspective on such comments, as demanded by Buxton and Foot, might focus on St Julians, the Huguenot church in Southampton, with its origins and buildings from the sixteenth century, where for nearly half a millennium services have been conducted in French. Is this a threat to the social fabric of local society? Is Southampton a fragmented community because there have been sermons in one of its most ancient churches delivered in the old and bitter enemy's tongue? The irony of this linguistic survival was certainly lost on anti-alienists such as William Evans Gordon who saw the ubiquity of Yiddish in the East End as proof that the East European Jews were beyond as-similation. In May 1903, William Moens, vice-president of the Hugue-not Society of London, was called, by Evans Gordon, to give evidence to the Royal Commission on Alien Immigration. Moens confirmed that 'in Southampton by licence of the Privy Council in 1567, a church was allot-ted to the Walloon congregation, and a French service is still held there every Sunday'.[91]

It might well be asked why the speaking of some foreign languages is later perceived as quaint and worthy of inclusion in the heritage industry (and in marked contrast, as we have seen, to how the speaking of French was regarded at the time of Huguenot settlement), while others are seen as problematic in the extreme.[92] Even that linguistic survival of French in the case of St Julians hides another aspect of the pressure to assimilate – in the late seventeenth and early eighteenth century the church was put under irresistible force to conform to the Anglican Church and away from its non-conformist, Huguenot roots.[93] As Bill Williams has argued, conditional acceptance, whether it be linguistic, religious or cultural, is 'the quintessential means by which British society accommodates ethnic minorities'.[94]

The fourth and final irony takes us back to Roche's comments con-cerning Indians and the 1968 Act: East African Asians, and especially those from Uganda, have become the third club in the elite league of refugees who we are now allowed and even encouraged to remember and who can, perversely, be utilised to attack today's undesirable new-comers. It is remarkable, for example, that the *Express*, the national daily newspaper at the forefront of the contemporary British media campaign against asylum seekers, could editorialise in 2003, without any sense of irony or self-awareness, that

> Back in 1972, according to Cabinet papers released last week, a Tory gov-ernment was secretly hunting for an 'island asylum' for Asians expelled from Uganda by Idi Amin. Thankfully, the plan came to nothing and Ugan-dan Asians continue to make a huge contribution to this country's culture and economy. Thirty years on, no respectable politician would consider transporting refugees against their will to some distant island.[95]

It is just feasible, though hard to envisage, that, in fifty years time, Home Secretary successors to Douglas Hurd, David Blunkett and others will be bemoaning the failure of green blobs from the Milky Way, victims of inter-galactic ethnic cleansing, to integrate properly unlike the example set by the now fondly remembered people of Pakistani background in Bradford. It might be argued that the difficulty in imagining such a scenario in the early twenty-first century is less to do with disbelief in there being life outside Planet Earth and more about the inability to perceive Muslims as good citizens, as 'one of us', especially post-9/11. From the nineteenth century onwards, the term 'alien' has developed from a legal term and status to one whose social and cultural reference point emphasises a problematic alterity, earthly or otherwise. Satirising such fears of otherness, Manchester punk poet, John Cooper Clarke, fantasised marriage to 'an alien being whose skin was jelly [and] whose teeth were green',

> [when] we walked out – tentacle in hand
> you could tell that the earthlings would not understand
> they'd go ... nudge nudge ... when we got off the bus
> saying it's extra-terrestial – not like us
> and it's bad enough with another race
> but fuck me ... a monster ... from outer space.[96]

In the early twenty-first century, however, it is the 'asylum seeker' who many in Britain fail to accept as fully human.

In a 2003 editorial entitled 'Way of Life at Stake', the *Sun*, Britain's best-selling newspaper, launched into a major attack on 'illegal immigration', by which it meant those who came to the country falsely as asylum seekers. There was, it suggested, a 'flood of shirkers, scroungers and criminals ... with their drugs, guns and vice' who were removing the Britishness of 'our cities'. Widespread fear about asylum seekers, it assured its three million-plus readers, was 'not racism. It is a fear that those who abuse our hospitality are stealing not just our money but our character and our culture.' The *Sun* then attempted to legitimise its anti-asylum seeker campaign by positive reference to non-white migrants but, in the process, continued the long tradition of differentiating past arrivals (good) from current entrants (bad):

> In the past half century, Britain has welcomed hundreds of thousands of Commonwealth and Third World citizens. They have enriched our lives, both materially, spiritually and culturally. Their children have been born here and have grown up as British in outlook as those whose lineage can be traced back for centuries.[97]

What is remarkable about such negative comments about asylum seekers is that they have been articulated not just by the populist right but also by those within the left-liberal world. A key example is provided by the 'progressive' monthly magazine *Prospect*. In several key articles *Prospect* has warned that current immigration influxes 'cannot continue at current rates without disturbing national culture and identities'. Again, the past has been directly instrumentalised. The numbers of people involved, suggests Bob Rowthorn, 'a leading left-wing economist', undermine attempts 'to teach a coherent national history'.[98] Asylum seekers within this discussion have been seen as particularly problematic. Immigrants to Britain, reminds *Prospect*'s editor, David Goodhart, 'come in all shapes and sizes. From the American banker or Indian software engineer to the Somali asylum seeker – from the most desirable to the most burdensome'.[99] Gordon Brown, Chancellor of the Exchequer, and second in the Labour government hierarchy, acknowledged this common ground between 'progressives' and the 'new right' in the growing debate about Britishness and immigration. In a speech delivered to the British Council in 2004, Brown talked of a tradition of tolerance in Britain, 'welcoming ... successive waves of settlers – from Saxons and Normans to Huguenots and Jews and Asians and Afro-Caribbeans'. It is significant that he did *not* include contemporary asylum seekers in his list of the 'included'.[100] Indeed, it is revealing that while the Labour party is committed to community cohesion and inclusion, refugees appear to be outside its vision of future Britishness. In 2005, at the beginning of a General Election campaign in which immigration and asylum was clearly becoming a key issue between the two major parties, while Labour promised to maintain the 1951 Geneva Convention, it pledged to re-examine the cases of all given refugee status after five years. The aim, given public concern, especially as manifest in opinion polls, was to encourage return and cut back numbers resident in Britain. In Labour's plans, temporary leave to remain would replace permanent refugee status.[101] Contemporary asylum seekers and refugees have thus been perceived as alien to Britain's history and future. In order to make opposition to them appear less racially prejudiced, asylum seekers in particular have been contrasted unfavourably to more recent arrivals from the New Commonwealth (or to past 'genuine' refugees) in their potential to assimilate within the nation.

Re-examining the aliens debate of the 1900s, Dorothy Buxton was painfully aware a generation later of 'the truth of how history repeats itself'.[102] Her problem in the late 1930s was to counter the collective amnesia of that debate, or more accurately, the selective memory that, at best, recalled only certain groups and, at worst, either problematised or denied the existence of past immigrant and refugee movements into Britain. Buxton was not the first to recognise this bias in history and memory. Indeed, half a century earlier, formal attempts were made to counter general ignorance in Britain and also to provide a usable past for descendants of former refugees and immigrants to gain pride and a sense of belonging.

Creating counter histories

Through dint of effort by those who set up the Huguenot Society of London (HSL) in 1885 and the Jewish Historical Society of England (JHSE) eight years later, not an alternative but more a gently pluralistic version of the British past was established, reflecting a broader trend in the 'invention of tradition' at this time.[103] The former, formed on the two-hundredth anniversary of the Revocation of the Edict of Nantes, wished to revive understanding and knowledge of the Huguenot contribution to Britain which its founders feared was fading into obscurity.[104] In the first presidential address to the latter, Lucien Wolf emphasised that 'a very large part of English history may be said to belong to Jewish history'. Wolf also highlighted the 'by no means inconsiderable role' of Jews both 'in England and abroad in the passage of this country from Roman Catholicism to Protestantism'.[105]

Integration, contribution and progress were the watchwords of these two societies, with the emphasis placed particularly on the deep history of these communities within Britain. The first publication of the HSL was devoted to the Walloon settlement in Norwich covering the period from 1565 to 1832. As its author, W.J.C. Moens (who later, as has been noted, gave testimony to the Royal Commission on Alien Immigration), suggested, Norwich was chosen because it was one of the first and 'most important settlements of the Protestant refugees to this country'. His painstaking research was, in addition, aimed at those descended from such refugees from Flanders who 'may wish to trace their families before they left their fatherland'. Creating such a genealogical resource reflected the fact that by the late nineteenth century the assimilation process had developed so far that often only the possession of a surname gave any hint of Huguenot origins.[106] The equivalent founding volume of the JHSE's *Transactions* had three articles devoted to the medieval period up to expulsion in 1290, two devoted to the re-admission of the Jews in the 1650s and the other two acting as a chronological and thematic bridge between each epoch. The exclusive focus of the JHSE on the medieval and the early modern eras was not accidental – it highlighted the concern both to document continuity of presence and to illustrate progress in English attitudes and responses.[107]

More recently in the British Jewish case, through ventures such as the Manchester Jewish Museum and the Museum of the Jewish East End, a more radical heritage was presented, allowing for the grassroots stories of ordinary, later, refugees, whether escaping Tsarist, Nazi, Communist or Arab nationalist persecution.[108] In his 1893 presidential address, Lucien Wolf had pleaded against 'the great-man-theory of history [which] can only afford a very inadequate ... clue to the general development of the social organism'.[109] His successors for the better part of a century ignored his advice on the dangers of elitism but, following the example of the early JHSE, rarely moved beyond the granting of emancipation to the Jews in the mid-nineteenth century. It took a new generation of scholars, Jewish and non-Jewish, to provide more inclusive and self-confident history and heritage as represented by the new social history museums in Manchester and the capital. In particular, they brought in the experiences of and responses to the East European Jews, half a million of whom settled in Britain for at least two years in the period from 1870 to 1914, forming the majority of British Jewry through the twentieth century.[110]

In contrast, other groups of refugee origin in Britain have had less permanence or resources to establish their own representation. The Heritage Centre in Spitalfields, for example, a proposed museum of immigration and refugee settlement in the East End, has been in the making for over two decades without the required funding to make it happen. Its lack of progress is strikingly different to that of the Ellis Island Immigration Museum in New York which was supported massively by private and public resources. Rob Perks, a leading oral historian in Britain who has been involved in various projects interviewing refugees and immigrants, visited Ellis Island in the early 1990s. He wondered whether '£8,000 could be raised in Britain for a museum about immigration, let alone the £80 million raised for Ellis Island'.[111] The development or non-development of the Heritage Centre has certainly confirmed Perk's prescience. In order to connect to wider and more popular discourses, those linked to the Heritage Centre (now styling itself the Museum of Immigration and Diversity) have made connections to the site, 19 Princelet Street, Spitalfields – a former eighteenth-century Huguenot house and later a Victorian synagogue – that have been totally bogus. In a remarkable example of distorted memory work they evoked iconic individuals, movements and events – Anne Frank, the *Kindertransport* and the Battle of Cable Street – to give status to a building whose particular immigrant and refugee past was clearly not seen by those concerned about its future and the media to make it sufficiently significant or newsworthy. The Holocaust, in particular, has become a reference point for 19 Princelet Street – it was, apparently, 'the nation's answer to the Anne Frank House in Amsterdam'. Similarly, references to the *Kindertransport*, as will emerge in chapter 4 of this study, have also become part of the mythology of

Britain's past redemptive refugee policy.[112]

The reality of New York's Ellis Island Immigration Museum stands in contradistinction to the grandiose but still frustrated aims of 19 Princelet Street which claims to be 'Europe's first museum celebrating diversity'.[113] It is also revealing to compare the project in Spitalfields to the Tenement Museum in the Lower East Side of New York. Developed from the late 1980s in a building that it is estimated housed in total some 10,000 people, largely Jews, its mission is to 'promote tolerance and historical perspective through the presentation and interpretation of the variety of urban immigrant and migrant experiences on Manhattan's Lower East Side, a gateway to America'. It focuses on six communities – 'free-African, Irish, Italian, Eastern European Jewish, German, and Chinese'.[114] This New York as world melting pot ideal clearly distorts the specific history of the actual building, but its intense success – both in raising funding and in attracting visitors – shows the power of the immigrant/refugee myth in (liberal) American culture as extolled by Kennedy in the late 1950s. The financial weakness and the desperate attempt to find a usable past in the case of 19 Princelet Street tells a very different story of British collective memory and the 'myths we live by'.[115]

The history of Huguenots and Jews in Britain has, through generations of scholars from within these communities and the politics of memory outside them, developed a relatively privileged status in comparison to other immigrant and refugee origin groups. Nevertheless, the recent story of 19 Princelet Street shows the continuing marginality of even Huguenot and Jewish memory. The exhibitions, museums, books and journals devoted to these two groups have created only the smallest of ripples within the general British historical and heritage worlds. The HSL commissioned Robin Gwynn to write a history of the Huguenots in Britain to mark the tercentenary of the Revocation of the Edict of Nantes. In 1985, even after a century of distinguished HSL publications, Gwynn acknowledged that 'the Huguenots have been shamefully neglected by English historians'. He added that

> Over the years, many immigrant groups have contributed to English society: amongst others, Flemish, Huguenot, Jewish, Welsh and Irish. Of these peoples, only the Jews have been adequately studied. The Huguenot refugees of the later Stuart period have been accorded more attention than Irish or Welsh migrants, but in general such groups are ignored, or summarily dismissed, or confined to the pages of specialist journals.[116]

A wider issue remains, however: why has the refugee experience in particular remained so elusive for historians?

The idea of refugee studies within academia is a relatively recent one, but is becoming increasingly established if still hardly mainstream. In addition to the Refugee Studies Centre at Oxford, linked to the *Journal of Refugee Studies* which began publication in 1988, there are now MA programmes at several British universities. It is significant, however, that when the *Journal* was launched it described its interests as being within 'anthropology, economics, health and education, international relations, law, politics, psychology and sociology'.[117] The absence of history from this list was unfortunate but perhaps realistic. Twelve years later, when the editor, Roger Zetter, was taking stock of its progress, he carried out a statistical survey of the many hundreds of articles submitted to his journal. History as a discipline came bottom, representing just 4 per cent of the papers published.[118] If, as Zetter argued in his first editorial, refugee studies 'for the most part ... existed on the periphery [rather than] the mainstream of academic enterprise',[119] its utter marginality in the history profession is doubly magnified. Revealingly, while *Refugees in an Age of Genocide* has been reviewed in law, literary, humanitarian and progressive journals, it has hardly been noted in history periodicals. It is also significant that what is clearly described as a history book has been shelved in the law sections of bookshops. Even the publisher forgot initially to put the book in its history catalogue, placing it instead in political studies. Taken together it suggests on the one hand actual resistance rather than simple apathy from the history profession to refugee studies and, on the other, from non-historians, the inability to see history and refugees as linked or relevant.

Defining the refugee: legal victories

The key to unravelling this antipathy rests, it will be argued, in the issue of fluidity against permanence, and, underneath, the desire, indeed the absolute demand, to control concepts such as time and place. In 1951, sociologist Jacques Vernant was commissioned by the United Nations High Commissioner for Refugees to write a comprehensive study of the 'refugee in the post-war world'. Attempting to define the 'problem', Vernant perceptively recognised that the refugee, while eliciting pity, also provoked

> an element of anxiety. The refugee is, in the first place, a symbol of *instability*. The legend of the Wandering Jew, the curse weighing upon him whose homeland is nowhere, is an indication of the survival in civilized minds of feelings which are frequently met with among primitive peoples.[120]

Similarly, Liisa Malkki highlights the 'pathologization of uprootedness in the national order of things' when refugees are referred to, even within scholarly literature.[121]

Refugees or asylum seekers, lacking the fundamental requirements of home and homeland, have to be defined into shape. Those best suited to controlling their messiness and, more than anything, their inherent instability, it is deemed, are not historians but lawyers. In contrast to the 'complex and ambivalent' social responses to the refugee, Vernant pointed to what he saw as the misleading clarity of the jurist, for whom 'a man's status as a refugee is determined first and foremost by the factors which led to his condition: expatriation and the breaking of ties that bound him to the State of his nationality'.[122] Hannah Arendt, herself a refugee from Nazism, wrote in *The Origins of Totalitarianism*

> All discussions about refugee problems [have] revolved around ... one question: 'How can the refugee be made deportable again?' The Second World War and the D[isplaced] P[ersons] camps were not necessary to show that the only practical substitute for a non-existent homeland was an internment camp. Indeed, as early as the thirties this was the only 'country' the world had to offer the stateless.[123]

Arendt was deeply influenced by the Nazi era, writing that 'contemporary history has created a new kind of human being – the kind that are put in concentration camps by their foes and internment camps by their friends'.[124] In fact, the internment of refugees went earlier than Arendt suggested and was a feature of the post-1918 world, but now one almost totally forgotten. It was the 1920s rather than the 1930s that saw the largest displacement and confinement of people in inter-war Europe.

Michael Marrus argues that while refugees 'have tramped across the European continent since time immemorial', it is only in the twentieth century that they have 'become an important problem of international politics, seriously affecting relations between states'. Numbers, the length of their exile and above all their hazardous legal status, argues Marrus, mark out the modern refugee 'from those of earlier times because their homelessness removed them so dramatically and so uniquely from civil society'.[125] Until 1951 and the Geneva Convention on the Status of Refugees, refugees had no rights or international protection. Before then they were at the mercy of the gatekeepers of each nation state. By 1933 most western countries, with only a few exceptions such as France, had implemented a policy of almost total control on alien entry.[126] Britain formally had no refugee policy or entry during the 1930s. In 1935, a Ministry of Labour official made explicit that government policy was 'not to vary the aliens administration in favour of or against the refugees'.[127] It did, subsequently, at best become flexible with its existing immigration procedures, though it proved unwilling to provide permanent rather than temporary refuge to Jews escaping the Third Reich. Indeed, re-inventing British tradition by coining a far more restrictive myth than that of a

country, pre–1905, that had offered the 'right of asylum' uncondition-
ally, Eaglestone's official mid-twentieth century narrative stated that it
had 'always been the practice to admit genuine transmigrants freely'.
Britain, he added, 'cannot provide a permanent home for any large mass
of refugees'.[128]

The 1951 United Nations Convention, which at least challenged, even
if it did not overcome such insularity, was created very much with the
Second World War in Europe, and its Cold War aftermath, in mind. It
defined a refugee as

> Any person who owing to a well founded fear of being persecuted for
> reasons of race, religion, nationality, membership of a particular social
> group or political opinion, is outside the country of his nationality and is
> unable, or owing to such fear, is unwilling to avail himself of the protec-
> tion of that country; or who, not having a nationality and being outside
> the country of his former habitual residence, is unable, or owing to such
> fear, is unwilling to return to it.[129]

Since then, as Patricia Tuitt has argued, 'International refugee law [has
been] established as the primary form of regulating and controlling ...
movements and, as such, refugee law has both directly and indirectly
been a guiding influence in discourses about the refugee'. She continues
that 'in seeking to portray the refugee as being for all practical intents
and purposes reducible to [the] definition under the Geneva Convention,
we have denied the refugee identity, and thus have denied adequate protection to refugees seeking asylum in Western Europe'.[130] Rather than
acting out of humanitarian impulse, international law does so only mar-
ginally and incidentally in spite of the rhetoric employed by developed
states. In this respect, James Hathaway suggests that

> Refugee law as currently administered allows Western states to maintain
> the facade of universal, humane concern without the necessity of afford-
> ing genuine protection. The failure to acknowledge the disharmony of law
> and social reality makes it possible to avoid the discussion of basic prin-
> ciples that would logically follow, and which would require developed states
> either to enhance their contributions to refugee protection or to temper their
> much prized discourse of humanitarianism and human rights.[131]

Rather than confront the needs and indivuality of refugees, Tuitt states
that 'One of the main functions of refugee law has been to shape or
construct an official or formal identity of refugee'.[132] Even then, as political scientist, Gil Loescher adds, 'International law seeks to define the
minimum that should be offered to refugees.'[133]

The 1951 Geneva Convention had as its reference point a European
conflict and post-war dislocation that had left huge numbers displaced –
over forty million in the war alone.[134] Michael Marrus places this starkly

in a historical context: 'Europe had never seen so many refugees'.[135] Since then, with notable exceptions after the fall of Communism and especially the break-up of Yugoslavia, the European continent has not been the major source of refugee movements which are now truly global and diverse. It is inevitable that 'Refugee identity varies from region to region'. Patricia Tuitt argues that in response 'Refugee law as a means of reducing the refugee identity is able to promote its overall cost reduction aim provided two important conditions exist. The first is that there must exist a dominant refugee identity – a dominant means through which the refugee is conceived ... The second is that this entrenched identity must be relatively narrow and inflexible.'[136]

Tuitt wrote in 1996, but her conclusions are clearly borne out by the current policies towards asylum seekers and refugees in the western world today, most recently and graphically illustrated by the Australian government's treatment of Afghans reaching its shores by boat, the success of politicians like Le Pen in France and, most recently, in Belgium, Holland and Denmark, as well as the desire of many governments to appease their electorates who are assumed to be hostile to asylum seekers.[137] If, concludes Tuitt, her two conditions exist, it 'becomes possible to portray refugees as illegal, bogus, fraudulent or at best on a second tier of humanitarian need, thereby justifying a limited range of assistance to refugees without that identity'.[138] Writing half a century earlier, Jacques Vernant pointed out that the refugee 'is the *unknown*. Every society seeks to classify foreigners, whether individuals or in groups, according to their "social coordinates", that is to say, the land they inhabited or the larger group to which they belonged'. The refugee has been cut off from his land, country and the 'State which is its legal expression'. Vernant believed that what singled out the refugee 'as a man apart', both legally and socially, was 'his *inferiority*; he is inferior both to the citizens of the country which gives him shelter and to all other foreigners, not refugees, living in that country'.[139] Ultimately, as Tuitt insists, 'international refugee law turns away from the needs of the refugee and towards the sovereign interests of Western States'.[140]

If the international legal construction of refugees has reinforced their social perception as 'unknowable', it is important to recognise the role of those who have worked against that status either as individuals or as collective campaigners on behalf of the persecuted. Historians have, in contrast to the attention they have given to anti-alienists, ignored those who have worked on behalf of the oppressed, such as the forgotten figure in refugee work and humanitarianism more generally, the independent-minded Anglican clergyman, James Parkes. Parkes, as will be explored in the Conclusion, worked ceaselessly on behalf of European Jewry during the Nazi era. He does not, however, feature in studies of twentieth-century British Christianity, let alone in general histories of modern Britain.[141]

Finding a place for the refugee beyond law?

Historians, through their silence on the subject, have failed to challenge the discourse generated by law on refugees or to respond to those such as Parkes who recognised the ethical imperative to help the persecuted, simply by acknowledging their common humanity. It was for this reason that the focus in *Refugees in an Age of Genocide* was on the lives of the refugees themselves, constructing their lives and responses to them through oral and written testimony. It was an attempt to break down the idea of refugees as either a constrained legal concept or the mass of undifferentiated miserable humans as often portrayed in the media. It thus in its sphere of historical writing runs alongside the growing number of literary and artistic representations that attempt to humanise refugees, whether through films such as in Michael Winterbottom's *In This World* (2003), oral history projects being carried out across the United Kingdom or Howard Davies' photographs.

In all these artistic and cultural representations and engagements, there is recognition of the huge political, legal and social barriers facing asylum seekers and refugees. Nevertheless, they are not shown as passive victims or without individuality. Indeed, it is in refugee self-expression that the contrast between outer perceptions and inner experiences is made blatantly clear. In her introduction to an anthology of refugee writing in Britain, *The Bend in the Road* (1997), Jennifer Langer notes how 'The media frequently portray refugees as a stereotypical group who are disempowered, uneducated, illiterate victims intent on exploiting the host society's welfare and other systems.' The literacy practices within *The Bend in the Road* reveal multi-layered and complicated realities, providing 'the opportunity to gain an insight not only into the pain of the refugee experience, manifested in alienation, marginalisation and loss of identity but also into the complexity and diversity of the experiences, concerns and issues of writers from different regions'.[142]

In Langer's anthology the genres of writing and the experiences are far from homogeneous, yet a common theme which remains unrecognised by legal definitions and within media representation – that of the uncertainty of displacement – runs throughout. In the words of Bosnian exile, Himzo Skorupan in his 'London Notes':

> this is the way things are: I am not really here, and over there, I am no more.[143]

Skorupan's prose stands as a warning against sentimentalising or romanticising the refugee and refugee experience. The bravery of Winterbottom's *In This World*, for example, is that 'no heart-warming relationships are established and no characters are registered as colourfully unforgettable'.[144] Many refugees manage to re-create new lives and they often contribute way beyond their proportion to their country of adoption. Yasmin Alibhai-Brown's family escaped from Idi Amin's Uganda. In Oxford she came into contact with Hugh Blaschko, a refugee from Nazism, who taught her that 'dispossessed people lose much less than they gain, that not having a nation, a country, a flag, is a liberation which enables you to see, feel and taste the whole world as an insider'.[145]

Alibhai-Brown's perspective is crucial in undermining the image of refugees as only pitiable. Yet it is also important to remember that the refugee experience always contains loss and frequently involves misery and suffering before, during and often after exile. The introduction to this study has explored the dangers of romantically portraying the status of 'refugee' as somehow liberating, freed from the normal restraint of the nation state.[146] One in six current refugees in Britain, for example, has a physical health problem severe enough to affect their everyday way of life. Roughly half of all asylum seekers have mental health difficulties 'associated with depression and post-traumatic trauma'.[147] Gil Loescher states the situation bluntly: 'Refugees … can rebuild their lives and start afresh, but many are unsuccessful, never emerging from the socially marginalized sectors of society'.[148] From the historian's perspective, it also needs to be kept in mind that while it is important to humanise history, the task is also to make sense of it, contextualising the experience. The potentially 'softer' approach of representing life stories in different media must not be at the expense of explaining where, and where not, they are situated in local, national and global developments – again, a success of *In This World*. The problem for historians, one that largely explains their unwillingness to engage, is that refugees do not readily fit, or rather they do not fit into their dominant assumptions of what the historical narrative should be about.

To conclude: putting the refugees back into history offers a major challenge. Refugees go beyond the black–white divide that crudely is seen as the faultline of racism but which ignores so many different forms of prejudices. Acknowledgement of their reality forces us to be more internationally-minded and to acknowledge that the local, the national and the global are intimately linked and socially constructed. Moreover, for the forcibly displaced, physical 'home' for many is a place lost and never to be recovered. As the Yugoslav refugee poet, Miroslav Jancic, states in his London exile: 'Language is my homeland'.[149] Examining critically the

past treatment of refugees challenges the tendency towards complacency
and the comforting assumption that 'our' noble tradition of granting
asylum can be taken for granted. It also, however, helps uncover the
many thousands of committees and millions of ordinary people who have
been involved in helping refugees in Britain and beyond.

From figures produced by the United Nations High Commission for
Refugees relating to the late twentieth and early twenty-first centuries,
of the 20 million-plus refugees in the world today, at least three-quarters
are being looked after in the developing world, with by far the greatest
numbers in the poorest countries.[150] In contrast, almost all asylum seekers are located in the western world. In other words, those least able
economically to deal with this massive issue are shouldering the vast
bulk of responsibility. Meanwhile, the prosperous West takes only a tiny
number of refugees and tries to stop more settling by creating the legal,
political and social construct, 'asylum seeker' – one that is almost unknown in the developing world. Nevertheless, according to a survey carried out by the *Reader's Digest* in 2000, four out of five adults in Britain
believed that asylum seekers came to this country because it is perceived
as a 'soft touch'. The sample overestimated the number of immigrants
and ethnic minorities by up to 500 per cent. Asylum seekers, to put all
these fears in context, represent less than one third of 1 per cent of the
UK population.[151] In 2002, a further poll suggested that 'on average people
think that 23% of the world's refugees and asylum seekers are in the
UK'. This was more than ten times greater than the reality 'which is
actually less than 2%'.[152] Worryingly for the future, for fifteen to eighteen
year-olds, the figure was even higher – 31 per cent.[153]

Fears about asylum seekers undermining the social security, education
and health services, taking our jobs and bringing crime, terrorism and
disease reveals much about insecurities within British identity today. The
absence and presence of refugees is thus a crucial but neglected part of
the country's history and construction of identity(ies). Forgetting, as
Jonathan Boyarin reminds us, is an active and not a passive process. He
suggests that the relationship between memory and forgetting is 'closer
to that of direct proportion' and not inversely related like plenty or famine. At times, the processes of 'forgetting and memory [are] so intermingled as to become almost one'.[154] Or, as Hyman Kaplan, Leo Rosten's
fictional East European hero, explains to his fellow students at the American Night Preparatory School for Adults, his brother Max 'is tarrible
smart. He got a wonderful mamory, only he forgats.' Stunned by his
logic or illogic, his long-suffering teacher, Miss Mitnick, asks him to explain, which he does triumphantly: 'Fects are fects! Foist, my brodder
has a wonderful mamory! Like a policeman! But – *sometimes* Max forgats.

So does dat minn he doesn't have a movvelous mamory *ven ve jost agreet he did?!*[155] For Max Kaplan, read the historical profession: the neglect of refugees has not been accidental – their history has been actively forgotten.

Notes

1 Hugo Gryn, *A Moral and Spiritual Index* (London: Refugee Council, 1996).
2 John Berger, *Keeping a Rendezvous* (London: Granta Books, 1992), p. 12.
3 Tony Kushner and Katharine Knox, *Refugees in an Age of Genocide: Global, National and Local Perspectives during the Twentieth Century* (London: Frank Cass, 1999), p. 1.
4 Most notably in his touring exhibitions, *Home and Away* and *Images of Exile*. For the latter, see *iNexile* no. 35 (January 2005), p. 20.
5 Liisa Malkki, 'Speechless Emissaries: Refugees, Humanitarianism and Dehistoricization', *Cultural Anthropology* vol. 11 no. 3 (August 1996), pp. 386–7.
6 *Daily Telegraph*, 21 May 2002.
7 Peter Mandler, *History and National Life* (London: Profile Books, 2002), p. 1.
8 Robin Gwynn, *Huguenot Heritage: The History and Contribution of the Huguenots in Britain* (London: Routledge, 1985), p. 1.
9 John Hope Simpson, *The Refugee Problem: Report of a Survey* (London: Oxford University Press, 1939).
10 Michael Marrus, *The Unwanted: European Refugees in the Twentieth Century* (Oxford: Oxford University Press, 1985); Gerard Noiriel, *La Tyrannie du national: le droit d'asile en Europe 1793–1993* (Paris: Calmann-Levy, 1991).
11 Peter Cahalan, *Belgian Refugee Relief in England during the Great War* (New York: Garland, 1982). See also Tony Kushner, 'Local Heroes: Belgian Refugees in Britain During the First World War', *Immigrants & Minorities* vol. 18 no. 1 (March 1999), pp. 1–28.
12 Kushner and Knox, *Refugees in an Age of Genocide*, chapter 2.
13 Agatha Christie, *An Autobiography* (London: Collins, 1977), pp. 256–7.
14 This is from the first description of Poirot in Agatha Christie, *The Mysterious Affair at Styles* (London: HarperCollins, 2001 [orig. 1920]), p. 35. I am grateful to Elisa Lawson for providing these references to Christie's work and for discussion of her representations of 'foreigners'.
15 Agatha Christie, *The Mystery of the Blue Train* (Glasgow: Collins, 1989 [orig. 1928]), p. 7.
16 Christie, *An Autobiography*, p. 256.
17 Hope Simpson, *The Refugee Problem*, p. 1
18 See, for example, the latest work of synthesis, aimed at a general audience – Martin Pugh, *'Hurrah for the Blackshirts': Fascists and Fascism in Britain between the Wars* (London: Jonathan Cape, 2005).
19 Robin Cohen, *Frontiers of Identity: The British and Others* (London:

Longman, 1994), p. 198.

20 See the special issue of *Patterns of Prejudice* vol. 37 no. 3 (September 2003) on 'Racism and Asylum in Europe'.

21 Tony Kushner, 'Meaning Nothing but Good: Ethics, History and Asylum-seeker Phobia in Britain', *Patterns of Prejudice* vol. 37 no. 3 (September 2003), pp. 257–76.

22 Editorial, 'The Distortion of a Proud History', *Daily Mail*, 30 November 2002.

23 See the obituaries and comment by Stephen Bates and Christopher Hitchens in the *Guardian*, 1 April 2002, which both refer to comments made by Woodrow Wyatt that the Queen Mother had 'some reservations about Jews in her old-fashioned English way'. For George V's decision to remove all German titles from the family name see Colin Holmes, *John Bull's Island: Immigration & British Society, 1871–1971* (Basingstoke: Macmillan, 1988), p. 99.

24 Schama himself, in volume 3 of his *A History of Britain*, entitled *The Fate of Empire 1776–2000* (London: BBC Worldwide, 2002) makes only one passing reference to refugees (p. 419).

25 Balfour in *Hansard* (HC) vol. 145 col. 799 (2 May 1905).

26 Bernard Porter, *The Refugee Question in Mid-Victorian Politics* (Cambridge: Cambridge University Press, 1979), p. 124.

27 Gwynn, *Huguenot Heritage*, chapter 7 'Opposition'; and Kushner and Knox, *Refugees in an Age of Genocide*, chapters 1, 5, 6 and 9 for the complex contemporary responses to these groups.

28 Kushner, 'Meaning Nothing but Good', pp. 266–8.

29 Cohen, *Frontiers of Identity*, p. 98.

30 Home Office, *Fairer, Faster and Firmer. A Modern Approach to Immigration and Asylum* (Cmd 4018, London: HMSO, 1998), p. 35.

31 Michael Howard, advert in *Sunday Telegraph*, 12 February 2005.

32 'Howard: My Grandad the "Illegal Immigrant"', *Daily Mail*, 12 February 2005.

33 London Committee of Deputies of British Jews, *Objections to the Aliens Bill* (London: London Committee of Deputies of British Jews, 1904), pp. 11–12.

34 Joseph Roth, *The Wandering Jews* translated by Michael Hoffman (London: Granta Publications, 2001 [1926]), p. 69.

35 Louise London, *Whitehall and the Jews 1933–1948: British Immigration Policy and the Holocaust* (Cambridge: Cambridge University Press, 2000).

36 Louise London, 'Whitehall and the Refugees: The 1930s and the 1990s', *Patterns of Prejudice* vol. 34 no. 3 (2000), p. 17.

37 Written answers in *Hansard* (HC) vol. 565 col. 83 (21 February 1957).

38 Michael Gilkes, 'The Dark Strangers', in Lesley Smith (ed.), *The Making of Britain* (Basingstoke: Macmillan, 1988), pp. 143–4.

39 See, for example, A.J.P. Taylor, *English History 1914–1945* (Oxford: Oxford University Press, 1965), pp. 514–15 and more recently Jeremy Black, *Modern British History Since 1900* (Basingstoke: Macmillan,

2000), pp. 323, 328 which deal exclusively and briefly with refugees from Nazism and their contribution and positive responses to them.

40 Zachary Irwin, review in *Library Journal*, 15 September 1999.

41 For the campaign, see Kushner, 'Meaning Nothing but Good', pp. 268–72 and for the eventual decision to abandon the project, *This is Hampshire*, 3, 4 and 5 February 2004 and *Financial Times*, 4 February 2004.

42 Sheila Rowbotham, *Hidden from History: 300 Years of Women's Oppression and the Fight Against It* (London: Pluto Press, 1973), p. x; Peter Fryer, *Staying Power: The History of Black People in Britain* (London: Pluto Press, 1984), p. 399.

43 Colin Holmes, *A Tolerant Country? Immigrants, Refugees and Minorities in Britain* (London: Faber & Faber, 1991), p. 1.

44 On the Portal family, see William Page (ed.), *The Victoria History of the Counties of England: Hampshire and the Isle of Wight* vol. 5 (London: Constable, 1912), p. 489; Barbara Carpenter Turner, *A History of Hampshire* (London: Darwen Finlayson, 1963), p. 68; Peter Mason, *Hampshire: A Sense of Place* (Crediton, Devon: Hampshire Books, 1994), p. 21 and William Portal, *Some Account of the Settlement of Refugees (L'Eglisse Wallonne) at Southampton* (Winchester: Jacob and Johnson, 1982 [orig. 1902]); web pages of Hampshire Record Office at www.hants.gov.uk/record-office/french.html, viewed 17 April 2002.

45 The building has been re-named 'Atlantic Mansions'.

46 *Southampton Times*, 11 November 1893.

47 The Wilson Line of Hull was responsible for this desperate transportation, part of the doctoral research of Nick Evans of Aberdeen University reported in *Jewish Chronicle*, 13 July 2001.

48 For a description of the dormitories, see the testimony of Albert Gibbs reproduced in Donald Hyslop, Alastair Forsyth and Sheila Jemima, *Titanic Voices* (Southampton: Southampton City Council, 1994), p. 175.

49 Ibid.

50 Built by the developers 'St George' and taken from their publicity material in 1998: 'Discover the Silk Quarter'.

51 Anne Kershen, *Strangers, Aliens and Asians: Huguenots, Jews and Bangladeshis in Spitalfields 1660–2000* (London: Routledge, 2005) is an extremely useful study of all three communities although it does not deal, other than in passing, with questions of comparative memory work concerning this geographical area.

52 Patrick Wright, *A Journey Through the Ruins: The Last Days of London* (London: Radius, 1991), p. 107; Gavin Stamp, 'A Culture in Crisis', *The Spectator*, 12 October 1985.

53 Stamp, 'A Culture in Crisis'. For brief discussion of this episode, see also Kershen, *Strangers, Aliens and Asians*, pp. 97–8.

54 Bill Fishman, *The Streets of East London* (London: Duckworth, 1979), pp. 10, 14, 83.

55 Tamsin Blanchard, 'Kitchen confidential', *Observer Magazine*, 3 February 2002.

56 Beth Wenger in Hasia Diner, Jeffrey Shandler and Beth Shindler, 'Introduc-
    tion: Remembering the Lower East Side – A Conversation', in idem (eds),
    Remembering the Lower East Side (Bloomington: Indiana University Press,
    2000), p. 3.
57 Robert Kennedy (ed.), *A Nation of Immigrants* (New York: Harper and
    Row, 1964 second edition [1958]).
58 Bill Williams, 'Heritage and Community: The Rescue of Manchester's Jew-
    ish Past' in Tony Kushner (ed.), *The Jewish Heritage in British History:
    Englishness and Jewishness* (London: Frank Cass, 1992), pp. 128–46, esp.
    pp. 140, 142–3.
59 Lucille Levi, 'Nostalgia or Pain?', *Jewish Gazette*, 28 September 1979. More
    generally see Tony Kushner, 'Looking Back with Nostalgia? The Jewish
    Museums of England', *Immigrants & Minorities* vol. 6 no. 2 (July 1987),
    pp. 200–11.
60 Barney Rosemarine, *Haimishe Laffs and Chaffs: A Book of English/Yid-
    dish Humour in Story and Modern Verse* (Altrincham: John Sherratt &
    Sons, 1962), p. 15.
61 See, for example, Ernest Krausz, *Leeds Jewry: Its History and Social Struc-
    ture* (Cambridge: Jewish Historical Society of England/W.Heffer, 1964),
    p. 127.
62 T.W.E. Roche, *The Key in the Lock: Immigration Control in England from
    1066 to the Present Day* (London: John Murray, 1969), p. 207.
63 John Solomos, *Race and Racism in Britain* (3rd edition Basingstoke:
    Palgrave, 2003), pp. 60–1.
64 Roche, *The Key in the Lock*, pp. 36–7.
65 William Evans Gordon, *The Alien Immigrant* (London: Heinemann, 1903),
    pp. 6–8.
66 W.H. Wilkins, *The Alien Invasion* (London: Methuen, 1892), pp. 6–7, 35.
67 'Notes towards a history of the Aliens Branch', Mr Eaglestone, 1950 (?), in
    National Archives, HO 213/1772.
68 Ibid.
69 Ibid.
70 Dorothy Buxton, *The Economics of the Refugee Problem* (London: Focus
    Publishing, 1939), pp. 24, 27.
71 'An Englishman's Home', *New Pioneer* vol. 1 no. 9 (August 1939).
72 London, *Whitehall and the Jews*, p. 12.
73 HO 213/1772.
74 Buxton, *The Economics of the Refugee Problem*, pp. 24, 27; London,
    Whitehall and the Jews, p. 12.
75 HO 213/1772.
76 Chaim Bermant, *Point of Arrival: A Study of London's East End* (London:
    Eyre Methuen, 1975), p. 33.
77 Quoted by Gwynn, *Huguenot Heritage*, pp. 167–8.
78 Colin Nicolson, *Strangers to England: Immigration to England 1100–1945*
    (London: Wayland, 1964), p. 69. See also the thorough treatment of an
    anti-alien tradition in the East End from the arrival of the Huguenots

onwards in Kershen, *Strangers, Aliens and Asians*, chapter 8.

79 Speech reproduced in Tom Stacey, *Immigration & Enoch Powell* (London: Tom Stacey Ltd, 1970), chapter 8, esp. pp. 113–14.

80 Television interview, 12 October 1969, reproduced in Stacey, *Immigration & Enoch Powell*, p. 65.

81 Powell, interview with David Frost, 3 January 1969, reproduced in Bill Smithies and Peter Fiddick, *Enoch Powell on Immigration* (London: Sphere Books, 1969), pp. 124–5.

82 Powell, Birmingham speech, 20 April 1968, in Stacey, *Immigration & Enoch Powell*, p. 95.

83 Hattersley in *Hansard* (HC) vol. 721 col. 359 (23 November 1965).

84 Zig Layton-Henry, *The Politics of Immigration: Immigration, 'Race' and 'Race' Relations in Post-War Britain* (Oxford: Blackwell, 1992).

85 Hattersley in *Hansard* (HC) vol. 709 col. 381 (23 March 1965).

86 Pedder, 28 May 1924, in National Archives, HO 45/24765/432156/17, quoted by David Cesarani, 'Anti-Alienism in England after the First World War', *Immigrants & Minorities* vol. 6 no. 1 (1987), p. 17. On Pedder see Jill Pellew, 'The Home Office and the Aliens Act, 1905', *Historical Journal* vol. 32 no. 2 (1989), pp. 374–5.

87 Tony Kushner, *The Holocaust and the Liberal Imagination: A Social and Cultural History* (Oxford: Blackwell, 1994), chapters 3 and 7.

88 Michael Foot in *Hansard* (HC) vol. 721 cols. 364–5 (23 November 1965).

89 See the *Guardian*, 26 October 2001 and *Daily Mail*, 7 February 2002 'Migrants Must Learn to be British'. In 1989 Douglas Hurd, then Conservative Home Secretary, at the time of the Rushdie affair, urged Britain's Muslims to 'be British'. See *Daily Mail*, 24 February 1989 and Tony Kushner, 'New Labour Old Racism?', *Jewish Socialist* no. 46 (Spring 2002), pp. 12–13 for further analysis.

90 David Blunkett, 'Integration with Diversity: Globalisation and the Renewal of Democracy and Civil Society' in Phoebe Griffith and Mark Leonard (eds), *Reclaiming Britishness* (London: Foreign Policy Centre, 2002), p. 77.

91 *Royal Commission on Alien Immigration: Minutes of Evidence* (Cmd 1742, London: HMSO, 1903), vol. 2, col. 849. The role of Evans Gordon in calling Moens is mentioned in Bernard Gainer, *The Alien Invasion: The Origins of the Aliens Act of 1905* (London: Heinemann, 1972), p. 154.

92 See, for example, Ian Broad, *The Illustrated Guide to Southampton* (Southampton: no publisher, 1982), p. 16.

93 Robin Gwynn, 'Huguenots and Walloons in Dorset, Hampshire and Wiltshire', *Hatcher Review* vol. 2 (1984), pp. 364–5.

94 Bill Williams, 'The Anti-Semitism of Tolerance: Middle-Class Manchester and Jews: 1870–1900', in A.J. Kidd and K.W. Roberts (eds), *City, Class and Culture* (Manchester: Manchester University Press, 1985), p. 94.

95 *Express*, 7 January 2003.

96 John Cooper Clarke, *(I Married a) Monster from Outer Space* (released as a single in 1979. See www.cyberspike.com/clarke/singles/gimmm.html, accessed 7 February 2005.

97 *Sun*, 18 August 2003.
98 Bob Rowthorn, 'Migration limits', *Prospect* no. 83 (February 2003).
99 David Goodhart, 'Too diverse?', *Prospect* no. 95 (February 2004).
100 Brown speech, 7 July 2004, in http://politics.guardian.co.uk/labour/story/0,9061,1256550,00.html viewed 9 July 2004.
101 The contradiction is highlighted by Maeve Sherlock, head of the Refugee Council, in an interview in the *Guardian*, 16 February 2005.
102 Buxton, *The Economics of the Refugee Problem*, p. 25.
103 Eric Hobsbawm and Terence Ranger (eds), *The Invention of Tradition* (Cambridge: Cambridge University Press, 1983).
104 Robin Gwynn, 'Patterns in the Study of Huguenot Refugees in Britain', in Irene Scouloudi (ed.), *Huguenots in Britain and their French Background* (Basingstoke: Macmillan, 1987), pp. 218–19.
105 Lucien Wolf, 'A Plea for Anglo-Jewish History' (delivered at the first meeting of the Jewish Historical Society of England, 11 November 1893), *Transactions of the Jewish Historical Society of England* vol. 1 ((1893–94), pp. 4, 6. See David Cesarani, 'Duel Heritage or Dual of Heritages? Englishness and Jewishness in the Heritage Industry', in Kushner, *The Jewish Heritage in British History*, p. 34 for further comment.
106 In the preface to *Publications of the Huguenot Society of London* vol. 1 (1887–88).
107 *Transactions of the Jewish Historical Society of England* vol. 1 (1893–94).
108 Kushner, 'Looking Back With Nostalgia?' and idem, 'Great Britons: Immigration, History and Memory', in Kathy Burrell and Panikos Panayi (eds), *Histories and Memories* (I.B. Tauris, forthcoming, 2006).
109 Wolf, 'A Plea for Anglo-Jewish History', p. 2.
110 Lloyd Gartner, 'Notes on the Statistics of Jewish Immigration to England, 1870–1914', *Jewish Social Studies* vol. 22 no. 2 (1960), pp. 97–102.
111 Rob Perks, 'The Ellis Island Immigration Museum, New York', *Oral History* vol. 19 no. 1 (spring 1991), pp. 79–80.
112 Kamal Ahmed, 'Jewish Refuge Under Threat', *Observer*, 7 July 2002; A.N. Wilson, 'A Princelet Among Houses', *Evening Standard*, 8 July 2002 and 'Newsnight', BBC 2, 9 July 2002.
113 Business card advertising the museum. It is a curious claim given, for example, the century-plus existence of Jewish museums in Europe.
114 Jack Kugelmass, 'Turfing the Slum: New York's Tenement Museum and the Politics of Heritage', in Diner et al., *Remembering the Lower East Side*, pp. 179–211, esp. pp. 182, 186.
115 Raphael Samuel and Paul Thompson (eds), *The Myths We Live By* (London: Routledge, 1990).
116 Gwynn, *Huguenot Heritage*, pp. viii, 1.
117 From Oxford University Press's abstract description of the *Journal of Refugee Studies*, 1988.
118 Roger Zetter, 'Refugees and Refugee Studies – A Valedictory Editorial', *Journal of Refugee Studies* vol. 13 no. 4 (2000), p. 352.
119 Roger Zetter, 'Refugees and Refugee Studies – A Label and an Agenda',

Journal of Refugee Studies vol. 1 no. 1 (1988), p. 2.

120 Jacques Vernant, *The Refugee in the Post-War World* (London: George Allen & Unwin, 1953), p. 13.

121 Liisa Malkki, 'National Geographic: The Rooting of Peoples and the Territorialization of National Identity among Scholars and Refugees', *Cultural Anthropology* vol. 7 no. 1 (February 1992), p. 32.

122 Ibid., p. 14.

123 Hannah Arendt, *The Origins of Totalitarianism* (London: George Allen & Unwin, 1958, 2nd edition), p. 284.

124 Arendt quoted by Michael Marrus, 'Introduction', in Anna Bramwell (ed.), *Refugees in the Age of Total War* (London: Unwin Hyman, 1988), p. 6.

125 Marrus, *The Unwanted*, p. 3.

126 Kushner and Knox, *Refugees in an Age of Genocide*, chapter 5.

127 Humbert Wolfe, minute, 5 March 1935 in National Archives, LAB 8/78.

128 National Archives, HO 213/1772.

129 The statute is reproduced in Vernant, *The Refugee in the Post-War World*, pp. 9–12.

130 Patricia Tuitt, *False Images: The Law's Construction of the Refugee* (London: Pluto Press, 1996), pp. 1, 2.

131 James Hathaway, 'A Reconsideration of the Underlying Premise of Refugee Law', *Harvard International Law Journal* vol. 31 no. 1 (Winter 1990), pp. 150, 180.

132 Tuitt, *False Images*, p. 14.

133 Gil Loescher, 'Introduction: Refugee Issues in International Relations', in idem and Laila Monahan (eds), *Refugees and International Relations* (Oxford: Oxford University Press, 1989), p. 9.

134 Malcolm Proudfoot, *European Refugees: 1939–52. A Study in Forced Population Movement* (London: Faber and Faber, 1957), p. 34.

135 Marrus, *The Unwanted*, p. 297.

136 Tuitt, *False Images*, p. 14.

137 For such electoral success, see *Patterns of Prejudice*, especially its special issue on 'Racism and Asylum in Europe', edited by Liza Schuster, vol. 37 no. 3 (September 2003). On the February 2005 Danish election and the success both of the increasingly restrictionist ruling Liberals and the growth of the anti-immigrant Danish People's Party see *Guardian*, 9 February 2005 and *Financial Times*, 8 February 2005.

138 Tuitt, *False Images*, p. 14.

139 Vernant, *The Refugee in the Post-War World*, p. 13.

140 Tuitt, *False Images*, p. 23.

141 See Colin Richmond, *Campaigner Against Antisemitism: The Reverend James Parkes 1896–1981* (London: Vallentine Mitchell, 2005) which attempts to rescue Parkes from obscurity.

142 Jennifer Langer, (ed.), *The Bend in the Road: Refugees Writing* (Nottingham: Five Leaves, 1997), p. 1.

143 Himzo Skorupan, 'Neither Here Nor There', in Langer, *The Bend in the Road*, p. 12.

144 Philip French, 'Passage to Kilburn', *Observer*, 30 March 2003.

145 Yasmin Alibhai-Brown, *No Place Like Home* (London: Virago, 1995), p. 194.

146 Phil Cohen, 'Rethinking the Diasporama' *Patterns of Prejudice* vol. 33 no. 1 (1999), p. 10 writes of the 'additional burden of utopian representation' carried by homeless and displaced people.

147 As reported in Jo Carlowe, 'The Doctor Won't See you Now', *Observer*, 24 June 2001.

148 Loescher, 'Introduction', p. 2.

149 Jancic quoted by Jennifer Langer in 'Introduction', *The Bend in the Road*, p. 3.

150 UNHCR figures reproduced in Refugee Council, 'Nailing Press Myths about refugees', in www.refugeecouncil.org.uk/news/myths/myth001.htm, viewed 21 May 2003.

151 Poll details in Tim Bouquet and David Moller, 'Are We a Tolerant Nation?', *Reader's Digest*, November 2000, pp. 62–8.

152 See http://www.mori.com/digest/2002/c020621.shtml, viewed 21 May 2003 and www.refugeecouncil.org.uk/news/myths/myth001.htm, viewed 21 May 2003.

153 Breakdown of figures in www.refugeecouncil.org.uk/news/june2002/relea070.htm, viewed 21 May 2003.

154 Jonathan Boyarin, *Storm from Paradise: The Politics of Jewish Memory* (Minneapolis: University of Minnesota Press, 1992), pp. 1, 4.

155 Leo Rosten, *The Return of Hyman Kaplan* (London: Penguin, 1979), p. 19.

2

Heritage and the refugees

The nature of heritage

The nature of the so-called 'heritage industry' has divided scholars and practitioners. Is heritage, as Robert Hewison argued, fundamentally reactionary and nostalgic for a lost but imaginary 'golden age'? Is it a strategy, in a period of intense and often traumatic de-industrialisation, of turning 'to the past ... both as an economic and a psychological resource'[1] to deal with 'Britain in a climate of decline'?[2] Patrick Wright, arguing from a less elitist cultural perspective than Hewison, nevertheless underlined in *Living in an Old Country* (1985) the potential for heritage to be instrumentalised to bolster the right-wing politics and culture of the Thatcher era. As a key example Wright neatly exposed the raising in Portsmouth of Henry XIII's flagship, the *Mary Rose*, as a 'usable past' during the South Atlantic military conflict of 1982:

> Just as the recovery of the *Mary Rose* was presented as giving 'us' something back – something which 'we' hadn't seen for 437 years – the Falklands war proved that 'we' are still powerful, still capable of rallying to one flag with confidence and moral righteousness, still, above all, capable of action and therefore no longer the 'waverers and fainthearts' of Thatcher's victorious Cheltenham speech.[3]

In contrast to Hewison and Wright, Raphael Samuel, while not denying the reactionary potential of heritage, argued in *Theatres of Memory* (1994) that its success represented a democratic and participatory triumph, enabling ordinary people to engage with and create their own sense and representation of the past. Heritage was, argued Samuel, ultimately inclusive and had the power to be even more so.[4] Others have argued that 'heritage is intimately related to the exercise of power ... being part of the process of defining criteria of social inclusion and – by extension – social exclusion'.[5] Recognising this negative/positive potential, the Heritage Lottery Fund (HLF) has explicitly allocated resources to enable 'communities to celebrate, look after and learn more about our diverse heritage'.[6] It has also recognised the need for debate on 'heritage and identity in the UK today' and has, since July 2004, provided a forum for this to occur.[7] The HLF's intervention is important not just at a practical level of policy implementation, but also at an intellectual level. The growing literature on heritage recognises its centrality in identity formation. Nevertheless, there has been no sustained analysis of how past diversity is represented, or is not represented, within the various public manifestations of heritage. This chapter will explore and develop further debates about exclusion and inclusion with specific regard to the presence (and absence) of refugees in local landscapes of memory. Refugees, it argues, provide a sensitive touchstone within the world of heritage, enabling the question, as the HLF puts it, of 'who do we think we are?', to be analysed acutely.[8] In turn it will allow further consideration of whether the conservative or progressive tendencies of heritage are dominant. It will confront these issues by interrogating specific places – the cities and wider regions of Manchester and Southampton – to indicate the dilemmas caused, but also the past uncovered, by confronting the refugee experience.

Manchester and Southampton are the two cities which I have lived in the longest. Yet rather than highlighting the autobiographical indulgently for its own sake, this chapter will reveal how the presence of refugees in past and present is often hidden, but not beyond reach. It is made possible if there is intensified 'local knowledge'[9] informed not only by a depth of historical awareness but also through an 'anthropology at home'.[10] Indeed, the nature of this hiddenness is itself significant, the processes of amnesia and remembering running alongside one another, sometimes in conflict, but more often, as argued by Jonathan Boyarin, in mutual reinforcement.[11] In this respect, Manchester and Southampton and their respective rural and small town hinterlands, differing in size as well as historical development and self-image, are good examples to explore. Such a focus, however, will not be exclusive – the chapter will make, where appropriate, comparisons and connections to other places (both national and international) – and to the representation of experiences beyond that of refugees. Such searching reflects the basic theme of this section of the book as a whole, that refugees legally, physically as well as metaphorically are everywhere and nowhere. They are invisible if we want to deny their existence; omnipresent if we feel threatened by them or, alternatively, simply part of the ordinary fabric of our everyday world of people and places where the local and global intersect.

Urban case studies

Manchester has often been constructed by those born in it and by visitors to it as the immigrant city par excellence. In an edited collection, *The Soul of Manchester* published in 1929, writer after writer emphasised the centrality of immigrants, especially Germans and Jews, in developing the city and its culture. For example, Neville Cardus wrote that it was 'nothing to Manchester's discredit that she owes much of her renown in music to the habits and devotion [of the] pre-War German colony' and especially Charles Hallé who formed its orchestra and Royal College of Music.[12] It was a view shared elsewhere by the Manchester critic and diarist James Agate who was convinced that it was the Jews, or rather German Jews, who were responsible for all the decent theatre and music in the city: 'In my time Manchester was a city of liberal culture, aware-ness and gaiety, which it owed almost entirely to the large infusion of German-Jewish brains and taste.' Nevertheless, revealing the tendency to bifurcate the image of 'the Jew', especially 'eastern' and 'western', Agate added that today (the 1930s) 'in place of the cultured Jews reigns the cheap and flashy Yid'.[13] The late W.G.Sebald continued such xenophilia (but without Agate's antisemitism and Cardus's elitism), writing in *The Emigrants* (1993) that

> Manchester is an immigrant city, and for a hundred and fifty years, leav-ing aside the poor Irish, the immigrants were chiefly German and Jews, manual workers, tradesmen, freelancers, retailers and wholesalers, watch-makers, hatters, cabinet-makers, umbrella makers, tailors, bookbinders, typesetters, silversmiths, photographers, furriers and glovers, scrap mer-chants, hawkers, pawnbrokers, auctioneers, jewellers, estate agents, stock-brokers, chemists and doctors.

Sebald concluded that in the nineteenth century 'the German and Jewish influence was stronger [there] than in any other European city'.[14] Pop DJ and writer Dave Haslam's *Manchester, England: The Story of the Pop Cult City* (1999) has a different point of musical reference than Neville Cardus – jazz, mod, punk, disco and the emergence, from the 1980s, of the sounds of 'Madchester'. Yet Haslam's portrayal of the city's 'myth of origins' follows closely in the pattern established by Cardus and expanded by Sebald:

> Unlike London, which was a thriving metropolis three hundred years ago, Manchester is a hybrid town, born all in a rush one hundred and fifty years ago, when those arriving looking for work in the fast-growing facto-ries, workshops, warehouses and foundries included large numbers of Catholic Irish, as well as Scots, and German and East European Jews. These migrations have been replicated since, with incomers from the Caribbean in the 1950s and from the Asian sub-continent in the 1970s.[15]

As these literary references drawn from across the twentieth century reveal, the formula that could be summarised as 'Manchester + immigrants
= culture' has become something of a recurring cliché. As Alan Kidd, one
of the city's most distinguished recent historians, has argued, 'The cosmopolitan character of Manchester's cultural life can be overdrawn'.[16]
Moreover, it is noticeable that in all these accounts, while the description
'immigrant' is embraced, the word 'refugee' is avoided. As we have seen,
there has been resistance to accepting that Britain has been a country of
immigration. In the examples just cited, it is noticeable in this respect
that many other important groups who came to Manchester, such as the
Italians and the Armenians, have been left out of the city's history.[17] Even
so, relatively speaking, while a history of immigration is hesitantly accepted, a tradition of refugee presence has been harder to acknowledge.

Partly it is a matter of numbers that explains the stress on immigrants
and not refugees. Manchester, for example, has had, if an elitist approach
is adopted, some notable immigrants who have settled and contributed
much to the city's life such as Charles Hallé and Hans Richter who made
'musical Manchester' world famous.[18] But it is the word 'settled' that is
perhaps the most salient. Historians, alongside the creators of local and
national heritages, have attempted in the main to describe or build a
single narrative experience. The domination of nationalistic history, which
extended beyond the Second World War,[19] has worked against a more
pluralistic approach. Liisa Malkki has argued that refugees are 'liminal
in the categorical order of nation-states'. It has led to an objectification
which is 'very evident in the scholarly and policy discourse on refugees'.
She concludes that 'One of the social and analytical consequences of the
school atlas, then, is the political sensitivity and symbolic danger of people
who do not fit, who represent "matter out of place"'.[20]

In Britain, local history, as typified by the Victoria History of the Counties of England, was aimed at highlighting national developments and
progress. Immigrants who settle and integrate and make their own contribution can, with relative ease, be assimilated into the story: in 1900 the
Victoria County history announced that its aim was to 'trace, county by
county, the story of England's growth from its prehistoric condition, through
the barbarous age, the settlement of alien peoples, and the gradual welding
of many races into a nation which is now the greatest in the globe'.[21]

This 'Whig' version is exemplified by Britain's largest 'local' heritage
centre, the Museum of London. Opened in 1976, it tells a linear story of
London's history from prehistoric times to the present day. In the late
1980s it recognised that its permanent exhibition galleries did not 'reflect
the important role played by settlers from overseas in the development'
of the capital. As preparation for change, the Museum of London launched

the largest exhibition and related programme on immigration within the British heritage industry: *The Peopling of London: 20,000 Years of Settlement* which opened in November 1993.[22] At the level of increasing social inclusivity, the exhibition was undoubtedly successful – nearly one hundred thousand visited it and the proportion of ethnic minority visitors increased four-fold to 20 per cent.[23] The exhibition covered a range of groups and through the use of oral testimony incorporated ordinary minority voices. Nevertheless, following a clear pattern within the historiography established by the Jewish Historical Society of England and the Huguenot Society of London, as illustrated in chapter 1, the emphasis was celebratory. It underlined 'the vast contributions of immigrants through the centuries of London's development'.[24] Themes that emphasised continuity of presence and (ultimate) integration were central to *The Peopling of London* – 'Arriving and settling down' was one of its major strands.[25] Refugees, however, were not prominent in the exhibition, in spite of London's role, in Samuel Smiles' lyrical description, as the 'world's asylum – the refuge of the persecuted in all lands, whether for race, or politics, or religion'.[26] There were exceptions in the exhibition, but these were predictable – Jews and Huguenots.[27] But in *The Peopling of London*, expulsion, restriction of entry and temporary settlement were hardly mentioned.

The rich tapestry of London's history was enhanced by the approach of this landmark exhibition in the representation of immigration to Britain. The idea, however, of emphasising the disrupted experience of refugees and other transient groups such as Gypsies, who challenge the more comforting concepts of continuity and place, has not been incorporated into the main exhibition of the Museum of London. The desire to embrace inclusivity and the eventual acceptance of all groups, to show that cultural diversity was compatible with being 'Londoners All', had its cost in the form of exclusion of groups or historical episodes that simply do not fit into this Whiggish perspective. The model provided by *The Peopling of London* is close to that of the 'Chicago School' of urban sociology in the inter-war period – initial mutual antipathy on behalf of both migrant and majority followed by adjustments on both sides (slower in some cases) and, a generation or two later, an enriched experience all round. As its leading figure, Robert Park, suggested in 1926, 'in relations of races there is a cycle of events which tends everywhere to repeat itself'.[28] This universalist and optimistic framework is echoed in the words of the curator of and principal researcher for *The Peopling of London*:

> As with many earlier communities, the first generation of migrants often retain close links with their country of origin and dream of an eventual return. In practice, post-war settlers such as Italians, the Poles, the Cypriots

and the South Asians, have put down their roots here and made London their home. They have raised families here, they have made homes and friends, and invested a great deal culturally, emotionally and financially in their adopted city. Their children and grandchildren have grown up to see themselves as Londoners, and often have little attachment to their parents' or grandparents' country of origin .... Through them, London is slowly absorbing another element in its rich history of cultural diversity, something we can all celebrate and of which we can be proud.[29]

The exhibition was partly inspired to counter the growing racism and xenophobia in Europe and within that context, which has deteriorated further in the decade since it was created, the desire to show immigration and diversity in a positive light is not only understandable but commendable.[30] Nevertheless, 'pride' in acceptance of past entry and current diversity runs the risk, returning to Louise London, of ignoring refusal of admittance, segregation and deportation, 'Because, even if it isn't proud, even if it doesn't fit the political message, this country also has a history of not taking in refugees'.[31]

The main heritage site telling Manchester's story at the city's Museum of Science and Industry, reveals similar tendencies to the Museum of London, though on a smaller scale. Viewed in 2002, two panels in its permanent exhibition, *The Making of Manchester*, were devoted to immigration out of a total of over sixty.[32] Immigration is certainly not seen as 'alien' to Manchester's history but, as with the Museum of London, it is integrated smoothly into the dominant, linear narrative of the progress and growth of the city:

> Centuries of immigration have created multi-cultural diversity, most noticeable in clothing, food and entertainment. Regeneration has brought both residents and tourists into [Manchester] city centre, adding to the cultural mix.[33]

This concluding text to *The Making of Manchester* provides the same comforting biography of the city as penned by writers from Neville Cardus to Dave Haslam.

In the new Urbis Museum in Manchester, opened in 2002, the parochialism of the Museum of London and the Manchester Museum of Science & Technology is avoided by adopting a global perspective to the experience of living in cities. Even so, when approaching the history of Manchester itself, similar tendencies to those in *The Peopling of London* and *The Making of Manchester* are apparent. In the floor of the exhibition devoted to 'arrive', the visitor 'can imagine what it was like to be an immigrant in Manchester and look around at the people who would [have] shared their lives'.[34] Such an approach within the museum would have been inconceivable thirty years ago – there was little or nothing on immigrants to Manchester in the original displays in the Science and Industry museum, for example. Indeed, Manchester's Pump House, the 'only national museum in Britain dedicated to people's history',[35] frankly acknowledges that it as yet 'does not have a satisfactory exhibition on the development of a multi-cultural society', explaining its absences due to the past failure to take the history of ethnic minorities seriously.[36] But it will take even greater effort and pain before we move from this more inclusive, pluralistic museum policy, to one that emphasises the fracturing experience represented by the presence, often only temporary, of refugees and asylum seekers, or for that matter, of transmigrancy in general. Even the Manchester Jewish Museum in its permanent display, now nearing its twentieth birthday, stresses immigration and settlement throughout, only mentioning 'refugee' at the very end.[37] Similarly, Urbis, which highlights the 'shock of the city', still focuses on the integration and contribution of immigrants. Following Neville Cardus, it emphasises the musical contribution of Germans in Manchester but blandly comments that 'Many Germans return[ed] home at the outbreak of World War One, but their legacy in music education continues.'[38] In contrast, Cardus acknowledged that in 1914 'crisis descended on musical Manchester. The Germans were driven underground, and the fate of the Hallé concerts hung in a terrible balance.' Cardus, writing prophetically in 1929 wondered whether 'in our post-War period … were a Charles Hallé to appear in Manchester now, or a Hans Richter, would Manchester not turn patriotically aside from them and decline their gifts?'[39] Indeed, in his *English Journey* (1934), J.B. Priestley wrote wistfully of the lost German Jewish colony in his native Bradford that had been destroyed by wartime xenophobia: 'I liked the city better as it was before … It seems smaller and duller now.'[40] Urbis has not the confidence, or perhaps the knowledge, to accept that the visibility of minorities in cities and elsewhere in the British landscape, especially that of refugees, has been removed not just by assimilation but also by forced removal.

More generally, refugees, if referred to at all, are usually and with much deeper significance mentioned only in two diametrically opposite contexts in the world of heritage. First (and dominantly), in the form of decline and decay in isolated and often confined sites. Second, through the prism of self-congratulation that highlights the decency and generosity through the granting of asylum in the past. Neither context, as will emerge, helps to humanise or individualise the refugee experience. In the one case, refugees are pathologised. In the other, they become objects to whom positive things were done – that is they relate to 'us' and not to 'them'. The scarcity of such references in the local landscape and heritage world necessitates microscopic research of places and spaces and

their multi-layered pasts. This is especially so as sites that through decline or re-development have, in many cases, been subject to the physical
obliteration of aspects of their past.

Memory wars in the countryside: the Hungarians

Styal's Quarry Bank Mill has been recognised in the post-1945 era as a
world heritage site. Quarry Bank Mill was originally developed by Samuel
Greg during the late eighteenth century, in what was then the Cheshire
countryside, as a 'model' cotton spinning factory. In the heart of the
industrial revolution the success of the venture led to the Greg family
taking over much of the local village and its surrounding land, creating
the Styal Village Colony for its workers. By the end of the nineteenth
century, however, the business was in decline, a victim of international
competition which even the gross exploitation of the company's workers, including many children, could not overcome. At this point, Dr John
Rhodes, involved in the Manchester orphanage movement, recognised
the potential of the Styal countryside to build a colony for those in his
charge. With the downturn in business, the Greg family and other local
people were unable to oppose successfully the development of this orphan colony, the Styal Cottage Homes, which was built in the late 1890s.
The orphanage was deliberately self-contained and as early as 1899 it
was being criticised by visitors who 'found that the children at Styal are
isolated from the rest of the world'.[41]

James Stanhope-Brown was born in Hulme, Manchester, in 1934 and
orphaned at the age of two. He spent the next fifteen years of his life
within the confines of the Styal Cottage Homes. In his memoir and history of the orphanage (1989) he concluded by comparing the fate of its
site with the neighbouring Styal Village Colony. In the 1950s, as will
emerge shortly, it was decided to close down the orphanage and to find
new uses for its buildings. Eventually it became part of one of the largest
prisons for women in Britain. For Stanhope-Brown, there was a certain
appropriateness in this evolution: 'Throughout the history of the Homes
in the generations of child residents, there has always been reference to
the comparison of Styal [Cottage] Homes to that of a prison.'[42] In contrast, 'Styal Village Colony ... has changed little during the past century
and thanks to the National Trust, its preservation for the future is assured.' Stanhope-Brown highlighted the battle over memory between the
two heritage sites and made clear who was the winner: 'Without doubt,
the famous Quarry Bank Mill at Styal is the focal point of the village,
with its acclaimed success attracting thousands of visitors from all over
the world.'[43]

In *Coronation Street*, the world's longest running 'soap opera', which is produced and set in Manchester, two female characters discuss the merits of living in Styal. One, a socially aspiring younger woman new to the area and from London, is considering moving from working-class 'Weatherfield' to nouveau-riche Styal, attracted no doubt by what Stanhope-Brown called its 'ability to hide behind the facade of a bygone era'. She is intrigued to find that the mother of her older friend, whose life ambitions have always been more limited, had once lived in Styal. The conversation continues amicably but at total cross-purposes – the mother had been a prison inmate and not a 'posh' resident of the village.[44] There are indeed two constructions of Styal, the confusion over which created the potential for *Coronation Street*'s comic interchange. On the one hand there is the upmarket, ex-urban Cheshire residence for Manchester professionals who relish its semi-rural tranquillity to which the beautifully restored Quarry Bank Mill and its Village Colony adds rather than detracts, in spite of its industrial and exploitative past. It is this Arcadian image that is marketed by the National Trust to woo tourists to the site: 'The essence of a visit to Quarry Bank Mill is the warm, friendly atmosphere [s]ituated in over 384 acres of the beautiful countryside of Styal Country Estate'.[45] On the other hand, is the hidden and unrespectable face of Styal typified by the Cottage Homes orphanage and the later prison. It is firmly within Styal's 'other' that its refugee connection is to be located, both in topography and in cultural construction.

Styal Cottage Homes were closed down in the summer of 1956, reflecting the slow post-war retreat from institutionalisation and isolation of those regarded as societal 'problems'. When the Homes were taken over by the Manchester Education Committee in 1930 up to six hundred children had been housed in over twenty cottages in Styal. This number slowly declined in the post-war era. In 1956, the remaining orphan children were dispersed into family homes and the Manchester Education Committee considered what new function the site should play. These included a 'boarding special school for educationally sub-normal boys' or a 'Summer Holiday Home' for children 'from more congested areas of the City'.[46] None of these options were deemed wholly satisfactory and in November 1956, a new possibility emerged – that of using the cottages for the thousands of Hungarian refugees entering Britain after the failed uprising against Soviet control. The reception centres, or 'first line hostels', as they were termed, in the south of England – mainly army camps and barracks – were overcrowded and the imminent arrival of British troops from the Middle East necessitated the creation of '"second line hostels"' in the industrial regions of the country and [the] transfer

[of] refugees to them as quickly as possible'. Styal, with its twenty-six large cottages, was deemed to be ideally suited for this task.[47]

By March 1958, eleven hundred Hungarian refugees had been accommodated at the Styal Cottage Homes, 425 maxium at any one time. While it was one of the largest hostels set up to deal with the 22,000 Hungarians who came to Britain after the failed uprising, it was, by January 1957, just one of 147 set up across the country with this purpose. Many thousands of local people were involved in helping the Hungarian refugees and, in this respect, Styal Cottage Homes was no exception. A report produced for Manchester City Council in February 1957 emphasised that 'From the first arrival of the refugees ... there has been a constant flow of goodwill ... from many voluntary organisations and private individuals'.[48]

As with many sites associated with temporary refugee settlement, those at Styal were in a state of decay. By 1956, over half a century after their original construction, the Cottage Homes were showing major signs of deterioration. Furthermore, when they were taken over for use for the Hungarians they had been empty for six months, almost all the furniture had been removed and 'public services were ... disconnected or run down'.[49] Nevertheless, with an echo of the workhouse origins of the Styal orphans, the limited facilities of the refugee hostel were not simply a reflection of this original decay and the rush to re-open the buildings. In March 1958 it was reported that the Hungarian refugees 'live a somewhat spartan life because the need to ensure that the Styal Hostel is merely a transit stage in their resettlement and not a permanent housing scheme [has] precluded any policy of providing excessive comforts and amenities'.[50] They were deliberately made to be basic and unattractive.

In spite of the numbers of the Hungarian refugee camps such as Styal, their history as well as the lives of these refugees in Britain, and responses to them, have received almost no attention from historians or the heritage industry.[51] Given the National Trust's fashioning of Quarry Bank Mill as a 'remarkable Georgian museum' in surrounds that are marketed for weddings and other social functions it is hardly surprising that it has no place in its narrative for the Hungarian refugees in the neighbouring Styal Cottage Homes.[52] Instead, the only reference to the refugee hostel available through the Quarry Bank Mill has been through selling the memoir of the former orphan resident, James Stanhope-Brown. Its availability in the site shop provides a note of disharmony amidst the celebratory commercial emphasis of the heritage world at Quarry Bank Mill, especially with Stanhope-Brown's conclusion that 'Like the novel "A tale of two cities", Styal, from the beginning of the 20th century became a divided community, with the emergence of "a village with two colonies"'. It is clear which side of the divide Stanhope-Brown places the Hungarian refugees, an empathy no doubt formed by an awareness of their marginality, temporariness and the conditions they would have experienced in the Cottage Homes that had echoes of the orphan experience.[53]

Since the closure of the Cottage Homes and the development of the women's prison at Styal, the divergent tale of the 'two colonies' has continued. Raphael Samuel, while, as has been noted, placing his emphasis on the inclusive potential of heritage, recognised that the 'mere fact of preservation aestheticizes … It makes backwardness visually appealing and turns subjects of study into objects of desire. The "dark satanic mills" no longer seem horrors when they are exhibited as historical monuments or reassembled in picturesque settings.' Quarry Bank Mills, argued Samuels, was a classic example of this 'cognitive dissonance':

> No one who visits the Greg mill at Styal, Cheshire, a National Trust property, can fail to be impressed by the giant water wheel, a veritable cyclops of Vulcan's arts. But no cotton waste sticks to the factory walls; the ground has been lovingly landscaped; and the restored looms, though 200 years old, are producing modern designer-ware …[54]

There is no place here for the desperate Hungarian refugees who, for short periods, were part of the same Styal landscape for over two years. Heritage, argued Samuels, has proved 'quite crucial in the construction of post-colonial identities'. He was confident that it 'helps to support both a multi-ethnic vision of the future and a more pluralist one of the past'.[55] Yet in this particular case, the Hungarian refugees represent the antithesis of everything that the National Trust's Quarry Bank Mill has come to represent – alien, decayed and transitory: unmarketable, it would seem, as public 'history'. Having sanitised its own past, there is little chance of considering Styal's other history – the orphans, Hungarian refugees and women prisoners of the Cottage Homes, all needing to be hidden from the public gaze in a village that now 'finds itself', as James Stanhope-Brown stated, with bitter irony, as 'one of the leading tourist attractions of the North West of England'.[56]

A similar multi-layered and contested memory process – significantly also relating to the Hungarian refugees – has occurred in Hampshire. *Spike Island* (2001), Philip Hoare's remarkable account of the Royal Victoria Military Hospital in Netley, the largest in Britain, is a superb analysis of its place in local, national and global memory work. Hoare locates its later function after dealing with the physical and psychological impact of the two world wars, as a gothic monument, rivalling its neighbouring site, the famous ruins of medieval Netley Abbey that had inspired generations of writers, painters and other visitors.[57] By 1956, all the patients at the Royal Victoria Military Hospital had been transferred elsewhere and 'the main building had finally given up its medical usefulness'. As with Styal, the arrival of Hungarian refugees in 1956 is given only the briefest of mentions in *Spike Island*. One half sentence is devoted to their presence – 'That year Cold War refugees from Hungary were housed in its draughty wards'. Of equal signficance is that they are used only to emphasise the degeneration of this site in Hoare's evocative narrative of history and memory:

> by then the great white elephant had become dilapidated, its bricks decaying in their mortar, slowly crumbling into the clay from which they came.[58]

The main hospital building, close to five hundred yards in length, burnt down in the 1960s. Today, the site has become a country park with a small exhibition in the surviving and imposing chapel, one that dominates the skyline when approaching Southampton along the Solent. The official guide to the country park, which tells briefly the story of 'a great military hospital', has a similar narrative of its later decline to that provided in *Spike Island*:

> Through the early years of the 1950's the Royal Victoria ran down ... When in 1956 the Red Cross took over the empty wards for Hungarian refugees in transit, beds had to be collected hastily from all over Hampshire.[59]

No effort is made in either of these references to research the background or experiences of these 'refugees in transit'. Highlighting this lucana is not a matter of point-scoring or taking the moral high ground. It is significant because Hoare's work otherwise is a superb example of writing back into memory the experiences of those excluded from 'mainstream' narratives. *Spike Island* is often uncomfortable reading for those who see the British past as essentially decent and tolerant. It reveals the hidden and often disturbing alternative histories of institutions and institutionalisation, of empire and the reality of British military might abroad. Furthermore, while the exhibition and guide at the current heritage site at Royal Victoria Country Park do not have such depth of understanding, they do attempt a social history perspective of this unique hospital and its changing military functions. The dismissal of the Hungarians at Netley thus requires deeper explanation.

W.G. Sebald, one of the most important voices in literary memory work in the late twentieth century, wrote of *Spike Island* that it provided 'everything a passionate reader could want – a subject that far transcends the trivial pursuits of contemporary writing, concerns both public and private, astonishing details, stylistic precision, a unique sense of time and place, and a great depth of vision'.[60] Sebald, however, as we have already seen and as will be explored further in this book, had a remarkable sensitivity to the exile and migrant experience in Britain. It is one that is largely absent in *Spike Island*. Nevertheless, it is telling that when Hoare does evoke sites of immigrant memory in relation to the buildings of Royal Victoria Military Hospital his reference point is American, not British:

> The great brick hospital on the shore had become an imperial processing plant, its raw material – its patients – arriving by sea to be admitted into its interior, like the red-brick buildings of Ellis Island in New York Harbour, to which it bore both stylistic and functional similarities. Both were insular buildings invested with hope and fear, fraught with medical and bureaucratic decisions on human destinies; individuals catalogued and assessed as they arrived from foreign lands. And, like Ellis Island, the hospital also had its own pier to receive its intake ...[61]

In fact Hampshire, as will emerge shortly, had its own 'Ellis Island', one of similar geographical scale to the Royal Victoria Military Hospital. Its history and memory have become hidden and thus have been beyond the cultural imagination of a writer even as sensitive and progressive as Philip Hoare. The black British artist, Lubaina Himid, has written in relation to the commemoration and recognition of slavery: 'when something is there you can talk about it, write about it, paint about it, but when something isn't there what can you say ...'[62] The 'British' Ellis Island, located just a few miles from Netley and its military hospital, has become both physically and culturally invisible. The reason for this invisibility has a similar explanation to the dismissive memory work associated with the Hungarian refugees in heritage sites in Britain. They are deemed to be alien outsiders, their temporariness adding to their perceived placelessness. The context of decay thus becomes their only point of location when juxtaposed with other narratives, mainstream or alternative. Nevertheless, the mixture of amnesia and problematic memory of the Hungarians in 1956, as typified by the two heritage sites examined here, requires particular explanation. Even within the marginalised memory of refugees in Britain, the Hungarians have achieved very limited recognition.[63]

The Hungarian refugees, as R.A. Butler's dismissive attempt to keep them out of the country revealed,[64] were never welcomed in Britain by the government. The Home Office did not want any to be allowed entry and then grudgingly bent to Foreign Office pressure and accepted a number that was small in international comparison – up to two hundred thousand left Hungary and just over 14,000 settled permanently in Britain.[65] In contrast to government and state antipathy, there was general public support for their cause, part of the Cold War culture of the 1950s and guilt concerning British non-intervention in the anti-Soviet uprising. As has been shown at Styal, it went beyond public declarations of support. Many activists aided their initial arrival in the local hostels. It remains

that the Hungarian refuge at Styal, however basic, provided some of the
best facilities made available in 1956 – many of the other temporary
hostels were even more isolated and decrepid. The fact that leading British politicians were determined to portray the country as not one of refugee entry had a practical impact: there were no facilities in place to cope
when influxes occurred. The sites chosen, following a pattern that had
been established earlier in the century and one that was to be repeated
later, were usually large-scale abandoned or semi-abandoned buildings,
often associated with the military. Even the happier situation at Styal
had a system to clear the refugees as quickly as possible and put them
into paid employment – nothing permanent was to be established. There
was thus little sensitivity to the traumas some of these refugees had experienced. Many were put straight to work down the coalmines and in
other large industrial concerns – in this respect they were a welcome
addition to a post-war economy still requiring more workforce. Only a
few Hungarians prospered in Britain and beyond the initial settlement,
little help was offered to help them integrate. All in all, for the 22,000
who came here, it was not a particularly happy experience. One-third
emigrated – mainly to Canada – hoping to find better opportunities as
well as a more open society. Many others were thwarted in their desire to
do so. In February 1957, an analysis of 167 refugees resident in Styal
found that less than 15 at that stage intended finding permanent work in
England.[66]

Two unpublished reports produced by the City of Manchester Council on the Hungarian hostel at Styal, written in February 1957 and March
1958, provide future clues as to why these refugees would subsequently
become forgotten. Both, understandably, portray the running of the hostel as a success. Leslie Lever, Lord Mayor of Manchester and later prominent in the Labour party, stated that the presentation of the later report
afforded

> opportunity to express to the officers of the Council and the various vol-
> untary organisations concerned the thanks of the City for the work they
> have done in caring for the unfortunate refugees and for the splendid ef-
> forts which have been made to resettle so many of them in new lives. It is
> also pleasing to record that the refugees have on numerous occasions ex-
> pressed their gratitude for the kindness shown to them by the citizens of
> Manchester and for the very real help given to them by the City Council
> since they first arrived in Manchester in December, 1956.[67]

The desire in both reports was, however, to show that the Hungarians
had been given initial support through the hostel only in order to maintain
'the Hungarians' morale until such time as they become self-supporting
citizens or move on to the next stage of their new lives'.[68] For those staying

in Britain the later report saw the way ahead as 'gradually learning English and being assimilated into the English way of life through their
outside employment contacts and attendance of their children at English
schools'.[69] To a large extent, for better or worse, this happened and, in
the process, the distinctiveness of their experiences were lost. The March
1958 report did recognise that not all the Hungarians would be smoothly
integrated. This recognition, however, was intolerant rather than
empathetic:

> There tends to be a hard-core of refugees comprising those who hesitate to
> leave the hostel because their large families cannot be accommodated out-
> side, those who shrink from facing an independent life in an unfamiliar
> community and those who cling pathetically to hopes that they may soon
> emigrate.[70]

As early as February 1957 it was feared that 'a hard core of homeless
refugees' might be left at Styal who could neither find employment nor
emigrate.[71] The shutting down of such hostels led to the dispersal of this
'hard core'. In 1979, a social worker who had later experienced some of
these Hungarian refugees confirmed their social isolation and mental
health problems, labelling them 'the lost sheep of migrations'.[72] There
were, alas, many such lost sheep amongst the Hungarians and no framework of support at that point within the wider society to help them cope
or adjust.

The speed with which the Hungarians were put into isolated hostels
and then pushed into employment or emigration, or left to fend for themselves, partly explains their subsequent obscurity. It is also significant
that, as the 1958 Styal report summarised, 'Most of the refugees are
artisans and members of the professions or students form only a very
small minority.'[73] Without ready access to the media, and with their relatively small numbers, the Hungarian refugees of 1956 were in a very
weak position to maintain the brief prominence they had enjoyed when
they first arrived. George Mikes, the Hungarian-born satirist of British
manners and character, quipped in 1960 that 'Everybody is Hungarian',
adding that 'London is a great English city, but it is also a small Hungarian village.'[74] Yet Mikes' attempt to 'out' the Hungarian in Britain only
highlighted their actual marginality and invisibility. Closer to this reality
of assimilation and placelessness were the experiences of the poet, George
Szirtes, who came to Britain as a child with his family. The Szirtes family
arrived from Hungary via an Austrian refugee camp and were first located in England at an army barracks in Tidworth. Failing to get to Australia, they moved around London. Szirtes writes that

> Once settled here, England was simply the place where we lived. I read
> English books, had English friends, watched English TV and went on

English holidays. Later, in my teens, when I began to write, it did not occur to me to write in Hungarian; it was far more natural to write in English, the language in which I thought and felt.[75]

Even in 1956, the Hungarian crisis was to an extent overshadowed by the Suez crisis which was perceived as having a more direct consequence on British politics and society. More generally, in a culture where memory of refugees is either minimal or highly selective, there has been almost nowhere for the Hungarians to be recognised and to become part of either national or local memory work. Indeed, at the level of the individual, the final chapter of this study explores the marginalised and largely negative image of Hungarians within life-story narratives of ordinary people in Britain. The 143 hostels set up for the Hungarians, of which Styal Cottage Homes and the Royal Victoria Military Hospital were but two, have largely been forgotten. Moreover, such amnesia will be harder to reverse as time progresses, especially given the decaying nature of the sites within which the Hungarians were initially placed.

Heritage construction and the Kosovans

The Hungarians are not the only group of refugees to be collectively forgotten in the world of British heritage and memorialisation. Growing up in Cheadle, a suburb of south Manchester, during the 1960s, the imposing building of Barnes Hospital (or Manchester Convalescent Home) dominated the landscape of memory, visible from my bedroom window and all approaches by road. Constructed in the 1870s as a convalescent home as part of the Manchester Royal Infirmary, it had a purpose in common with the Styal Cottage Homes – sending its charges away from the obnoxious fumes of the world's first modern industrial city and to the recuperating atmosphere of the Cheshire countryside. 'It would be difficult to overestimate the benefits it has confirmed upon thousands of sufferers', argued an 1898 report on the Manchester Convalescent Home, 'who, on leaving the parent institution, have been in urgent need of fresh air … occupy[ing] a pleasant situation in its own grounds at Cheadle, one of the most pleasant and healthy districts in the neighbourhood of Manchester'.[76]

Today, it is hard to imagine it as a source of tranquillity and pollution-free breathing. *Around the M60*, by Matthew Hyde, Aidan O'Rourke and Peter Portland, is both a history and travelogue of Manchester's orbital motorway, built over forty years and completed in 2000. They write of Barnes Hospital that 'This great gaunt pile of a building, abandoned and all dark at night, except for the lonely light in its tower-top clock, is not just near Junction 3 but embraced by it. If you come off the M60

Eastbound onto the A34 you gyrate right around it.'[77] Its contemporary proponents generously described Barnes Hospital as 'a handsome and spacious building'.[78] It was more cruelly, though more accurately, described by the arch-modernist architectural historian and refugee from Nazism, Nikolaus Pevsner, as 'Large, Gothic, and grim.'[79] In a local newspaper article from 1986 entitled '"Forgotten" Hospital', even its manager was forced to concede that while Barnes was a 'very cheerful and happy hospital … the old building does look a little gloomy'.[80] Indeed, the gothic potential of Barnes Hospital had been recognised in the gory, cannibalistic conclusion to a horror movie, *The Living Dead at the Manchester Morgue* some twelve years earlier. The work of Spanish director, Jorge Grau, who wrote of it that 'I hope you get very scared and that you suffer profoundly',[81] *The Living Dead* has been described as a 'seminal example of 1970s Eurohorror'.[82]

The film, which has now achieved alternative cult status, has been criticised for its simplistic anti-authoritarianism and simplistic warnings about the ecological danger of modern technology. Nevertheless, *The Living Dead* has also been widely praised for its 'intelligent handling of locations [in which] England becomes a very bleak place indeed, full of sinister quietness'.[83] Recognition of the 'striking originality of [Grau's] location choices'[84] has led to a search to identify them all.[85] One of the film's more supportive critics has suggested that 'famously, there *is* no Manchester morgue in *The Living Dead at the Manchester Morgue*'.[86] In fact, Barnes Hospital is the setting for the Manchester morgue where the zombie cannibalism takes place. It is possible that Grau spotted Barnes Hospital's sinister potential when travelling towards either the Peak District or Lake District for filming the bulk of his film. Hyde, O'Rourke and Portland conclude their book on the M60 with a haunting photograph of Barnes Hospital 'eerily lit up at night, even though the building has long since been out of use'.[87] Similarly, Grau recognised its sense of gothic decay – bold, ugly and menacing.

This excursion into the 'cheerfully brazen Euro-gore twist on *Night of the Living Dead*' has a purpose.[88] The authors of *Around the M60* see their 'chosen themes [as] forgetting and remembering'. They were drawn to the 'monstrous exterior' of Barnes Hospital within the topography of the motorway and, as with many of the buildings in their study, its current state of decay. No doubt they would have approved of Grau's filmic exploitation of the site had they been aware of *The Living Dead*. Hyde, O'Rourke and Portland situate their 're-remembering' in relation to Barnes Hospital in its function as a convalescent home. Yet while *Around the M60* sets itself the task of exploring what is forgotten and why, it also sows the seeds of further amnesia itself. At the close of the book's narrative on Barnes Hospital is a sentence that resonates strongly of Philip Hoare's description of the Hungarians at Netley: 'The hospital carried on its original function until about 1993, including treating wounded soldiers in the First World War, and was also used briefly to house "asylum seekers"'.[89]

As we have seen, the Home Office had no intention of taking Hungarian refugees in 1956. It was pushed into doing so through an amalgam of looming international embarrassment if it did not follow the example of others, as well as pressure from below: significant and vocal sections of the British public wanted to show that they cared. In 1999, the British government was similarly hostile to the entry of Kosovan Albanians, refugees from Serbian mass 'ethnic cleansing' which left over one million people internally displaced or forced out of Kosova. The horror of media images of the persecuted, however, stimulated popular demand, including from the right-wing and normally anti-asylum seeker press, to bring Kosovan Albanians to Britain. This campaign, alongside international pressure from the UNHCR, led eventually to just over four thousand being granted entry under a temporary admission scheme specifically aimed at the vulnerable, ill and injured.[90]

The then Labour Home Secretary, Jack Straw, was reluctant to consider anything other than a token entry of refugees. It meant that when a decision was made to allow several thousand Kosovan Albanians to recuperate in Britain a panic ensued to find suitable accommodation for them. It repeated the situation with the Hungarians in 1956 and other sudden refugee movements such as the Basque children in 1937.[91] When faced with the reality of mass refugee movements emanating from inside and outside Europe and its inability through pressure – both domestic and international – to isolate its borders from them, the net result has been an unpreparedness in Britain for large-scale arrivals. Old, abandoned and decaying buildings have thus been brought into use at short notice.

Various immigrant groups settling in Britain have often been accused of bringing into disrepute neighbourhoods that were, in reality, already in a state of decline. John Garrard, in his comparative study of the responses to East European Jews in the 1900s and New Commonwealth migrants in the post-1945 era, points out how both groups were accused of 'somehow interrupt[ing] and destroy[ing] an earlier golden age' in the development of particular neighbourhoods. As an example he quotes a contemporary response in the West Midlands during the 1960s: 'Edgbaston Road used to be a lovely road ... you used to have nannies up that way you know ... Now they've taken over, and the place is a slum. It's horrible.' alongside testimony from the Royal Commission on Alien Immigration (1903) on an East End street where 'In the afternoons you would see the steps inside cleaned, and the women with their clean white aprons ... Now is a seething mass of refuse and filth ... the stench is disgraceful ... They are such an unpleasant, indecent people'.[92] In contrast to such settlement in residential locales, refugee and asylum seekers have often been housed initially in large-scale and isolated reception centres. The buildings utilised as reception centres have, however, in many cases, played in the past a prominent civic or military role. They have subsequently become important in the making of local/national memory and place identity. Yet the sheer presence of refugees and asylum seekers in such buildings, even if only fleetingly, can call into question the reassuring narratives associated with the construction of place identities. Such placing of refugees and asylum seekers can evoke emotions as powerful as those coming out of the perceived impact of migrants settling into specific residential areas. In this respect, Barnes Hospital provides a good example of the complexities of local memory work and the linked processes of remembering and forgetting.

Tens of thousands of Mancunians were treated in Barnes Hospital in its one hundred and fifteen years as a convalescent centre. Many more came to the hospital to visit friends and relatives. Within the village of Cheadle, local people played an important role in directing visitors to what was, pre-motorway and dual carriageway, a relatively remote semi-rural site.[93] The significance of the hospital in the Manchester region, including for the residents of Cheadle, the convalescents and their visitors, is exemplified by the variety of postcard images sold portraying the building and its gardens.[94] The hospital formally closed in 1999, leading to concern over its future. In response, a local residents' group sought and achieved listed (and thereby, to some extent, protected) building status (Grade 2). The chairperson of the residents' group stated that 'Barnes Hospital is a landmark for Cheadle because it is the first thing that you see when you turn off the motorway'. In short, post-closure, the hospital still maintained its importance in constructing local place identity. The hopes of the resident' group were that 'It should become luxury apartments, a hotel, or to be used as a future hospital as long as the building is left untouched'.[95] The launching of this conservation campaign coincided with the decision to use Barnes Hospital to accommodate the Kosovan Albanians.

In May 1999 it was reported that one hundred Kosovan refugees would be flown into Manchester airport and settled in the neighbouring Stockport region.[96] The spreading of these refugees across Britain mirrored a wider policy of dispersal being implemented by the Home Office in response to what it saw as the dangerous concentration of asylum seekers in southeast England.[97] In the case of Stockport, two former hospitals, St Thomas' and Barnes, were chosen as the initial reception centres for the Kosovans. Rather than one hundred, just 83 refugees arrived and most of these were sent to Barnes Hospital.[98] One of these was Fadil Gashi, a thirty-five year-old who had, with his family, been expelled from his home by Serb paramilitaries. The Gashi family were put on a train and kept in brutal conditions in a camp for two months.[99] Contrasting such distressing descriptions of 'ethnic cleansing', the local media portrayed Barnes Hospital and St Thomas' as a 'sanctuary in Stockport'[100] and as 'safe-havens' for those who had escaped persecution.[101]

As with the Hungarians, local people made great efforts to make the Kosovan Albanians feel welcomed. Of great significance in relation to the contemporary campaign against asylum seekers, the Kosovan refugees were presented as genuine. Great emphasis was placed on the horrors that they had witnessed and experienced at home as well as the sympathy and support they had received in Stockport. Rather than being presented as in any way problematic (for example, in danger of being provided with better care than that given to local people in need), the description of the facilities provided for them were seen as fitting and deserving:

> Accommodation at Barnes is made up of comfortable three-bedroom flats in the hospital grounds, with lawns for the children to play on and cooking equipment for the increasingly self-sufficient families to use.[102]

Barnes Hospital was thus represented as being part of a redemptive process, returning the refugees' sense of self-dignity and restoring their trust in other human beings. After three weeks in Barnes Hospital, the Gashi family was portrayed in the *Stockport Express*, along with the other refugees, as settling into a routine:

> Over the next few weeks they'll all be gradually familiarised with the area until they're confident enough to get about themselves. But at the moment, the unit at Barnes is a cocoon, a haven of safety and a place where English lessons are taught.

In response, Fadil Gashi was keen to emphasise his gratitude: 'These have been very hard days. Now I feel liberated and have found a great humanity here.'[103] This narrative, comforting all round, was confirmed when he added that while he was 'very happy to stay here for now [that] when all the circumstances are ok to go back then I will'.[104] Not surprisingly, however, given the havoc wrought on their homeland and its instability, destruction of infrastructure and continuing ethnic tensions, these refugees were hesitant to return. Notwithstanding such dangers and unease to go back 'home', the British government wanted them to return – their exceptional status, post-NATO victory, was removed. Over the next years, legal battles would ensue as half these refugees, particularly those with major ongoing health problems, attempted to stay in the Stockport region – struggles that were echoed elsewhere in Britain with the Kosovan refugees.

In June 2000, the *Stockport Express* reported on the family of Mehedin Bekteshi who, just over a year earlier, had fled their 'war-torn village. Aged 31, he spoke no English. He could barely walk from the three bullet wounds to his arm and hip. His pregnant wife led the couple's two toddlers by the hand as the family settled into rooms at Barnes Hospital, Cheadle.' Mehedin Bekteshi had applied to extend his stay in Britain on compassionate grounds relating to his own health and that of two of his children. The local newspaper was sympathetic to his case and emphasised Mr Bekteshi's integration: he liked 'Coronation Street, football commentary and English food'. It also highlighted how his wife, Mehrem, 'gave birth to one of Stockport's Millennium babies ... on new year's day'. Mr Bekteshi's gratitude was stressed throughout the article: 'I would risk my life for the people of Stockport. They are wonderful.' Again the narrative was made more palatable by having an end point back 'home' and not in Stockport: 'I want to go back to Kosovo, I don't want to live in England forever.'[105] Another year on, the majority of the original eighty families had been returned, and only a handful were fighting on to stay in the Stockport region. As Arun Parmar of the Stockport Refugee Asylum Team commented in April 2001: 'They all desire to remain here as they say that the state of affairs in Kosovo is still not good and it continues to be a very dangerous place. A lot of them have lost their homes and have nothing to go back to.'[106]

The tedious, frustrating and anxiety-inducing delays in making decisions about the remaining Albanian Kosovans inevitably proved less newsworthy than their original settlement in Barnes Hospital. It is significant that in references to the site itself the Kosovans were represented as essentially 'other' to the building's past, present and future. In November 1999 it was reported that Barnes Hospital had been 'empty since the summer except for a large group of refugees who still occupy part of the premises'.[107] Three years later, a planning application to re-develop the site as luxury apartments and houses omitted all reference to the presence of the Kosovan refugees. Instead it emphasised the building's architectural distinction as a fine example of the 'French Gothic Revival Style' as well as its historic importance as 'an early example of a convalescent hospital'.[108] Heritage was overtaking history. The humane representation in the local media in 1999 and 2000 of the refugees as individuals with particular pasts, as well as their local integration and the dedicated work of those who cared for them, was speedily forgotten. Finally, in *Around the* M60, they ceased to be 'refugees' who had become part of the local landscape – including Rita Bekteshi, the Stockport millennium baby. Rather than being personalised and placed as victims of the last geno-cidal surge of twentieth-century Europe, they were now simply labelled 'asylum seekers', a term of widespread opprobrium in contemporary Britain and, in this particular case, erroneous in describing their initial legal status. Its negative qualities and otherness are further underlined in this text by being placed in quotation marks, as if, through punctuational device, somehow to cast doubts on their authenticity.[109] The narrative of a middle-aged woman in Cheadle, a part-time technician, written in sum-mer 2000, shows how easily these victims of ethnic cleansing could be transformed into unwanted and unassimilable 'asylum seekers':

> Locally we have had about 60 Kosovan families housed in an old hospital. About half have not gone home and seem to be quite settled and have no intention of returning, as they were intended to. They don't seem to be learning English (judging by the fact that they can't speak it in the local supermarket and charity shops where I see them), so could never get jobs here. One was interviewed in the local paper and said he had nothing in his own country and wanted to stay here. I thought that in fact he has nothing here but the prospect of never ending charity from the state, which he has done nothing to be entitled to …
>
> I do not see why we should support a community of 30 families indefi-nitely when with help they could return home. If they are economically worse off there it is not our problem, they were only well off here because of the charity they received off us. If there are Kosovans who would be in danger if they returned to the same part of their own country that they came from … there must surely be a part of their country where they would be accepted and they should be rehoused there, rather than thou-sands of miles away in England.[110]

Keeping the refugee out of sight

The use of abandoned buildings for refugees, keeping them outside the public gaze, has therefore been common but has been largely unrecorded in history and problematised or ignored within heritage. As V.S. Naipaul writes in *The Enigma of Arrival* 'refugee' or 'asylum' has the association 'of things kept decently out of sight and mind'.[111] Such buildings include Warth Mills near Bury, north of Manchester – a rat-infested and filthy disused cotton mill, which housed several thousand enemy aliens (largely Jewish refugees from Nazism and British Italians) in May/June 1940 and, after the war, became a paint factory. Norbert Barrett came to Britain from Germany in 1939 as a seventeen year-old on a temporary permit. In

1940 he was living in a Manchester refugee hostel and then interned by the authorities in Warth Mills:

> It was characterised nationally for its dilapidated conditions, incompetence, squalor and antisemitism. Warth Mills gained notoriety for being the worst internment camp in Britain. It lacked bedding, heating, electric light and toilet arrangements. The building held 2,000 people who were served by 20 taps and basins and 20 latrines ... Our crime appeared to be that we had fled to Britain from Nazi persecution.[112]

An infamous place for the refugees and the Italians, its brief life as internment camp has subsequently largely been forgotten – the site itself provides no indication of its past role. It was one that was particularly devastating for the Italians, many of whom were to drown soon after their departure from Warth Mills. They were on board the *Arandora Star*, a ship taking them, along with other Italian internees, to be interned in Canada. The *Arandora Star* was torpedoed by a German submarine with the loss of over 400 lives.[113] Warth Mills features briefly as 'Bury' in a list of British camps drawn in a sketch by a refugee interned in the Isle of Man in 1940, now in the permanent exhibition of the Manchester Jewish Museum, but it has only the briefest of mentions in the heritage displays in the town of Bury itself.[114]

Moving again from north to south, what was the site of one of Southampton's oldest schools and is now the home of Humanities at the University of Southampton, was also used briefly as an internment camp. The principal lecture theatre, once the school gym, was used to house all male refugees from the area in May 1940, mainly from Bournemouth where they had begun to start new lives. Here they were guarded closely and surrounded by barbed wire, and, as at Warth Mills, found themselves without basic facilities such as a water supply. Fritz Engel, an Austrian Jewish dentist, recalled his stay at Taunton's College 'already surrounded by electrically loaded barbed wire joining about 20 other refugees with whom I was locked up in a large room. A soldier, armed with rifle and bayonet, guarded the only door. Outside stood a bucket to receive our excrement.'[115] His account is taken from an unpublished testimony discovered by chance. Many other temporary internment sites have been lost now from future memory work as the generation of refugees who experienced them passes away. Taken together such camps formed an important aspect of the modern refugee experience but they are hidden, disguised, ignored or neglected in heritage production and the construction of collective memory. The ice rink in Southampton and Belle Vue zoo and amusement park in Manchester are fondly remembered as centres of everyday leisure for much of the twentieth century. Both, however, in the First World War and Second World War respectively, were used as internment camps.[116] And these are simply examples emerging from a close reading of the urban landscape in two particular cities. Hundreds of other cases could be exposed if the search was to be extended nationally. Yet in terms of the British heritage world, only the Isle of Man, through the Manx Museum in Douglas, has, if somewhat belatedly, recognised the importance of alien internment during both world wars. The domination of these camps in the local landscape was exceptional and can now be marketed as heritage. In this case it would have proved much harder to ignore their past presence in a place where they were located in 'all four corners of the Island'.[117]

A much larger and longer lasting camp, but one equally subject to the general amnesia outlined so far, was Atlantic Park, situated at what is now Southampton International Airport. It acts as a site revealing a battle of memories, and one in which, not surprisingly, a great icon of modern Britain overwhelms that of the refugee experience. Told briefly, Atlantic Park was created in 1922 by the major shipping companies in the hope that Southampton was to be *the* place of departure for the new world after the war in the previously lucrative business of transmigrancy. Due to the implementation of rigid and racially constructed immigration controls across the world, especially the United States through its quota laws of 1921 and 1924, Atlantic Park ended up being Europe's, if not the world's largest transmigrant camp in the 1920s.[118] It has never been referred to in British history books and has mainly been noted in local heritage because its physical presence blocked the attempt to create an airport for Southampton during and beyond the 1920s. For the people in the camp, however, some of whom were confined there for the best part of a decade, it was a pivotal experience. An increasing number of descendants of those quasi-interned there, including those of Ukrainian Jewish and Mennonite origin, have contacted me, as, so far, the sole historian of Atlantic Park. Such individuals are trying to make sense of their family history and the impact of the camp on later generations. Indeed, the whole life cycle of events happened in the camp – births, barmitzvahs, marriages and sadly death.

The site itself would not have merited much attention after its conversion into an airport in the early 1930s had it not been intimately connected to the most famous British aircraft, the Spitfire. The Spitfire has become a symbol of British resistance to the Nazis, especially in perhaps the most important moment in twentieth-century national mythology, the Battle of Britain. This remarkable plane was developed in Southampton by R.J. Mitchell who tragically died before the war but after the Spitfire had first been tested at the site of what was still called Atlantic Park. It is possible that Mitchell might have been familiar with the transmigrant presence as he tested out earlier planes at the camp in the 1920s. Southampton now prides itself as the 'home of the Spitfire' and major commemorations have taken place linked to anniversaries staged around its memory. Indeed, the focal points of Southampton's heritage promotion and modern historical identity are the *Titanic* and the Spitfire.[119]

When the old buildings, which housed the Jewish refugees in the 1920s, were knocked down some seventy years later to be replaced by the new airport, a display mentioned in passing its past history as Atlantic Park. More recently the memory of the Spitfire at the airport has become totally dominant and there is no mention at all of what was a very special place in British and global refugee policy and experience.[120] The refusal of the British government to let settle less than one thousand Jews who had escaped mass murder in the famine and civil war ridden Ukraine tells its own story. As the Conservative Home Secretary, William Joynson-Hicks unambiguously stated: 'under no circumstances will I permit these unfortunate people to be absorbed into our population. It is quite impossible. They are the class of people who come from the east of Europe that we do not want, and America does not want them either'.[121] It is not an episode, however, that British historians have found worthy of relating. Its general narrative runs counter to the myth of British, or more frequently English, tolerance and decency towards those in need. In this respect, the Spitfire, a representation of pluck, sacrifice and victory against the odds, provides a far more usable past.

These examples show how the presence of refugees in heritage sites, or alongside heritage sites, have been perceived as a problem. They are an embarrassment to be airbrushed out of the narrative; a sign of later decay; or as a passing curiosity meriting the briefest of mentions. Taken together they represent, often through absence, the dominant treatment of heritage and the refugee. And such use of heritage does not exist in a political vacuum. The local campaign in the town of Lee-on-the-Solent (close to Portsmouth) from 2003 to 2004 to oppose a proposed asylum seeker camp at the former naval airbase, HMS Daedalus, blatantly instrumentalised patriotic war memory: 'So this is why they died', as one banner on the site put it.[122] Another deviously and insidiously added to this already explosive mixture by playing on the sexualised fears often associated with the incoming 'alien':

DEAR DADDY

WHILE YOU WERE AWAY IN THE GULF SERVING YOUR COUNTRY LOOK WHAT THE GOVERNMENT HAS DONE TO ME AND MUMMY. THEY GAVE US 400 ASYLUM SEEKING MEN.[123]

Through the covering of the perimeter of HMS Daedalus with such posters

the heritage site itself became a crudely constructed exhibition of hatred.[124]

Not surprisingly in a context of a government anxious to appease any
signs of anti-asylum sentiment, the xenophobic and frequently racist campaign of the Daedalus Action Group (DAG), to stop the creation of the
camp, which was supported by the local press and council, was ultimately successful.[125] Nevertheless, at a grassroots level, the attempt to
mobilise heritage in an explicitly exclusive and racialised manner was
not uncontested. 'Bannerman', a local anti-racist, became notorious for
re-appropriating these makeshift displays of execration and storing them
in his garage. Hidden in the Portsmouth area is, with this garage, what
might be termed a private museum revealing Lee-on-the-Solent's dab-
bling with the politics of prejudice. It moved to the public sphere when
the anti-asylum campaign was exposed in a Channel 4 documentary,
Keep Them Out, described by one critic as a 'wake up call for anybody
who may have deluded themselves into believing that Britain is quite a
tolerant, multi-cultural sort of place'.[126]

Largely through the actions of DAG, Portsmouth, in the words of the
Guardian, 'gained a reputation as a hotbed of hostility towards asylum
seekers'.[127] For all the popular support garnered by DAG (and the weakness of its local opponents, 'FriendLee'), this was a distorted portrayal of
the wider area. It ignored, as one pro-refugee campaigner, Eleanor Scott,
a Liberal Democrat councillor, reminded the *Guardian*, Portsmouth's 'long
history of giving shelter to vulnerable incomers'. It was a tradition that
was most recently manifested (January 2005 onwards) in a remarkable
campaign of school children to stop the deportation of a fifteen-year-old
classmate, a Kurdish asylum seeker.[128] Scott's claim, however, that 'many'
of Portsmouth's past refugees are 'venerated in monuments throughout
the city, its cemeteries and parks', however desirable in principle, is, in
reality, wide of the mark, reflecting the relative absence of refugee heritage mapped throughout this chapter. On closer inspection it extends no
further than a private memorial to the post-war Poles in a specific Portsmouth cemetery.[129]

Counter-representation of the refugee: the Huguenots

In contrast to the negative imagery of Lee-on-the-Solent, or the general
void when confronting/avoiding the refugee past/present, there is a counter
form of representation that is, true to the general thrust of the heritage
industry, one of celebration. In the previous chapter the politicisation of
Britain's alleged 'proud tradition of sheltering the persecuted' has been
analysed. There is a heritage counterpart to this positive approach and it

is increasingly manifest with regard to those who helped the refugees
from Nazism. It highlights the support given to the child refugees, and
especially those coming on the *Kindertransport*, as will be explored further in chapter 4. Recent examples include the eulogising, and quasi-
canonization, of those involved in refugee work during the 1930s. Both
the civil servant, Frank Foley, and the businessman, Nicholas Winton,
have, for example, recently been re-discovered and described as 'Britain's
Schindler' for their work in helping to save Jewish lives in the desperate
months before the outbreak of the Second World War.[130] In these two
cases, the books, documentaries and, with Foley, the statue in his home
town of Highbridge, Somerset, have created saint-like figures whose work
for refugees is portrayed as redemptive, morally distancing Britain, or
England, from the evil persecutions taking place on the continent.[131] Such
commemoration builds on the much quieter celebration of George Bell,
Bishop of Chichester throughout the Nazi era. His death was marked in
1958 by the unveiling of a plaque in the church of St Michael and All
Angels, north London, 'as a thank offering by men and women who
found in Britain a refuge from tyranny ... and as a tribute to George
Kennedy Allen Bell who ... was tireless in his activities on their behalf'.[132]
There are, however, limits to the reference points of such heritage work
and also to its impact. A brief overview of the representation of the Huguenot refugees will illustrate this point clearly.

It has already been noted in chapter 1 that the Huguenot Garden in
Southampton is unique in Hampshire in its public recognition of the refugee presence and contribution to the county. In the post-1945 era, Elsie
Sandell emerged as the most popular writer of Southampton's heritage.
An internationalist and more specifically, a Francophile, she was particularly drawn to the French church in Southampton that has featured in
chapter 1. In *Southampton Cavalcade* (1953) she concluded a chapter
devoted to 'Links with France' with a tribute to those who had escaped
Catholic persecution on the continent:

> It requires but little imagination to see those Huguenot refugees wending
> their way along our old High Street to Winkle Street and their quiet church
> whence they drew spiritual help and encouragement. They had reached a
> safe haven here and they wrought industriously for the town of their adop-
> tion. School teachers, ministers, serge-makers, silk weavers, paper-mak-
> ers, merchants, soldiers, sailors and government officials.

What is especially remarkable about Sandell's narrative of local Huguenot integration is its conclusion: 'the pattern of their lives is woven for
ever into the story of Southampton'.[133]

Whether many other Sotonians, either in the 1950s or subsequently,
shared Sandell's vision and the ease with which she included the Huguenot

refugees within her mental picture of Southampton's past is debatable. It
has been noted that only the exceptional Henri de Portal has featured,
and usually in passing, in the historiography of Southampton. Sandell
would no doubt have been delighted by the creation of the Huguenot
Garden in the heritage zone of Southampton. Twenty years on, however,
the garden is tatty and the plaque close to indecipherable. The failure, in
the Hampshire countryside, to acknowledge the most dramatic Huguenot contribution, further reveals a continuing marginality and invisibility.

The story of Henri de Portal (but later anglicised to Henry Portal) and
his family has the classic features of a refugee success story suitable for
integration into a celebratory version of heritage construction in Britain.
It consists of a heroic break for freedom, local support, and contribution
of first and later generations. It is related with verve by Elsie Sandell:

> [I]n 1705, one Henri Portal a Protestant refugee from France who had, it
> is said, in order to escape, been hidden in a barrel and thus smuggled on
> board a vessel, landed at Southampton and found help and shelter amongst
> the Huguenots here. He went out to the mill at South Stoneham under
> Gerard de Vaux, also a French Protestant, and there learnt the craft of
> paper-making; so well, indeed that he was able in 1718 to establish his
> own mill at Laverstoke [near Whitchurch] in the north of Hampshire.
> Such was his skill that in 1724 he obtained the monopoly for manufactur-
> ing the special paper for the Bank of England notes, a privilege which his
> descendants, who carry on the mill, still hold. The Portals have indeed
> served their adopted country well, not only in Hampshire but in a national
> way in war and peace.[134]

William Cobbett, in his *Rural Rides*, penned throughout the 1820s, visited Whitchurch often and, true to his idiosyncratic, and often prejudiced, Tory radicalism, suggested a reading of the historical topography
very different from that later presented by Sandell, reflecting his con-
spiratorial hatred of the Bank of England. Through Whitchurch, wrote
Cobbett, ran a stream 'which turns the mill of Squire Portal ... [T]his
river, merely by turning a wheel ... has produced a greater effect on the
condition of men, than has been produced on that condition by all the
rivers, all the seas, all the mines and all the continents in the world'.[135]
Rather than celebrating this part of the rural Hampshire landscape,
Cobbett hoped that the time would come

> when a monument will be erected where that mill stands, and when on
> that monument will be inscribed *the curse of England*. This spot ought to
> be held accursed in all time henceforth and for evermore. It has been the
> spot from which have sprung more and greater mischiefs than ever plagued
> mankind before.[136]

Samuel Smiles, in his advocacy of the Huguenots as a group extolling his virtues of hard work and self-improvement, quoted Cobbett's comments on 'Squire Portal's' mill selectively, thereby highlighting only the recognition of the site's importance and not the evils of monetary capitalism that it had allegedly brought forth.[137] Today, however, in Whitchurch and its surrounds, neither the demonisation of this Huguenot site by Cobbett nor its appreciation by Smiles and Sandell, is present. Instead, there is simply a failure to consider its Huguenot connections, as exemplified by the major heritage centre in the area. 'Keeping alive the traditions and quality of a bygone age' is the goal of the Whitchurch Silk Mill – its future is 'based on maintaining strong links with the past'.[138] The local past that is portrayed, however, is selective and exclusive.

The silk industry was brought to Britain from the continent by Protestant refugees. Yet the opportunity to explore this theme, particularly significant because of the huge impact of the Portal family locally, is not taken up in the Whitchurch Silk Mill – its neighbour in the town, Bere Mill, was where Henri de Portal first made his banknote paper. Indeed, in an informal history of Whitchurch, it is acknowledged that in 1712 'the fortunes of the town improved … with the arrival of a Huguenot refugee named Henri de Portal, who brought the skill of paper-making to Whitchurch'.[139] This absence of reference is more the remarkable as in the Mill's display on the 'story of silk', the geographical focal points of the English trade, corresponding closely to Huguenot settlement, are made clear though the precise refugee connection remains unstated: 'Silk has been woven in England since the 15th century, mainly in Spitalfields in London, and in Norwich.'[140] Moreover, in Laverstoke itself, while the whole landscape was shaped and re-shaped by the Portal family business and largesse,[141] only the name lingers in the form of 'Portals Social Club'. There is no recognition within the landscape of the intimate link to its Huguenot refugee heritage.[142]

The most prominent, long-lasting and obvious refugee contribution to Hampshire is thus ignored or marginalised. The same is true within the Manchester region where the Huguenot impact has been, if anything, more intense. Manchester's fortune as the first large-scale industrial city was built on cotton spinning, building on a sixteenth-century foundation partly laid by Flemish refugees.[143] In contrast, Macclesfield, fifteen miles to the south, was a 'town built on silk'.[144] Today, the silk industry in Macclesfield is miniscule but the moniker 'silk town' still dominates its external and internal image. Through a 'silk trail' and four interconnected museums, the 'silk town story' is told and re-told in an impressive example of topographically integrated heritage work.[145]

Given the central role of the Protestant refugees in the creation of the

British branch of this industry, it might be assumed that some prominence would be given to them in what is the foremost heritage site relating to the silk industry in Britain. In fact, the references in Macclesfield
to these refugees are rare. Only in the Macclesfield Heritage Centre is
there brief mention of the role played within the expansion of the silk
industry through 'the arrival of weavers fleeing from religious persecution on the continent. Flemings settled in Norwich, Huguenots at Can-
terbury and London'. It is also acknowledged that 'By the 1680s, many
more Huguenots had come from France. Though not silk weavers, many
brought capital which *benefitted the London industry* [my emphasis].'[146]
This connection of the Huguenots to London is itself revealing – within
the Heritage Centre, silk production in Spitalfields is presented as somehow 'other' to Macclesfield. Indeed, it is remarked that 'Spitalfields was
a close community where large numbers worked in the silk trade'. In
fact, whatever the restrictions imposed within the Spitalfields industry,
from the late eighteenth century the two places were intimately connected.
Raw silk was sent from London and returned from Macclesfield as yarn
to Spitalfields. This inter-dependence was even marked by an informal
process of topographical naming. As one historian of Macclesfield has
remarked, 'So important was the London market to the town that the
district between Roe Street and Newgate was called Little Spitalfields.'[147]
Nor was it simply a case of the Protestant refugees developing the London and East Anglian trade without any role in its production in
Macclesfield. In *Silk Town*, Gail Malmgreen suggests that 'Local tradition traces the beginnings of large-scale silk-spinning in Macclesfield to
the enterprise of one Peter Orme, a Huguenot, who is said to have opened
a spinning workshop in the market-place'.[148] It is also clear that when
large-scale production began in Macclesfield, Huguenot workers played
a key role: 'A number of these weavers were brought to Macclesfield by
Leigh and Voce [probably the first weaving-masters in the town], looms
were installed in a workshop in Back Street and the production of silk
cloth was commenced under conditions of great secrecy.'[149] It was these
'immigrant workers' who were soon to 'instruct local workers in the
art'.[150]

    Later, in the nineteenth century, Spitalfields Huguenot silk weavers
would move north to Macclesfield in search of work.[151] Indeed, there is a
certain irony in the representation at the Macclesfield Heritage Centre of
the Spitalfields silk colony as a closed and restrictive world. It was only
in 1729, with the decline of the silk button business, that Macclesfield
Corporation reversed its 'long-standing protectionist and xenophobic
stance', revoking restrictions against 'ingenious strangers' starting busi-
nesses in the town.[152] Neither these Huguenot contributions nor the

xenophobia against earlier 'strangers' are mentioned in the Macclesfield museum world. The relative failure to engage and 'localise' the Huguenot experience in these Hampshire and Cheshire case studies requires further consideration.

In his *Huguenot Heritage*, Robin Gwynn outlines how it was 'from Spitalfields and through Spitalfields connections that the skills introduced by the refugees were later spread ... to other parts of Britain like Edinburgh, Macclesfield and Sudbury (Suffolk)'.[153] Gwynn's version of 'heritage' was inspired by the tercentenary of the Revocation of the Edict of Nantes. He concluded his study of the 'history and contribution of the Huguenots in Britain' by pleading that it showed

> that the right of a minority to exist is more than a moral rule. It is also, as Philippe Joutard remarked, 'the most certain means of enriching a civilization and increasing its dynamism'. At a time when there are more refugees than ever before in human history, yet when governments all around the world are setting up barriers against immigration, the reminder is salutary.[154]

Thirty years on, it is even more politically relevant to emphasise Gwynn's 'salutary reminder'. Furthermore, there is no sign that thirty years from now a future scholar will not still have to be making such calls to memory. The issue here is not to naively ponder why we don't 'learn from the past' but to explore why the Huguenot heritage work of Gwynn has not been followed in the local memory work explored in this section.

In *The Rings of Saturn* (1995), W.G. Sebald's exploration of the landscape and people of East Anglia, a vision is provided that makes the separation of the local from the global impossible. It is illustrated in one case through the Strangers Hall Museum in Norwich. Sebald was drawn to the 'marvellous strips of colour in the pattern books' kept in the Norfolk museum which was 'once the town house of ... a family of silk weavers who had been exiled from France'. Sebald did not romanticise their occupation, pointing to the mental and physical pain associated with weaving. The wooden frames they worked on are, he suggested, 'reminiscent of instruments of torture or cages'. It is, however, the ability to connect places that makes Sebald's place imagination so exceptional:

> Until the decline of the Norwich manufacturers towards the end of the eighteenth century, these catalogues of samples, the pages of which seem to me to be leaves from the only true book which none of our textual and pictorial works can even begin to rival, were to be found in the offices of importers throughout Europe, from Riga to Rotterdam and from St Petersburg to Seville. And the materials themselves were sent from Norwich to the trade fairs at Copenhagen, Leipzig and Zurich, and from there to the warehouses of wholesalers and retailers, and some half-silk wedding

shawl might even reach Isny, Weingarten or Wangen in the pannier on a Jewish pedlar's back.[155]

Can heritage replicate Sebald's ability to do justice to migration, exile and diaspora? Can it accept, as historical geographer, Doreen Massey, insists, that the 'local is always a product in part of "global" forces'[156] and that 'The global is everywhere and already, in one way or another, implicated in the local'[157]?

Towards an inclusive form of heritage?

David Lowenthal has attempted to move the 'heritage versus history' debate further by arguing that the two have to be fundamentally distinguished from each other. It is a mistake, he argues, to view heritage as 'bad' history. Instead, Lowenthal believes that 'heritage is not history at all; while it borrows from and enlivens historical study, heritage is not an inquiry into the past but a celebration of it, not an effort to know what actually happened but a profession of faith in a past tailored to present-day purposes'.[158] History, concludes Lowenthal, is a critical engagement and re-engagement with the past, whereas heritage is celebratory. Heritage is, by nature, biased, but unlike history, makes no attempt to correct that bias. Ultimately 'Prejudiced pride in the past is not a sorry consequence of heritage; it is its essential purpose. Heritage thereby attests our identity and affirms our worth.'[159] Robert Hewison dismissed heritage, 'for all its seductive delights', as 'bogus history'.[160] In contrast, Lowenthal attempts to take heritage on its own terms, and not as an inferior or counterfeit version of something else.

Lowenthal may be criticised for overdrawing so clearly the division between heritage and history which are, perhaps, better understood as closely related relatives under the broad family of 'memory work'. Nevertheless, his distinction – that heritage is a 'celebration' of the past and history as a critical perspective on it – is crucial. It still raises the question of *whose* heritage is to be celebrated. Like Raphael Samuel, Lowenthal believes that heritage has the potential to be inclusive by incorporating those previously excluded from representations of the past such as ethnic minorities. Even then, however, the celebratory mode often leads to exclusion of unsavoury aspects of the past: 'Hence New York's Museum of Immigration on Ellis Island makes no reference to the immigrant underworld of Sicilian mafiosi and Jewish prostitutes.'[161] How then does one become part of heritage's world of the included?

Lowenthal puts particular emphasis on what he calls 'time-honored stability'. Heritage pride, he suggests, inheres no less in precedence than in perpetuity – unbroken connections, permanent traits and institutions. Maintaining or restoring such links confirms that the groups we belong to are not ephemeral but enduring organisms ... Since any breach in a lineage might jeopardize heritage transmission, stewards exalt continuity.[162]

As we have seen in chapter 1, historians of minority groups in Britain such as Jews, Huguenots, African Caribbeans and Asians have made great effort to prove their subjects' long-standing presence within Britain and thus to take their rightful place in representations of the country's past. More recently, the heritage world in Britain has increasingly accepted the need to attract a more diverse audience. *Power of Place: The future of the historic environment* (2000) was a review bringing together the large heritage bodies in England. One of its five main messages was that 'Because people care about their environment, they want to be involved in decisions affecting it. And, in a multi-cultural society, everybody's heritage needs to be recognised.'[163] Such a perspective has been encouraged, through carrot and stick, by the British government. In January 2001, Chris Smith, then Secretary of State for the Department for Culture, Media and Sport in a document *Libraries, Museums, Galleries and Archives for All* (and subtitled 'Co-operating Across the Sectors to Tackle Social Exclusion'), stated that there had been some comments that it was 'not the business [of such bodies] to be involved in social regeneration by serving a wider and more diverse audience'. Smith disagreed and argued that it was 'clearly right that these national treasures should be available and accessible to all citizens'.[164]

In such policy-orientated documents, emphasis has been placed on bringing ethnic minorities into the existing world of heritage, rather than addressing the nature and ability of such collections and environments to be able to do so. For example, rather lamely, the Department for Culture, Media and Sport suggests that 'where appropriate, museums', galleries' and archives' collections and exhibitions should reflect the cultural and social diversity of the organisation's actual and potential audiences.'[165] *Power of Place* highlighted how a survey revealed that 'Only a quarter of Black people said they had made a special trip to the countryside in the past year, and both Black and Asian people were less likely than White people to visit stately homes.' The message drawn from this evidence was that 'Perceptions of a lack of welcome are significant and should be taken to heart by public and private owners alike.'[166]

In the desire to promote 'a greater appreciation of the value and importance of heritage for our future well-being',[167] there is a hesitation to confront that the past 'celebrated' in stately homes may itself be offensive and thereby exclusionary. Stately homes rarely reflect critically on the source of their wealth that enabled their creation and maintenance, including the riches from colonial exploitation and slavery or local expropriation. It raises the wider point about heritage – the catastrophic past can be represented, but generally only if 'we' are not implicated, or, even better, if 'we' were part of the redemptive process of righting the wrong.[168] Hence the anti-slavery movement has been commemorated, leading to often crude representations of the 'peculiar institution', but less so Britain's key economic role in the slave trade. In this respect, cities and towns such as Bristol, Liverpool, London and Lancaster are still struggling to come to terms with their past. Their prosperity at critical stages of development owed much to slavery but the heritage industry struggles to confront this distressing history.[169] At a totally different level of connection, the growing commemoration of the Holocaust in Britain tends to distance itself from what was not done in this country to help the Jews and instead, as we have seen, to celebrate those who helped rescue refugees. In the Imperial War Museum's impressive permanent Holocaust exhibition (2000), the largest visual image by far relates to British troops and their liberation of Belsen concentration camp. As with slavery, the horror is not celebrated in any way, but the righteousness of the cause of those fighting against it is. Similar images from Buchenwald are used at the United States Holocaust Memorial Museum in Washington.[170]

The desire amongst its leading practitioners to make heritage inclusive is genuine and sincere:

> People are interested in the historic environment. They want to learn about it. They want to help define it. They want their children to be taught about it. They want to be involved in decisions affecting it. They want to take part. But many feel powerless and excluded. The historical contribution of their group in society is not celebrated. Their personal heritage does not appear to be taken into account by those who take decisions[171]

It is also, in the spirit of Raphael Samuel, fundamentally optimistic:

> If the barriers to involvement can be overcome, the historic environment has the potential to strengthen the sense of community and provide a solid basis for neighbourhood renewal. This is the power of place.[172]

In contrast, this chapter has shown how the 'power of place' in relation to refugees and heritage has been used to *exclude* – continuing in the social and cultural sphere the political processes which have been designed to keep out, or keep to a minimum (with maximum invisibility), the persecuted from other lands. In the *Power of Place* the landscape architect, urban designer and environmental planner, Kim Wilkie, is quoted from his *Indignation!* (2000) that 'A sense of continuity does not have to stop new ideas – just the opposite. The deeper the root, the greater the range of nutrients.'[173] It is, however, the lack of continuity, the lack of continued presence that has led to the exclusion, marginalisation and problematisation of refugees in the heritage landscape.

More often than not, refugees, especially those whose stay has been temporary, have been portrayed as essentially *anti-heritage*.[174] Yi-Fu Tuan argues that 'if we see the world as process, constantly changing, we should not be able to develop any sense of place'.[175] The confusing reality of such flux can be mitigated by constructing place as unchanging. Edward Relph in his seminal *Place and Placelessness* (1976), while recognising that landscapes can change dramatically, also suggested that 'the persistence of the character of places is apparently related to a continuity both in our experience of change and in the very nature of change that serves to reinforce a sense of association and attachment to those places'.[176] It is against the dominant tendency of constructed continuous lineage that the recognition of refugee presence has to contend. Ian Baucom has suggested that only in the late twentieth century was there a turn, through figures such as Enoch Powell, to define Englishness racially. Before, 'localist discourse identified English place, rather than English blood, as the one thing that could preserve the nation's memory and, in preserving its memory, secure England's continuous national identity'.[177]

In contrast, this chapter suggests that 'English place', could and has been defined exclusively. John Urry oversimplifies when he suggests that 'It is part of the culture of those living in a given geographical area that there is a distinction drawn between those who are local, "people like us", and those who are non-local, "outsiders", "offcomers", etc.'[178] The thousands of local refugee committees set up in Britain across the twentieth century, which involved huge numbers of ordinary people, points to the possibility of collapsing the categories of 'local' and 'non-local'. Nevertheless, the equal, if not greater potential for the 'local' to become a mechanism of exclusion, including racial exclusion, has also to be acknowledged. It is particularly relevant to this chapter's geographical focus to take on board the comments of Dave Russell in his study of northern England and the national imagination – that 'regional loyalties ... have the capacity to add a potent ingredient to banal racism'.[179] In the interrogation of the British local landscape in this chapter, it is largely the helpers of the refugees, and then mainly those who helped Jews escape Nazism, who have been *celebrated*. Even the Huguenots, whose narrative could easily become part of a heritage success story, have been marginalised. As with the writing of history, the myth that Britain is not a country of past diversity and settlement have, so far, proved too strong for their ready inclusion in the local heritage industry.

Is it, therefore, feasible to imagine a world of British heritage that would include sites such as Atlantic Park and the Hungarian settlement in Styal that went alongside the so-far dominant and celebratory narratives associated with these places? It would require the world view of a W.G. Sebald to enable this radical alternative to be realised – one that recognised that the local and the global are inseparable, or, rather, as Derek Gregory suggests, that our 'imaginative geographies' are both. The 'global', he adds, 'is not the "universal", but is itself, as the 'local', 'a situated construction'.[180] Furthermore, the radical alternative requires an acceptance of Sebald's understanding that exile and migration, as a traumatic as well as an enriching experience, are core to the past as well as shaping the present. Ironically, sites such as Atlantic Park point to continuity – one of the core ingredients of heritage – that of the confinement of refugees, immigrants and minorities in the modern world, a tradition that Britain, at home and abroad, has certainly not been immune from (indeed, it has often taken the lead). It is not a tradition, however, that it is easy to imagine as being the example the Heritage Lottery Fund had in mind when it highlights the need for 'communities to celebrate their past'.[181]

To incorporate the refugee experience will therefore require the extension of the bounds of heritage so that their contribution, and those who supported (and opposed) them, can be recognised. Simultaneously, however, it also necessitates the need to create a form of non-triumphalist counter-heritage where impermanence, absence and reflection of past (and present) exclusion is accepted. Only post-war Germany (or, until 1990, West Germany) comes close to providing such a model in a situation that was exceptional – a politics and culture based on an official, if not always a popular, acceptance of guilt. Even then responsibility for past actions has been contested, partly through denial.[182] In Britain, no such self-reflection has taken place or has been politically necessary. Moreover, its war memory works against a non-celebratory approach, especially as the country has collectively constructed the conflict, post–1945, as one fought against a racist, as opposed to a militarily aggressive, enemy.[183] The xenophobic political potential of this inward-looking and self-congratulatory war memory was exposed in the disturbing campaign fought by the Daedalus Action Group in Lee-on-the-Solent.

And yet there is a counter-tradition in Britain that is suspicious of all types of nationalism, even forms that attempt to construct a Britishness or Englishness that is inclusive and, indeed, tolerant of pluralism.[184] It is within an alternative, internationalist but locally sensitive, anti-heroic and anti-celebratory tradition that a counter-heritage movement could possibly develop, building on the self-reflexive 'new museology' practice.[185] It is only within such counter-heritage that those whose stay in Britain was brief – such as the Kosovans in Barnes Hospital and the Ukrainians in Atlantic Park – could be incorporated. At best, when refugees are included it is briefly (particularly in comparison to those labelled as immigrants) and without destroying the sense of local harmony emphasised elsewhere through continuity of presence. Generalising from the case studies outlined in this chapter, it is clear that larger urban centres have been more willing to represent immigrants in their heritage construction than has been evident in smaller towns and rural areas. Even then Manchester and London have been hesitant to place refugees in their landscapes of memory, including the innovative take on city living, 'Urbis'.[186]

George Szirtes writes of his refugee father that he

> spoke some English before he left Hungary, the only one of us to do so. I have watched him grow older, seen his name anglicised to Surtees at work and then de-anglicised again since his retirement. I have seen him move through the suburbs of London, remarry and return to Hungary with his old scout associates. His journey, like mine, has been through culture and language. Above all, his has been through history. That history is part of the English landscape now.

Szirtes adds that the sonnet *Portrait of My Father in an English Landscape* 'attempts to place, realise and annotate his journey as a human document':[187]

> Particularities, hard luck and guilt
> compose him. Mention his patience too,
> also his kindness.[188]

Szirtes' work as a poet without a fixed place identity has produced the dilemma of 'inbetweenness': 'I may envy the rooted but I cannot enter their territory.'[189] That placeless marginalisation has been true of many refugee groups in Britain, including, as we have seen, the Hungarians. Rather than being unintended, the many examples of local memory work in heritage construction presented here reveal how ignoring the presence of refugees (and sometimes their absence of presence), has often necessitated an active process of amnesia. It will thus take effort and pain to incorporate Szirtes' 'human document' into meanings more generally associated with 'an English landscape'. Yet that his work, and that of the late W.G. Sebald, has gained (albeit belated) recognition in literary and cultural circles suggests that it is far from impossible to include the memory of exile from other places within a British local context.[190]

What the next chapter reveals, through the writings of ordinary people, is that any attempt to bring the refugees into British history and heritage (or counter-heritage) is not distorted or what is now so often, so easily and so lazily rejected as 'politically correct'. Refugees have been part of the everyday world in Britain and responses to them have been positive, negative and, more often than not, ambivalent. Such responses, and their very complexity which make them hard to categorise, show an *engagement* with refugees rarely featured in the world of heritage.

Notes

1 Robert Hewison, 'The Heritage Industry Revisited', *Museums Journal* vol. 91 no. 4 (April 1991), p. 23.
2 Robert Hewison, *The Heritage Industry: Britain in a Climate of Decline* (London: Methuen, 1987).
3 Patrick Wright, *On Living in an Old Country: The National Past in Contemporary Britain* (London: Verso, 1985), pp. 164–5 and chapter 5 generally.
4 Raphael Samuel, *Theatres of Memory* vol. 1 *Past and Present in Contemporary Culture* (London: Verso, 1994).
5 Brian Graham, G.J. Ashworth and J.E. Tunbridge, *A Geography of Heritage: Power, Culture & Economy* (London: Arnold, 2000), p. 34.
6 Heritage Lottery Fund, *Who Do We Think We Are?* (London, Heritage Lottery Fund, 2005).
7 This was begun at a HLF conference held on 13 July 2004 at the British Museum.
8 Heritage Lottery Fund, *Who Do We Think We Are?*
9 Clifford Geertz, *Local Knowledge* (London: Fontana, 1983).
10 Anthony Jackson (ed.), *Anthropology at Home* (London: Tavistock Publications, 1987).
11 Jonathan Boyarin, *Storm from Paradise: The Politics of Jewish Memory* (Minneapolis: University of Minnesota Press, 1992), chapter 1.
12 Neville Cardus, 'Music in Manchester' in W.H. Brindley (ed.), *The Soul of Manchester* (Manchester: Manchester University Press, 1929), pp. 176–7.
13 James Agate, *Ego: The Autobiography of James Agate* (London: Hamish Hamilton, 1935), p. 44.
14 W.G. Sebald, *The Emigrants* (London: Vintage, 2002 [orig. in German, 1993), pp. 191–2, 198.
15 Dave Haslam, *Manchester, England: The Story of the Pop Cult City* (London: Fourth Estate, 1999), p. xi. See also the comments of Alan Lawson, '*It Happened in Manchester': The True Story of Manchester's Music 1958–1965* (Bury: Multimedia, no date), p. 59: Liverpool was 'Nothing like as cosmopolitan as Manchester and a very insular and parochial place'.
16 Alan Kidd, *Manchester* (Keele, Staffs: Keele University Press, 1993), p. 164. For an overly romanticised picture, see W.M. Crawford, 'A Cosmopolitan City', in N.J. Frangopulo (ed.), *Rich Inheritance: A Guide to the History of Manchester* (Wakefield: S.R. Publishers, 1969 [1962]), pp. 109–23.
17 See Antonio Ria, *Italians in Manchester* (Aosta: Musumeci Editore, 1990);

B. Jenazian, 'The Armenian Merchants and the Armenian Community in Manchester' (unpublished typescript, 1965, Manchester Central Reference Library, F301 45 Je1).

18 Cardus, 'Music in Manchester', pp. 176–7.

19 Peter Mandler, *History and National Life* (London: Profile Books, 2002), p. 151 suggests that in Britain 'At least through the 1930s, and in certain respects right up to the 1960s, professional historians thought the one surviving public justification for history was its value for citizenship'.

20 Liisa Malkki, 'National Geographic: The Rooting of Peoples and the Territorialization of National Identity among Scholars and Refugees', *Cultural Anthropology* vol. 7 no. 1 (February 1992), p. 34. Her last phrase is taken from Mary Douglas, *Purity and Danger: An Analysis of the Concepts of Pollution and Taboo* (London: Routledge, 1966).

21 William Page (ed.), *The Victoria History of the Counties of England: Hampshire and the Isle of Wight* (London: Archibald Constable & Co, 1900), p. 1.

22 See the exhibition catalogue, edited by its curator, Nick Merriman (ed.), *The Peopling of London: Fifteen Thousand Years of Settlement from Overseas* (London: Museum of London, 1993) and the comments of the Museum's director, Max Hebditch (pp. x–xi). For an insightful overview informed by international comparisons see David Kahn, 'Diversity and the Museum of London', *Curator: The Museum Journal* vol. 37 no. 4 (1994), pp. 240–50.

23 Figures from the Museum of London files on 'The Peopling of London'.

24 Nick Merriman and Rozina Visram, 'The World in a City', in idem, *The Peopling of London*, p. 13.

25 See Anon., 'Maybe it's Because I'm a Londoner', *History Today* (November 1993), p. 3.

26 Samuel Smiles, *The Huguenots* (London: John Murray, 1868, 2nd edition [1867]), p. 107.

27 See, for example, Merriman, *The Peopling of London*, pp. 43–6, 138–48.

28 Robert Parks quoted by Peter Rose, *The Subject is Race: Traditional Ideologies and the Teaching of Race Relations* (New York: Oxford University Press, 1968), p. 72.

29 Merriman and Visram, 'The World in a City', p. 25.

30 See the comments of Nick Merriman in 'Maybe it's Because I'm a Londoner'.

31 Louise London, 'Whitehall and the refugees: the 1930s and the 1990s', *Patterns of Prejudice* vol. 34 no. 3 (2000), p. 18.

32 The Museum of Science & Industry in Manchester, *Souvenir Guide* (Manchester: Museum of Science & Industry, no date), p. 16 summarises the historical section but does not mention immigration as a major theme.

33 Text in final section of the exhibition, sponsored by Central Manchester Development Corporation, visited in March 2002.

34 *Manchester Metro News*, 12 April 2002; Urbis Museum, visited July 2002.

35 *The Pump House: Peoples History Museum, A Guide* (Manchester: National Museum of Labour History, 1998), p. 1.

36 Introductory video, 'The Pump House Museum', visited March 2002.
37 Permanent exhibition of the Manchester Jewish Museum, visited March 2002.
38 Urbis, 'Changing City', visited July 2002.
39 Cardus, 'Music in Manchester', pp. 178, 180.
40 J.B. Priestley, *English Journey* (London: Victor Gollancz, 1934), pp. 160–1.
41 James Stanhope-Brown, *A Styal of Its Own (1894–1964)* (Manchester[?]: Christine Pothecary, 1989), chapter 7 (no page references).
42 Ibid., 'Epilogue'.
43 Ibid.
44 *Coronation Street* (Granada Television), story line, 2004.
45 National Trust website, www.quarrybankmill.org.uk/, accessed 27 February 2005.
46 Report of the General and Parliamentary Committee, 5 September 1956, City of Manchester Council Minutes, 1956/57, vol. 2, appendix, p. 506, Manchester Central Reference Library Local Studies Unit.
47 'Hungarian Refugees: Styal Cottage Homes', Report of the Town Clerk, February 1957, in General and Parliamentary Committee, City of Manchester Council Minutes, 1956/57, vol. 2, appendix, p. 1765.
48 'Hungarian Refugees', Town Clerk report, February 1957.
49 Ibid.
50 Town Clerk report, 26 March 1958.
51 There is, however, a brief and celebratory mention in W. Crawford, ' A Cosmopolitan City', pp. 120–1.
52 National Trust website, www.quarrybankmill.org.uk, visited 27 February 2005; Quarry Bank Mill exhibition, visited 1994.
53 Stanhope-Brown, *A Styal of its Own*, chapter 13.
54 Samuel, *Theatres of Memory*, p. 304.
55 Ibid., p. 308.
56 Stanhope-Brown, *A Styal of Its Own*, chapter 13.
57 Philip Hoare, *Spike Island: The Memory of a Military Hospital* (London: Fourth Estate, 2002 [2001]), passim.
58 Ibid, pp. 280–1.
59 John Holder, *Royal Victoria Country Park: The Story of a Great Military Hospital & Royal Victoria Country Park* (Winchester [?]: Hampshire County Council, no date), p. 17.
60 Sebald on inside cover of the paperback version of *Spike Island* recommending it as one of the *Sunday Telegraph*'s books of the year.
61 Ibid., p. 115.
62 Alan Rice, 'Exploring Inside the Invisible: An Interview with Lubaina Himid', *Wasafari* no. 40 (Winter 2003), p. 24.
63 This amnesia was highlighted in Colin Holmes and Sean Kelly, '"A Question of Ways and Means": Hungarian Immigrants to Britain 1956–7', paper at 'Immigration, History and Memory in Britain' conference, De Montford University, September 2003.
64 See chapter 1.

65 Ibid. and Tony Kushner and Katharine Knox, *Refugees in an Age of Genocide: Global, National and Local Perspectives during the Twentieth Century* (London: Frank Cass, 1999), chapter 8.

66 Kushner and Knox, *Refugees in an Age of Genocide*, chapter 8; report on Hungarian refugees in Styal, February 1957.

67 Leslie Lever, 3 April 1958 in City of Manchester council minutes, 1957/58, vol. 2, appendix.

68 'Hungarian Refugees', Town Clerk Report, February 1957.

69 'Hungarian Refugees', Town Clerk Report, March 1958.

70 Ibid.

71 'Hungarian Refugees', Town Clerk Report, February 1957.

72 'Hungarian welfare', March 1979, Refugee Council archives, RH/QU61.

73 'Hungarian Refugees', Town Clerk Report, March 1958 report on the Hungarian refugees in Styal.

74 Reproduced in George Mikes, *How to be a Brit* (Harmondsworth: Penguin, 1987 [1960]), pp. 177, 179.

75 George Szirtes, 'Preface', in idem, *The Budapest File* (Newcastle: Bloodaxe Books, 2000), pp. 11–12.

76 *Manchester Convalescent Home, Cheadle* vol. 9 (September 1898) in Cheadle library, files on Barnes Hospital.

77 Matthew Hyde, Aidan O'Rourke and Peter Portland, *Around the M60: Manchester's Orbital Motorway* (Altrincham, Cheshire: AMCD Publishers, 2004), p. 31.

78 *Manchester Convalescent Home, Cheadle*, vol. 9.

79 Nikolaus Pevsner and Edward Hubbard, *The Buildings of England: Cheshire* (London: Penguin, 1990 [1971]), pp. 128–9.

80 *Stockport Messenger*, 15 August 1986.

81 Quoted in 'Neil Young's Film Lounge', www.jigsawlounge.co.uk/film/manchestermorgue2.html, accessed 9 February 2005.

82 By its video version distributors, Blackstar. See www.blackstar.co.uk/video/item/7000000069394, accessed 18 April 2002.

83 John Pym (ed.), *Time Out Film Guide* (London: Time Out, 2000, 8th edition), p. 608.

84 'Neil Young's Film Lounge'.

85 See http://us.imdb.com/Locations?0071431, accessed 18 April 2002.

86 'Neil Young's Film Lounge'.

87 Hyde, O'Rourke and Portland, *Around the M60*, pp. 170–1.

88 'Neil Young's Film Lounge'.

89 Hyde, O'Rourke and Portland, *Around the M60*, pp. 31, 35.

90 Kushner and Knox, *Refugees in an Age of Genocide*, Afterword, pp. xxvii–xxxvii; Elspeth Guild, 'The United Kingdom: Kosovar Albanian Refugees', in Joanne van Selm (ed.), *Kosovo's Refugees in the European Union* (London: Pinter, 2000), pp. 67–90.

91 Kushner and Knox, *Refugees in an Age of Genocide*, passim.

92 John Garrard, *The English and Immigration: A Comparative Study of the Jewish Influx 1880–1910* (London: Oxford University Press, 1971), pp. 5, 51.

93 Dora Steele, *Cheadle Remembered* (Manchester: Neil Richardson, 1983), pp. 28–30.
94 Charles Makepeace, *Cheadle and Gatley in Old Picture Postcards* (Zaltbommel, Netherlands: European Library, 1988), images 126 and 127.
95 *Stockport Express*, 24 November 1999.
96 *Stockport Express*, 12 May 1999.
97 Guild, 'The United Kingdom', pp. 82–3. For a critique see Audit Commission, *Another Country: Implementing Dispersal under the Immigration and Asylum Act 1999* (London: Audit Commission, 2000).
98 *Stockport Express*, 28 July 1999.
99 *Stockport Express*, 23 June 1999.
100 Ibid.
101 *Stockport Express*, 2 June 1999.
102 Ibid.
103 *Stockport Express*, 23 June 1999.
104 Ibid.
105 *Stockport Express*, 21 June 2000.
106 *Stockport Times*, 5 April 2001.
107 *Stockport Express*, 24 November 1999.
108 Turley Associates: Barnes Hospital Planning Proposals, September 2002, Cheadle Library: 'Historic Buildings' files.
109 Hyde, O'Rourke and Portland, *Around the M60*, p. 35.
110 Mass-Observation Archive, University of Sussex: DR J931, Summer 2000.
111 V.S. Naipaul, *The Enigma of Arrival* (London: Penguin, 1987), p. 182.
112 Testimony reproduced in *Jewish Telegraph*, 12 April 2002.
113 Terri Colpi, 'The Impact of the Second World War on the British Italian Community', in David Cesarani and Tony Kushner (eds), *The Internment of Aliens in Twentieth Century Britain* (London: Frank Cass, 1993), pp. 176–81.
114 Manchester Jewish Museum, visited March 2002. In the newly refurbished and re-fashioned Bury Art Gallery Museum (which opened in May 2005, visited September 2005), there is a table made at Warth Mills within the 'Changing Communities' section. In the description of this object in accompanying 'Interpretation' material, it is identified as being the work of an Italian internee in 1945. In fact, it was produced by one of the prisoners of war who was housed at Warth Mills after it was used briefly as an internment camp. See Ken Inman and Michael Helm, *Bury and the Second World War* (Warrington/Formby: Inman and Helm, 1995), chapter 10. I would like to thank Ronan Brindley, Bury's Museum Development Officer, for discussing this display and for showing me other items made by the Italian prisoners of war.
115 Fritz Engel, 'A Chain of Events' (unpublished memoir), pp. 118–19.
116 See Kushner and Knox, *Refugees in an Age of Genocide*, pp. 45, 173–4.
117 Yvonne Cresswell (ed.), *Living With the Wire: Civilian Internment in the Isle of Man during the two World Wars* (Douglas, Isle of Man: Manx National Heritage, 1994).

118 Kushner and Knox, *Refugees in an Age of Genocide*, chapter 3.
119 See Tony Kushner, 'Not That Far? Remembering and Forgetting Cosmopolitan Southampton' in Miles Taylor (ed.), *Southampton: Gateway to Empire* (London, forthcoming).
120 Site visits to Southampton International Airport, 1990 to the present.
121 In *Hansard* (HC) vol. 180, cols. 313–14, 11 February 1925.
122 *Southern Daily Echo*, 15 February 2003.
123 Image of this poster reproduced in 'Closing the Door? Immigrants to Britain 1905–2005', exhibition, Jewish Museum, London, March–August 2005.
124 The early campaigning is dealt with in Tony Kushner, 'Meaning Nothing But Good: Ethics, History and Asylum-Seeker Phobia in Britain', *Patterns of Prejudice* vol. 37 no. 3 (September 2003), pp. 268–72, and the final stages and aftermath by Michelene Stevens, unpublished undergraduate dissertation, University of Southampton (History), 2005.
125 *This is Hampshire*, 4 and 5 February 2005; *The Express*, 4 February 2004.
126 David Modell, *Keep Them Out*, Channel 4, 6 May 2004; review by Kathryn Flett, *Observer*, 9 May 2004. The collection of 'Bannerman' featured in the documentary.
127 Description in the *Guardian*, 24 January 2005.
128 Eleanor Scott, Liberal Democrat councillor, Fratton, in letter to the *Guardian*, 27 January 2005.
129 Ibid. and Councillor Scott in discussion with the author, 29 January 2005, at public protest meeting in Portsmouth to keep Lorin Sulaiman and her family in Britain.
130 For more general comments, see Tony Kushner, 'The Search for Nuance in the Study of Holocaust "Bystanders"', in David Cesarani and Paul Levine (eds), *'Bystanders' to the Holocaust: A Re-evaluation* (London: Frank Cass, 2002), pp. 70–1.
131 For local commemoration in Highbridge, including a new street name and the statue, see BBC Television West, 'Inside Out', 28 February 2005.
132 Reproduced in Paul Foster (ed.), *Bell of Chichester (1883–1958)* (Chichester: University College Chichester, 2004), p. 106.
133 Elsie Sandell, *Southampton Cavalcade* (Southampton: G.F. Wilson, 1953), p. 137.
134 Elsie Sandell, *Southampton Through the Ages* (Southampton: G.F. Wilson, 1960), p. 93.
135 G.D.H. and Margaret Cole (eds), *Rural Rides … by William Cobbett* vol. 1 (London: Peter Davies, 1930 [orig. 1830]), pp. 311–14.
136 Ibid., p. 120.
137 Smiles, *The Huguenots*, p.335.
138 Brochure, *Whitchurch Silk Mill* (Basingstoke: Whitchurch Silk Mill, no date).
139 Anne Pitcher, *Whitchurch* (Basingstoke: Bird Brothers, 1984), p. 21 and also the entry in Whitchurch Town Council in www.hants.gov.uk/parish/whitchurch/history.html, accessed 14 March 2005.
140 Permanent exhibition of Whitchurch Silk Mill, visited February 2004.

141 William Portal, *The Manors and Churches of Laverstoke and Freefolk, in Hampshire* (no place of publication: Hampshire Field Club, 1908), passim.

142 There are, however, references to Portal's refugee connections in various Hampshire County Council websites on Laverstoke. See, for example, www.hants.gov.uk/localpages/north_west/whitchurch/laverstoke/, accessed 14 March 2005.

143 Crawford, 'A Cosmopolitan City', p. 110 highlights this role but cautions against overstating the Flemish connection.

144 Gail Malmgreen, *Silk Town: Industry and Culture in Macclesfield 1750–1835* (Hull: Hull University Press, 1985), chapter 1.

145 Macclesfield Museums Trust, leaflet, 'Silk Town Story', summarises the musuems and heritage infrastructure.

146 Macclesfield Heritage Centre, visited February 2005.

147 C. Stella Davies, *A History of Macclesfield* (Manchester: Manchester University Press, 1961), p. 124.

148 Malmgreen, *Silk Town*, p. 13.

149 Davies, *A History of Macclesfield*, p. 128.

150 Malmgreen, *Silk Town*, p. 21.

151 Ibid., p. 199 note 93.

152 Ibid., p. 13.

153 Robin Gwynn, *Huguenot Heritage: The History and Contribution of the Huguenots in Britain* (London: Routledge, 1985), p. 68.

154 Ibid., p. 175.

155 W.G. Sebald, *The Rings of Saturn* (London: Harvill Press, 1998 [orig. in German 1995), pp. 282–6.

156 Doreen Massey, 'Places and Their Pasts', *History Workshop* no. 39 (spring 1995), p. 183.

157 Doreen Massey, 'Double Articulation: A Place in the World', in A. Bammer (ed.), *Displacements: Cultural Identities in Question* (Bloomington, IN: Indiana University Press, 1994), p. 120.

158 David Lowenthal, *The Heritage Crusade and the Spoils of History* (Cambridge: Cambridge University Press, 1998 [1996]), p. x (Preface to the paperback edition).

159 Ibid., chapter 5, esp. p. 122.

160 Hewison, *The Heritage Industry*, p. 144.

161 Ibid., p. 160.

162 Ibid., p. 184.

163 English Heritage, *Power of Place: The Future of the Historic Environment* (London: English Heritage, 2000), p. 1.

164 Department for Culture, Media and Sport, *Libraries, Museums, Galleries and Archives for All* (London: Department for Culture, Media and Sport, 2001), p. 4.

165 Ibid., p. 8.

166 *Power of Place*, p. 25.

167 Heritage Lottery Fund, *Who Do We Think We Are?*

168 For a brief discussion of 'heritages of disinheritance and atrocity', see Graham

et al., *A Geography of Heritage*, pp. 62–73.

169 Gabriel Gbadamosi, 'So Much Misery Condensed', *Museums Journal* vol. 9 no. 9 (September 1990), p. 25; Marcus Wood, *Blind Memory: Visual Representations of Slavery in England and America, 1780–1865* (Manchester: Manchester University Press, 2000).

170 Tony Kushner, 'The Holocaust and the Museum World in Britain: A Study of Ethnography' in Sue Vice (ed.), *Representing the Holocaust* (London: Frank Cass, 2003), pp. 27–30.

171 *Power of Place*, p. 23.

172 Ibid.

173 *Power of Place*, p. 5; Kim Wilkie, 'Indignation tomorrow' in Mavis Batey, David Lambert and idem, *Indignation! The campaign for conservation* (London: Kit-Cat Books, 2000), p. 55.

174 This is made explicit in the quarterly magazine *This England* which claims to be the largest selling heritage publication in Britain. Non-white immigrants, and more recently the figure of the 'asylum seeker' has been used to illustrate the undermining of Englishness.

175 Yi-Fu Tuan, *Space and Place: The Perspective of Experience* (London: Arnold, 1977), p. 179.

176 Edward Relph, *Place and Placelessness* (London: Pion, 1976), p. 31.

177 Ian Baucom, *Out of Place: Englishness, Empire, and the Locations of Identity* (Princeton: Princeton University Press, 1999), p. 16.

178 John Urry, *Consuming Places* (London: Routledge, 1995), pp. 73, 153.

179 Dave Russell, *Looking North: Northern England and the national imagination* (Manchester: Manchester University Press, 2004), p. 284.

180 Derek Gregory, *Geographical Imaginations* (Oxford: Blackwell, 1994), pp. 203–4.

181 Heritage Lottery Fund, *Who Do We Think We Are?*

182 Ian Buruma, *The Wages of Guilt: Memories of War in Germany and Japan* (London: Jonathan Cape, 1994); Mary Fulbrook, *German National Identity after the Holocaust* (Cambridge: Polity Press, 1999); and William Nevin, *Facing the Nazi Past: United Germany and the Legacy of the Third Reich* (London: Routledge, 2001).

183 Tony Kushner, *The Holocaust and the Liberal Imagination: A Cultural and Social History* (Oxford: Blackwell, 1994), chapter 7.

184 See, for example, Julian Baggani, 'Here's what it really means to be British', *Guardian*, 16 March 2005 in response to 'progressive' attempts to define Britishness and Englishness by leading Labour party figures, Gordon Brown and David Blunkett.

185 Peter Vergo (ed.), *The New Museology* (London: Reaktion Books, 1993 [1989]).

186 In the *Making of Manchester* there is, for example, a powerful photograph with the caption 'Ukrainian refugees at the Displaced Persons camp at Inskip near Preston in May, 1947. These refugees were dressed in traditional Ukrainian folk costumes to give a concert. Central and Eastern European immigrants were accepted in Britain under the European Volunteer Workers

scheme. They were usually placed in special camps, like this one, until work and proper accommodation could be arranged.' Museum of Science and Technology, Manchester, visited March 2002.

187 Szirtes, 'Preface', pp. 14–15.
188 From 'Portrait of My Father in an English Landscape' (1998) reproduced in Szirtes, *The Budapest File*, p. 191.
189 Szirtes, 'Preface', p. 15.
190 Szirtes won the T.S. Eliot prize for poetry in 2004 for his collection *Reel*.

3

Writing refugees: memory work during the Nazi era

Introduction

In his breezy and upbeat account of the development of 'cosmopolitan' Manchester, W.M. Crawford devoted a paragraph to the 1930s:

> the dictatorship of Hitler caused an exodus of political and religious refugees from Germany. One of the most distinguished scholars of modern times who exchanged the inhibiting intellectual atmosphere of Berlin for the freer air of Manchester University was Michael Polanyi, Professor of Chemistry, 1933–48, and Professor of Social Studies, 1948–58. In this pre-war period there existed an unofficial group of university teachers in this country – among whom were university teachers in Manchester – who voluntarily raised funds and organized assistance for refugee scholars.[1]

A.J.P. Taylor, Professor of History at Manchester during these years, in his classic *English History 1914–1945*, confirmed this narrative with its two key elements – the positive reception of the refugees and their subsequent achievement. The refugees 'received a warm welcome in England', Taylor adding that each one 'was walking propaganda against the Nazis'.[2] Crawford and Taylor were writing in the 1960s, some thirty years after these refugees had arrived in the city. As we have seen, Manchester has taken particular pride in its self-image of being a liberal, tolerant and hospitable city. It has acted as an intensive micro version of a national mythology in which the treatment of refugees from Nazism plays an increasingly central role. This chapter does not set out to debunk for its own sake such celebratory approaches to these refugees and responses to them. Instead, it explores how ordinary people confronted the presence of refugees in the Nazi era through their contemporary analysis of the situation, thereby creating the complex framework for later remembering (and forgetting) of those who have sought asylum in Britain.

The two types of material to be studied in this chapter – directive responses and diaries – are very different. They are united under the

umbrella of the Mass-Observation project and archive, set up in 1937 to
be an anthropology of everyday life in Britain 'of ourselves by ourselves'.[3]
Mass-Observation, as Dorothy Sheridan, Brian Street and David Bloome
emphasise, whether in its historic form (1937 to 1951) or since its revival
in the 1980s, is 'primarily about writing'. Mass-Observation is 'consti-
tuted by the writings, observations and insights of ordinary people who
both individually and collectively make claims about the purposes, practices and policies of Mass-Observation'. As they add, its reflective quality 'makes inquiry about literacy practices and Mass-Observation a particularly useful telling case for gaining insights into the nature and relationships of writing, knowledge, power and social life in Britain'.[4]

The purpose of this chapter is to examine through the presence (and
absence) of refugees, how members of the British public constructed and
re-constructed their place in the world. The narratives that will be analysed
in their different genres are often equivocal, fluid and multi-layered, especially when 'local', 'national' and 'global' identities were juxtaposed –
sometimes in harmony, often in conflict. While the positive features highlighted a generation later by Crawford and Taylor were certainly not
absent, there is far more uncertainty and confusion in these contemporary sources. Nevertheless, the very complexity of the Mass-Observation
material points towards the importance of engagement with the refugees
from Nazism, whether experienced in person, media or everyday discourse. In some cases, the absence of such engagement is equally significant. Such 'instant' memory work was far from static at the time even
within the written sources utilised here. As Sheridan, Street and Bloome
argue, 'people are continually modifying established literacy practices,
adapting them to new situations'.[5] The range of contemporary responses
and the fundamental ambivalence towards refugees, the ongoing struggle
to come to terms with them, is a perspective often missing from subsequent reflections on their presence, as will emerge in subsequent chapters. Rather than 'correcting' later memory work, which is, after all, as
much (if not more) about 'now' rather than 'then', this chapter will attempt to unravel the intricate processes of 'writing refugees' within the
specific context of Britain during the 1930s and the Second World War.

The Mass-Observation directives and the refugees

The propaganda war between contemporaries justifying the entry of refugees from Nazism and their exclusion has been analysed earlier in this
study. The 'mainstream' media in Britain also provided contrasting accounts of their desirability – the Rothermere and Beaverbrook press 'em-
pires', including the *Daily Mail* and the *Daily Express*, were largely hostile

whereas left-liberal dailies such as the *Manchester Guardian* and *News Chronicle* were generally sympathetic to the plight of those attempting to escape Nazism. From the *Anschluss* in March 1938 through to the first year of war, refugees, and refugee-related issues, were newsworthy items in Britain. While lacking the intensity of media scrutiny as is the case at the end of the twentieth century and into the new millennium, refugee issues were still prominent some sixty years earlier. As now, during the Nazi era the number and circulation of newspapers hostile to newcomers was much greater than those which were sympathetic.[6] The British government was wary of public opinion on the 'refugee question', especially fearing the possibility of antisemitism which it believed the fascists would exploit.[7] In fact, the British Union of Fascists, with its explicit campaign against the 'refujews', was relatively weak in the immediate pre-war period. Indeed, the only notable public campaign in relation to refugees at this point was *in favour* of the admittance of children, as will be explored in chapter 4. From its perspective of maintaining law and order and minimising civil unrest, however, it was anti-alien sentiment that occupied the government as well as the Jewish and refugee organisations which worked closely in tandem with it.

With hindsight it is possible to argue that the fears of domestic antisemitism, and particularly its potential to manifest itself in an organised movement, were overstated. Yet with politicised antisemitism spreading across the continent of Europe such concerns were understandable. Moreover, detailed contemporary evidence of public opinion was thin on the ground; in this context negative attitudes and responses, whether expressed violently by fascists and other antisemitic groups or in hostile newspapers, were more likely to be taken seriously by politicians and those in the state structure than humanitarian sentiment in favour of the refugees. Opinion polls were still in their infancy and regarded with suspicion.[8] Furthermore, only one public poll relating to refugees was carried out before the war and its findings were so vague that they could have been utilised by those supporting either liberalisation of refugee policy or those demanding further restrictions.[9] In late July 1939 the British Institute of Public Opinion (BIPO) carried out a survey of whether refugees should 'be allowed to enter Great Britain'. Some 70 per cent answered 'yes' and 26 per cent 'no'. Of the majority who responded positively, a follow-up question asked whether they should 'be allowed to enter freely or with restrictions designed to safeguard British workers and taxpayers'. Not surprisingly, only 15 per cent wanted refugees to be allowed to enter 'freely'.[10]

A few months earlier, but outside the public realm (its work for the government began only with the war), Mass-Observation had asked its directive respondents to comment on 'the effect of Jewish refugees on British life'. Over four hundred people replied and a rough statistical analysis would confirm the general trend identified by BIPO. Three-quarters of the Mass-Observers were generally positive about refugees being allowed entry. There was a small minority, less than one in ten, who believed that there should be no restrictions on entry to Britain or activities once in the country. At the other extreme, an even smaller percentage argued that it had been a mistake to allow in any refugees, regardless of the safeguards that had been imposed.[11] Yet even though the findings of the rival bodies of BIPO and Mass-Observation generally tallied, as they would do later with regard to the treatment of 'enemy aliens' in the first year of the war, it is dangerous to read too much into such statistical findings. That only 4 per cent of the BIPO sample had 'no opinion' on whether refugees should be allowed to enter or not is significant in itself with regard to the level of public engagement with the issue. Nevertheless, crudely categorising the British population as either in favour or opposed to refugee entry was far too simplistic. Moreover, BIPO's follow-up enquiry to the positive majority produced results that were of limited use through what was, even if unintended, a leading question.[12]

In the case of Mass-Observation, the material generated was ultimately more of qualitative rather than quantitative use. It is hard to make the case that the people writing for the organisation were statistically representative of the population as a whole. There is no doubt, for example, that there was a relative absence of working-class Mass-Observers. Moreover, its respondents were, on the whole, left-liberal leaning with initially three times as many men as women. But it is, as the leaders of the organisation recognised sooner or later, the *subjective*, individualised nature of its archive that makes it such a rich source for the study of everyday literacy practice rather than, as they initially hoped, an objective, scientific tool to measure 'Britain'.[13]

The question on Jewish refugees was part of one of Mass-Observation's first directives. Started in 1939, the directives served the function of getting the Mass-Observers to write about their own beliefs and feelings about a range of everyday as well as political issues. The directives marked a shift within the young organisation towards encouraging autobiographical writing.[14] Sent out in March 1939, the question on refugees was under the broad heading 'racial research' which had begun a month earlier. In essence, the large part of Mass-Observation's second and third monthly directives were devoted to the subject of antisemitism, part of a wider project on attitudes towards Jews in Britain, including anthropological fieldwork in the East End of London. The two directives taken together encouraged both a life history approach – the Mass-Observers were asked to write about 'what first influenced you in your ideas about Jews' – as well as to respond to more specific questions, including the impact of Jewish refugees. As with so much material generated by Mass-Observation, it reflected the encouragement given by its leaders for its respondents to write about themselves *and* to report on the views of others. Many at the time and subsequently have criticised Mass-Observation for the dual function it required of its Observers, especially as they were given no training to act as anthropologists 'at home'. Yet it is the reflexive quality of much of their writing, whether analysing their own attitudes and behaviour or those around them, that makes the Mass-Observation archive so significant. I have argued at greater length elsewhere that it is the massive diary collection that came closest to realising the goals of Mass-Observation. The material analysed later in this chapter confirms such an analysis. Even so, the February–March directive material is, at its best, richly textured, moving way beyond the crudity of the BIPO survey on refugees, especially when the directives encouraged autobiographical responses. All in all, the two directives on Jews/antisemitism generated over half a million words.[15] The questions on Jewish refugees were a relatively small part of this total and some of the 451 directive responses were frustratingly brief on this specific topic. The majority, however, even with their limitations, provide valuable glimpses into the way Mass-Observers felt about refugees or perceived the responses and attitudes of others to them.

Proponents of Mass-Observation have suggested that it provided an 'extra dimension' in understanding the views of ordinary people in contrast to the 'flat' material generated by opinion polls.[16] In the case of the March 1939 directive, the breadth is provided by the tensions, often within the responses of each respondent, with regard to three major interlocking areas of concern – economics, national identity and morality. As we will see, all three were used to support or reject the case of the refugees, and, most commonly, to respond ambiguously towards them. There is, however, the presence of the fourth dimension, time, to further complicate the directive responses and their underlying ambivalence.

Mass-Observers took their role very seriously – they were attracted to the organisation not only because it gave a forum for them to express their opinions but also because they wanted to make a difference to the world around them. The specific question asked by Mass-Observation – on the effect of the Jewish refugees – put them in a quandary. Many of the directive respondents, not without good reason, argued that it was, as yet, hard to assess the particular impact of the refugees from Nazism. As one Observer from Chelmsford argued, 'it was too early to judge'. Furthermore, as yet he had 'no personal experience' of refugees.[17] To

counter this absence of perspective and/or experience the Mass-Observers drew upon and combined two sources. First, they referred to contemporary debate on refugees and the contributions of politicians, activists
and the media, as well as to discussions with their friends and relatives.
Second, they constructed past precedents in which to contextualise the
specific arguments around them.

When searching for a usable past, especially for those who were
favourable to those escaping Nazism, the explicit historical reference point
in the directives was, almost exclusively, the Protestant refugees from the
continent who came to Britain from the sixteenth through to the eighteenth centuries. In every such reference, these refugees were regarded
positively: 'I always supposed in a vaguely liberal way that England's
prosperity was possibly due to refugees, Huguenots and so on, who
brought trades [with them]'.[18] A London male respondent believed that
while the short-term impact of the refugees from Nazism was presently
only beginning

> I remember how this country has benefited by giving sanctuary to the
> Huguenots and the Walloons etc, and there is little reason to suppose that
> the present refugees will not add further to the crafts produced in this
> country. In fact I believe I am right in saying that they have already begun
> to do this.

Nevertheless, even this positive account was tempered by the comment
that 'it will largely depend on [the refugees'] attitude'.[19] Indeed, in many
of the responses, it was the nature of the refugees themselves that would
determine whether they were perceived as 'good' or 'bad' for Britain. In
such thinking, the Jewishness of the refugees was rarely regarded as a
neutral feature.

There were some within the Mass-Observers who refused to differentiate between types of refugees. A male, London, Mass-Observer suggested that the effect of the Jewish refugees would be the same as any
other:

> We already have historical evidence of the benefits conferred upon our
> economic life and culture from the influx of the Huguenots on words.
> Today we have Jewish (and other) refugees from Germany, Austria and
> Czechoslovakia bringing the fur trade, new manufacturing processes, and
> arts ... and scientific benefits to the country.

The British Union of Fascists' claim that refugees stole British jobs was,
he believed, simply a 'red herring'.[20] Similarly, a Surrey Observer asked if
'England has benefited from the Flemings, Huguenots and others ... why
not the Jewish[?]'[21] and a historically well-informed teacher from Watford
rejected the 'Britain for the British' argument against the refugees by

concluding her case that 'our country will eventually benefit by having and using the ability and talents of the Jews, just as in the past we have gained an enormous amount from Flemish weavers, and Huguenot silk, leather and wood workers'.[22] With rather crude culinary allusion, an author in London, while moaning that Golders Green and Hampstead were 'getting cluttered up' with Jewish refugees, added 'But we have absorbed other lumps of refugees before without indigestion'. Indeed, it had increased 'the variety of life'.[23] Yet for many others, the Jewishness of the refugees *did* matter.

A left-wing Observer from Leeds believed the effect of refugees was 'probably many-sided'. His response, a desperate and failed attempt to provide Marxist 'objectivity', revealed an internal struggle between a theoretical commitment to internationalism and a personal disdain of cosmopolitanism. It was tinged and made even more distinctive by cross-fertilising antisemitism aimed at 'rich' Jews with a heavy dose of anti-Americanism. On the one hand, he believed that the effect would be 'enriching us, as other refugees have done i.e. the Huguenots; Marx!; the Flemings from Holland'. Yet even his 'positive' assessment was informed by a negative discourse about Jews: 'Naturally the Jews try to enrich themselves, but in economic theory this also enriches the community by providing employment, though a Jewish capitalist is as bad as any other'. On the other hand, he was deeply concerned about the possible 'denationalizing' impact of the refugees. Leeds, which he described as an 'English town', was, with its large Jewish population, in danger, he feared, of 'becoming bastard-megalopitan [sic]' on the American model. Jewish shops in Leeds 'display like cheap and vulgar American stores and they are a denationalizing influence which is bad'.[24]

What is significant here is the Observer's fear that allowing in too many refugees would create a problem of excessive 'Jewishness'. While not explicit (as was the reference to Protestant refugees), his antipathy had, as its historical reference point, East European Jewry – the origins of most Jews in Leeds.[25] And although his combination of socialism and nationalism was idiosyncratic, his antipathy to un-English Jews and their alien ways was not. Indeed, a sympathetic Observer from Surrey, an admirer of Jewish 'business ability', was one of only two within the sample who explicitly and positively referred to the earlier arrival of Jews from eastern Europe. He stated that 'We have had Jewish influxes before (ie from Russia) and I have not heard anyone pointing out any lasting change of any kind as a result.'[26] In fact, much of the material collected by Mass-Observation in the February–March 1939 period suggested that the memory of this pre-First World War migration and its subsequent legacy was far from positive.

Typical of many accusing British Jewry of ostentation and vulgarity was an Observer from Runcorn who urged the organisers to 'Go and have a look at the Midland Hotel [in] Manchester one day if you want to see how unpleasant Jews are.' For those minority who were totally opposed to the arrival of Jewish refugees, believing that whatever the total, it was 'too much',[27] the anti-alienism of the turn of the century was updated. It now incorporated not only second-generation East European Jews in Britain but also the new arrivals from Nazi Germany. To a housewife in Gateshead the only solution was to 'keep them out – only more to suck the life blood of the country and more to fight against us when (and if) we do finally remove them'.[28] Another believed that pogroms carried out by the 'English race' would happen if controls were not instituted and warned 'that if we allow any more Jewish refugees to enter the country they are going to alter the whole of our national life and character'.[29]

Others used such arguments in favour of the refugees, suggesting that 'mixing' them with the British population 'may lead to an invigorating of our race',[30] or suggested that Jews' 'Easternism should be a valuable antidote to the bad influences of Westernism in Britain'.[31] Jews, it was suggested by a London shipping clerk, like Arabs, were 'Semites' and therefore 'above the ordinary in intelligence'. Therefore Jewish refugees would be 'enormously beneficial to Britain'.[32] Yet race discourse within the directive responses, either in favour of or against the refugees, was rarely explicitly influenced by 'scientific' thinking.[33] Indeed, it occurred only once in this survey, in the writings of a female doctor from London:

> *Racially* as a member of the Eugenics Society I regard Jews as low grade
> Orientals of poor physique, as undesirable immigrants ... To my mind the
> Jews in general and refugees in particular are an undesirable influence on
> the national life and we should work to get them out of public life and to
> prevent them starting up any industries here.[34]

This diatribe was unusual not only in its source of influence, but also in the animosity expressed which contained no element of ambiguity, backed, as it was, by an absolute belief in the certainty of 'race'. More common within the March 1939 directive responses was to bifurcate the refugees. As an Observer from Shropshire put it: 'The better class and the learned refugees will have a beneficial effect, the lower classes which are the greater majority will have a very bad effect.'[35] Time and again in the directive responses the names of Freud and Einstein were used to write positively about the 'better type' of refugee and how Germany's loss of such figures would be Britain's gain. Fears lingered, however, about the masses of refugees who were regarded as a potential menace on the same grounds, and indistinguishable from, the earlier *ostjuden* and their offspring.

In this respect, the response of a masseuse from Surrey is revealing because she was aware of her own tendency to fuse all Jews together. In an attempt to weigh the good and ill effects of refugee entry to the latter category 'one thinks chiefly of the business methods'. She then gave examples of alleged Jewish malpractice she had heard about but then added that these cases were 'probably not refugees'.[36] As will emerge in the second half of this chapter, female Mass-Observers were more likely to be reflexive over their own attitudes and literacy practice in general. A London journalist whose diaries will be part of this analysis, Rebecca Lowenstein, was similarly self-aware, even if she was unable to overcome a tendency to rationalise her prejudices. Her ambivalent response is particularly interesting as she described herself as 'half-Jewish':

> Many Jews do ... raise in me an 'instinctive dislike'. It is difficult to find a reason for this. My natural bias should be the other way round. I am very proud of the various accomplishments of the Jewish race, its genius, courage, faith. But the noisy, loud, flashy type of Jew seems to have little in common with ideal Jewry.[37]

Even more extreme in this respect were the comments of a respondent of orthodox Jewish background living in north-west London: 'I fear them ... because I realise that they are increasing the anti-semitism which already exists here, and by their swaggering arrogance, they fan the flames of destruction in which all British Jewry may perish'.[38]

An implicit class snobbery underpinned the racialised division of refugees and those perceived desirable and undesirable. It was further cemented by gender categorisation within the directives. The praise for the talented elite, who were regarded as assimilable, focused on the *male* refugee scientists, industrialists, artists and writers – Lowenstein's 'ideal Jewry'. Only in one response was their equivalent praise of women – for the actresses Bergner, Mannheim and Rotha.[39] Even here, the sexualised image of the Jewish female, a powerful trope in literature and culture in general, may have played a part. It was more explicit and negative in another directive response that combined class, gender and race prejudices.[40] It came from a female Observer of 'independent means' whose comments typified hostility towards the 'wrong sort' of refugee: 'My feelings about the refugees changed after I had seen two of them in Chelmsford who must have come from abroad, peroxided, cheaply fur-coated, blatant type.'[41] No evidence was provided of why they must have been foreign, or indeed Jewish, but the assumptions of this upper-class Observer show the complex processes by which the newcomers were regarded. Rather than being simply opposed to refugee entry she wrote that 'Naturally I admire and sympathise with Jews but there is a subconscious resentment against them.' With equal honesty she admitted that her initial horror at the injustice meeted out by Nazi Germany had now faded. The Observer then tried to rationalise her antagonism by putting the emphasis on the nation that had produced the refugees: 'I do not see why we, or any other country, should support Germany's cast-offs.'[42] Indeed, much of the debate within the directives depended on whether the Mass-Observers regarded the refugees as undesirable 'cast-offs' or, alternatively, as economic assets.

Keynesians such as Roy Harrod, with strong links to the Labour move-ment, argued that the refugees would help the British economy through their particular skills and also by stimulating demand. The latter factor was especially important, they suggested, because Britain had a declining population. Harrod had difficulty in getting the higher echelons of the Labour party to accept his analysis. One senior figure rejected further debate on the 'positive' economics of the refugee question late in 1938 because he did 'not see the slightest prospect ... of the TUC endorsing these views. The Unions would certainly reject them.'[43] The Home Secre-tary, Sir Samuel Hoare, in similar vein a few weeks earlier in the House of Commons, in its major pre-war debate about refugees, reminded his fellow MPs about the dangers of liberalising entry policy:

> In this country we are a thickly populated industrial community with at the present moment a very large number of unemployed. Competition is very keen with foreign countries, and it is difficult for many of our fellow-countrymen to make a livelihood at all and keep their industries going.

Hoare concluded that it was 'quite obvious that there is an underlying current of suspicion and anxiety, rightly or wrongly, about alien immi-gration on any big scale'.[44]

Hoare warned those motivated sympathetically by concern about 'the fortunes of particular refugees' to 'avoid anything in the nature of mass immigration which, in my view, would inevitably lead to the growth of [an antisemitic] movement which we all wish to see suppressed'.[45] His seamless slippage in terminology from the individual *refugee* (deserving) to mass *alien immigration* (dangerous) mirrored the concerns of many Mass-Observers. The respondents rarely saw the refugees as personal competitors in the job market or the economy as a whole. Nevertheless, some maintained a paternalistic attitude of protection towards ordinary British workers who they believed might be adversely affected by the refugees. Again, an earlier discourse from the aliens debate was employed to point out the danger: 'these incomers may, unless prevented, adopt the methods of their kinsmen already here – i.e. to occupy the key positions in certain lines of business. There is quite enough of this as things are at present'.[46] Similarly, another male Observer, while not overly concerned about the threat posed by the newcomers, made an explicit link to an occupation intimately connected to the East European Jews in Britain: 'There are no doubt abuses of hospitality by people working illegally, and at cut rates, notably in the tailoring trade'.[47] In reality, very few refugees during the 1930s worked as tailors, legitimately or otherwise. Other Mass-Observers, however, were more worried about resulting unemployment rather than the alleged methods of business. A Jewish respondent from Hackney had no doubt that en masse the refugees would increase unemployment and 'no matter how small is a step in the wrong direction'. He recognised that the elite, like 'Dr Freud[,] can only be a gain for any community' but the Observer wondered whether 'these few people, by giving us their theories and plans, compensate us for the additional expense of the others'.[48]

Nevertheless, the large majority of Mass-Observers believed that the refugees would be good for the economy. If Harrod had failed to influence the Labour party or the trade union movement as a whole, his analysis – popularised by pro-refugee campaigners such as Dorothy Buxton, Norman Angell and Louis Golding in widely circulating 'Penguin specials' such as *You and the Refugee* (1939) and *The Jewish Problem* (1938) – was highly influential in arguing the case for a more liberal entry policy.[49] Refugees had *created* employment and their impact was positive, argued one Observer – 'to argue otherwise is the "old work fund" theory [ie that there were only a limited number of jobs to go round] that is false'.[50] Where the respondents differed was in their faith of the British public to accept such economic 'truths'.

From an optimistic perspective, one Mass-Observer was scathing about the restrictions that were being imposed on the refugees, such as confining the women to positions in domestic service where there was a shortage of British labour. He dismissed 'all this Blimpian bleating about displacing English workers, this parish pump claptrap about "our two million" unemployed', concluding that it showed 'only one thing – that the country is not administered in a manner which can even remotely be considered intelligent'.[51] Another was more basic in his Keynesianism: 'They have got to eat, drink, dress, so they will not cause unemployment, or at any rate, increase it.'[52] Even so, a greater number of respondents, while positive about the economic potential of the refugees, were not hopeful that such 'truths' would be understood at a popular level. They believed that xenophobia and antisemitism would undermine what they saw as a rational response to the entry of refugees and their freedom to operate in the British economy. A clerk in Kent believed bluntly that the refugees were disliked by the working class on the basis that they 'take our bloody jobs away'.[53] A student in Cambridge who, while 'working on behalf of refugees' and believing them to be an economic asset, feared that each one that 'enters this country is sowing a potential seed of anti-Semitism'.[54] If Jews were allowed to compete in the job market, worried another respondent, 'it is very likely to cause strong anti-Semitic feeling among the working class, a feeling which can be used to advantage by the Fascists'.[55]

Such fears of intolerance from below made many Observers accept and often welcome the restrictions enforced by the government on refugee employment. There was also an awareness and lack of dissent about the transitory status imposed by the state on most refugees – immigration procedures which were intended to ensure that few would settle permanently in Britain. Yet to a small but articulate minority, the temporariness and marginality imposed on the refugees was regarded as unfortunate, not because of economic arguments in their favour, but because it undermined any claims to morality on behalf of the British nation.

There were those who argued that in any ethical equation drawn up, it 'seems a great pity that money should be willingly subscribed to help Jewish refugees when the public conscience with regard to our own social refugees is not very troubled'.[56] Other respondents agonised whether or not 'charity begins at home'. One Observer outlined how his theoretical response was, in the name of humanity, that 'we should doubtless offer refuge to them'. In practice, however, he was concerned that 'we have our own unemployed, homeless and destitute to care for, and we are not doing that job properly'. His conclusion was, even when recognising Jews and Englishman were equal 'human beings', that universalism was not possible 'while the world remains divided into nations'.[57] It took those whose identity went beyond such pragmatic nationalism to incorporate the refugees within their universe of moral obligation.

Typical of the undifferentiated humanitarian approach was a respondent from Welling who dismissed any 'material considerations', stressing instead that 'I think we have a moral duty to shelter the oppressed and to help them recreate their lives.' Such actions, he added, would ultimately have a beneficial impact at 'home': 'The world is now such a small place that if injustice and intolerance breed in one part they will spread far … Helping refugees is a tangible demonstration of our hatred of intolerance'.[58] Combining sympathy and self-interest further, and thereby undermining the division between 'us' and 'them', a female teacher Observer stated categorically that 'Compassion is never wasted'.[59]

If the majority of respondents believed that energy should be spent in differentiating the 'right sort of refugee', there were others who saw the implications of such elitism. For them it undermined the mythology of Britain as a country of asylum for *all* those in need of refuge. A film-strip producer in London was thus

> sorry for refugees who may not be quite so desirable, folk who would go along well enough in the ordinary way, but who cannot make ... as good a case as those who do get in. I realise the feeling about providing for our own people first, but think there would be a great loss to the spirit and character of the nation if the generous impulse to help the even more un-fortunate [was] lost.

She concluded that 'Some of the most honourable chapters in British history have been those in which a haven has been offered to refugees.'[60] Another female respondent was determined not to know the numbers involved which she thought was irrelevant. As she eloquently stated: 'if they need help that should be a sufficient passport'.[61]

For those of a strongly internationalist outlook who took the threat posed by the fascist regimes seriously, the refugees were valued further as people whose very presence would break down British insularity. One consequence of having refugee entry would be, according to a male librarian, 'a slight broadening of the minds of certain citizens towards a greater interest in the continent and political problems, especially opening some people's eyes re-Germany'.[62] 'Their presence [by] extending social contacts', argued another Observer, was 'helping to emphasise the effects of racial tyranny. Their knowledge of Europe is enlarging many people's vision.'[63] A social worker from Surrey argued that such broadening of outlook would extend beyond the immediate issue of foreign affairs. The impact of refugees, she wrote, could only be a 'good one for the British people as it should help to break down their insularity and make them more alert and energetic in their thinking. Out of the breaking down of insularity should come sympathy and an effort to understand the point of view of other people.'[64] A male respondent was of a similar mind: helping refugees 'helps to create a bond between the peoples of the world [and] makes us realise that there are other people besides ourselves'.[65]

In contrast to those who argued that the presence of Hitler's victims would destroy 'provincialism, parochialism ... excessive narrow-mindedness [and] excessive nationalism',[66] a London telephonist warned starkly that refugees were 'responsible for a lot of war-mongering'.[67] Her response was, however, the only one in the whole directive which was negative with respect to such international considerations. Statistically, less than 10 per cent of the Mass-Observers supported the refugees on grounds of Britain's international moral responsibilities. Conversely, those objecting to refugees did so on grounds related almost exclusively to the alleged *domestic* damage they would do to the economy, culture and racial make-up of Britain. There were few if any respondents who had any truck with the Nazi regime as a whole, a reflection of the progressive bias of Mass-Observation and the general revulsion at what was happening in Germany. But one last set of issues remains to be explored in this analysis of the Mass-Observation directives: how much actual contact was there with refugees and ordinary people in Britain and, for those who did encounter them in person, did it make a difference in attitudes and responses?

The number of refugees allowed entry into Britain had, compared with the early years of Nazi rule, increased in the last months of 1938 and would remain relatively high until the outbreak of war. Indeed, up to 50,000 arrived from March 1938 through to the start of September 1939.[68] It is significant, however, that only a minority of Observers wrote about experiencing refugees themselves. Furthermore, in a follow-up question in the directive which asked how many refugees had come into Britain in the past twelve months, most suggested between two and five thousand. The lower figure, ironically (given the general tendency in Britain to overestimate the number of incomers) was, in reality, roughly 10 per cent of the actual total. While there were some who wildly exaggerated the number of refugees granted recent entry, the low totals reflected, especially for those outside the major cities, a lack of contact with refugees en masse *and* a deep suspicion of the anti-alien press with its scare-mongering stories about the 'flooding' of Britain. A Somerset respondent had 'no idea about the number of refugees' but was patronisingly scathing about his brother who believed it was very high: 'I have no doubt [that his] information came from the popular press.'[69]

In contrast, but representing a smaller number of the directive, was the hostile response of a male Observer that 'judging by the numbers of illegal landings reported (in the press) and the numbers to be seen in Central London the number must be considerable'.[70] For the 1930s at least, although the sales of daily newspapers with an antipathy towards the refugees was immense (over five million for the *Daily Express* and *Daily Mail* in combination alone), not all their readership accepted their message uncritically.[71] One respondent was candid that he had no idea about numbers 'but papers such as the "Daily Express" would lead me to believe that the total is astronomical. I do not believe this as I can find no support in more moderate channels of information'.[72] More generally a female respondent added that 'The only source from which I could get such information [about numbers] would be the newspapers and they are often unreliable.'[73] To reinforce the point, another quoted an article in *News Chronicle* 'which said there had been far fewer refugees than people imagined'.[74] Such independence of mind and unease with the popular media had encouraged many of the respondents to become Mass-

Observers. As we will see in the final chapter, media representation of asylum and refugee matters some sixty years later has been subject to far less critical engagement, as is revealed in a Mass-Observation directive on this subject carried out in summer 2000.

An engineer commented that he had very little contact with the refugees and therefore his comments were based on 'impression rather than observation'. He was certain, however, that 'The whole problem of Jewish refugees seems ... to have been greatly exaggerated by the Press'.[75] This Observer came from Greenock, Renfrewshire, and is a reminder that even as late as March 1939, there were towns and rural areas where there were few refugees from Nazism in Britain. The refugees tended, much to the anxiety of the bodies set up to deal with them, to concentrate in large urban centres, especially London.[76] The greater number of refugees as 1939 progressed, as well as the attempt to disperse them, increased the number of places where they settled in noticeable numbers. The first year of the war was to have an even greater impact on the distribution of refugees. On the one hand, there were areas that became restricted on security grounds (followed in mid-1940 by mass internment) for the refugees. On the other, evacuation and the eventual breaking down of employment restrictions (including, eventually, in the armed forces) pushed refugees into many different areas of the country and the war effort as a whole. Indeed, the war diaries of Mass-Observation, which form the second case study of this chapter, provide a markedly different picture of contact than the snapshot provided by the March 1939 directive. But for those directive respondents who did meet or even simply witnessed the presence of refugees before the war, the impact could be profound – whether negatively or positively.

A male Observer from Winchester provided a narrative account close to that constructed by A.J.P. Taylor with which this chapter started. 'The Jewish refugees I have met', he reported, 'have been excellent people. I should think that they will give to the English families with whom they stay a breadth and true outlook on foreign affairs ... in Germany etc than is possible by any other means.' Significantly he added that 'Their stories have authenticity.'[77] The impact of their experiences under Nazism was brought home to a clerk in Margate when he saw those who were housed in the nearby camp at Richborough, Kent: 'occasionally we see them in the streets, rather small and stockily built, the younger ones bright and silent, the older people grave and silent, and they look round before they speak a word'.[78]

A less passive image was presented, though with an element of ambiguity, by a power loom turner (and poet) from Huddersfield. He believed the refugees to be clever, perhaps overly so, reporting how 'we have a

refugee who comes into Toc H, he speaks 9 languages ... and I can detect
a certain difference in the tone of the meeting when he is there'.[79] Similarly, while the refugee children were generally the focus of universal
pity, especially through press and newsreel imagery, which will be explored in chapter 4, several Observers commented on their successful
integration into local schools, moving beyond pathos in the way they
were described. One respondent, for example, reported that his children's
school had some twenty refugees out of a total of 150 boys and girls, and
they played 'a full part in the school life'.[80]

For those who were hostile to refugees, however, their presence did
not necessarily break down antipathy. The antagonistic telephonist in
north-west London referred to earlier stated that she had no idea of their
number 'but as I live in Hampstead [the district in Britain with the highest concentration of refugees] it seems like millions'.[81] Another was candid that while she felt sympathy when seeing the newsreel images of
Jewish refugees, she was still antagonistic to their actual presence. She
tried to rationalise her hostility by asking whether 'the rich Jews hands
[were] clean on hoisting Hitler to power?'[82] Indeed, a lingering suspicion
of whether the Jews were still somehow responsible for their own misfor-
tune was present, either explicitly or implicitly, in many of the responses.

There were some who unambiguously denounced Nazi antisemitism
and could only explain it as an irrational aberration with the only precedent being the superstitious world of the deep past.[83] As a London chemist put it: 'In my own opinion, the treatment of the Jews by Hitler and
other dictators is absolutely unjustifiable and smacks of Medievalism.'[84]
Yet others, while not defending Nazi methods and violence, did not exempt the Jews from blame. The Jews, argued one Observer, were '"stir-
rers up" of trouble ... They have a strong sense of race but no sense of
national unity. I consider them definitely bad citizens.'[85] Refugees, suggested another, 'may eventually be the root cause of anti-Semitism in this
country'.[86] A Stockport Observer added that 'If they come in large numbers they will probably capture all-important posts in trade, industry,
finance, and fields of science, medicine, law etc, and this will give rise to
antisemitic feeling in the country as it has done on the Continent.'[87] Similarly another female Observer in north-west London feared that 'the
qualities that have made them so hated abroad may work against them
here'. She added that she had been told by a Jewish refugee worker that
there were 50,000 refugees in Britain and had responded that 'they must
all be in Hampstead'.[88]

In their role as observers of others, the respondents provided further
evidence of an ambivalence towards the persecution of the Jews. A South
Wales respondent commented on the sympathy after the November 1938

pogrom 'but it was tempered by a curious sense that perhaps the Jews deserved it'.[89] A London office worker was also concerned that while pity had been generated 'English people won't let a little thing like the refugee problem interfere with their life, so apart from various donations … the refugees have little effect on their lives, I imagine, and are too soon forgotten when the newspaper headlines find some new topic of interest'.[90] Her analysis, as we will see, is confirmed when the Mass-Observation war diaries are analysed.

The most striking aspect of the directives as a whole, however, was the lack of personal contact with refugees. Refugees, as described in the March 1939 Mass-Observation material, were still more likely to be 'experienced' through newspaper articles and other printed sources, newsreels and political debate. Even for some of those who encountered refugees directly, the impact could be muted. Another respondent from Hampstead commented that it was 'just as commonplace to hear German spoken as English' there but that in spite of this proximity of so many refugees, he had only managed to chat briefly to members of the three German Jewish families in his small close.[91] Finally, however, while the directive provided a wealth of interesting material on how contemporaries responded to Jewish refugees, it was not a format that encouraged extensive self-reflexivity. In some responses a snobbery existed in which 'common' prejudices towards refugees were seen to be the preserve of the working classes. The format of the directives, however, did not encourage the Observers to explore whether they were, in fact, projecting their own concerns onto the 'lower orders'. Moreover, the specificity of the question asked in March 1939 did not promote a life story response. Nevertheless, despite such lacunae and limitations, the directive responses are an intriguing source. They reveal that the engagement *and* the failure to engage with refugees (and the related persecution they were escaping from), were important aspects of how ordinary people in Britain constructed their local and global identities, and, critically, their inter-relationship, in a world in increasing crisis. The Mass-Observation diaries for the Second World War provide both a different context and a different genre to explore such contemporary memory work further. Most significantly, the contrast between the two sources reveals how varieties of literacy practices produced different perspectives on the refugees. It further illustrates the many-layered and complex responses and reactions in Britain to the victims of the Nazis.

The Mass-Observation diaries and the refugees

By the outbreak of war, 78,000 refugees were present in Britain.[92] Nevertheless, as with the directives, what the writings of the Mass-Observation diarists reveal was an ongoing struggle to comprehend who these refugees were – the nature of their past lives, the reasons they had come to Britain and their status in the place of refuge. The leaders of Mass-Observation believed that if its respondents wrote war diaries it would be possible to measure the public mood, and thereby identify issues that were concerning ordinary people. Some, including the co-founder, Charles Madge, felt that such measuring of morale, with its close links to the government, was against the independent and radical vision of Mass-Observation. In fact, the Mass-Observation diaries, some five hundred of which were written at some stage during the war, proved too huge and complex a source to be used in the utilitarian manner envisaged by Tom Harrisson, the dominant force in the organisation. Filed in monthly installments and divided into men and women, the diaries were organised as if they were directive responses with the agenda set by the changing context of the home front. Eventually, however, even Tom Harrisson began to recognise that the strength of the diaries was in their subjective and dynamic nature.[93] The analysis of the material here will return the individuality of the diary writing and restore its life story perspective which the organisation of the material mitigated against. In order to do justice to the reality that 'a diary reveals not one person, but many different selves, a chorus of voices',[94] it will focus on a small number of diarists and their ongoing confrontation with refugees during the war.

The close reading of the Mass-Observation diaries serves several purposes. First, they provide a unique source revealing interaction between ordinary people and the refugees, evidence that varied immensely at different stages of the war. Second, although focused through the subjective gaze of the Observers, these diaries supply contemporary material, hardly available elsewhere, of the everyday life of the refugees.[95] Third, and most relevant to this chapter, they bring to light how the process of diary writing was crucial for those trying to come to terms with the often confusing presence of the refugees, enabling a comparison to the literacy practices within the earlier directive responses.

The Mass-Observer Janet Neal was a London journalist and writer in her early thirties who had frequent contact with refugees. Her diaries in the first months of the conflict reflect close relationships with some of these refugees and a degree of friendship with many more. Yet while they reveal an acute understanding of the situation faced by the refugees they also highlight her own internal ambiguities towards them. In early October she wrote of two Austrian refugees coming to tea. Rather than a contrived or patronising meeting of people from different backgrounds which so often typify social gatherings involving host and newcomer, there appears to have been mutual affection between the women, and, as

Janet wrote, 'we laugh[ed] a lot'. The friends went out to a restaurant only to find it was dark when they had finished. The two refugees saw her home, the irony of which was not lost on the Mass-Observer: '"Good job I have a couple of Enemy Aliens to look after me", I say, and we all laugh.' Janet Neal understood the damage caused through the refugees being given the legal status of enemy aliens at the start of the war with regard to practical matters of ordinary life as well as to their self-esteem. 'I know it hurt them to begin with, so now I joke about it, and they relax. One of the refugees, Gerta, added, 'It's funny, isn't it? ... So many people of the enemy country in a land, and all of them wanting the "enemy" country to their own to win?'[96] The somewhat forced nature of the humour and laughter as reflected in these diary entries reflected a deeper tension and unease of the situation within which the refugees were placed.

Janet was also acutely aware of the situation from which the refugees had escaped and had made an effort to familiarise herself with their background:

> I asked Gerta how she felt when she left Austria and she said that there were three refugees in the [railway] carriage and two Nazis, and that the two Nazis – also on their way to England – said 'In ten days we shall be in Prague' and that the refugees did not speak. But she said the moment they left Aachen and were on Belgian soil, they all said everything they could think of against the Nazi regime, and the Nazis said nothing, and remained quiet.

Yet it is significant that Janet ended her diary entry by giving the story not only a redemptive ending but also a patriotic twist, reporting Gerta's words that 'It is lovely to walk about and hold your head up again, instead of creeping about wearing your oldest clothes.'[97]

Other Mass-Observation diaries had a tendency to refer to refugees only as a way of expressing a form of national self-congratulation. A chemist in Luton witnessed the ease with which a Hungarian exile was registered. It was, he wrote with satisfaction, 'characteristically English ... We don't believe in making people miserable in this country'.[98] Similarly, Rebecca Lowenstein recorded in November 1939 how she

> went with the German maid, an elderly widow from Bremen, to the Alien Tribunal in Croydon [and] was struck by the courtesy of the officials and their genuine consideration. From my own considerations, specially in connection with refugees, the treatment by English people of those in distress is something to be proud of ... I was asked what I thought of Mrs W, how long I had known her, whether I thought her a fit person to be granted exemption. Her passport was stamped, and the whole thing finished in 5 minutes. I saw a little man so excited with his freedom that he put his hat on sideways as he came out and didn't know it.[99]

In this extract the refugees were referred to solely in order to show the superiority of the English. But when it came to her own reactions to Mrs W, as will be shown later in this chapter, Rebecca's attitude reflected a deep ambivalence.

Janet Neal was also acutely aware that her understanding of the plight of the Jews and others persecuted by the Nazis was not shared by the majority of the population and that even her awareness, gained through her work as a journalist and contact with refugees, was still incomplete. Indeed, her role as 'objective' observer of the British and her 'subjective' views as one of them inevitably became blurred. Almost a year to the day after *Kristallnacht*, on 9/10 November 1938, when synagogues and other Jewish buildings were destroyed, scores of Jews murdered and tens of thousands arrested, Gerta came to see Janet Neal. Gerta wanted Janet's help to translate an article written by another Austrian refugee which he wanted to publish in an English newspaper:

> I told her that it was not explicit enough – the writer would say 'On this day …' and I would say 'which day' and Gerta would reply 'The day of the pogrom …' Then I'd have to say 'which pogrom? When?' 'The pogrom on the anniversary of the Munich putsch' 'Which day was that?' I tried to point out to her – which she saw immediately – that although all these events were so overwhelmingly important to the man who had lived through them, to the people in England they were foreign history, and that life had been flowing on at the same time in England.

There was both understanding of the refugees' isolation as well as exasperation at their insistence on difference when Janet concluded to Gerta, not without some vexation, that it had to be remembered that 'their eyes had not been fixed entirely on Austria'.[100]

Three days later, on 8 November 1939, such aggravation came out explicitly in her diary. Janet expressed her irritation at the Germans and Austrians she knew, claiming that their innate Prussian characteristics were starting to reveal themselves: 'I felt as if I would like to sweep all the refugees out of the country – having found somewhere nice for them to go, of course – and have an "England for the English" campaign, which is the antithesis of everything I have previously felt, and is, of course, just a passing mood.'[101] In this entry, the writing process could be regarded as a form of safety valve of emotions. Another Mass-Observation diarist, the writer Naomi Mitchison, was explicit about such tendencies, observing how with friends in Oxford their mutual annoyance with the alleged behaviour of refugees was said in private 'so that one can get it off one's chest and not say them in public'.[102] But there was more to Janet Neal's comments than letting off steam. On one level her entry of 8 November was honest and self-critical. On another, by passing it off as 'of course, just a passing mood', she was glossing over a tendency towards anti-alienism and exclusive English nationalism that she had observed in others but was hesitant to probe within herself.

When entertaining her two refugee friends a month earlier she was pleased with the progress they were making with their English. Janet was concerned that 'They will speak German in the streets, which they have been forbidden by the Government to do (all Germans must speak only English in public)'.[103] In fact, Janet Neal was mistaken – the German and Austrian Jews had simply been strongly advised by the refugee organisations, who worked closely with the state apparatus, to speak German only in private so as not to provoke antagonism amongst the public at large.[104] The diarist, however, seemed to share the refugee bodies' concern. Janet told Gerta that it was 'better that she should obey; in any case, public feeling might get stronger later.' She added, again eclipsing the division between her own views and those as an observer of others, but also with keen foresight, that 'in any case, public feeling might get stronger later'. Nevertheless, rather than distancing herself totally from anti-alienism, she added that 'It is something understandable, that sudden irritation or resentment of German language, everything German – not at the beginning of a war, but after it has been getting on everyone's nerves after a bit.'[105]

In Janet Neal's own case, as we have seen, that irritation did not take much time in coming, even if it was confined, at least in her own understanding, to the private realm of the diary. Yet rather than being a result solely of war strain, her form of anti-alienism had ideological and cultural roots revealed within her own writings. At the end of October 1939, the British government published a White Paper on German atrocities which aroused a mixed response from the public.[106] Janet Neal was suspicious not of the contents of the document, which she had no doubts about, but of the government's motivation in publishing it only after war had been declared. She assumed, rather idiosyncratically, that such propaganda was being used as a warning by politicians that such atrocities could happen in Britain in the future. Janet experienced the verbal expression of antisemitism on a regular basis on the Home Front, and generally reprimanded those who articulated it, later denouncing them in her diary. Even so, she felt that at a collective level the British public would never stand for the ill-treatment of others.[107] In contrast, however, she firmly believed that 'quite a number of Germans are involved [in causing atrocities], which shows that a percentage of the race is "like that" – cowardly and cruel'.[108]

By early November Janet wrote that 'Prussianism [was] popping his head up'. She had read in the paper 'that Jews being evacuated from

"German Poland" into "Russian Poland" were thrown into the river if they couldn't pay the price demanded', adding that it seemed 'fantastic – the old epithet of barbarians seems the only one to use'.[109] Five days further on she was tarring the refugees themselves with the label of Prussianism.[110] Clearly such thoughts did not hinder her active pro-refugee work and close association with individuals such as Gerta. Yet alongside the friendship and intimacy was a self-constructed barrier of race in which behaviour was liable to be explained by essentialised national characteristics. The diarist constructed the tolerant Englishman on the one hand and the brutal Prussian on the other. For Janet, the attempts of Gerta to speak English were commendable, if somewhat comical. If not constrained, their Prussianism would out.

In contrast to such ambivalence towards her friends who were somewhat confusingly victims of the Nazis yet Germanic in origin, Janet could not resist a sense of pride in a mystically defined Britishness. After spending the day with Gerta and her fellow refugee friend, Janet went to bed and wrote 'a patriotic poem called "The British Flag will always Wave"'. At first she dismissed it as being a 'rehash of all the patriotic poems ever written', but then admitted that she felt 'better for having written it, like a Girl Guide who has done her good deed for the day'. Janet then confessed in her diary that 'I *did* mean it. I had a sudden feeling while I was in the pictures, that it *would*, somehow, always wave'.[111] Janet's Mass-Observation diaries highlight a self-awareness and critique of the prejudices of the Home Front. She was unwilling to challenge fully her own belief in Britain's and the British people's natural superiority and sense of decency. Nevertheless, her diary writing neatly exposed her inner wrestling over the expression of nationalistic rhetoric.

The strength, as well as the fragility, of the bonds between the refugees and the British public were revealed in such diary writings. In the late spring of 1940 it was not only the power of an unrestrained xenophobia of sections of British society and state but also the ambivalence of those more positively inclined to refugees that was exposed. The privately expressed antipathies, if rarely transformed into public hostility, were more often articulated in the form of a silence to protest against state measures of internment, perhaps reflecting tacit agreement in what some saw as a humane way of removing the refugees. Janet Neal's earlier malicious imaginings of an 'England for the English' campaign came to fruition. Indeed, Janet herself wrote extensively and revealingly on the internment episode.

In early May 1940 the first mass measures of internment were made by the British state, reflecting a state of panic relating to the military catastrophe after the collapse of Holland and the threat of invasion and an underlying political and economic crisis.[112] In such an atmosphere, anti-alienism flourished, manifesting itself violently in the form of riots against the British Italian community. In the middle of May Mass-Observation reported that with stories of aliens acting as a fifth column in Holland

> Now the enemy in our midst is easily visualised. The always latent antagonism to the alien and foreigner began to flare up. Nearly everyone ... is latently somewhat anti-semitic and somewhat anti-alien. But ordinarily it is not the done thing to express such sentiments publicly. The news from Holland made it quite the done thing, all of a sudden.[113]

Some of the male relatives of Janet Neal's refugee friends were amongst the first to be caught up in the first wave of mass arrests. One of these was Max whose sister Hedi phoned Janet in a state of great distress. Using her connections, Janet found out that Max may have been sent to the Isle of Man, but it was not possible to find out his exact location owing to the chaos of the first stages of internment and military secrecy. Janet's reaction, as related in her diary, again reflected complex interwoven layers of empathy and irritation, understanding and antipathy:

> I was so sorry for Hedi – not because of Max being interned, but because of the suspense. He was taken away once before by the Gestapo, and once, after being released, was shot at, while Max's sister went out and 'rescued' him. However, as she said they have had seven years of it and it seems it never ends.

Yet in contrast to this sensitive awareness of the background of the refugees, their current woes were still understood through a discourse of exclusive nationalism and ethnic stereotyping in which their suffering had, in the view of Janet, to be contextualised:

> I told her that while Englishmen were going to be shot to keep the Nazis away, I was not worried about anyone being interned, only for her suspense. After all, so many of the refugees were very critical of the English methods for fighting Germany but did nothing but worry about how to keep their own lily-white bodies safe.[114]

To another refugee in the same situation, Janet responded in similar vein, adding that 'at least [the internees] were all safe and had free board and lodging, which was more than a lot of English had at the moment, and that I did not feel they had the right to moan while English boys were being sent to the Front'. But as her diary reveals, Janet was not wholly at ease with the policy of mass internment, or, for that matter, with her own attitudes towards refugees. She added, almost as a way of apologising to the reader for the bluntness of her views, that 'Actually, I only wanted to shock [the relatives of the internees] into feeling better about it'. The diarist was dismayed to hear that a woman had refused to work for some refugees and turning the situation round in a moment of close identification, wrote that 'If the English were made refugees, they would lump together me and the maid who steals, and the butcher's wife, and Lady Doo-Dah, and the Reddest of communists – all under the heading "refugees" – yet it never seems to occur to people that the German and Austrian refugees are equally mixed.' Nevertheless, such expressions of positive sentiment and empathy were still followed by another attempt to justify mass internment – 'I told [another refugee] that if there were only six of the Fifth arm [column] among 60,000 of them, they had to be put away'.[115]

In the penultimate section of this revealing diary entry, Janet turned to the causes of anti-refugee sentiment. As with Janet's earlier entries (and in similar vein to the 1939 directive respondents who blamed the 'masses' for any prejudice towards the newcomers), she attempted to turn the focus away from her own antipathies and became, instead, what she saw as the objective but critical observer of those around her:

> I have often wondered how it was that the Germans turned so savagely against the Jews, and now I understand – in part. Everywhere I went [in Britain] I heard the most apparently good-natured people tearing the refugees orally limb from limb. Most of them had never seen even one refugee. They did it without reason, not stopping to think that the real refugees were the last to want Hitler to win, and most of them were talking about suicide already. To these people the refugees were all fifth-arm merchants ... the people here, unhappy and worried at the way the war was going, in a spasm of relief turned all their unhappiness against the refugees.[116]

It is significant, however, that her diary entry of 8 May 1940 finishes on a note which leaves the reader pondering how far the Mass-Observer was projecting her own feelings about the refugees onto the general public. She referred to her friend Gerta who had not yet been interned. Janet had suggested to Gerta that internment might be a good option – again stressing the free board and lodgings as against the refugee's increasing struggle to make a living through the restraints imposed as an enemy alien.[117] Yet it was the constant emphasis placed on what Janet insisted would be the benign experience of internment that suggest that her desire expressed some six months earlier, of removing the refugees, but to, as she put it, 'somewhere nice',[118] lurked beneath the surface of her defence of the government's policies. For Janet, in spite of all her intimate knowledge of the refugees and their situation, it was a policy that could be justified beyond the needs of national security. Her insistence that internment would be carried out in a sympathetic manner reflected her faith in the essential decency of the British people and its government.

Moreover, while Janet Neal was capable of collapsing the division between 'us' and 'them' and acknowledging the shared humanity between
the British and the refugees, there remained a lingering suspicion about
the danger of their 'difference'.

Janet Neal's belief in British 'fair play' was only partially merited.
With hindsight, it is possible to point to the academic, artistic and cultural achievements of the internees that were facilitated by the government. It would be wrong, however, to ignore the abuses they indured,
including the poor conditions in the initial camps, being mixed with genuine Nazis and, especially, the robbery and harsh treatment endured when
deported to Canada and Australia.[119] Self-aware, at some levels, of her
own ambivalence, Janet's diary writing did not resolve her inner tensions. Yet it was important in itself in validating aspects of her outlook
and everyday life which in the specific crisis of the first year of war were
increasingly coming into conflict. Only those of a more internationalistic
outlook, such as Naomi Mitchison, could criticise (if not, even in her
case, in public) the success of anti-alienism, writing in her diary that the
failure to differentiate between anti-Germanism and anti-Nazism represented 'The return of nationalism'.[120]

What the Mass-Observation diaries reveal from the period September
1939 to May 1940 is the processes by which anti-alienism became dominant in British society, albeit its expression and self-justification were far
from simple. While many reported the hostility of those around them,
few were willing to express their own antipathies as openly as a librarian
in Devon, who launched into a diatribe against Belgian war refugees,
writing boldly that 'We have our own mouths to feed. Let them stay
under Germany'.[121] More common was the response of a teacher in Ply-
mouth who, when commenting on a big round-up of aliens in the town,
couched his anxieties in more diplomatic terms, justifying the internment
of one of his own students, Hans M. He was, the schoolteacher suggested, a 'nice boy, but far too clever to be about. The 16 years age limit
[on internment] seems to be rather high. I know plenty of 14 year olds
who'd make magnificent spies'. But in similar fashion to Janet Neal, the
teacher justified mass internment on liberal grounds as being in the best
interests of the refugees: 'it would be better surely to take all aliens into
internment camps for protective custody – for their own sake if they're
reliable'.[122]

Even those who seemed critical of the government's measures were
silent on the issue, perhaps fearful of the consequences of speaking out.
Indeed, two Mass-Observation diarists, both of whom had close contact
with the refugees (to the extent in one case of helping them pack their
bags before being sent away), felt great unease in actually writing about

what had happened. A middle-aged office worker, a pacifist, wrote what
was for him a very brief daily summary of what he called the month's
'unusual happenings', not providing any commentary or personal reflection. He added a note at the end of his monthly submission that he was
fearful that by even mentioning the processes by which internment had
been carried out 'I have laid myself open to suspicion as a "5th Colum-
nist" but trust that anything sent to Mass-Observation is privileged and
confidential'.[123]

Taking the period from the start of the conflict to the end of the 'pho-
ney war', the Mass-Observation diaries are a revealing source, divulging
the intricate and multi-layered interaction between individuals confronting on an everyday basis the confusing presence of the refugees. In addition, fulfilling their obligation to their sponsoring body, they offer often
astute observation of attitudes and responses of those around them at a
time when definitions of national identity, both legal and cultural, were
becoming increasingly exclusive. In addition, the tensions between what
people felt they should be thinking and their own antipathies and prejudices were exposed through the act of writing. If not all the ambiguities
and contradictions were resolved by such literacy practices, it is still the
case that the diaries provide valuable evidence of the complex mecha-
nisms by which ordinary people in Britain made sense of aliens and anti-
alienism in the context of their own identities at a time of crisis.

Not surprisingly, given that nearly half the refugee population was
interned, and several thousand were sent to Australia and Canada, the
contact of Observers with refugees declined in this period. But it certainly did not disappear after May 1940. Several Observers had friends
who were interned in Britain and its dominions. They were aware of the
hardships of the internment camps and of the refugees' attempts to make
the most of their time there, through such initiatives as the creation of
kindergartens for the children in the Isle of Man.[124] As late as January
1942, Naomi Mitchison reported on the fate of her friend, Paul, who had
just been released from an internment camp, noting that, while his partner was 'so happy', Paul himself looked 'pale and queer still'.[125] Few
would have had Mitchison's range of contacts, however, and it remains
that, as explored in previous chapters, alien internment remains hidden
in the history and heritage of the British 'Home Front' experience.

Given the vulnerable, temporary and marginal status of the refugees,
interaction between them and the general population was bound to be
distorted by issues of power as well as cultural difference. It was much
easier, however, before the restrictions on aliens gathered momentum in
the first year of the war. Nina Masel had worked for Mass-Observation
in the East End during the Blitz. Before then, as a working-class schoolgirl

of Jewish origin, who had 'poured her heart' into first the Mass-Observation directives, and then her war diary, Masel was acutely aware of both the dilemmas facing the refugees and the gulf that separated her experiences from those who, at the outbreak of hostilities, had been cut off from their former homeland and families and friends. In mid-September 1939 she visited an acquaintance, writing with immense maturity (Nina was only seventeen) about the reality of refugee life and her relationship to it:

> She was pleased to see me because she is extremely unhappy. She is actually only fourteen, but is so abnormally highly developed that … she looks a good nineteen and behaves it too. The trouble is that a permit for work is not usually given to a refugee until she is sixteen (At present she is partly at school, partly nursemaid) and she feels [strongly] that she is wasting her time. Then, like all refugees, she is intensely worried about her parents. She spoke about dying and insanity.

Masel added, with a self-awareness much more developed, it must be said, than Janet Neal, that 'I did my best to comfort her, which was not much'.[126]

Many Mass-Observers had contact with the twenty thousand refugees, almost all women, who had come into Britain as domestic servants, cooks and nursemaids. Some, like Nina Masel, clearly made a conscious decision to visit them to ease the isolation they were experiencing in a foreign land. Other Observers were employers of refugees within their homes. Their diaries provide a deep insight into the interplay between class, 'race' and the construction of national identity. And once more they reveal the importance of the writing process itself in Mass-Observers' attempts to confront the difference of others and their own tolerance and intolerance of this difference.

Rebecca Lowenstein's directive responses and diary entries have already featured in this chapter. In late October 1939 she provided a candid account of the domestic arrangements in her family home which, while perceptive in its analysis, is remarkable for its lack of human engagement with the refugee whom she encountered on a daily basis. Its fascinating mixture of frankness and distance make it worth quoting at length:

> Our German refugee maid is inclined to make her chief virtue her claim on our sympathies: in fact she is damned inefficient [she added 'and rather indifferent to being helpful' then crossed it out]. It is necessary to keep on a morning girl to get any work done at all. The two complain about each other separately and there is no love lost, various unfortunate incidents exacerbating the feelings of both. My mother tells the English girl, 'You must look upon it as your contribution to war work'. The girl agrees, and says 'yes she thinks it's war work all right.' She probably resents the foreigner

to some extent, but there is no feeling, I think, against an *enemy* alien. We used to own 2 Seelyham bitches, who when they got old used to share a fight whenever they got a chance. Rather the same quality of nature in the raw can be felt in the kitchen now.

My mother's chief reason for keeping the German is her feeling that 'It is my contribution. We must do what we can at a time like this'. She does not like foreigners much, but sees no strangeness in her contribution to the well-being of an enemy alien. Rather interestingly the German is a widow of our own 'class'. My mother's sympathies are to some extent poised between the class sympathies (horizontal) which oppose her to the English 'daily', and her *English* feelings (vertical) which oppose her to the foreigner. It is a kind of triangular balance of forces, with the mistress of the house at the apex.[127]

On the surface, keeping a Mass-Observation diary gave the writer the option of simply observing the reactions and behaviour of those around them. It is evident, however, that in attempting to focus the attention of the reader on firstly the maid and then her mother, Rebecca was revealing much about her own feelings. Indeed, the very attempt at a clinically objective approach, rather than turning attention away from herself, actually achieved the reverse. What emerges, alongside her clear irritation at the failings of the refugee in her function as maid, is an equal lack of empathy with her mother's honest, if rather patronising, attempt to help a victim of Nazism.

The refugee domestics were caught between the two differing statuses that their title implied. Some employees clearly expected both good service and a degree of gratitude from their new servants. When this was not forthcoming, irritation could soon emerge. In January 1940, a young Surrey housewife described the visit of a friend who had come in order to escape from her German Jewish maid who was 'so pushing and ungrateful'.[128] A few months later, when the government's restrictions on aliens were at their height, the amalgam of obligation and utility came out neatly in the diary of a female ambulance driver in London. She wrote how a friend had gone to Worthing 'to fetch her sister's German maid who is banned [from] the coast. Bit of a problem to know what to do with her. Still, we need a maid here, so shall probably keep her for a bit.'[129]

Some of the Mass-Observers like Lowenstein used their diaries to problematise their reactions to the 'alien presence' of these women in their own homes. Others adjusted with remarkable ease to their 'difference', discounting it and, for better or worse, treating the refugee women simply as servants to be used and disposed of. A teacher in Sussex commented with much surprise on a letter from her aunt who, from being a 'rabid anti-Jew' was now 'reasonable' and delighting in the excellence of her German Jewish maids.[130]

Most of the refugee women were anxious to leave domestic service and to contribute their particular skills to the war effort more directly. Some were successful, but many had little choice other than to stay in service. Miss French, a member of the Glasgow Association of University Women, which had been very active in helping female refugees, reflected on the case of a woman who had been given 'a testimonial saying she was far the best dietician they had ever had'. Nevertheless, this refugee had been unable to get a position other than in service.[131] Even after the disruption of the anti-alien panic in summer 1940, when many refugee domestics had to leave protected areas, there were thousands still in the occupation.

Before leaving the world below stairs and its interrelation with the refugee movement, one final diary entry is worth consideration. Mrs Jones was a young widowed housewife in central London. Her extensive voluntary work in London depended on sophisticated household management involving a group of servants. The foreignness/Jewishness of some of the maids, however, made the management of her servants a cause for ongoing concern. Mrs G, a 'daily' help, had got into a row with two of the foreign live-in domestics. Mrs Jones decided to sack Mrs G only when she 'was quite sure there wouldn't be any upsets over the advent of an enemy-alien non-Aryan from the other two'. 'I said that I quite understood the difficulty of getting on with foreigners'. It remained that household needs came above national solidarity: 'as I found the two Hungarians perfectly satisfactory, and couldn't risk being left without living-in maids, it was Mrs G whom I must sacrifice'.[132]

It emerged later that another servant, Mrs B, had 'blown the gaff' about Mrs Jones' decision to employ another foreign maid – a German Jew. Mrs B had 'deliberately invited trouble by animadverting upon the girl's nationality – a subject which I'd intended to introduce most carefully, in case of any racial or national feeling which might upset my whole household apple-cart'. Mrs B had apparently told the two 'English' maids in the house that she 'couldn't think how the two girls would be able to stand living and working with an enemy in the house, and a Jew at that'. Fortunately for Mrs Jones, it emerged that neither of the 'English' girls had 'any strong anti-Jew or anti-German feeling to overcome, as I'd feared likely'. Manipulating pity partly for her own ends, Mrs Jones wrote in her diary that she was 'easily able to enlist their positive sympathies for [the German Jewish maid] by telling them how her husband and father had been killed by the Nazis, and she herself had only escaped with difficulty'.[133] Matters came to a head a few days later. Mrs G was picking a row with one of the Hungarian maids and Mrs Jones intervened. Mrs G launched into a 'torrent of abuse to the effect that she'd no intention of taking orders from *foreign* girls – she was *English*, and this was *England*, wasn't it, when all was said and done'. Again the plea for national solidarity was turned down: 'I cut her short ... by saying I was also English and she would please take orders from me, namely, to leave at once and without argument.'[134]

These diary entries show how difficult it is to generalise about racial attitudes at a popular level. Mrs Smith expected the worst from her 'English' maids and, while two clearly justified their opposition to the foreigners on grounds of 'race' and nation, they could not influence their compatriots. She made clear the complexity of running a household, a priority which took precedence over all other factors. The very fact that Mrs Smith was eager to employ refugee domestics suggests at least a lack of inherent bias, although self-interest was again to the fore – at a time when it was very difficult to obtain live-in help, the homeless and often very talented refugees were a great asset. Yet beyond pride in her household management skills, her diary also points to a satisfaction at running a home that was so diverse. Ironically, the time saved by employing domestics enabled Mrs Jones to engage in voluntary work running vans to provide refreshments for auxiliary workers, most of whom were German and Austrian aliens. Exchanging broken German and broken English, Mrs Jones reflected after one shift in Whitechapel that 'If only this contact between members of different nations could be general, I'm sure it would be the death of most of that national and racial hostility and mistrust which is a major cause – if not *the* cause – of wars'.[135]

Mrs Jones' Mass-Observation diary reveals her belief that the servant classes were understandably prone to prejudice but that she herself could envisage a more tolerant and inclusive world. She had a clear understanding of the background of the foreign domestics but sympathy alone was not the basis of her employment of three refugees. She treated the refugee domestics as individuals with specific skills but did not use her diary as a mechanism for explicitly exploring her own attitudes towards them. Nevertheless, her future optimism stemmed from living with difference on a daily level, a fact to which her Mass-Observation diary is clearly intended as a detailed testimony.

The Mass-Observation diaries show both irritation and empathy with refugees, often from the same person. Some expected the refugees to be eternally grateful, thereby strengthening the diarists' faith in the decency of the English and Englishness in general. Others reflected more deeply on the plight of refugees and how their experiences and background separated them from the general population. Late in 1943 a nurse in Blackburn wrote about a refugee colleague whose boyfriend had just died. Rather than simply another story of a heart-breaking war romance, the Mass-

Observer commented in her diary that 'She is a refugee from Occupied Europe and has lost her parents which makes things doubly hard for her. She has no home and no parents, her relatives may or may not be still alive. No wonder she is taking it so badly.'[136] Many diarists were in-between, reflecting some understanding of the plight of the refugees but unable to empathise with them fully through the barriers of Englishness they had constructed. A young solicitor's clerk in the Lake District went to a meeting where the possibility of creating a Czech refugee club was discussed. His mother was uneasy and wondered, whether, if 'we were in exile we'd do the same'. He responded positively, using the example of the colonies to prove his point. The Mass-Observer closed off the debate, however, by stating categorically that 'in the first place, we wouldn't have been driven out of England'.[137] The Mass-Observation diaries were thus a site of reflection in which it was possible to discuss the specific issues raised by the presence of refugees. They also provided the individual with a chance to reflect on their place in the world. Refugees, although experientially far removed, were nevertheless often close to the everyday lives of Mass-Observers. The Mass-Observation diaries were a forum through which this simultaneous distance and closeness could be explored, if never fully reconciled.

Conclusion: writing about difference

In September 1940 Miss French reported on a meeting of the Glasgow Association of University Women. The Association had received an appeal for support from a Polish refugee, anxious to resume her studies. There was a feeling at the meeting, she wrote in her diary, 'that we would rather help someone whom we could meet and not someone whom we should never see'.[138] In November 1939 Rebecca Lowenstein went for a morning shift at her London first aid post. She introduced a refugee boy who had been in Sachsenhausen concentration camp to the others in the post – 'a group of 10 pub going Englishmen'. She wrote in her diary later that one 'could almost cut with a knife the atmosphere of inarticulate sympathy. After a short silence, one said "But what's it *like* in a concentration camp?"[139] Lowenstein, as with her writings on her mother's response to the refugee domestic, avoided direct comments on her own response and projected the inarticulacy and fascination described onto those she clearly saw in snobbish terms as 'below' her. A young woman from Sheffield was more self-critical when she described her recent encounter with a refugee friend whom she had persuaded to visit a doctor: 'As he was too young to normally have false teeth I had previously cherished the idea that he'd had them pushed out in a concentration camp' –

in fact, he had fallen over after a drunken evening.[140]

Such diary entries reflect a contemporary engagement with those who were victims of Nazi persecution which was both inclusive and exclusive. On the one hand, there was ordinary contact with individual refugees in what were everyday encounters on the Home Front. On the other, it was often distorted by a sense that the refugees came from 'over there', reflecting a total otherness to Britain – the concentration camp. Other Mass-Observers used their diaries to explore, if not always to fully confront, the nature of their own racial prejudices. A teacher in Kent, at the time when the news of the extermination of European Jewry was at its most intense, reflected uneasily about the roots of her antisemitism. She and her friend were irritated by a Jewish man they had met. After the man had gone she said to her friend 'Look here, I'm getting absolutely anti-semitic, and I don't like it'. The friend replied, trying to reassure her: 'Well he was a loathsome specimen, German Jewish extraction. His father was probably born in a ghetto in Mannheim'. Neither seemed convinced that their views were justified and she concluded her diary entry by commenting that 'We both wondered about our growing Jewish antipathy'.[141]

Both the March 1939 directive responses and the Mass-Observation diaries for the war years provide, in their different ways, unique insights into how the 'refugee' was experienced and imagined. There are occasions when the two sources reinforce the importance of themes that would continue to dominate later memory work, one in particular being that of gratitude. It is clear that thankfulness was expected from the refugees and whether it would be given, beyond the short term, was a major factor in determining attitudes towards their entry. On the positive side, a London bank clerk believed that the Home Office would keep out undesirable refugees 'so that those who come in should be decent citizens arriving with a sense of gratitude'.[142] In contrast, another respondent, believing that the number of refugees allowed into Britain was 'too many', argued that 'however grateful they are for sanctuary at the present time, in years to come they will live and act on the assumption that they have equal rights with the natives of the land'.[143] The requirement of gratitude, no matter how demeaning the position in which refugees found themselves, has also been illustrated acutely in the case of the diary entries relating to domestic servants. These refugees were not only expected to perform their gruelling daily duties below stairs but also had to be thankful for the opportunity to do so.

There are two important points to note here. First, the acceptance of refugees on behalf of many was conditional – their entry was a privilege, not a right, and depended upon them behaving in a certain manner. Second, and coming out of this expectation, many of the refugees themselves, unsurprisingly, internalised such pressure and responded with a 'cult of gratitude' made manifest in the 'Thank You Britain Fund' set up largely through the auspices of the Association of Jewish Refugees (AJR) in 1964.[144] The historiography and heritage representation of the refugees from Nazism relating to their experiences in Britain has increasingly become dominated by the triple criteria of showing loyalty, contribution and gratitude. The articulation of these principles is especially notable in the histories, autobiographies, memorials and exhibitions produced by these refugees themselves or their offspring in recent decades.[145] Such representation contrasts to the harder hitting analysis produced just after the war in the monthly journal of the AJR. *AJR Information*, which began publication in 1946, was not afraid to outline the problems of immigration control procedures and to analyse the range of popular responses and reactions to refugees from Nazism, including antipathy, that slowed down their integration and settlement in Britain.[146] The dilemmas created over refugee self-representation will be explored further in the following chapter in relation to the memory of the *Kindertransport*.

As well as commonalities, there are major differences that emerge in the writing within the directives and the diaries. The most basic is that the 'refugee' in the directive is largely an abstract figure, rarely personalised beyond reference to famous figures such as Einstein and Freud. In the diaries, the refugees become 'real', ordinary people. While the refugee 'voice' is articulated through the writings of others, at their most sensitive the Mass-Observers reveal an empathy with the dilemmas facing those who had often left all their family and friends behind. Even then, for many of the Mass-Observation diarists, discourses of nation, race, class and gender shape and often warp the representation of the refugees. What is fascinating within the diaries is how, at their best, they enable a long-term perspective of the Mass-Observer wrestling with the presence of the refugees and their mutual place in the world.

Ultimately, in contrast, the directive responses are a static source. They contain concentrated information that supplements and further complicates the contemporary debate about refugees that was articulated in politics and print. It enables a 'history from below' of the 1930s refugee crisis and acts as a reminder to take the views of ordinary people seriously. Nevertheless, the literacy practice contained within the responses is relatively limited – in the particular case of the question on refugees it was generally brief and to the point. The directive responses are substantial enough to allow conflicting emotions and attitudes to be revealed, and they emerge as a far richer source than the rival contemporary opinion polls. Generally, however, the directive responses did not encourage the working out of inner tensions and uncertainties about the refugees – even if such ambiguities are laid out clearly to the reader. The temporal element is not missing – a close reading reveals the importance of the past as constructed by the Mass-Observer, in responding to the current refugees. But how that individual response itself changes over time was inevitably missing in the directive responses.

In contrast, diaries are, by nature, dynamic and, as a genre, suggests Felicity Nussbaum, they articulate 'modes of discourse that may subvert and endanger authorized representations of reality in its form as well as its discourse of self or subject'.[147] In this respect, one specific aspect deserves analysis before the close of this chapter – the issue of gender and literacy practice. The bulk of the material in the section on directives features the writing of male Mass-Observers and that on the diaries from females. Partly this bias is a matter of numbers – there were three times as many men as women before the war while that balance shifted during it. By the end of the conflict female Mass-Observers outnumbered their male counterparts. There are other factors at work, however, than the purely numerical.

A close reading of the March 1939 directives reveals little major difference between male and female responses. The proportion of those sympathetic, ambivalent and hostile to the refugees was similar as were the reasons given for the attitudes expressed whether they be based on ideas of economics, nation or morality. Only in one respect is there a contrast, and even then it is only in a minority of the female respondents – the greater self-reflexivity in literacy practice, especially when dealing with the articulation of prejudice. Its significance is that it points towards a factor that is manifest most strongly in the Mass-Observation diaries – women used this genre to explore their own identities and relationship to the outside world. Such self-questioning was relatively rare in the diaries of male Mass-Observers. It is therefore particularly through female Mass-Observation diaries that the huge contemporary struggle to confront the refugee presence is articulated in its full complexity.

While the earlier directive responses provide more focus, enabling a clinical dissection of the factors operating in favour of and against the entry of refugees, it is the diaries that enable a more nuanced construction of memory work during the Nazi era. As has been noted with regard to the expectation of gratitude, this contemporary engagement with refugees has been subsequently smoothed over, allowing a self-congratulatory narrative to become dominant. That there was, at the time, ambiguity, indifference and antipathy expressed alongside empathy and sympathy, however, only points further to the importance of the refugee in constructing identities in one of the most pivotal periods of modern British history and, of equal importance, the subsequent evolution of collective memory. It is the Mass-Observation diaries in particular that show how experiencing refugees during the 1930s and the Second World War could be both an enriching and a confusing experience. The desire to show compassion was often compromised by conditional acceptance, irritation with the ordinary human failings of the refugees, and the inability to overcome a belief in innate British/English superiority which ran alongside a residual fear about the menace posed by the 'alien' presence. The Mass-Observation diaries, and to a far lesser extent, the directives, became sites where such ambivalence could be explored and articulated if never fully resolved. They are thus perhaps the most fitting contemporary memorial to Britain's confrontation with what has subsequently become constructed as the most famous of refugee crises. Within that refugee movement the *Kindertransport* has developed special status in collective memory both inside and outside Britain. The next chapter is devoted to the memory work associated with these child refugees.

Notes

1   W.M. Crawford, 'A Cosmopolitan City', in N.J. Frangopulo (ed.), *Rich Inheritance: A Guide to the History of Manchester* (Wakefield: S.R. Publishers, 1969 [1962]), p. 120.

2   A.J.P. Taylor, *English History 1914–1945* (Oxford: Oxford University Press, 1965), p. 419.

3   Tony Kushner, *We Europeans? Mass-Observation, 'Race' and British Identity in the Twentieth Century* (Aldershot: Ashgate, 2004), part 1.

4   Dorothy Sheridan, Brian Street and David Bloome, *Mass-Observation and Literacy Practices* (Cresskill, NJ: Hampton Press, 2000), p. 2.

5   Ibid., p. 5.

6   There is no detailed study of the British media and the refugees during the 1930s although there is useful material presented, if not always accurate in its detail, in Andrew Sharf, *The British Press & Jews under Nazi Rule* (London: Oxford University Press, 1964), chapter 6. On the ownership and circulation of the British press for this period see Royal Commission on The Press 1947–1949, *Report* (London: HMSO, 1949 Cmd. 7700).

7   In the House of Commons the Home Secretary, Sir Samuel Hoare, warned that 'I know it from my own experience that there is a making of a definite anti-Jewish movement'. In *Hansard* vol. 341 col. 1468 (21 November 1938).

8   Robert Worcester, *British Public Opinion: A Guide to the History and Methodology of Political Opinion Polling* (Oxford: Blackwell, 1991), part 1.

9   See Sharf, *The British Press*, p. 199 for comment.

10 The poll results were initially published in *News Chronicle*, 31 July 1939. See also Hadley Cantril (ed.), *Public Opinion 1935–1946* (Princeton: Princeton University Press, 1951), p. 1150.

11 Based on the author's analysis of the March 1939 Mass-Observation directives.

12 Cantril, *Public Opinion*, p. 1150.

13 Kushner, *We Europeans?*, part 1.

14 Ibid., chapter 4.

15 This is my own estimate, confirmed by Mass-Observation's own analysis of these directives in Mass-Observation Archive (M-O A): FR A12.

16 N.S. Stanley, '"The Extra Dimension": A Study and Assessment of the Methods Employed by Mass-Observation in Its First Period, 1937–40', (unpublished PhD, Birmingham Polytechnic, 1981).

17 M-O A: DR 5010, March 1939.

18 M-O A: DR 1421, March 1939.

19 M-O A: DR 1135, March 1939.

20 M-O A: DR 2015, March 1939.

21 M-O A: DR 1227, March 1939.

22 M-O A: DR 1048, March 1939.

23 M-O A: DR 1403, March 1939.

24 M-O A: DR 1597, March 1939.

25 R.O'Brien, 'The Establishment of the Jewish Minority in Leeds' (unpublished PhD thesis, Bristol University, 1975).

26 M-O A: DR 1285, March 1939. In DR 1328, March 1939, a male, Sheffield respondent, who was generally positive towards those escaping Nazism, commented that 'My own tailor is an elderly Eastern European Jew – a refugee from the Great War – and both he and his son are exceptionally likeable people.'

27 M-O A: DR 1986, March 1939.

28 M-O A: DR 1016, March 1939. For more on this individual, see Kushner, *We Europeans?*, chapter 6.

29 M-O A: DR 1423, March 1939.

30 M-O A: DR 1098, March 1939.

31 M-O A: DR 1088, March 1939.

32 M-O A: DR 1147, March 1939.

33 More generally see Nancy Stepan, *The Idea of Race in Science: Great Britain 1860–1960* (Basingstoke: Macmillan, 1982) and Elazar Barkan, *The Retreat of Scientific Racism: Changing Concepts of Race in Britain and the United States between the World Wars* (Cambridge: Cambridge University Press, 1986).

34 M-O A: DR 1551, March 1939.

35 M-O A: DR 1616, March 1939.

36 M-O A: DR 1329, March 1939.

37 M-O A: DR 1039, March 1939.

38 M-O A: DR 1164, March 1939.

39 M-O A: DR 1437, March 1939.

40 For an exploration of this trope within the work of Anthony Trollope see Bryan Cheyette, *Constructions of 'the Jew' in English Literature and Society: Racial Representations, 1875–1945* (Cambridge: Cambridge University

Press, 1993), pp. 32–5.
41 M-O A: DR 1070, March 1939.
42 Ibid.
43 Scott to Gillies, 13 December 1938, WG/REF/69/ii–iii, Labour Party archives, National Labour Museum, Manchester.
44 In *Hansard* (HC) vol. 341 col. 1468, 21 November 1938.
45 Ibid.
46 M-O A: DR 1592, March 1939.
47 M-O A: DR 1361, March 1939.
48 M-O A: DR 1275, March 1939.
49 Norman Angell and Dorothy Buxton, *You and the Refugee* (Harmondsworth, Middlesex: Penguin, 1939); Louis Golding, *The Jewish Problem* (Harmondsworth, Middlesex: Penguin, 1938).
50 M-O A: DR AJ, March 1939.
51 M-O A: DR 1130, March 1939.
52 M-O A: DR 1304, March 1939.
53 M-O A: DR 1133, March 1939.
54 M-O A: DR 1596, March 1939.
55 M-O A: DR 1423, March 1939.
56 M-O A: DR 2008, March 1939.
57 M-O A: DR 1986, March 1939.
58 M-O A: DR 1394, March 1939.
59 M-O A: DR 1048, March 1939.
60 M-O A: DR 1075, March 1939.
61 M-O A: DR 1057, March 1939.
62 M-O A: DR 1383, March 1939.
63 M-O A: DR 1250, March 1939.
64 M-O A: DR 1036, March 1939.
65 M-O A: DR 1097, March 1939.
66 M-O A: DR 1597, March 1939.
67 M-O A: DR 1464, March 1939.
68 Tony Kushner, *The Holocaust and the Liberal Imagination: A Social and Cultural History* (Oxford: Blackwell, 1994), p. 51.
69 M-O A: DR 1223, March 1939.
70 M-O A: DR 1350, March 1939.
71 Royal Commission on the Press, *Report*.
72 M-O A: DR 2026, March 1939.
73 M-O A: DR 1390, March 1939.
74 M-O A: DR 1420, March 1939.
75 M-O A: DR 1587, March 1939.
76 Marion Berghahn, *Continental Britons: German-Jewish Refugees from Nazi Germany* (Oxford: Berg, 1988), pp. 126–9.
77 M-O A: DR 1379, March 1939.
78 M-O A: DR 1133, March 1939.
79 M-O A: DR 1257, March 1939.
80 M-O A: DR 1125, March 1939.

81 M-O A: DR 1464, March 1939. On Hampstead and the refugees see An-
    thony Grenville, *Continental Britons: Jewish Refugees from Nazi Europe*
    (London: Jewish Museum, 2002), p. 31 and Graham Macklin, '"A Quite
    Natural and Moderate Defensive Feeling"? The 1945 Hampstead "Anti-
    alien" Petition', *Patterns of Prejudice* vol. 37 no. 3 (September 2003), pp.
    277–300.
82 M-O A: DR 1393, March 1939.
83 For this tendency more generally see Patricia Skinner, 'Confronting the "Me-
    dieval" in Medieval History: The Jewish Example', *Past & Present* no. 181
    (November 2003), pp. 232–3.
84 M-O A: DR 1237, March 1939.
85 M-O A: DR 1014, March 1939.
86 M-O A: DR 1428, March 1939.
87 M-O A: DR 1250, March 1939.
88 M-O A: DR 1978, March 1939.
89 M-O A: DR 1281, March 1939.
90 M-O A: DR 1076, March 1939.
91 M-O A: DR 1217, March 1939.
92 For the most recent analysis of numbers, see Louise London, *Whitehall and
    the Jews 1933–1948: British Immigration Policy and the Holocaust* (Cam-
    bridge: Cambridge University Press, 2000), p. 12. London estimates that
    up to 10,000 refugee Jews had re-emigrated and that of the 78,000 present
    at the outbreak of war some 70,000 were Jewish.
93 For a detailed analysis of the nature of Mass-Observation diaries see Kushner,
    We Europeans?, chapter 5 and the articles in the special issue of *Feminist
    Praxis* nos 37 and 38 (1993). The following section of this chapter is devel-
    oped further in chapter 7 of *We Europeans?*
94 Margaret Kertesz, 'To Speak for Themselves? Mass-Observation's Women's
    Wartime Diaries', *Feminist Praxis* nos 37 and 38 (1993), p. 78.
95 See, however, Lori Gemeiner Bihler, 'German-Jewish Refugees in London
    and New York, 1935–1945: A Comparative Study of Adaptation and Ac-
    culturation' (unpublished PhD thesis, University of Sussex, 2004) in which
    everyday culture features prominently.
96 M-O A: D C5291, 4 October 1939.
97 M-O A: D C5291, 23 November 1939.
98 M-O A: D 5179, 1 January 1940.
99 M-O A: D K5349.
100 M-O A: D C5293, 5 November 1939.
101 M-O A: D C5291, 8 November 1939.
102 M-O A: DR 1543, March 1943.
103 M-O A: D C5291, 4 October 1939.
104 See, for example, *Whilst You are In Britain* (London: Bloomsbury House,
    1939).
105 M-O A: D C5291, 4 October 1939.
106 *Papers Concerning the Treatment of German Nationals in Germany 1938–
    9* (Cmd. 6120, HMSO, London, 1939).

107 For her confrontation with domestic antisemitism see M-O A: D C5291, 9 September, 3 November 1939, 8 May, 10 June 1940. For her criticism of the White Paper, see her diary entry for 31 October 1939.

108 M-O A: D C5291, 31 October 1939.

109 M-O A: D C5291, 3 November 1939.

110 M-O A: D C5291, 8 November 1939.

111 M-O A: C5291, 4 October 1939.

112 See David Cesarani and Tony Kushner (eds), *The Internment of Aliens in Twentieth Century Britain* (London: Frank Cass, 1993).

113 M-O A: FR 107. 'Feeling About Aliens', 14 May 1940.

114 M-O A: D C5291, 8 May 1940.

115 M-O A: D C5291, 8 May 1940.

116 M-O A: D C5291, 8 May 1940.

117 M-O A: D C5291, 8 May 1940.

118 M-O A: D C5291, 8 November 1939.

119 See the contributions in Cesarani and Kushner, *The Internment of Aliens*, especially Burletson's.

120 Dorothy Sheridan (ed.), *Among You Taking Notes … The Wartime Diary of Naomi Mitchison* (London: Gollancz, 1985), p. 64 entry for 7 June 1940. See also her entry of 11 June 1940 in M-O A: D5378.

121 M-O A: D 5263, 28 May 1940.

122 M-O A: D5057, 26 May 1940.

123 M-O A: D G5092, May 1940. See also the comments of M-O A: D AC5239.

124 M-O A: D5095, 4 September 1940; D5220, 10 September 1940.

125 M-O A: D5378, 16 January 1942.

126 M-O A: D M5370, 14 September 1939. On the first day of war Nina had spent the day with a close refugee friend, possibly her boyfriend, and the evening with other refugees. She reported on his concern about his status as an alien and his desire to prove his gratitude by joining the Army. Nina concluded her entry by stating that 'They were all terribly upset'. See *New Statesman*, 31 May 1985 and Nina Masel's obituary in the *Guardian*, 5 June 2004 for further details of her life as a Mass-Observer.

127 M-O A: D K5349, 27 October 1939.

128 M-O A: D5363, 14 January 1940.

129 M-O A: D5385, 18 June 1940.

130 M-O A: D5376, 7 March 1941.

131 M-O A: D5390, 17 September 1940.

132 M-O A: D5427, 1 February 1941.

133 Ibid.

134 M-O A: D5427, 7 February 1941.

135 M-O A: D5427, 22 February 1941.

136 M-O A: D5344, 17 December 1943.

137 M-O A: D5226, 1 December 1941.

138 M-O A: D5390, 17 September 1940.

139 M-O A: D5349, 18 November 1939.

140 M-O A: D5395, 4 February 1945.

141 M-O A: D5412, 5 January 1943.
142 M-O A: DR 1325, March 1939.
143 M-O A: DR 1178, March 1939.
144 See *AJR Information*, September 1964 to December 1965 for discussion of the setting up of the Fund and Berghahn, *Continental Britons*, p. 142 for general discussion.
145 See, in particular, the work of Anthony Grenville. See, for example, Marian Malet and Anthony Grenville (eds), *Changing Countries: The Experience and Achievement of German-Speaking Exiles from Hitler in Britain from 1933 to Today* (London: Libris, 2002) and Grenville, *Continental Britons*, based on an exhibition at the Jewish Museum, London (May to October 2002).
146 For an analysis of the approach of *AJR Information*, first published in January 1946, see Tony Kushner, 'Comparing Antisemitisms: A Useful Exercise?', in Michael Brenner, Rsiner Liedtke and David Rechter (eds), *Two Nations: British and German Jews in Comparative Perspective* (Tubingen: J.C.B. Mohr, 1999), pp. 104–9.
147 Felicity Nussbaum, 'Toward Conceptualizing the Diary', in James Olney (ed.), *Studies in Autobiography* (New York: Oxford University Press, 1988), p. 137.

4

The *Kinder:* a case of selective memory?

The narrator in the late W.G. Sebald's last novel remembers a visit to the Belgian fort of Breendonk, used by the Nazis from 1940 to 1944 as a reception and penal camp. His mood became dark as

> I think how little we can hold in mind, how everything is constantly lapsing into oblivion with every extinguished life, how the world is, as it were, draining itself, in that the history of countless places and objects which themselves have no power of memory is never heard, never described or passed on.[1]

The subject of the novel, Jacques Austerlitz, arrived in Britain in the summer of 1939 as a five-year-old on the *Kindertransport*. His Christian hosts decided to bring him up erasing all memory of his past history and identity. Only on retirement does Austerlitz decide to reverse his earlier avoidance of his hidden past. Based loosely on a BBC documentary on a real former *Kind*, Susie Bechhofer, the themes of suppressed and denied memory, of loss, of rupture in the movement of people leading to the intimate but surpressed connections between the local and the global, permeate Sebald's work.[2]

There is a certain irony that Sebald, who shared with Bechhofer a birthday, a birthplace, and what he called the 'seas of silence' over the war, should choose to write about the lost memory of the *Kinder*.[3] Of all refugee movements in twentieth-century Britain, both large and small, it is the arrival of what turned out to be close to ten thousand children in the last ten months of peace that has produced the largest number of histories, memoirs, exhibitions, plays, documentaries, films (including the Academy award-winning *Into the Arms of Strangers*), and memorials. It is possible, for example, that in bringing written life histories, both published and unpublished, together with oral and video testimony that as many as one thousand former *Kinder* have provided some permanent account of their lives.[4] That up to 10 per cent of those involved in a major historical experience should record their experiences is perhaps unprecedented – in stark contrast, for example, to accounts from Belgian refugees in Britain during the First World War which are scarce, even though 250,000 came to this country. More broadly, we would expect literally millions of memoirs from participants in the two world wars even when confined to the United Kingdom if the same percentage held true as with the *Kinder*, rather than the few thousands that exist in reality.[5] And yet, for all its relative prominence in the memory of refugees, Sebald was right to reflect on the persisting absences that surround the memory of the *Kinder*. These lacunae are particularly noticeable, in spite of (or even because of) the amount written about this refugee movement, in the field of critical history writing and other forms of memory work. It is an intriguing case study in which the initial entry of these refugees, then an iconic moment, was soon to be lost in a wider narrative of Britain at war, only to be rediscovered some sixty years later. Only recently and incompletely, for example, has a recognition taken place of the *Kinder* at the level of post-war collective memory in Britain. Ken Livingstone, mayor of London and veteran proponent in principle (if not in practice), of anti-racism, confessed when addressing a Holocaust memorial event in January 2002 sponsored by the Pink Triangle Coalition, at Liverpool Street Station, site of what was to become a major memorial to the *Kinder*, that 'Until today, I did not know that Jewish children had escaped to London before the Second World War'.[6] This chapter explores the interrelated, if not inversely proportioned processes of remembering and forgetting that have surrounded the *Kindertransport*. How have the *Kinder* been remembered and represented, including by themselves, and why has interest recently grown so markedly in their experiences at an international level? Is this apparent surplus of memory a reflection of our belated coming to terms with the losses of the Holocaust or, alternatively, a failure to confront the full horror of the past and, more specifically, Britain's past record of refugee entry and exclusion?

Memory and the persecution of children

It is estimated that of the six million Jews who perished in the Holocaust, one and a half million were children. Given that little was written of the victims, other than by the survivors themselves in their memorial books, or in privately published memoirs and by obscure publishers in small print runs, as was the case with Primo Levi,[7] and given also the general failure until recently to accept the importance of the history of childhood,[8] it is not surprising that these Jewish children would fail to achieve recognition for so long. The first major history, *Children With A Star: Jewish Youth in Nazi Europe*, by Deborah Dwork, was published as late as 1991.[9]

Reflecting on why, some fifty years on, in spite of what had developed as a massive literature on the Second World War, Nazism and the Holocaust, 'Children are conspicuously, glaringly, and screamingly silently absent', Dwork concluded that it was

> not surprising that this should be so. When we think of 'society' we understand this to mean the world of adults. Our dominant paradigm is that society consists of productive, or voting, or participatory members. The only place children have in that scheme is as future participants, the citizens of tomorrow … Indeed, the usual theme of children's history has been child-rearing practices and education, in other words, how adults develop the next generation of adults.[10]

It is asked of adult victims, either implicitly or explicitly, why they did not do more to resist. Such questions, however inappropriate, cannot be asked of the defenceless child. It is obvious, remarks Dwork, 'that the only meaningful question is not "why did you allow this to happen to you?" but "why was this allowed to happen?"'.[11] Dwork thus explains the absence of attention to children through our attachment to the core of civilised values – studying the persecution of children enables 'an understanding of the *Shoah* stripped bare of all rationalizations, explanations, or justifications, in other words, with an apperception of the quintessence of this evil'. The *Shoah*, argues Dwork, represents the 'most radical challenge our society has experienced' and the failure to focus on the 'heart of that catastrophe', the murder of the children, reflects our failure to confront that challenge.[12]

Dwork embraces the 'emotional difference' relating to the one and a half million who, she suggests, her fellow historians have failed to confront and 'so, like everyone else, they have been loath to pursue the subject'.[13] Dwork is right to point to this absence in the literature, one that has been distressful particularly to the young survivors of the Holocaust. The young undoubtedly experienced their persecution differently, and were treated in specific ways by the perpetrators. Her book is a brave one, stripping away the moral failure to confront such a huge and distressing part of the Holocaust. Nevertheless, there are potential dangers if sentiment, as demanded by Dwork, comes to the fore: there is the implication, however indirect, that adult victims, especially men, were somehow less innocent than the children and the possibility that mawkishness might, unless one is careful, replace critical engagement. Aware of these pitfalls, the film maker Claude Lanzmann, whose film *Shoah* (1985) avoids any form of sentimentality, has refused to accept that the murder of the children was somehow worse or different from the murder of adults.[14] Not surprisingly, however, more commercially oriented representations of the Holocaust do use the murder of the children differently, as exemplified in Steven Spielberg's *Schindler's List* (1993). Filmed in black and white, only one Jewish figure amongst the multitude – a little girl dressed in red – is differentiated. Such individualisation culminates with her being shot dead in the liquidation of the Cracow ghetto. The girl becomes the only personally identifiable victim in the mass murder, enabling a gesture towards the humanisation of the Jewish masses but also part of the film's descent 'into an irredeemable sentimentalism'.[15] But it remains the case that the progress made in the areas of women's and children's experience of the Holocaust has left other areas under-researched – for example there is also a need for the study of older victims in the Nazi era. Moreover, while most of the studies of the Holocaust have in their general focus been biased towards males, there are few if any studies on men *as men* and the impact of persecution on their sense of masculinity.[16] In short, we require an inclusive gender analysis of the Holocaust and similarly a life cycle approach rather than regarding children as the only group with age-specific experiences.

Whether sentimental or not, there has been some attempt since Dwork's book was published to confront the murder of the children. Taking the case of Anne Frank, the most famous victim of the Holocaust and of the Second World War more generally, there has been a move away from the Broadway and Hollywood portrayals in the 1950s, which ended on notes of optimism and within the secret annex, to Oscar-winning documentaries and television serialisations in the 1990s and in the twenty-first century which at least accept her and her sister's death in the filth and misery of Bergen Belsen.[17] Similarly, the desire amongst critics and public alike that Benjamin Wilkomirski's *Fragments* be an authentic autobiographical account of a Holocaust childhood, rather than fiction, reflected at least in part the hope that the child victims had found a true voice to communicate their collective experiences.[18] Nevertheless, it is extremely doubtful whether we are yet ready to confront the searing questions posed by Dwork in relation to the million and a half Jewish children.

One indication of that failure is the attention given to those who were successfully hidden during the war. In 1993, *The Hidden Children: The Secret Survivors of the Holocaust*, by Jane Marks, was published, prompted by a reunion of survivors held in New York in 1991. Its preface was written by Abraham Foxman, National Director of the Anti-Defamation League and himself a former hidden child. Her book was, according to Foxman, 'an extraordinary contribution to an understanding of the Holocaust'. The first-person accounts 'by those who survived the war against Jewish children preserves for history the courage and resources of the hidden as well as those who rescued them'. For Foxman 'these inspiring accounts symbolize the triumph of good over evil … [it]

is also a story of hope. Those who survived depended on the goodness and kindness of others'.[19]

The desire for a happy ending is also revealed in Roberto Benigni's *Life is Beautiful* (1998). For all of its powerful attributes, the success, popular if not critical, of this Oscar-winning film is based on the survival ultimately of the hero's son, Giosue. The film is self-consciously and explicitly a fable or fairy tale; it is, as the director has stated 'a story about a father who is trying to protect a child' and not, as he has made clear, 'a story about the Holocaust'.[20] The story of the Holocaust is about the utter impossibility of parents to protect their children, a fact that the influential child psychologist, and Jewish refugee, Bruno Bettelheim totally failed to understand in relation to his criticisms of Otto Frank.[21]

The post-1945 memory of the murdered and hidden children in the Holocaust thus fits within a complex and dynamic matrix made up of longstanding ignorance and marginalisation, celebration, sentimentality and hope for the future. It will be argued here that the parallel memory of the *Kinder* can be understood within a similar framework. It is one that has allowed intense contemporary engagement, followed by a period of amnesia and then the present abundance of memory leading, on the one hand, to the beginnings of heritage construction and, on the other, to the absence of history and critical reflection. If, as has been suggested in previous chapters, the refugees from Nazism have received privileged status in recent memory construction, the children amongst them have become doubly set apart, both special and celebrated.

The origins of the *Kindertransport*

Some refugee movements in the twentieth century have been largely and deliberately hidden from the public gaze – the state, whether at a national or local level, has regarded the invisibility of refugees as the second best option if exclusion has proved impossible or illegal. In the Labour Party's White Paper on asylum, immigration and citizenship, *Secure Borders, Safe Haven* (2002), for example, the government maintained that dispersal was right – in spite of the appalling failings of its policy in sending asylum seekers to depressed areas where they have been isolated and subject to extreme violence, including murder.[22] Dispersal was 'designed to ensure that the burden on services is shared across the country ... This principle will be upheld as new trial Accommodation Centres are developed'.[23] In contrast, there have been specific groups of refugees from particular places at critical moments whose arrival and settlement in Britain has not only been officially acknowledged but also highlighted and triumphed. This was true, at least initially, with the Belgian refugees during the First World War, the Ugandan Asians in the 1970s, the Vietnamese boat people in the 1980s and most recently the Kosovans in 1999. But by far the most blatant case was with the *Kindertransport* late in 1938 and early in 1939. In each example there was also opposition to these arrivals at all levels of British society, including within Westminster and Whitehall. Yet it was the positive virtues of the British response that were stressed both at the time and subsequently.

In May 1938, following the *Anschluss*, the Permanent Under-Secretary at the Colonial Office, Sir Cosmo Parkinson, wrote that however much one sympathised with, as he put it, 'the wretched Jews in Austria', the fact remained that it was 'not specially for His Majesty's Government to find homes for Jewish refugees'.[24] Both legally in terms of the absence of international protection of refugees and in practice in relation to post-1918 British immigration policy, there was no reason for Britain to embark on any scheme of mass rescue of refugees. The right to asylum for those 'seeking admission to this country solely to avoid persecution or punishment on religious or political grounds' had been inserted into the Aliens Act of 1905.[25] It was absent in the Aliens Restriction Act of 1919. The Labour Home Secretary, J.R. Clynes, told a delegation from the Board of Deputies of British Jews in 1930 that 'The "right of asylum" in so far as it exists or ever existed is not a right attaching to an alien, but is a right of the Sovereign State to admit a refugee if it thinks fit to do so'. Clynes outlined that *individual* applications for refuge might be looked upon sympathetically, but that was as far as he could go.[26] His Conservative predecessor, William Joynson-Hicks was less circumspect in his language: 'The entry of aliens to this country was not a right, it was a privilege'.[27] From 1933 through to the summer of 1938, assisting a relatively small number of carefully selected individual refugees, helped by a guarantee provided by British Jews in 1933 that such arrivals would not become a charge on the state, was government policy with only a few thousand refugees allowed entry into Britain.[28] Why then was a decision made to help not individuals but a *group* of Jewish refugees in November 1938?

In the parliamentary debate on refugees in late November 1938, when the scheme to help the children was officially announced, the tradition of Britain offering asylum to 'the afflicted and the distressed' was a recurring theme.[29] Throughout the 1920s Home Secretaries had told Jewish delegations that asylum could only be offered if the domestic situation allowed for it and if those seeking entry were worthy of entry. As late as July 1938 at the international conference on refugees at Evian, the British representative, Lord Winterton had warned that 'the United Kingdom is not a country of immigration. It is highly industrialised, fully populated and is still faced with the problem of unemployment.'[30]

The other fear was of domestic antisemitism, one that particularly concerned the Home Secretary, Sir Samuel Hoare, as we have seen in chapter 3. Hoare, however, had been convinced in November 1938 by Jewish refugee workers who had pointed out the successful integration of Belgian refugee children during the First World War. The maintenance of the children, the Jewish delegation assured, would be met by the refugee organisations and by generous individuals. Hoare told the Commons that 'So also with these Jewish and non-Aryan children, I believe that we could find homes in this country without any harm to our own population.' The parallel to the Belgians had a wider significance: through granting asylum 'we played an invaluable part in maintaining the life of the Belgian nation'.[31] The child refugees from Nazism were to be a generation kept safe but the intention was to grant only a temporary home – temporary transit visas were granted to the *Kinder*, as was the case with almost all Jews entering in the 1930s. Nevertheless, in contrast to the official line of governments since 1919, the impression was given in the Commons debate that the post-war aliens legislation had never been intended to keep out those being persecuted abroad.

The re-discovery of the concept of asylum in November 1938 depended on the combination of several factors. First, there was widespread repulsion, amongst the public as well as at parliamentary level, against the *Kristallnacht* pogrom. While the anti-alienism of sections of the press and society as a whole did not disappear after 9/10 November 1938, there were few who could justify (or sufficiently explain) the open viciousness of this night of terror and the Nazis' subsequent actions against the Jews. Many, such as Prime Minister Chamberlain, who were critical of the Jews and uneasy with their presence, were nevertheless genuinely appalled by the details of the pogrom.[32] Yet such sympathy (if not empathy) was a necessary but not sufficient factor in opening up the doors of entry. The intense antisemitic violence accompanying the *Anschluss*, for example, some eight months earlier, had not led to a major shift in policy, and the Evian conference led only to small modifications in British immigration procedures. Even so, such concessions to generosity put Britain ahead of many other countries that had attended the international gathering.[33] Rather than the response to the pogrom alone, other inter-related factors have to be taken into account in explaining why the *Kindertransport* scheme came into existence. Guilt (and an attempt to compensate for it) has been the motivating force for most of the generous moments of British refugee policy in the twentieth century, whether in the case of the failure of Britain to intervene militarily as with the Belgians in the First World War, the Czechs in 1938, the Hungarians in 1956, and former Yugoslavs in the early 1990s, or with the Poles after

1945 and British tacit acceptance of Communist control in the country.[34] In the case of the Jews in the latter part of 1938, the open-ended *Kindertransport* scheme has to be seen alongside the failure to protest meaningfully at a diplomatic level against the intensification of Nazi antisemitism and also the closing of the doors of Jewish entry to Palestine. Indeed, the scheme for children to be allowed into Britain came at the same time that demands for a similar project for Palestine were being turned down.[35]

Such contextualisation does not remove the significance and importance of the *Kindertransports*. For example the British government could have followed the example of its American counterpart and rejected a child refugee scheme. The Wagner-Rogers Bill was introduced in February 1939 and called for the entry of 20,000 German children over a two-year period *above* normal immigration quotas. The scheme was rejected. President Roosevelt refused to challenge the restrictionists in Congress and in the American public as a whole – in spite of much evidence of humanitarian sentiment in support of the Bill.[36] One of the great failings, for example, of W.D. Rubinstein's best-selling *The Myth of Rescue: Why the Democracies Could Not Have Saved More Jews from the Nazis* (1997), is its failure to give contemporaries any choice.[37] It was not inevitable that the Wagner-Walters Bill would have been defeated nor that the proposal put forward by Jewish campaigners in November 1938 would have met the approval of the nervous Home Secretary who, in the parliamentary debate, stated that there was 'an underlying current of suspicion and anxiety ... about alien immigration on any big scale'.[38] Nevertheless, the generosity of the *Kindertransport* scheme cannot simply be seen as a response to the increasing desperation of its recipients – those had largely been ignored before the pogrom. Nor can the specific focus of the scheme be explained by particular need; it was essentially Jewish male adults who were especially vulnerable after the pogrom with up to 30,000 interned in concentration camps such as Dachau and Buchenwald.[39] It is thus important to focus on the question that few now seem willing to ask: why *just* the children?

The question was in fact raised from the start. Sir Samuel Hoare himself stated in the House of Commons 'I could not help thinking what a terrible dilemma it was to the Jewish parents in Germany to have to choose between sending their children to a foreign country, into the unknown, and continuing to live in the terrible conditions to which they are now reduced in Germany.' Having been told by a Quaker representative that the parents would be willing to part with their children, the Home Secretary announced that 'we shall put no obstacle in the way of children coming here'.[40] The former Prime Minister, Lord Baldwin, in his famous radio broadcast on behalf of the child refugees in December 1938, which itself became the stuff of instant and iconic memory work (with, amidst other promotions, a record of it sold to raise money), echoed Hoare's comments: 'Thousands of parents are appealing to the refugee committees to take their children out of Germany, even though they may never see them again'.[41] But Baldwin and Hoare were not probing very far: while it was, of course, the Nazis who were responsible for persecuting the Jews, and making the process of emigration as tedious and humiliating as possible, it was the receiving or potential receiving countries that were ultimately determining who could and could not leave. From 1938 through to autumn 1941, emigration, alongside maximum financial extortion, remained the official Nazi policy towards the Jews of Greater Germany. The dilemma outlined by Hoare was one that his government and state apparatus had created. The scheme to rescue children alone had been suggested by the Jewish refugee workers not out of callousness but from a calculated assumption that it was as far as the government could be pushed.[42] As both shared an obsessive, and mutually reinforcing, fear of domestic antisemitism it also suited their mutual nervousness. As Louise London states bluntly: 'Admission saved the children's lives. Exclusion sealed the fate of many of their parents.'[43]

Early histories and representations

Right from the start, rather than acknowledge the inherent problem with the scheme, policy was couched in the most positive and humane terms. Hoare told the Commons that 'Here [was] the chance of taking the young generation of a great people'. Rather than ignore reference to their mothers and fathers, Hoare emphasised that we might 'mitigat[e] to some extent the terrible sufferings of their parents and friends'.[44] The parents were presented as fundamentally damaged by Nazism and fatalistically beyond rescue, taking us back to the gothic 'living dead' of chapter 2, and a theme that was to re-occur in later memory work on the *Kindertransport*.[45] Similarly the organisation set up to administer the scheme – the Movement for the Care of Children from Germany, later to become the Refugee Children's Movement, or RCM – was anxious both in terms of its contemporary reputation, and, it must be argued, for the sake of posterity, to justify its actions. Its first annual report, covering the period from November 1938 to December 1939, started in defensive mode, arguing that it was 'thought worth while for the benefit of all to restate some of the facts that made it necessary to bring into this Country nearly 10,000 children, between the ages of 2 months and 16 years and to explain to the more critical why mistakes were made and why delays occurred'.[46]

This annual report was the first attempt to claim legitimacy for the RCM and its actions. It involved outlining the RCM's historical precedents, most specifically the Inter-Aid Committee which, since 1936, had been helping on a small scale to rescue vulnerable children. In the Commons, earlier examples of aid to refugee children were cited for similar reasons.[47] Further, the RCM's annual report outlined the desperate letters that had been received from Germany and Austria 'begging for help'. Many, the report added, 'were so touchingly written that it required a hard heart to consign them to files and indexes'. Nevertheless, the RCM had to show it had responded rationally and responsibly to such pleas. It legitimised its actions by highlighting how permits were granted on grounds of prioritising those children who were at particular risk and whose parents approved of their emigration.[48] Third, it did so by employing the voice of the refugees themselves by including the condensed diary entries of Leo W., a fourteen-year-old boy 'who is now in England'. His diary covered the anxious days before the declaration of war.

On 20 August 1939, Leo's diary outlined his fear which could only be solved by emigration: 'At the first answer I have I shall go away from Germany, no matter what country it will be, only to be far from this hell'. The innocence of the Jews was then emphasised in the published extract, thereby confronting the unevenness of contemporary understanding in Britain about why the Jews were being persecuted, as was apparent in the Mass-Observation directive responses analysed in the previous chapter. '[W]e are driven away like animals, but where is our guilt?'. The day after his permit to Britain arrived 'God thank! … I am so glad, I can't describe it'. Four days later he arrived by ship from the Hook of Holland in a group that was tired, seasick, but relieved to be away from danger.[49]

The reproduced diary entry appears unspontaneous, written after the arrival in Britain and most likely with encouragement and input from members of the RCM. Its tone is almost apologetic and the build up towards gratitude provides a comforting narrative. The diary entries do acknowledge Leo's parting from his mother who went with him to the station where 'we separated for years'. Yet the trauma of such separations, which have grown exponentially with time, is mitigated in his account. Rather crudely, an opportunity is taken to stress the previous patriotism and good citizenship of German Jewry. The diarist's father had died two years earlier 'suffering from wounds he received in the war. He fought for the country which now sends us out'. The mother, however, is not left to her fate in Germany. She has a visa for America and was to depart the following day. The loss of his father enables the boy to be presented as even more vulnerable and therefore in need of temporary British refuge. Nevertheless, the possible cruelty of separating Leo from his mother through the *Kindertransport* is mitigated: their parting would not be permanent – only the Atlantic and not the Nazi state would stand between them being united. Ultimately, Leo's story has a redemptive ending: 'we were happy to be on English and free ground'.[50]

The same approach to the RCM's first annual report was adopted by Gladys Bendit, writing under the pseudonym of John Presland, who published an account of the organisation in 1944. Significantly its title was more suited to a 'Boy's Own' tale than the harrowing one it described: *A Great Adventure: The Story of the Refugee Children's Movement*. In this first history of the RCM, the *Kindertransport* was domesticated and made palatable to a British Home Front audience. Again, the persecution of Jewish and non-Aryan children in Nazi Germany, as opposed to adults, was highlighted:

> They were set apart from other children in the class rooms, they were forbidden to join in sports or games and the pupils were encouraged, sometimes even instructed by the teachers, to torment them in a hundred ways. Reliable witnesses stated that the number of child-suicides greatly increased in these years and was a sad indication of their suffering.[51]

Emphasis was also placed on 'Generous British hospitality', especially from ordinary people, Jewish and Christian, and how this helped over 9,000 be 'saved', a term used frequently in recent years in relation to the *Kinder*, especially in the Hollywood documentary *Into the Arms of Strangers* (2000).[52] 'Saved' had clear Christian connotations but it is also implied that the rest, the adults, were, in the depths of the Nazi beast, beyond reach. *A Great Adventure* was thus an early example of what has become a powerful trope of Holocaust representation – the portrayal of rescuers of Jews as redemptive figures or, more unusually, as redemptive communities – in this case the British nation. The potential for such saviours to be presented through a Christian discourse was realised, many argue, through Spielberg's depiction of Oskar Schindler.[53] The charge of Christian influence on the RCM, as will emerge shortly, was also levelled by its contemporary critics.

Bendit ended by acknowledging that 'Nothing ha[d] been said of the personal histories of all these children, of the miseries from which they escaped; of the fear and bewilderment with which they found themselves refugees in a strange land, having different habits, ways of thoughts and speech'. Instead, the emphasis was that through the 'untiring efforts of the Movement's workers, the natural kindliness of the public and the humanity and patience of the authorities has restored to a large number a sense of security in this society of ours'. In turn, the *Kinder* had shown intense loyalty and contributed intensely to the forces and war work.[54] Without the Movement, however imperfect, Bendit stated categorically 'these children must have suffered death, or a fate far more horrible than death, if they had been left within the frontiers of the Greater Reich'. Anticipating so much recent commemoration, she concluded by stating that while 'In the appalling total of refugees with which post-war Europe will be faced, the figure of ten thousand is a small one', it was still the case that 'each one of these ten thousand [was] a sentient human being' who had been rescued and saved.[55]

Throughout *A Great Adventure*, reference to the children's parents is notable by its absolute absence. This silence is not accidental but crucial to the dynamics of the RCM's and government's justification of the project: in essence a younger generation had found what Bendit called 'not only an abiding place among us, but a spiritual home'.[56] What had happened to the parents, or the children's grief and anxiety over their fate, were not allowed to interfere with the overarching narrative of the RCM's achievements.[57] Indeed, in only one of its printed documents, and in this case an internal one from 1940 offering 'instructions for the guidance of regional and local committees', was explicit reference made to the *Kinder*'s parents. Even then it was relegated under the medical sub-heading 'Problem Children'. It warned that 'bed-wetting, petty pilfering, lying and similar signs of instability of character are sometimes symptoms of deep-seated nervous disturbance and should not be lightly dismissed or treated by penal methods'. It added that 'Often their emotional disturbance is due to anxiety for the fate of their parents in Nazi Germany.' It was these specific children who became, in the RCM's words, exceptional 'problem children who need and deserve kindness and patience to help them overcome their difficulties'.[58] Otherwise, however, it was the restorative qualities of British society and the successful adjustment to it by the children that dominated the RCM's version of their 'great adventure'.

The first arrival of the *Kinder* in Britain in late December 1938 and early in 1939 generated much public and media interest. Photographs in the press alongside newsreels emphasised the vulnerability of the children, some clutching teddy bears and dolls, the pathos and marginality highlighted further by their number labels around their necks given to them by the refugee organisations.[59] The headline and accompanying photograph in the *Mirror* some sixty years later as the carefully selected Kosovan refugees arrived in Britain hardly differed in tone or content: 'Safe but Shattered' and, one might add, implied but never stated openly, utterly innocent.[60] Recent artistic representations of the *Kinder*, including the national memorial in Liverpool Street station, replicate this childhood vulnerability.[61] Such visual representation conforms to what Liisa Malkki has referred to as the 'expectation of a certain kind of *helplessness* as a refugee characteristic'.[62] The arrival of the *Kinder* merited international attention, a phenomenon recently revived with the growing interest in this refugee movement especially in the United States. *The New Yorker*'s British reporter covered the *Kinder*'s arrival, as one commentator has put it, 'one of the many journalists who turned up regularly at Liverpool Street in search of a heart-warming story'.[63] Other common images of the *Kinder* emphasise their smiling on arrival at Harwich and Southampton – as *Picture Post* argued, they may have left their country, their parents, their friends and everything they had, 'But they are free. They are in a land where they will not be despised on account of race'.[64]

The narrative of *Picture Post* and its feature on the Dovercourt camp set up in December 1938 for the *Kinder* was somewhat different from other contemporary media accounts. While it paid due respect to British decency and generosity, it focused more on emphasising that the children had a future. Through re-training in Britain as useful workers they could then 'help to fill up those empty spaces in the Empire, which are at present in need of men and women equally to develop and defend them'. In contrast to many other representations in the press which were of female *Kinder* or the very young, *Picture Post* produced a more challenging image of young, athletic boys who were 'lively, sturdily built, intelligent'. It was clear, however, that the journal recognised that its readers might have been challenged by this strident representation of the boys' masculinity. This potential threat was countered by emphasising that their future might well be in the Empire. Generally, however, even *Picture Post* accepted the logic of the government's position on helping youngsters at the expense of their parents: 'They have had to abandon their homes and families, perhaps for good, for it is easier to assimilate children into the nation's life than grown-up people'.[65]

Picture Post, with its strong refugee connections – its founder was Stefan Lorant, one of 'Hitler's emigrés' – was willing to make a less defensive statement about the *Kinder* and their permanent future place in Britain or its empire.[66] This, in some ways, was a risky decision of what was an innovative and progressive example of British photojournalism. It must not be assumed, with the benefit of hindsight, that the entry of the *Kinder* was without controversy. A reminder of contemporary tensions is provided by the Mass-Observation directives of March 1939 and responses they gathered specifically relating to the child refugees.

Contemporary responses to the *Kinder*

Norman Angell and Dorothy Buxton's *You and the Refugee*, which outlined positively 'the morals and economics of the problem', was published at the same time as the Mass-Observation directive. It began by outlining how

> Each morning's paper brings us usually further news of further miseries
> inflicted upon ever-increasing numbers of civilised men and women at our
> doors. We see pictures of even tiny children at our ports, labelled like
> parcels, bundles of forlorn and helpless childhood, homeless, parentless,
> seeking refuge and sanctuary from the storm of cruelty and oppression
> which has swept their parents to penury, imprisonment, torture, death.[67]

The Pathé newsreels and newspaper photographs of the children arriving and settling into hostels undoubtedly made a profound initial impact
and the directive responses provide evidence to support Angell and
Buxton's analysis. It was typified by an engineer's draughtsman from
Surrey who, combining his own feelings with those he perceived around
him, wrote that 'Personally, the pitiful scenes depicted in newspapers of
child refugees hugging their pathetic little goods and chattels has done a
lot, I think, to influence British public opinion. It has brought home to
one the sorrow and suffering wrought by the Fascist countries against
the Jews.'[68] It was often through reports of the arrival of small numbers
of *Kinder* that Observers gained a sense of the overall scale of refugees
coming to Britain, thereby tending to underestimate the total.[69] The directives also provide evidence of the successful integration of the *Kinder*
at local schools and more generally. A Jewish respondent from Newport,
South Wales, had talked to a child refugee taken in by a Jewish family
and 'he says he is treated with the greatest possible kindness and consideration at his school'.[70] An Observer in Kent reported on a local hostel
and school that had been set up for Jewish refugee boys, commenting
that 'They are particularly well behaved and have created a good impression as compared with the Basque refugee children here, who are somewhat unruly.'[71] Yet such positive sentiments were not unchallenged. The
fears and ambivalence outlined over the impact of Jewish refugee adults
were also present, if articulated slightly differently, with regard to the
children.

A Scottish steelworker commented on his 'sympathy when [watching]
Pathé newsreels', but added that it was tempered with an uneasy feeling
that 'charity begins at home'.[72] Others were less cautious about their
opposition to funds given to the *Kinder* and other refugees, believing that
it had damaged support for 'our own unemployed from the distressed
areas' as such donations were less 'glamorous'.[73] A nurse, and reader of
the ultra-conservative and antisemitic weekly, the *Patriot*, believed that
the money given to support each child refugee through the Baldwin fund
and other collections was three times that of the British unemployed, and
five times that of British children in need of relief. She 'expect[ed] a revolution in Britain over this'.[74] Most striking in melding the alleged threat

posed by the *Kinder* and older refugees was the response of a female Observer from Hampstead:

> I think people feel sorry for the children now, but they won't like it when their children start to find work and they find so many Jews in the market at the same time. I think thousands of people feel, too, that these refugees are having a far better time than the children of the unemployed – I do.[75]

In the USA, the wife of the Commissioner of Immigration was to express such concerns less politely, arguing semi-privately that the problem with the Wagner-Rogers Bill was that '20,000 children would all too soon grow up into 20,000 ugly adults'.[76] While such blatant antipathy on either side of the Atlantic was rarely articulated publicly, it was still the case that support for the refugee children did not go unchallenged.

It was in this context of ambivalent responses that the government, refugee organisations and campaigners, in spite of the huge sympathy and offers of help that the child refugee movement had made manifest, were cautious to move beyond the specific fate of the *Kinder*. The underplaying, dismissal or silence of the separation from the parents thus ran across contemporary representations of the *Kinder* whether establishment or more radical as with *Picture Post*, domestic or international. We have seen how this could be manipulated to include the refugees themselves as was the case with the RCM's first annual report and Leo W.'s diary contained within it. In the case of another refugee diary, which has subsequently achieved some degree of fame, the content was not directly dictated. Nevertheless, it is even more revealing in that it discloses how the refugee children *thought* they should relate their experiences.

The Harris House diary was written by a group of young girls from February 1939 until February 1940. Harris House was a small hostel set up under the auspices of the RCM in Southport on the north-west coast of England. It initially housed nine girls and at its height held eighteen young refugees. It was closed down in 1940 as the coast became a protected area and all 'enemy aliens' had to be removed from it. The diary, or more accurately a general history of the home, was the product of many hands. As has been shown in the previous chapter, no diary, no matter how intimate and personal, is written without some kind of reader in mind, even if the intention is for it never to be put in the public realm. The Harris House diary was clearly written for an audience, although its preservation owed more to good fortune than design.

It is possible that the number of local refugee committees created in twentieth-century Britain could be as high as ten thousand, including, as has been noted, over two and a half thousand for the First World War Belgian refugees alone. It is telling that there has not been a detailed history written of even one of these committees.[77] The lack of value placed by society as a whole, especially by politicians, on refugee work, is reflected not only in this absence of historical reference but at a more basic level by the preservation or otherwise of relevant material. The fact that the Harris House diary remained in an attic for many decades and then was transferred to a junk stall says something about the place such material occupied in popular memory until recent years. But it was fitting that the diary should then be given to the Manchester Jewish Museum, the first body, as we have seen, to respect the heritage and history of ordinary refugees in Britain, whether they were of East European origin in the nineteenth and early twentieth century or from Nazi Germany in the 1930s. It has been part of the permanent display of the museum since it officially opened in 1984.[78]

In 1985 Yorkshire Television traced some of the girls who had lived in Harris House and an emotional reunion was organised with the matron, Margaret Stone, née Margarete Steinberg. Steinberg, who had been in charge of a larger Jewish children's home in Germany, acted as editor of the collective account, completed on the first anniversary of the hostel. In a brief analysis of the diary in her account of the *Kindertransport*, Rebekka Gopfert suggests that it 'was obviously put together under the supervision if not the instruction of an adult' and its overarching theme is one of gratitude towards Britain.[79] At a witness seminar held on the diary at the Manchester Jewish Museum in 1985 Margaret Stone emphasised that the entries were in fact written without interference. There is no reason to doubt the former matron's account, but what also emerged, perhaps not surprisingly, in the witness seminar from some of the former *Kinder* was that they wrote what they *thought* was expected of them. Their response was one that clearly shocked the former matron and was a poignant if difficult moment within the meeting.[80]

The matron's report in the diary stressed the progress made by the girls emotionally, educationally and physically, even including an indication of their weight gain.[81] The entry of the girls, however, in spite of the genuine gratitude expressed both at a general level to Britain and more specifically to those running Harris House, reveals their lives being dominated by two forces. The first was the need to get on, retrain and make a living within Britain (most were aged between fourteen and sixteen). In this respect, their accounts are positive and matter of fact, no matter how mundane the careers they were trained for, including domestic service – the occupation, alongside nursing, in which few barriers were placed by the Ministry of Labour. It allowed some 20,000 refugee women to come to Britain, if only several hundred men.[82]

The second theme exposes how in spite of the desire to write for their audience of the Harris House committee, the individual entries were still deeply personalised. The force of separation from parents was such a dominant part of their everyday lives that inevitably it shaped the testimony they provided of their first year in Britain, even if it ran counter to the narrative that no doubt was expected of them. The account of Lottie Gross within the diary is the most intensive in this respect. Her father was a farm manager near Vienna. As with so many autobiographical accounts of the *Kinder* or refugees in general where the years before persecution become idealised and 'home' constructed as a place of safety, love and warmth, Lottie related that she 'spent a very happy childhood at home'. In the four-page account, 'happy' is used five times, but by the end it is clear that it is the least appropriate word to describe her state of mind. Twice Lottie relates how 'I could be ever so happy if I would only know my parents [were] safe'. Since the outbreak of war her father had been imprisoned and she did not know where he was. She concluded her account by stating 'I do hope with all my heart that the time is not too far away when I can see my dear parents again and then I shall tell them all about the wonderful experiences I have had in England, amidst kindness, understanding, sympathy and loving care'.[83]

Gina (already Jean) Bauer, wrote in similar vein. Fifteen years old, she came from Vienna, 'a happy family ... I think I have the best parents in the world ... I never worried much about my future.' With the Nazi regimes 'all my hopes were destroyed'. When her father was taken to a concentration camp 'I felt that this was the end of my childhood and everything that went with it', reinforced when her mother and she were forced out of their home. In contrast to this grim portrayal of life under the Nazis, the tone changes to a rather forced cheerful tone when Gina relates her life as a refugee in Southport: 'I was very glad to be in England, in a free country. I love England very much'. In Southport she 'felt at home rightaway. I was glad to know that kind people had taken care of me'. This brief optimistic interlude was then followed by the final section of her entry relating to the outbreak of war – 'a big blow to all of us'. In her case it was especially tragic as her sister had arranged for her parents to come to England on 6 September. The war was thus 'a great shock for my sister amd me. God knows if we shall ever see our parents again. But yet I shall hope'.[84] Eva Reise from Magdeburg, who was training to be a chemist, outlined her busy day training and then coming back to do domestic chores. She ended her 'diary' entry simply and as evocatively as Jean: 'In the evenings I send my good wishes and dreams to my parents'.[85]

There is, in the early sections of the diary, a subtle and revealing struggle between the desire of the children to relate their individual testimony with all its heartbreaking separation and the desire to present an acceptable narrative to their hosts. In the later stages such wrestling with diverse voices disappears. Individuality is removed and the children write as a collectivity with the expectations of the readership coming more obviously to the fore. In an entry scripted together and entitled 'War', the children state briefly how their hopes were destroyed of their parents leaving Austria and Germany. There is no comment on this tragic state of affairs and instead, in what are the most contrived sentences in the diary – revealing their acute awareness of their marginal status as refugees who were tolerated in a conditional manner, especially now as enemy aliens – they write 'But we could not only think of ourselves, we cannot only think of ourselves! England, the country which we learned to love, the country which gave us hospitality is at war!'[86]

The war and after

During the war, the neat narrative structure of the *Kinder* was broken down. Evacuation, internment inside and outside the UK, re-emigration for several thousand, mainly to the USA, and general dispersal to war work and eventually for some, the armed forces, made it hard for the RCM to keep track of their charges in an organisation which, from its inception, struggled to deal with the scale and complexity of its operation alongside the scarcity of its funding and largely volunteer staff.[87] The major public issue with regard to the *Kinder* concerned their spiritual welfare which led to a bitter communal battle between the Jewish members of the RCM and sections of the orthodox community. It came to a head in 1944 when the Union of Orthodox Hebrew Congregations published an unrestrained attack on the RCM, *The Child Estranging Movement*, written anonymously by the Chief Rabbi's son-in-law and leading force behind the Chief Rabbi's Religious Emergency Committee, Solomon Schonfeld.[88]

Schonfeld had acted as a one-man rescue mission in the late 1930s, bringing to Britain close to one thousand children.[89] He was an irritant to the RCM partly because of his politically unorthodox techniques which were largely to act and then to contrive the official paperwork later, and partly because the RCM was often left to clear up the administrative and financial mess he left behind.[90] A separate memory of Schonfeld's rescue efforts, especially linked to those he helped rescue, has developed, one that remains very much within the very orthodox private domain.[91] The neglect of Schonfeld's rescue work in secular accounts of the *Kinder*, including Barry Turner's best-selling version, ... *And the Policeman Smiled*, published in 1990, where it is covered briefly and aside from the main narrative,[92] and most recently in the Imperial War Museum's permanent

Holocaust Exhibition (2000) where he is totally absent, is on the surface surprising.[93] The domination of the organisational successors to the RCM, the Central British Fund for World Jewish Relief, in the construction of *Kindertransport* memory – they sponsored Turner's book as well as histories of their own organisation written by Turner and Amy Gottlieb – partly explains Schonfeld's marginality in such semi-official memorialisation.[94] It is also to be explained at a more general level through the form of Jewish particularity he relentlessly pursued which was at odds with the more assimilationist tendencies of British society – ones that continue to influence policy with regard to the treatment of asylum seekers and refugees as well as ethnic minorities as a whole.

The battle between Schonfeld and his orthodox supporters and the RCM was on two levels. One was very practical – who should be looking after the children now and in the future, especially as in 1944 the question of the legal guardianship of the children was put to parliament.[95] The second was at the level of memory. It is no coincidence that *The Child Estranging Movement* and *The Great Adventure* were published in the same year – the former in January and the latter in July. The offensive nature of Schonfeld's pamphlet was matched by the defensive qualities of the RCM's response. Outside the Jewish community, however, these debates received little if any attention. Both the history and the counter-history were low level small publications and if Schonfeld had hoped to embarrass the RCM over the guardianship issue, he failed – guardianship for the children whose parents did not survive the war passed in 1944 to Lord Gorrell, chairman of the RCM.[96]

The concern of the RCM had always been to rescue as many children as possible and to put them in homes that were suitable, although suitability was largely determined by the foster parents' ability to cope financially with the cost of the children. For the Schonfeld camp, the refugee children were a saved remnant of the Jewish world, whose Jewishness, defined solely in religious terms, had to be preserved at all costs. In contrast, he proffered the accusation that the RCM's intention was 'to make these children forget all their past, to send them as ambassadors into the homes of Christian foster-parents where they will assimilate and create Christian-Jewish good-will'.[97] It ended by warning that unless action was taken against the RCM's policies, Anglo-Jewry would be 'blamed by the parents and by posterity for the tragedies that will ensue from the wholesale estrangement from Jewry and Judaism'.[98] To the RCM, a more universal aim was present in their hopes for the children which, as *A Great Adventure* concluded, was 'to have given to ten thousand children the opportunity to grow up in an atmosphere of decency and normality, to work, to play, to laugh and be happy and to assume their rightful heritage as free men and women'.[99]

Both the universal and the particular aims were sincerely held by people who had worked extraordinarily hard for the children and what they thought were their pressing needs; for the RCM practical matters of coping in Britain and for the Union of Orthodox Hebrew Congregations maintaining a Torah true faith. Oral histories and written testimonies of the *Kinder* as well as contemporary materials reveal on the one side many who adopted the practice if not the faith of Christianity in order to please their hosts, or sometimes, as with Susi Bechhofer, were forced to do so.[100] On the other, many children, of mixed parentage and secular upbringing, were thoroughly miserable in orthodox hostels.[101] What is significant, however, is that the trauma of separation from parents that the war years intensified massively, was not the major concern of either extreme of the refugee organisation camps. In the *Child Estranging Movement*, for example, the children were referred to as orphans at one point and with their parents surviving at others. Such apparent thoughtlessness confirms how adult Jews under Nazi control had ceased to be perceived as an active force by many involved in the *Kindertransport* scheme.[102]

It was to be another two decades before attention would again focus on the *Kinder*, their stories lost in different post-war narratives of the Nazi era. In 1966 Karen Gershon, a poet and former *Kind*, published her collective autobiography of the *Kindertransport, We Came As Children*. She explained her motives in a letter to her publisher: 'At the time of the twenty-fifth anniversary of the first children's transports I discovered that most of the documents of those days had been destroyed, and that many of the people who were concerned with our rescue no longer remember the events clearly or, like Anna Essinger, are dead. I decided then to collect what material I could before it was too late.'[103] There was no organisational structure of former *Kinder* and Gershon advertised in the national press for people to contact her. Some three hundred responded and her anthology uses the words of 234 of them. Emphasising further the fluidity of the movement, Gershon stressed how 'We all came in transit and there is no record of how many of us eventually stayed.'[104] Recent *Kinder* commemoration, organisationally and in terms of representation, has been international. It is telling that Gershon's account was confined within the nation state: 'Most of us had a choice at the end of the war; I have confined my enquiry to those who chose England. With their help I have compiled this record, in gratitude and as an explanation.'[105]

Gershon's last phrase, 'in gratitude and as an explanation', neatly summarises the internal tension in *Kinder* testimony that has existed since she compiled the volume in the 1960s. The need to express gratitude was there from their arrival in England, as has been shown in the contemporary diaries analysed earlier, and has never gone away, producing an ambivalence among the refugees. As one contributor put it:

> I shall always be grateful *now* for what was done for us then, although I wish it had not been rammed down my throat so much as a child who after all does not understand what wars and being refugees are all about. Now I understand better and I could have given my love and gratitude even in those early days if love had been given to me more freely.[106]

The need to explain was equally complex. Within the collection, it emerges as the need to explain to friends, acquaintances and especially family of who they were and where they came from. It was reflected in a review in the Association of Jewish Refugee's journal in 1962 of the first fictionalised account of the *Kinder*, Kenneth Ambrose's *The Story of Peter Cronheim*:

> Twenty odd years ago [this book] would have fulfilled the most important task of explaining to English children why so many young Central Europeans were turning up in their classrooms and at their playgrounds. It would have answered the recurring question, 'But *why* did you leave?', quite convincingly, and those teenage readers could then have passed on that explanation to their parents, who still did not know what this Hitler business was all about.[107]

But most striking is the richness of Gershon's deeply moving and desperately unsentimental collection created by the desire of the former *Kinder* to explain to themselves who they were. The anonymous contributions are terse and therefore do not reveal fully the complexities of each of the 234 individuals that would have emerged from a full life story. Nevertheless, they are artistically crafted together by Gershon, a neglected talent in the post-war British literature scene, to produce not one smooth narrative, but an astonishing collection of voices that show the complexities of belonging and not belonging and the contradictory pressures past and present operating on the former *Kinder*.[108] Floating between history, biography, literature and psychology, it offers one of the most profound insights into being a refugee in twentieth-century Britain. In the final section, 'Summing Up', the former *Kinder* reflect on that status: 'A refugee is someone who is not wanted in one place and given shelter in another out of pity. He is therefore forced to choose between death and charity'; 'If we had not remembered that we were refugees there were always others to remind us'.[109] As Gershon herself wrote in a later edition of the collective biography, from her home in Cornwall: 'I feel more at home in Israel than I do in England, but I don't feel at home there either, and that is worse, because I still expect to be able to feel at home. Here I am reconciled.'[110]

One of the most important chapters in the collective autobiography is entitled 'Death and Survival'. It opened with a quotation from Ambrose's *The Story of Peter Cronheim*, a didactic novel aimed at British children:

'"I won't go!" he shouted at his parents. "Why should I have to be pushed out on my own? I've done nothing wrong! I hate the Germans and I hate you"'. *We Came as Children* provided the first public forum for the grief of separation from parents before September 1939 and anxiety and depression caused by the lack of contact with parents after the outbreak of war.[111] The pattern of knowledge in *Kinder* accounts is relatively similar. Letters became increasingly infrequent and were replaced at best by messages from the Red Cross, eventually with the information for most, either in the war or after it, confirming the death of parents. But each individual reacted differently: from total denial at one end to publicly expressed grief at the other and including elements of anger, shame, guilt and heartbreak. Vera Schaufeld, who came to Britain from Czechoslovakia, was 15 when the war ended. Vera relates how she:

> then started having fantasies that really they were alive, and that they's started a new life in Shanghai or one of the places that they'd tried to get to, and had another family but just didn't want me ... I couldn't accept the reality ... I never saw anything [confirming their death]. [When the letters stopped from my parents] that was dreadful ... I think that I always thought somehow I hadn't written ... back enough [or] that they hadn't wanted to write ... I thought that they could come to me if only they wanted to enough.[112]

The impact of the news is disturbingly described in Sebald's *The Emigrants* (1993) when dealing with the semi-fictionalised refugee artist, Max Feber, who lives in Manchester. Feber had kept the news of his parents' death at bay but he tells the narrator that 'the fact is that the tragedy in my youth struck such deep roots within me that it later shot up again, put forth evil flowers, and spread the poisonous canopy over me which has kept me so much in the shade and dark in recent years'.[113]

The *Kinder* rediscovered

Gershon's volume was an isolated reminder of the *Kinder* in the first decades after the war. In the late 1970s and early 1980s, oral history projects, including at the Imperial War Museum and Manchester Jewish Museum reflected a general growth of interest in the refugee movement in the Nazi era, reflecting the growth of non-elitist history.[114] As we have seen in chapter 1, it was typified in the area of Jewish history by the pioneering work of Bill Williams and his talented Manchester Studies team, including Rickie Burman, later the curator of the London Museum of Jewish Life which was to create the first exhibition devoted to the *Kinder*, *The Last Goodbye: The Rescue of Children from Nazi Europe* (1996).[115] This successful touring exhibition, aimed particularly at schoolchildren, reflected the growing interest in the *Kinder* and went alongside a growing number of memoir publications. Such autobiographical practice was stimulated by demand for their writing which in turn validated the desire to record as the *Kinder* reached the end of their careers. Retirement provided both the time to reflect as well as the incentive to record for future generations before it was too late.[116]

Yet just as Karen Gershon had been alone in attempting a commemoration of the *Kinder* for its twenty-fifth anniversary, Bertha Leverton in 1988 realised that there were no plans to celebrate the jubilee of the scheme. A huge reunion took place in 1989 achieving national prominence – indeed, the success of the meeting reflected the initial media attention given to the idea of a reunion. For the first time, the *Kindertransport* was becoming part of the national history and heritage of Britain and was more generally connected to what were by then the beginnings of the huge growth in interest in the Holocaust. A collection of autobiographies was published, *I Came Alone* (1990) which was similar to Gershon's *We Came as Children* only in the large number of contributions that made it up – 243. In this later anthology, however, the autobiographical fragments were self-contained and presented alphabetically.[117] The individuality, as indicated in the title, reflected the growing interest in the life stories of ordinary people.[118] Unlike the earlier collection, however, the truncated stories reveal little of the emotion and complexity of the *Kinder* experience. Perhaps the best summary of this somewhat unwieldy collection is that provided in its original cover: 'It is a fitting tribute to the *Kindertransportees* and the generosity of their hosts, that so many survived to become upright and useful citizens of the countries in which they settled.'[119] Indeed, the success of the scheme and of the individuals in rebuilding their lives, creating their own families and successful careers is an increasing feature of *Kinder* representation, including the television documentary, *Rescued: A Sixty Year Journey* (2000).[120] Similarly, the organiser of the sixtieth anniversary, Bea Green, entitled her entry into the accompanying brochure 'Survival and Achievement'.[121]

In *Children Writing the Holocaust* (2004), Sue Vice has suggested that in *I Came Alone*, 'especially in contrast with Gershon's, appears barely edited'.[122] It is certainly the case that the testimonies in *We Came as Children* are artistically crafted and such skill is absent in the later anthology. Nevertheless, there was a strong editorial process at work in *I Came Alone*. The representation of Annette Saville's testimony within it provides an interesting case study of the collective narrative that was forged in the anthology and how testimonies that run counter to it were re-shaped. Although the frustrations of a musically-gifted person who missed out on utilising her talents professionally are made clear in her contribution,[123] the trauma of separation from her parents that pervades her longer autobiography, *Only a Kindertransportee* (2002) are absent in *I Came Alone*. Her impetus for writing this account of her life in Britain was to present 'the plain unvarnished truth of what happened to me in England'. Her autobiographical impulse also had a clear desire to balance the increasingly Whiggish representation of the *Kinder* experience: 'I have seen the damage, mental and emotional, which a lot of the "*Kinder*" still show, even to this day.'[124] Her autobiography ends bleakly in reflecting on the *Kindertransport*: 'Most of us would rather have died with our parents in concentration camps, or in my case, gone to Shanghai with them. The Jewish belief is that children's lives must be saved, but not at the cost of psychological damage, thank you very much!'[125] Saville's testimony in *I Came Alone* is not alone in being re-shaped – it has been suggested that the editing of Inge Joseph's testimony in the anthology omits 'large sections on Jacoby's homesickness to concentrate on a wider range of issues'.[126]

The reunion of 1989 had its own specific impact, leading to the formation of the Kindertransport Association. Its membership is based mainly in Britain. Nevertheless, reflecting the temporary legal status initially given to the *Kinder* before the war, many settled outside the UK. The Kindertransport Association has close to one thousand members in Canada, the USA and Israel alone with a complex form of *Kinder* diaspora belatedly developing.[127] Indeed, one of the entries in *I Came Alone* stresses that now she has her 'first *real* identity': 'I AM ONE OF THE KINDER'.[128] The poet, Lotte Kramer, who came to Britain from Mainz in July 1939, reflects the strength generated by such mutual activities in 'Kindertransport Reunion':

> A doddery crowd with the same history,
> We hug shoulders and clasp hands,
> Weeping, laughing at new nearness.[129]

The recognition and respect given to the *Kinder*, if belatedly, has, almost uniquely in twentieth-century refugee movements into Britain, allowed a pride rather than an embarrassment in refugee origins, a factor very much absent in the identity of the former children in Gershon's 1960s collection. An even earlier example of *Kinder* autobiographical practice – a school essay written during the Second World War – highlights further how the label 'refugee' during the Nazi era, rather than being embraced, was more often avoided as it implied inferiority. Anne Kopel came on a *Kindertransport* and then was reunited with her parents in Britain before moving on to America. Arriving in London, Anne was introduced to her foster family, and it was the first time I heard myself referred to as a refugee. It was a funny feeling, because I had never before considered myself as a refugee. It hurt, but when I thought it over, I knew that I was a refugee to these people who did not know me, to whom I was just a tired girl with a suitcase and a layer of dirt from the train and boat rides.[130]

Yet by the time of the first *Kinder* reunion in 1989, the condescension of the 1930s and 1940s, and then the indifference and invisibility of the post-war years, had given way to respect and increasing interest.

In June 1999, Bea Green organised the unveiling of a plaque at the House of Commons: 'In deep gratitude to the people and Parliament of the United Kingdom for saving the lives of 10,000 Jewish and other children who fled to this country from Nazi persecution on the Kindertransport 1938–1939'.[131] At a time when rampant anti-refugee sentiment was beginning to develop exponentially in the media, as well as in public discourse and in government behaviour, the prominence given to this plaque provided an intriguing example of memory work where the past and present were brought together in potential conflict. In September 2003 Flor Kent's memorial to the *Kindertransport* outside Liverpool Street station, *Für das Kind*, was unveiled with an almost identical message, with only the words 'and parliament' removed.[132] By this stage, the campaign against asylum seekers had reached fever pitch. That connections were not generally made between British refugee policy then and now was an indication of the respectability and acceptability of the *Kinder*. Some sixty years on there had been time enough for them to become viewed as decent citizens of Britain and no longer somewhat undesirable or pitiable aliens.

The *Kinder*, by the start of the twenty-first century, had become a safe story, put together neatly and with a redemptive ending. In the case of the Oscar-winning *Into the Arms of Strangers* (2000) even the losses were minimised with some of the children featured reunited with their parents after the war.[133] Sadly, this was not a very typical experience, and when it did happen, it was not always an easy one for all concerned, a theme deftly explored in Diane Samuel's *Kindertransport*, first performed in London in 1992. Samuel's play explores the tension between mother and daughter when the former returns from the camps. Neither can overcome their trauma based on the guilt of survival on the one hand and anger at being abandoned on the other. It leads to the daughter suppressing all recognition of her origins.[134] It still remains the case, however, that Samuel's play, which owes much to the testimonies in Gershon's *We Came as Children*,[135] and more critical individual autobiographies act counter to the increasingly dominant representation of the *Kindertransport* in which there are few questions asked about the generosity and wiseness of the scheme as a whole.

The *Kinder* have been incorporated into a Holocaust narrative, one with a powerful American influence. *Into the Arms of Strangers* is to be firmly located within this context, the cover of its book version proclaiming it tells the story of 'The British scheme that saved 10,000 children from the Nazi regime'. And just as with the earlier Hollywood blockbuster, *Schindler's List*, it has its happy ending in the form of the former child refugees successfully re-creating their lives across the world. Unusually for Hollywood, Britain emerges as the hero, with America as the (minor) villain for refusing to emulate the scheme in 1939. In the film, one of the arguments used against the Wagner-Rogers Bill, that separating children from their parents ran 'contrary to laws of God', is dismissed as a puerile excuse. Nowhere is it asked why Britain excluded their mothers and fathers.[136] *Into the Arms of Strangers* is thus 'Heartbreaking, but also inspiring and not without humour'. It consists of

> the stories of those who survived with the help of others; they are stories of courage and hope, stories about the strength and resolve of children; and most astonishingly, they are stories not yet heard about the impact of the Holocaust.[137]

More generally, we have seen in chapter 2 how, in the British context, the Christian rescuer has been personified in the form of Nicholas Winton, a British businessman who helped set up the *Kinder* scheme in Czechoslovakia. In documentaries, media features and now in biography, Winton, who has always downplayed his role and not sought recognition, has been transformed into 'Britain's Schindler', as has Foreign Office bureaucrat, Frank Foley. Vera Gissing, one of the Czech girls brought to Britain by Winton, states that 'He has become the much cherished father-figure of the largest family in the world, because our own parents had perished in the holocaust as surely we would have done without his swift and timely intervention. To him we owe our freedom and life'.[138] The complexity of the actions of Foley, Winton and of course Schindler himself are lost sight of in the desire to create what are in essence 'secular saints', or for the orthodox, a Jewish equivalent in the form of Solomon Schonfeld, perhaps one of the most difficult people to have operated at an organisational level in British Jewry during the twentieth century. In one testimony he appears almost as a timeless Golem, rescuing the Jews from their violent oppressors:

> Where is this Rabbi Dr Schonfeld? ... A man has entered. But no, he is not really a man, he is more like a giant. Like the giants in the Bible stories our father used to tell us on Friday nights. He is big and tall and broad-shouldered with a firm, strong stride and a ruddy beard and an undulating voice that is craggy like mountain ridges. He is quite old, like our father,

forty at least. But no, on the other hand he seems quite young, in fact ageless.[139]

The narrative structure is thus completed – the innocent children are rescued by the righteous nation and specific righteous individuals. They become a saved remnant of a lost people whose parents sacrificed their own happiness for the wellbeing of their children who subsequently made good. It is a neat storyline and one that is understandable given the need to respond positively to the unfathomable scale of the Holocaust. Its appeal, however, explains the lack of critical history on the subject and in such narratives we forget the essence of being a refugee, that of loss, and in the specific case of the *Kinder*, the irreparable fracture of their parents' absence. As Louise London puts it: 'We remember the touching photographs and newsreel footage of unaccompanied Jewish children arriving on the *Kindertransports*. There are no such photographs of the Jewish parents left behind in Nazi Europe, and their fate has made a minimal impact.'[140] Self-contained and self-congratulatory, the story becomes cut off from the messiness of modern refugee movements, including the existence of enormous numbers of unaccompanied refugee children today who can be counted not in the thousands but in the millions. Indeed it has been estimated that 'approximately one-half of the global refugee population comprises children under the age of 16'.[141]

Conclusion: struggles over *Kinder* memory

It is worth at this point returning to Karen Gershon's *We Came as Children* which remains the most powerful exploration of the identities and experiences of the *Kinder* in any genre. When the anthology was reviewed in 1966 there were those who desired to place it within the context of the general refugee experience and others who linked it more specifically to the Holocaust. The critic, John Carey, writing in the *New Statesman*, while putting the emphasis on the latter, was not oblivious to the former:

> Over here they froze in converted seaside chalets, then went to foster-homes. Often they were treated as servants by the wife. Still, they lived. Brothers and sisters who stayed behind were made into fertiliser at Auschwitz. Some who got as far as Holland were returned to Germany and used for medical experiments.[142]

The anonymous reviewer in *The Times* similarly raised the problems they faced in Britain but ultimately dismissed them with the crude moral sledgehammer of the alternative raised by Carey: 'the overriding moment must come from Auschwitz and Buchenwald. They did survive'.[143]

Not surprisingly, it was only within the refugee world itself that there was full appreciation of Gershon's success in documenting the dilemmas of adaptation. In the monthly journal of the Association of Jewish Refugees in Great Britain, Lucie Schachne focused solely on this aspect of *We Came as Children*. In particular she wrote of the difficulty in 'trying to keep their identity in spite of the handicap of a double labelling as "Jew" and "Refugee"'. Schachne believed that while focusing on the *Kinder*, many 'aspects of refugee mentality and present-day existence are highlighted in these pages [of Gershon's book], reflecting like a mirror problems and thoughts of the entire German Refugee Community here.'[144]

In terms of the contemporary reception of *We Came as Children*, attention focused more on 'How the refugees found us',[145] rather than an 'aware[ness] that the holocaust that had swept Hitler-Europe is by no means a thing of the past and forgotten, but a painful scar still vivid in the memories of its victims'.[146] Gershon, as Sue Vice has argued, turned her collective text into an examination of Englishness. Vice suggests that England takes on 'the role of promised land' in the 1966 anthology. It is true that the focus of the book, by excluding those *Kinder* who left Britain, is on England (even for those who had settled in Scotland). Yet rather than aspiring to Englishness, as Vice concludes, it is more convincing to view the testimonies as articulating its exclusive nature and ultimate impenetrability. As Vice herself concludes, 'If *We Came as Children* is a "thank-offering to Britain" it is an ambivalent one'.[147]

A generation later, the *Kinder* experience has increasingly been placed in the Holocaust context, the former children describing themselves as 'survivors' and unwittingly or not, a barrier drawn up with other refugee experiences. Bertha Leverton introducing *I Came Alone* in October 1989 wrote to her 'Friends and Readers' that 'Most of the children lost their parents in the Holocaust and thus became part of history.' She continues that 'If some of the stories seem repetitive, please realize that our experiences were often identical; for instance the journey … was a trauma, as was the realization of having become orphans when the rest of the world celebrated victory'.[148] Lotte Kramer's poem, 'Kindertransport Reunion', quoted earlier, continues with similar themes of uniformity under the impact of the Holocaust:

The same faces with stencilled age
We are survivors of circles of hell
Having slid through some six decades.[149]

The use of the *Kindertransport* as a pedagogic tool reveals much about the struggles over its collective and public memory at the end of the twentieth century and beyond. Educational resources such as *The Last Goodbye* (1996 and 2004), *Our Lonely Journey* (1999) and *Journeys to*

Freedom (2000), all contextualise the *Kindertransport* solely through the Nazi persecution of the Jews rather than the history of refugee movements – indeed, the rescue of the children has become a major way of tackling the Holocaust at school level. Such a focus enables an identification across time with those who were a similar age and also, as with *The Diary of Anne Frank*, avoiding direct confrontation with the murder process itself.[150] There is a danger that when linkages are made to contemporary events, attempts to 'learn from the past' may be weakened by the insistence upon the specificity of the Jewish experience of persecution. In *The Last Goodbye*, there is recognition that 'In Britain today, at the start of the twenty first century, several thousand unaccompanied children are arriving each year, fleeing from violence and abuse ... Many have witnessed terrible atrocities and have lost close family members.' Pupils are tasked to 'find out what happens to unaccompanied child refugees when they arrive in Britain today. What organizations exist to help them? Are they always able to stay in Britain? How can they adjust to a new life?' Yet immediately after having been asked, after 'Reflecting on the experiences of children who came on the Kindertransport', whether they think more could 'be done to help unaccompanied child refugees today', they are reminded that 'The Kindertransport is, however, a unique episode in history. Under the Nazis, children were not simply caught in the crossfire of war but were coldly targeted for destruction, as they represented the future of the Jewish people.'[151]

The requirement of uniqueness inevitably undermines any attempt at comparison and the genuine desire to show contemporary relevance. Nowhere in these educational resources is the question asked why Britain refused to accept the parents of the *Kinder*. Moreover, the ambivalence towards Britain articulated in the early years of the Association of Jewish Refugees' journal, and in Gershon's collective testimony, has, in recent memory of the *Kindertransport*, given way to eulogy towards the new 'promised land'. Thus at the end of *Into the Arms of Strangers* 'grandfather and granddaughter walk past the [House of Commons'] plaque commemorating the rescue endeavour'.[152] The failure to confront the *selectivity* of British refugee procedures during the Nazi era leads to a failure to make connections with contemporary policies where certain types of asylum seekers are privileged over others. More generally the fatalism towards the (non)-rescue of the parents and other adults during the 1930s is replicated in the paralysed response to the millions suffering in the world today who we convince ourselves we cannot help. The hermetically sealed moral universe that has developed in Holocaust commemoration, in which the *Kindertransport* is now largely placed, has enabled mainstream politicians who have been at the forefront of anti-asylum

seeker policies to engage in celebration of Britain's past generosity towards refugees. Martha Blend in her autobiography, *A Child Alone* (1995),
writes with pride, rather than unease, at the presence of a Home Office
minister at the 1989 reunion, a man 'whose predecessor had authorised
the *Kindertransport*'.[153] Even Annette Saville, whose *Kinder* autobiography is perhaps the most critical of Britain and the scheme as a whole, is
at pains to emphasise that she does not want to be accused of 'being
ungrateful'. With such a cult of gratitude towards Britain having developed over the collective memory of the *Kindertransport*, criticisms relating to the country's past or present exclusion of refugees and asylum
seekers carry less weight.

   In *Our Lonely Journey*, three former *Kinder* agree that the treatment
of refugees at the end of the twentieth century is appalling. The text
concludes that the testimonies included are important 'Not just because
it is interesting to learn about their experiences, but also because they
really could be anyone, anywhere; at any time.'[154] The desire for
universalising the experience of the *Kinder*, however, sits awkwardly with
the otherness of the Holocaust experience in the same educational pack.
'How would you feel if you had waited to see your parents for six years
and then found that the Nazis had killed them?' is a suggested point for
discussion.[155] It is hard to imagine this question stimulating anything but
the most obvious response. There are few former *Kinder* who have publicly articulated that 'Present-day immigrants are treated much better
than we were.'[156] Significantly this statement appears in one of the few
testimonies that is critical of Britain during the 1930s. Otherwise, the
desire, as in *Into the Arms of Strangers*, to celebrate not only 'Britain as
saviour country', but also to show the international uniqueness of this
act of rescue, is dominant.[157] In this context, any criticisms of Britain,
including of its later refugee policy, are bound to have less impact.

   Ultimately, the sense of obligation and feelings of thankfulness have
led to *Kinder* memory being more about 'the British' and less about the
experience of being a child refugee. It has been suggested that 'it is easier
to write with some confidence about childhood than about children'.[158]
So far, only Karen Gershon's *We Came as Children* has had the self-
confidence to turn the focus onto the refugees, and to be able to do justice to both the collective and the individual story, as well as the particular and the universal contained within the story of the *Kindertransport*.
Gershon shaped her anthology to interrogate and question all forms of
exclusivities – whether based on race, religion or nation. In particular,
she raises the concept of 'home' and its fragile nature: 'Home is where
you have been living and consider you belong. But if all your family went
away, I don't think it would be home any more.'[159] The temporariness of

the *Kinder* experience is emphasised and thereby links made to all those forced to become refugees. Gershon focuses on England and the limits of Englishness, themes explored by Diane Samuels' play which 'follows the subtle pressures of assimilation to the limits'.[160] Dislocation is also the major theme of *War Games* (2002), children's author, Jenny Koralek's interpretation of the *Kinder* experience, which is strongly influenced by Gershon's anthology.[161] The work of Gershon, Samuels, Koralek and Sebald, with whom this chapter began, provide the antithesis to the more internationally-focused commemorations of the *Kindertransport* since the 1989 reunion which have placed the scheme within the mythology of the country's innate decency, tolerance and sense of fair play.

In contrast to *We Came as Children*, in the late twentieth and early twenty-first centuries the dominant memory work associated with the *Kinder*, whether in the form of memorials, publications or pedagogic work, rather than connecting to present refugees, creates a chronological and experential distance to them. As will be shown in the final chapter, the impact of this re-remembering raises doubts about the authenticity of contemporary asylum seekers. Such a celebratory reading of the past also undermines the success of the *Kinder*, not by denying their undoubted achievements, but by underplaying the forces of indifference, antipathy and conditional acceptance that for so long they faced and the ongoing impact of the forced separation from their parents. It ignores what was denied to the *Kinder* – the rights of a child. Such rights, as Brian Klug argues, 'are not simply human rights for the young; they are specifically rights for a child: for a child to *be* a child'. As Klug adds, in contrast to Peter Pan, 'Real children come from the womb'.[162] The *Kindertransport* scheme, by choice, denied the right of the children to their natural parents: it gave them back the fundamental human rights denied by the Nazis – to live without persecution – but not the freedom to be a child. It has been suggested that 'Children, in all sorts of ways, in all kinds of circumstances, have adulthood thrust upon them before they have had the chance to be children.'[163] Nazi antisemitism, but also British refugee policy, inhibited that chance. The absence was painfully expressed in Karen Gershon's poem, 'Cast Out' (1966):

Sometimes I feel I am a ghost
adrift without identity
what as a child I valued most
for ever has escaped from me
I have been cast out and am lost.[164]

Nor does the increasingly dominant redemptive *Kindertransport* narrative do justice to the thousands of ordinary people who worked tirelessly on their behalf by focusing on only a handful of famous (and especially male) rescuers. Trevor Chadwick, for example, is largely forgotten, yet he carried out much of the dangerous work in Prague alongside the now more famous Nicholas Winton who has always stressed that it was 'a very small part of my life'.[165] Chadwick, before and after this work, in which he helped to arrange eight Czech transports, was, at best, a lovable rogue, a playboy who for once in his life found a clear purpose: 'one of those enchanting men, but no saint', according to his niece.[166] His testimony in Gershon's anthology ends not on a note of self-congratulation or desire for recognition but with the sad reflection that 'I shall always have a feeling of shame that I didn't get more out.'[167] Even more neglected is Doreen Warriner who became the focal point of all British refugee work in Prague from October 1938 through to spring 1939. Warriner flew out from England with 'no idea at all of what to do, only a desperate wish to do something'. Delegating the child refugee work to Winton and Chadwick, the two relied on the expertise she had quickly amassed. The role of other female refugee activists has similarly been subject to amnesia.[168] The key point, however, is that many of those involved in the *Kindertransport* and other refugee activities were ordinary people with normal human flaws and contradictions. But in common with Warriner, they possessed an overriding concern 'to try and help in some way'.[169]

As has been highlighted throughout this chapter, creating a 'safe' *Kindertransport* narrative necessitates a downplaying of the vulnerable adults left behind in the Third Reich who lacked, in the eyes of the receiving countries, the appeal of childhood innocence. Even then, the children were regarded with some suspicion. In November 1938 the Home Secretary, Sir Samuel Hoare, justified the *Kindertransport* scheme as being 'Without any harm to our own population'.[170] The Home Office's official history of British refugee policy, written in 1950, hurried through this movement in one paragraph and simply outlined how this damage limitation was to be achieved. The children were allowed in 'on condition that they would be emigrated when they reached 18 … [and] no encouragement was given to them to qualify for the professions or for "black-coated occupations"'.[171] Until there is a film, book or memorial echoing such official proclamations, rather than redemptively desiring that they first witnessed Britain as a place where *The Policeman Smiled* before falling comfortably *Into the Arms of Strangers*, we will not have done justice either to the experience or to the legacy of the *Kinder*.

Notes

1 W.G. Sebald, *Austerlitz* (London: Hamish Hamilton, 2001), pp. 30–1.
2 Maya Jaggi, 'Recovered Memories', *Guardian*, 22 September 2001. See

Jeremy Josephs, *Rosa's Child: The True Story of One Woman's Quest for a Lost Mother and a Vanished Past* (London: I.B. Tauris, 1996) for Bechhofer.

3 Jaggi, 'Recovered Memories'.

4 Mona Korte, 'Bracelet, Hand Towel, Pocket Watch: Objects of the Last Moment in Memory and Narration', *Shofar* vol. 23 no. 1 (Fall 2004), p. 115 suggests that 'If one compares the immense corpus of Shoah-related autobiography with that related to the *Kindertransport*, one immediately notices the paucity of such works by the former *Kinder*.' In fact, proportionately, there is a higher percentage of *Kinder* testimony. What is of greater significance is that Holocaust and *Kinder* testimony have gone through similar patterns with a massive growth since the late twentieth century. It is the increase in Holocaust consciousness, I would argue, that has enabled interest in the *Kindertransport* to expand.

5 See, for example, the collection of testimonies and other autobiographical writings in the Imperial War Museum archives.

6 Quoted in *Jewish Chronicle*, 1 February 2002.

7 See Donald Bloxham and Tony Kushner, *The Holocaust: Critical Historical Approaches* (Manchester: Manchester University Press, 2005), Introduction and chapter 1 on Holocaust memory and survivors.

8 Hugh Cunningham, *Children and Childhood in Western Society since 1500* (London: Longman, 1995), pp. 4–18 provides a succinct overview of historiographical development. See also Kathleen Alaimo, 'Historical Roots of Children's Rights in Europe and the United States', in idem and Brian Klug (eds), *Children as Equals: Exploring the Rights of the Child* (Lanham, Maryland: University Press of America, 2002), pp. 1–24.

9 Deborah Dwork, *Children with a Star: Jewish Youth in Nazi Europe* (New Haven: Yale University Press, 1991).

10 Ibid., p. 253.

11 Ibid., p. 256.

12 Ibid., p. 254.

13 Ibid., p. 256.

14 Claude Lanzmann, *Shoah: An Oral History of the Holocaust* (New York: Pantheon Books, 1985) and in discussion about the film.

15 See Yosefa Loshitzky, *Spielberg's Holocaust: Critical Perspectives on Schindler's List* (Bloomington: Indiana University Press, 1997) and especially Bryan Cheyette, 'The Uncertain Certainty of *Schindler's List*', pp. 230, 237.

16 See, for example, the essays in Dalia Offer and Lenore Weitzmann (eds), *Women in the Holocaust* (New Haven: Yale University Press, 1998) which deal with gender but only with regard to women's experiences.

17 See, for example, Jon Blair's Oscar-winning *Anne Frank Remembered* (1995) and comment on it in G. Jan Colijn, 'Anne Frank Remembered', *Holocaust and Genocide Studies* vol. 10 no. 1 (spring 1996), pp. 78–92.

18 Benjamin Wilkomirski, *Fragments* (Basingstoke: Picador, 1996) and for sensitive analysis of the 'affair", Elena Lappin, 'The Man With Two Heads', *Granta* no. 66 (summer 1990), pp. 9–65 and Blake Eskin, *A Life in Pieces*

(London: Aurum Press, 2002).

19 Jane Marks, *The Hidden Children: The Secret Survivors of the Holocaust* (London: Bantam Books, 1995 [1993]), pp. viii, x.

20 Benigni quoted in Melanie Wright, 'Don't Touch My Holocaust: Respond- ing to *Life is Beautiful*', *Journal of Holocaust Education* vol. 9 no. 1 (sum- mer 2000), p. 29.

21 Bruno Bettelheim, 'The Ignored Lesson of Anne Frank' in idem, *Surviving and Other Essays* (New York: Knopf, 1979), pp. 246–57.

22 See Alice Bloch, *The Migration and Settlement of Refugees in Britain* (Basingstoke: Palgrave Macmillan, 2002), pp. 53–4.

23 Home Office, *Secure Borders, Safe Haven: Integration with Diversity in Modern Britain* (London: HMSO, 2002 Cmd 5387), p. 15.

24 Parkinson to Dufferin, 16 May 1938 in National Archives, CO 323/1605/2.

25 *Aliens Act, 1905* (11 August 1905), 5 EDW.7.

26 Clynes to D'Avignor Goldsmid, 26 February 1930, in Board of Deputies of British Jews papers (BD), E3/80, London Metropolitan Archives (LMA).

27 Board of Deputies delegation to the Home Office, 6 February 1925 in BD, E3/80, LMA.

28 Louise London, *Whitehall and the Jews 1933–1948: British Immigration Policy and the Holocaust* (Cambridge: Cambridge University Press, 2000), chapters 2 and 3.

29 Commander Sir Archibald Southby in *Hansard* (HC) vol. 341 col. 1457 (21 November 1938).

30 Winterton's speech is reproduced in Norbert Kampe (ed.), *Jewish Immi- grants of the Nazi Period in the USA* vol. 4 Part 2 *Jewish Emigration from Germany 1933–1942* (Munich: K.G. Saur, 1992), p. 338.

31 Hoare in *Hansard* (HC) vol. 341 cols. 1473–4 (21 November 1938).

32 For further discussion see Tony Kushner, *The Holocaust and the Liberal Imagination: A Social and Cultural History* (Oxford: Blackwell, 1994), chapter 1; Dan Stone, *Responses to Nazism in Britain, 1933–1939* (Basingstoke: Palgrave, 2003), chapter 3.

33 A.J. Sherman, *Island Refuge: Britain and Refugees from the Third Reich 1933–1939* (Berkeley: University of California Press, 1973), chapter 5.

34 See the conclusion to Tony Kushner and Katharine Knox, *Refugees in an Age of Genocide: Global, National and Local Perspectives during the Twen- tieth Century* (London: Frank Cass, 1999).

35 Sherman, *Island Refuge*, pp. 172–3.

36 Henry Feingold, *The Politics of Rescue: The Roosevelt Administration and the Holocaust, 1938–1945* (New Brunswick, NJ: Rutgers University Press, 1970), pp. 148–53; Richard Breitman and Alan Kraut, *American Refugee Policy and European Jewry, 1933–1945* (Bloomington: Indiana University Press, 1987), pp. 66, 73, 107, 232; and Judith Tydor Baumel, *Unfulfilled Promise: Rescuee and Resettlement of Jewish Refugee Children in the United States 1934–1945* (Juneau, Alaska: Denali Press, 1990), chapter 2.

37 W.D. Rubinstein, *The Myth of Rescue: Why the Democracies Could Not Have Saved More Jews from the Nazis* (London: Routledge, 1997).

38 Hoare in *Hansard* (HC) vol. 341 col. 1468 (21 November 1938).

39 For the best overview see Saul Friedlander, *Nazi Germany & the Jews: The Years of Persecution 1933–39* (London: Weidenfeld & Nicolson, 1997).

40 Hoare in *Hansard* (HC) vol. 341 col. 1474 (21 November 1938).

41 Baldwin's broadcast of 8 December 1938 was printed as *The Plight of the Refugees* (Ottowa: Canadian National Committee on Refugees, 1939), p. 9 for this quote. For the gramophone record version see *The Times*, 15 December 1938.

42 For further analysis of the role and mindset of the refugee organisations, see Claudia Curio, '"Invisible" Children: The Selection and Integration Strategies of Relief Organizations', *Shofar* vol. 23 no. 1 (Fall 2004), pp. 41–56.

43 London, *Whitehall and the Jews*, p. 118.

44 Hoare in *Hansard* (HC) vol. 341 col. 1474 (21 November 1938).

45 Beate Neumeier, 'Kindertransport: Childhood Trauma and Diaspora Experience', in Ulrike Behlau and Bernhard Reitz (eds), *Jewish Women's Writing of the 1990s and Beyond in Great Britain and the United States* (Trier: Wissenschaftlicher Verlag Trier, 2004), pp. 64–9 comments on the gothic influence on two very differing readings of the *Kindertransport*, the film *Into the Arms of Strangers* (2000) and the play, *Kindertransport* (1995) both of which will be explored later in this chapter.

46 Movement for the Care of Children from Germany, *First Annual Report: November 1938–December 1939* (London: MCCG, 1940), p. 3.

47 Ibid., p. 3.

48 Ibid., pp. 4–7.

49 Ibid., p. 20.

50 Ibid., pp. 20–1.

51 John Presland [Gladys Bendit], *A Great Adventure: The Story of the Refugee Children's Movement* (London: Bloomsbury House, 1944), p. 3.

52 Ibid., pp. 3–4.

53 Loshitszky, *Spielberg's Holocaust*, passim.

54 Bendit, *A Great Adventure*, p. 16.

55 Ibid.

56 Ibid.

57 Andrea Hammel, 'Representations of Family in Autobiographical Texts of Child Refugees', *Shofar* vol. 23 no. 1 (Fall 2004), pp. 119–20 indicates how this tendency has continued in recent *Kinder* testimony.

58 Movement for the Care of Children from Germany, *Instructions for the Guidance of Regional and Local Committees* (London: Bloomsbury House, 1940), p. 17.

59 See the photographs reproduced in Barry Turner, *... And the Policeman Smiled: 10,000 Children Escape from Nazi Europe* (London: Bloomsbury, 1990), facing p. 150.

60 *The Mirror*, 26 April 1999.

61 This was true also of a 1999 First Day Cover celebrating the 60th anniversary of the scheme. Included in the *Kindertransport* exhibition, Jewish Museum, Finchley, visited May 2005.

62 Liisa Malkki, 'Speechless Emissaries: Refugees, Humanitarianism and Dehistoricization', *Cultural Anthropology* vol. 11 no. 3 (August 1996), p. 388.
63 Turner, ... *And the Policeman Smiled*, p. 86.
64 'Their First Day in England', *Picture Post*, 17 December 1938.
65 Ibid.
66 On Lorant, see Daniel Snowman, *The Hitler Emigres: The Cultural Impact on Britain of Refugees from Nazism* (London: Chatto & Windus, 2002), p. 158.
67 Norman Angell and Dorothy Buxton, *You and the Refugee* (Harmondsworth: Penguin, 1939), p. 11.
68 Mass-Observation Archive (M-O A): DR1108, March 1939.
69 See, for example, M-O A: DR1048, March 1939.
70 M-O A: DR1983, March 1939.
71 M-O A: DR1018, March 1939.
72 M-O A: DR1393, March 1939.
73 M-O A: DR1488, March 1939.
74 M-O A: DR2049, March 1939.
75 M-O A: DR1981, March 1939.
76 Quoted by Feingold, *The Politics of Rescue*, p. 150.
77 Gertrude Dubrovsky, *Six from Leipzig* (London: Vallentine Mitchell, 2004) provides information on the Cambridge Refugee Children's Committee although it is not a history of it.
78 See *Jewish Gazette*, 22 August 1986 for the story of the diary. The diary featured in a 1985 Yorkshire Television documentary. It is in a permanent display at the Manchester Jewish Museum with a microfilm copy available at Manchester Central Reference Library Local Studies, MF2845.
79 Rebekka Gopfert, *Der Judische Kindertransport von Deutschland nach England, 1938/39: Geschichte und Erinnerung* (Frankfurt: Campus Verlag, 1999), pp. 127–8.
80 Manchester Jewish Museum, Harris House witness seminar, 27 October 1985.
81 Harris House diary, Manchester Jewish Museum.
82 See Tony Kushner, 'An Alien Occupation – Jewish Refugees and Domestic Service in Britain, 1933–1948', in Werner Mosse (ed), *Second Chance: Two Centuries of German-speaking Jews in the United Kingdom* (Tubingen: J.C.B. Mohr, 1991), pp. 553–78.
83 Lottie Gross, entry in Harris House diary.
84 Jean [Gina] Bauer, entry in Harris House diary.
85 Eva Reise, entry in Harris House diary.
86 Collective entry, 'War', Harris House diary.
87 Turner, ... *And the Policeman Smiled*, chapters 8 and 11. For an uncritical account of the Jewish refugee organisations and the RCM, see Amy Gottlieb, *Men of Vision: Anglo-Jewry's Aid to Victims of the Nazi Regime* (London: Weidenfeld & Nicolson, 1998).
88 *The Child Estranging Movement: An Expose on the Alienation of Jewish*

Refugee Children in Great Britain from Judaism (London: Union of Orthodox Hebrew Congregations, 1944). Copies of this eight-page pamphlet are
held in Schonfeld papers, University of Southampton archive, MS 183/344/
10.

89 See David Kranzler and Gertrude Hirschler (eds), *Solomon Schonfeld: His
Place in History* (New York: Judaica Press, 1982); Pam Shatzkes, *Holocaust and Rescue: Impotent or Indifferent? Anglo-Jewry 1938–1945*
(Basingstoke: Palgrave, 2002), pp. 5–7 and 224–5 provides a positive reading of Schonfeld's activities.

90 See the comments about Schonfeld's approach in C.Robinson memorandum to Sir Alexander Maxwell, 15 August 1945, National Archives, HO
213/781.

91 See the testimonies collected in Kranzler and Hirschler, *Solomon Schonfeld*.

92 Turner, *... And the Policeman Smiled*, pp. 23, 75.

93 Schonfeld's absence from the Imperial War Museum Holocaust exhibition
was highlighted in a feature presented by Sacha Berg on the BBC Radio 4,
'Today' programme, 29 May 2000.

94 Barry Turner, *The Long Horizon: 60 Years of CBF World Jewish Relief*
(London: CBF, 1993), pp. 25–34; Gottlieb, *Men of Vision*. More generally
on this roots of this warped historiography, see Paula Hill, 'Anglo-Jewry
and the Refugee Children 1938–1945' (unpublished PhD thesis, University
of London, 2001).

95 See, for example, *Hansard* (HC) vol. 396 cols 1576–81 (4 February 1944).

96 Turner, *... And the Policeman Smiled*, chapter 13; idem, *The Long Horizon*, p. 29 where it is acknowledged 'That he was not a Jew was seen as
another point in his favour'.

97 *The Child Estranging Movement*, p. 2.

98 Ibid., p. 8.

99 Bendit, *A Great Adventure*, p. 16.

100 Josephs, *Rosa's Child*; Annette Saville, *Only a Kindertransportee* (London:
New Millennium, 2002); Vera Schaufeld, oral testimony in National Sound
Archives, C410/008, British Library on temporary conversion to Chris-
tianity.

101 See the correspondence over a complaint concerning an orthodox hostel
with the Chief Rabbi's office in Rothschild archive, RAL, 00/315C.

102 See the subtitle on the cover of *The Child-Estranging Movement*: 'Defend
the Religious Rights of Jewry's Orphans'.

103 Karen Gershon (ed.), *We Came as Children: A Collective Autobiography
of Refugees* (London: Gollancz, 1966), p. 7, Gershon to Gollancz, September 1965.

104 Ibid.

105 Ibid.

106 Ibid., p. 151.

107 Egon Larsen, 'What Every Child Should Know', *AJR Information*, June
1962; Kenneth Ambrose, *The Story of Peter Cronheim* (London: Constable,
1962).

108 Karen Gershon, *A Lesser Child* (London: Peter Owen, 1994); obituaries in the *Guardian*, 22 April 1993 and *The Times*, 15 April 1993. See also Peter Lawson, 'Three Kindertransport Poets: Karen Gershon, Gerda Mayer and Lotte Kramer', in Ulrike Behlau and Bernhard Reitz, *Jewish Women's Writing of the 1990s and Beyond in Great Britain and the United States* (Trier: Wissenschaftlicher erlag Trier, 2004), pp. 87–9.

109 Gershon, *We Came as Children*, pp. 150, 155.

110 1989 edition (London, Papermac), p. 9.

111 Gershon, *We Came as Children*, p. 111; Ambrose, *The Story of Peter Cronheim*, p. 58.

112 Testimony of Vera Schaufeld in National Sound Archives, C410/008, British Library.

113 W.G. Sebald, *The Emigrants* (London: Vintage, 2002 [1993]), p. 191.

114 Neither the interviewing at the Manchester Jewish Museum nor that of the Imperial War Museum's 'Britain and the Refugee Crisis' focused on the *Kinder* but both included former child refugees.

115 It initially ran from September to November 1996 at the Jewish Museum's Finchley site.

116 *The Last Goodbye: The Rescue of Children from Nazi Europe: An Educational Resource about the Kindertransport* (London: The London Museum of Jewish Life, 1996). On examples of relatively 'early' *Kinder* memoirs see Hannele Zurndorfer, *The Ninth of November* (London: Quartet, 1983); Vera Gissing, *Pearls of Childhood* (London: Robson Books, 1988).

117 Bertha Leverton and Shmuel Lowensohn, *I Came Alone: The Stories of the Kindertransports* (Lewes, Sussex: The Book Guild, 1990).

118 Mary Chamberlain and Paul Thompson (eds), *Narrative and Genre* (London: Routledge, 1998).

119 Leverton and Lowensohn, *I Came Alone*, front cover illustration.

120 For a review of this documentary directed by Sue Read see Ronald Channing, '*Kinder*'s Lifetime Odyssey', *AJR Information*, July 2000.

121 *Kindertransport 60th Anniversary* (London: Reunion of Kindertransport, 1999), p. 6. See also Hammel, 'Representations of Family', p. 132 for the emphasis on successful integration in *Kinder* autobiographies.

122 Sue Vice, *Children Writing the Holocaust* (Basingstoke: Palgrave, 2004), pp. 42–3.

123 Leverton and Lowensohn, *I Came Alone*, pp. 291–2.

124 Saville, *Only a Kindertransportee*, p. viii.

125 Ibid., p. 323.

126 Caroline Sharples, 'Reconstructing The Past: Refugee Writings on the Kindertransport' (unpublished MA dissertation, University of Southampton, 2002), p. 16. See Leverton and Lowensohn, *I Came Alone*, pp. 159–61 and I. Jacoby, *My Darling Diary* (Cornwall, no place: United Writers, 1998). The diary appears reconstituted.

127 Membership figures in *Kindertransport 60th Anniversary*, pp. 8–9.

128 Entry of Elfriede Colman in Leverton and Lowensohn, *I Came Alone*, pp. 59–61. See also the comments of Ruth Barnett, 'The Acculturation of the

Kindertransport Children: Intergenerational Dialogue on the Kinder-transport Experience', *Shofar* vol. 23 no. 1 (Fall 2004), p. 101 which describes the first reunion event as an 'epiphany'.

129 In Lotte Kramer, *The Phantom Lane* (Ware: Herts: Rockingham Press, 2000); see Lawson, 'Three *Kinder*transport Poets', p. 93 for comment.

130 Anne Kopel, 'Citizenship None', p. 10 (Leo Baeck Institute, New York, AP 5791, A28/n).

131 *Jewish Chronicle*, 18 June 1999. The plaque features in the film *Into the Arms of Strangers* (2000) and on the cover of *Kindertransport 60th Anniversary*.

132 The statue and installation are outside the Liverpool Street station where many of the *Kinder* arrived and were organised by the RCM. At the time of writing (autumn 2005), the future of this memorial is unclear and may be replaced by another devoted to the *Kindertransport*.

133 Produced by Deborah Oppenheimer and directed by Mark Jonathan Harris. See idem, *Into the Arms of Strangers: Stories of the Kindertransport* (London: Bloomsbury, 2000).

134 Diane Samuels, *Kindertransport* (London: Nick Hern Books, 2004 [1995]), Act Two, Scene One. See Neumeier, 'Kindertransport', pp. 66–9 for an interesting reading of this text.

135 Samuels, *Kindertransport*, p. xviii.

136 Baumel, *Unfulfilled Promise*, p. 27 on this argument against creating an American equivalent of the *Kindertransport*. For an incisive analysis of the film and its gothic renderings with influences from the genres of film noir and thriller, see Neumeier, '*Kindertransport*', pp. 64–5.

137 Inside cover of Harris and Oppenheimer, *Into the Arms of Strangers*.

138 Gissing, *Pearls of Childhood*, p. 11.

139 David Kranzler and Gertrude Hirschier (eds), *Solomon Schonfeld: His Place in History* (New York: Judaica Press, 1982), p. 84, testimony of Frieda Stolzberg Korobkin.

140 London, *Whitehall and the Jews*, p. 13.

141 Fred Ahearn, Maryanne Loughry and Alastair Ager, 'The Experience of Refugee Children' in Alastair Ager (ed.), *Refugees: Perspectives on the Experience of Forced Migration* (London: Continuum, 1999), p. 215.

142 John Carey, 'Digging in the Sand', *New Statesman*, 20 May 1966.

143 'Innocents Abroad', *The Times*, 26 May 1966.

144 Lucie Schachne, 'It Takes More than One Generation', *AJR Information*, July 1966.

145 Raymond Mortimer in *Sunday Times*, 15 May 1966. See also *Times Literary Supplement*, 9 June 1966.

146 Lucia Pollman Strangwick, 'A Painful Scar', *The Jewish Quarterly* vol. 14 no. 4 (Winter 1966/67), p. 55.

147 Vice, *Children Writing the Holocaust*, p. 43.

148 In Leverton and Lowensohn, *I Came Alone*, p. 8.

149 Kramer, *The Phantom Lane*, p. 13.

150 *The Last Goodbye: The Rescue of Children from Nazi Europe* (Jewish

Museum); Sheila Chiat, *Journeys to Freedom* (Leo Baeck College Centre for Jewish Education); *Our Lonely Journey* (Beth Shalom Holocaust Centre).

151 *The Last Goodbye*, p. 66.
152 Neumeier, '*Kindertransport*', p. 68.
153 Martha Blend, *A Child Alone* (London: Vallentine Mitchell, 1995), p. 167.
154 Stephen Smith (ed.), *Our Lonely Journey: Remembering the Kinder-transports* (Newark, Notts: Paintbrush Publications, 1999), p. 22.
155 'Our Lonely Journey', resource guide for teachers.
156 Saville, *Only A Kindertransportee*, pp. vii-iii.
157 Neumeier, '*Kindertransport*', pp. 64–5.
158 Cunningham, *Children and Childhood*, p. 3.
159 Gershon, *We Came as Children*, p. 160.
160 Neumeier, '*Kindertransport*', p. 66.
161 Jenny Koralek, *War Games* (London: Egmont Books, 2002).
162 Brian Klug, 'Wendy and Peter Pan: Exploring the Concept of the Child', in Alaimo and idem, *Children as Equals*, pp. 30, 39.
163 Ibid., p. 39.
164 Gershon, *We Came Alone*, p. 174.
165 Winton quoted in *Jewish Chronicle*, 25 March 1998.
166 Elizabeth Cooper, 'The Pimpernal of Prague', *Observer*, 10 July 1988.
167 Gershon, *We Came as Children*, p. 25. See also Cooper, 'The Pimpernal of Prague', and *Sunday Express*, 14 July 2002 in which his niece, the children's author, Jenny Koralek, also describes him as a 'mixed bag'. Chadwick's role is included in Koralek's novel, *War Games*.
168 For further comments on the neglect of women refugee workers, see Sybil Oldfield, '"It is Usually She": The Role of British Women in the Rescue and Care of the Kindertransport Kinder', *Shofar* vol. 23 no. 1 (Fall 2004), pp. 57–70.
169 Doreen Warriner, 'The Winter in Prague', in Imperial War Museum, Department of Documents.
170 Hoare in *Hansard* (HC) vol. 341 col. 1474, 21 November 1938.
171 In National Archives, HO 213/1772.

5

Remembering to exclude: a turn of the twenty-first century immorality tale

Introduction

In his eloquent synthesis, *Bloody Foreigners: The Story of Immigration to Britain* (2004), Robert Winder writes that hostility towards contemporary asylum seekers and others is

> as powerful as the ancient fears that have disfigured these islands many times in the past before fading, almost invariably, into indifference. The debate has followed the same lines as previous uproars, and there is little to suggest it will not subside along the same lines, too. One can fly in the face of the facts only for so long. It is childlike economics, for instance, to argue that migrants are stealing 'our' jobs, 'our' houses and, in the most frenetic arguments, 'our' women. Economies are neither static nor fixed: they thrive on movement and change. The arrival of more mouths does not mean less for everyone if the new mouths produce more than they consume. Today's migrants come, like the Flemish weavers in the Middle Ages, in search of jobs, but they create as many jobs as they fill ...[1]

Winder's last sentence might have been taken directly from one of the Keynesian-influenced, pro-refugee publications of the late 1930s featured in chapter 1. To such an analysis Winder has added a belief that widespread migration in a global economy is inevitable. His narrative also possesses a Whiggish self-confidence, arguing that, in the long term, history will be on the side of those 'new foreigners' attacked today as being both undeserving and undesirable. Optimism and the ability to think beyond the ongoing moral panic about asylum seekers is a necessary condition of moving beyond the scare-mongering, anxiety and hatred that has typified responses from the late twentieth century onwards.[2] Winder's account is also comforting in pointing out how hindsight has overturned the perspective of those contemporaries who opposed the entry of newcomers in earlier times. He is undoubtedly right to emphasise the tedious unoriginality of anti-alienists past and present. The alien will take what is 'ours', whether it be jobs, housing, women or security, and bring in what is bad for 'us' – criminality, revolution, terror or disease. The nature of such 'ills' may have mutated – for example, from anarchist to fundamentalist, from typhus to AIDS – but the perception of the threat is similar.

Nevertheless, there are several potential problems with Winder's sanguine model, no matter how attractive it appears, if more progressive asylum policies are to be encouraged. First, his study gives little attention to the *success* of anti-alienism in British history – the moments in which individuals and groups were denied entry, expelled or restrained in their freedom within Britain. More than anything, *Bloody Foreigners* is a forceful testimony to the contribution of refugees and immigrants in British culture and society. The *absence* of those disqualified from playing such a positive role is not allowed to interfere with the dominant narrative in Winder's account. Second, and refining the first point, his thesis does not recognise how immigration procedures generally, and refugee entry policy specifically, have tended towards bifurcation – often allowing in one carefully chosen group (or part of it) and refusing entry to another. *Selectivity* has been the basis of British refugee policy since the 1905 Aliens Act, even since 1951 and the context of international agreements about the rights of those seeking refuge. Third, Winder's writerly version of the Chicago school cyclical model of migration does not allow for the possibility that the current animosity against the 'asylum seeker', for all the familiarity of its hostile rhetoric, could be unprecedented.

A historical perspective, especially one that embraces, as does Winder's, several millennia, may well lead to the assumption that there is nothing new under the sun (or indeed invented by the *Sun*). The recent accusations (utterly fictitious) that asylum seekers have spit-roasted swans and donkeys 'owned' by the Royal Family is novel only in its precision and in the surrealist or absurdist undertones of the allegations.[3] Aliens/foreigners/refugees/immigrants/minorities have been accused for many centuries of failing to understand, and of undermining British (or more frequently English) 'tradition', including through a lack of respect for the monarchy and an inherent cruelty to animals. And yet, in spite of such continuity in anti-alienism, there is strong evidence suggesting the singularity of the current situation.

Historians, even (or perhaps especially) contemporary historians have been notoriously unsuccessful in predicting the future. This book has been conceived and constructed in the middle of a relentless campaign against asylum seekers. Writing in the middle of the first decade of the twenty-first century there is no indication of when this already drawn out moral panic will end. In 2005, asylum issues, which were at the heart of the Conservative party's campaign, loomed larger than they had in any previous general election in Britain. It is possible, but far from certain, that asylum-seeker phobia has now peaked and will fade only for another form of xenophobia to emerge at another time in Britain with another target. It is, however, not necessarily the longevity of the current hostility that sets it apart – the anti-alienism aimed largely at East European Jews a century earlier was also notable for its durability, encouraged in its growth rather than climaxing with the 1905 Act. It is the intensity and increasing hegemony of the sentiment against asylum seekers in Britain today that makes it unusual, if not unique – even within a century of 'closing the door' against the foreigner.

This final chapter of *Remembering Refugees* explores the complex inter-relationship of politicians and the state apparatus, the media, and public opinion on the 'asylum seeker'. As ever, the focus is on 'then and now' and the confrontation with the past in the construction of contemporary policies, attitudes and responses. There are two temporal moments that are explored in relation to one another – the start of the twenty-first century and the Second World War. The particular focus will be the memory work associated with two particular groups of refugees/asylum seekers, Jews and Roma. Both were genocidal victims of the Nazi regime's nihilistic destruction. In the post-war world, the survivors of both communities were dispersed, often far from their original homes. But it is the Roma, rather than the Jews, who, some two generations later, are, along with those from former Yugoslavia, Europe's largest group of internally-generated asylum seekers. History and the selective memory of the past and its political and their social instrumentalisation is the basis of this chapter.

There is an abundance of sources to carry out such recent and ongoing issues, enabling an exploration and analysis of responses and reactions at high level politics through to the views of ordinary people. The problem facing the contemporary historian in this instance is not the absence of evidence (if anything, it is too plentiful), but more the dilemma of locating a theoretical and ethical framework in which to operate. To find an appropriate language, terminology and sociology of knowledge to explain hostility towards contemporary asylum seekers, especially the Roma, is far from easy. There is the problem of confronting the *Through the Looking Glass* aspect of contemporary debate in which, through the media and such stories as the *Sun's* 'Swan Bake', we are asked to believe 'as many as six impossible things before breakfast'.[4] The ludicrousness of so much contemporary hostile discourse about asylum seekers is intensified by the conviction, by those articulating it, that adhering to such nonsense and absurdity is fundamentally reasonable. A recent study, *Asylum: Understanding Public Attitudes* (2005) concludes that 'Constant

use of the term "asylum seeker" in the media and by politicians has ...
created the impression that they are a distinct group about whom it is
acceptable to express extreme forms of prejudice. There appears to be
very little social sanction against negative remarks about asylum seekers.'[5]
There is thus a huge gulf between, on the one hand, the perception of
fairness, and, on the other, the hostility, prejudice and violence that is
being enunciated and put into practice. Rather than mirroring the harm-
less and self-conscious twaddle written about Elvis Presley being found
alive and well on the dark side of the moon, the lies told about asylum
seekers matter in relation specifically to the actual and increasingly brutal treatment of them. More generally, there is the danger inherent when
prejudice is allowed to reign without restraint – the real problems of
society are masked and the moral well-being of those articulating it is
compromised. What is also remarkable is the consensus that has developed in this moral panic, enabling what might at other times to be regarded as extremist views to become mainstream and unchallenged. A
parallel thus has to be found with an extraordinary situation. The comparison that has been chosen is that of collaborationism and especially
the complex insights that have been gained from case studies from the
Second World War. While the circumstances, contexts and effects are
radically different, it is the ethical dilemmas facing contemporaries, and
the issue of choice, that will be highlighted. In turn, such a focus forces
the historian to confront the relationship between her/his own discipline
and the specific subject matter, thereby putting into sharp focus underlying ethical considerations. It has recently been asked: 'do historians *as*
historians have an ethical responsibility, and if so to whom?'[6] This chapter, by providing an important case study in such matters, will serve as a
prelude to a more focused consideration of ethical issues in the conclusion to this study of refugees, refugee studies, history and memory.

The nature of collaboration

For historians collaboration has become a dirty word, provoking images
of cowardice and moral culpability during the Second World War. It represents the 'wrong choices' that were made during Nazi occupation, evoking the reverse emotions to the memory of 'heroic' figures involved in
resistance.[7] Such 'collaboration' stands in contrast to the term's potentially positive reading in relation to those working together in a literary
or artistic production. Even then, however, such processes also involved
compromises and difficult choices. Indeed, in the cases of the writers
Henry Williamson and Francis Stuart, as Mark Rawlinson has explored,
the two definitions overlap when one is confronted in the Nazi era with

'literary productions which side with the enemy'.[8] It is the historians' rather than the literary critics' meaning of collaboration that is the obvious point of comparison in this chapter. Nevertheless, it is the voluntary aspect of so much anti-asylum rhetoric and action that provides the justification for the linkage to the Second World War, and a bridge between the two meanings of collaboration. In short, I will argue that the public as well as the state, politicians and the media have collaborated in Britain, with a decreasing amount of opposition, in the creation of a socio-cultural-political bogeyman – the stigmatised asylum seeker. Its particular focus is on the campaign against Gypsies, especially Czech and Slovak Roma, which has led to daily violence in word and deed, their partial expulsion from Britain and a largely successful legislative effort to exclude their entry. Yet, as with individuals under Nazi occupation, it is also the ambiguities and sometimes blatant contradictions that often make the categories of 'collaborator' and 'resister' hard to draw and the subject matter so fascinating if disturbing. In this case, it is the ambivalences exposed when the theoretical commitment to the right to asylum is juxtaposed with hostility towards asylum seekers themselves, or support for one group and opposition to another, that will be subject to close analysis.

In late 1945, a Foreign Office official, exasperated at Zionist rhetoric against Britain's Palestine policy, reminded his critics that 'His Majesty's Government were not responsible for countless Jewish deaths and suffering. The Nazis were responsible.'[9] Likewise it is the actions of eastern and central European countries and their state apparatus and popular antipathy that has created a Gypsy refugee population. Even so, there is determination from the British state that such people should not settle and that they should be kept out of the UK and returned. Such successful, if specific and localised, 'ethnic cleansing'[10] in a stable liberal democracy appears, on the surface, to be surprising, even more so when the Home Office's operation to prevent the arrival of Czech Roma has subsequently been labelled by the country's law lords, Britain's highest legal authority, as 'inherently and systematically discriminatory on racial grounds' – a judgment we will return to in the conclusion to this chapter.[11] Such a clear ruling runs counter to the country's self-mythology of tolerance, moderation and decency which has been a central element, since the eighteenth century at least, in the construction and re-construction of 'Englishness'.[12]

The paradox of this gap between the myth of 'fair play' and the reality of a discriminatory and mean-spirited asylum policy will be explored and explained through Britain's vital and unique 'special relationship' with the Second World War. It has enabled, through a process of selective, and relatively uncontested, collective memory, ordinary people, the press and government alike to see themselves as possessing an inherent and almost natural anti-Nazism. Equally powerful is the assumption of a similarly innate anti-racism in Britain which, it will be suggested, rather than acting as a barrier against all forms of prejudice has enabled its free articulation against certain but not all ethnic groups and minorities.

It is not surprising that after the trauma of the Second World War there was a desire to avoid ambiguity and to remember only heroes and villains or the crude categories of perpetrators, their collaborators, resisters and victims. Post-liberation France is perhaps the most analysed case study of the legacy of war and its impact on collective memory in a country in which notoriously after 1944 almost everyone claimed resistance status and only the unlucky few were labelled and publically punished as collaborators.[13] Soon after 1945, as Philippe Burrin argues, 'Thanks to the cold war, the myth of an entire people committed to resistance logically enough soon led to an amnesty designed to bring peace through the integration of a handful of traitors.'[14] Recent work on the 'myth of resistance' in France suggests that at all levels of society resistance *and* collaboration were an everyday occurrence. The same person, not just in different phases of the war but within a daily routine, could reveal contradictory tendencies.[15] Individual choice, whether it be altruistic or selfish desire for personal gain and ideological acceptance of collaboration, thus needs to be put alongside the fear of punishment by the Vichy regime or the German authorities in explaining the complex range and nature of human behaviour. Julian Jackson concludes in his history of the 'dark years' that the 'Occupation should be written not in black and white but in shades of grey … The Resistance was never monolothic, and the lines dividing it from Vichy were not always well defined.' Highlighting the ambiguities of the period, Jackson refers to the unexpected figures that made up Vichy:

> A pro-Petainist resister; a pro-British and anti-German Petainist; a pro-Jewish Petainist; two anti-Semitic resisters … They reveal the complexity of reactions to the Occupation and the extent to which antagonists might share as many assumptions with their enemies as with those on their own side. People who made different choices often did so in defence of similar values.[16]

Similar ambiguities are now generally accepted in explaining the acquiescence of literally hundreds of thousands of individuals in the implementation of the 'Final Solution'. According to Daniel Goldhagen, ordinary men, and to a lesser extent, women, carried out orders to murder Jews and others because, simply, they wanted to. Goldhagen argues that it was not only the Nazi elite but large sections of the German population

that believed in the exterminationist antisemitic ideology and practice of
the Third Reich. More convincingly, Christopher Browning argues that
such 'ordinary men' took part in mass murder through group solidarity
and rarely through racist fanaticism.[17] But whatever the disagreements
of such historians, there is now little doubting that if these people had
not wanted to carry out orders to kill, usually at the closest of proximities,
men, women and children, the sick and the infirm, then no direct punishment would have resulted.

Such collaboration, then, even at its most extreme and emotional level
and at the height of the bloodiest of European civil wars, was still largely
voluntary. Those pure in their innocence who consistently did the 'right
thing' were as rare as the sadistic figures who actually relished torture
and murder. Oskar Schindler, now the most famous 'righteous' figure
during the Second World War, remained, in spite of the best efforts of
Steven Spielberg to suggest otherwise, a flawed and ambiguous character as he slowly embarked on saving 'his' Jews.[18] In Britain, however,
acceptance of the type of ambiguity described by Jackson, especially in
relation to the former enemy, is still anathema. The conflict is still too
central in the formation of national identity to enable the acceptance of
contradictory motivation in the fighting of the 'people's war': it is, even
more than the 'myth of resistance' in France, an 'either/or' affair with no
ambivalence permissible.

Germany remains the former enemy and all ties with it, whether economic and political (as with the European Union and more recently the
single currency, or most blatantly in relation to popular culture manifested through the national game – soccer) are viewed through the prism
of the conflict. Indeed, every international football match between the
two countries becomes a re-run of, as one tabloid put it after a remarkable and untypical 5–1 victory in a 2001 World Cup qualifier, 'Our Fin-
est Hour'.[19] The fact that another tabloid alongside a quality paper could
quip, echoing the fictional comic xenophobe, Basil Fawlty, 'Don't mention the score', suggests the *acceptability* of Germanophobia: it is, at
worst, a little naughty, but not regarded in as in any way beyond the pale
of respectability.[20]

If it was confined simply to the worst word-play the headline makers
could muster, such 'humour' would be of no great significance. But
Germanophobia matters because it effects the treatment and response to
Germany on an official level as well as attitudes and behaviour towards
ordinary Germans at home and abroad. Indeed, anti-Germanism is one
of the most unrecognised and virulent forms of racism in contemporary
Britain, scarring the lives of people of both recent and distant German
origin. In December 2002, following assaults on German schoolchildren

in London and other anti-German incidents in Britain, the newly-appointed German ambassador, Thomas Matussek, pleaded for a more balanced teaching of history in which the successes of the post-war period were placed alongside the Nazi period and the Holocaust.[21] The war has acted as an obstacle to the reassessment and rejection of such prejudice, perhaps not unsurprisingly given the massive durability of its mythic status. Moreover, the Holocaust itself has become part of the armoury of anti-German racism. A few weeks before the German ambassador's comments, two German computer experts left their jobs in Swindon, Wiltshire, complaining that colleagues 'had goosestepped around the office and made references to gas chambers'.[22]

Less obvious to explain, however, is the totally unreconstructed racism aimed at the Roma in British politics, culture and society. Britain is far from being alone in this respect. Indeed, 'The Roma population of former Eastern Europe is at the cutting edge of what is often termed the democratic deficit of Europe.'[23] The focus of this chapter will be on the virulence of anti-Roma prejudice in contemporary Britain, showing the complex inter-relative collaboration between private and public worlds in its production. Ultimately it asks what function such remarkable hostility is playing in the making and remaking of individual as well as national identity. In this respect, it follows Colin Clark and Elaine Campbell's analysis of newspaper reporting of the 'Gypsy invasion' in October 1997, who emphasise that their research 'is *not* primarily ... about the Romani asylum-seekers from the Czech Republic and Slovakia themselves; it is ... more about *gadzhe* (non-Gypsy) reactions to them'.[24]

Problematising Roma asylum seekers

In the summer of 2001, British Home Office immigration officers in Prague screened all passengers to Britain in order to stop Czechs of Roma origin reaching the country and claiming asylum.[25] A monitoring operation carried out by the European Roma Rights Centre revealed that only 14 out of 6,170 non-Roma boarding flights to Britain from Prague airport were stopped by British officials in contrast to 68 out of 78 Roma.[26] The Home Office can carry out such screening in spite of the clauses of the Race Relations (Amendment) Act, 2000, outlawing institutional racism, because state discrimination in immigration control procedures was exempted from the new legislation. Home Office guidelines state that 'This exemption reflects a unique requirement for immigration and entry clearance officers to discriminate on grounds of nationality or national origin as set out in instructions'. As John Solomos comments, 'It is perhaps a sign of the times that this statement was made in good faith and with no sense of irony.'[27] What is perhaps the strongest piece of anti-racist legislation in the world enables one form of discrimination to take place freely and legally – or at least until queried by the law lords in December 2004.

The specific background to this campaign against the Roma came in 1997 when the Canadian authorities imposed new visa requirements on Czechs and Slovaks. According to both the 'broadsheet' and popular press in Britain, such moves coincided with a Czech television programme outlining the attractions of life in Britain to potential Roma asylum seekers. As Clark and Campbell point out, the focus on Britain as a 'gravy train' ignored the discrimination, violence and other human rights violations that the Roma were experiencing and fleeing from.[28] The idea that the Roma were 'cherry-picking'[29] destinations misses the basic point that they were embarking, in the words of a Refugee Council study, on an 'unwanted journey':

> If the migration of Roma in Europe has any special characteristics, they are not the wanderings of exploitative nomads of popular myth, apt to move at the vaguest scent of a welfare benefit scam ... Their recent migration is rather characterised by their desperation to seek safety and normality, to take huge risks despite no recent history of significant migration. The Roma did not want to leave their homes and come to the UK. They left countries which have spent centuries making it painfully clear that they were not wanted there.[30]

More appropriately, this small movement to Britain has to be put in the context of a much larger and desperate Roma search for asylum during the late twentieth century. From 1990 to 1996, for example, between 50,000 and 150,000 Roma from Romania, Macedonia and Bosnia-Herzegovina applied for asylum in western Europe.[31] The legislative response to them also needs to be put into a longer time frame – from the early 1900s, when German Gypsies were expelled, the British state has shown itself capable of draconian measures against foreign Gypsies (as well as domestic travellers). '[T]he debate over the Gypsy question witnessed the concerted action of anti-alien forces, at a time when alien immigration issues were in the air, to exploit the Gypsy "invasion" in order to secure a tighter measure of control over the entry of immigrants into Britain'. Writing in 1980, Colin Holmes could have been describing the moral panic some quarter of a century later about Romani asylum seekers. In fact his focus was the 1900s.[32] While there were periods of less hostile responses to foreign Gypsies in Britain during the twentieth century, state (and popular) antipathy did not disappear. In the mid–1990s, for example, and as a foretaste of responses to the Czech and Slovak Roma, it was reported that the British government was putting pressure on its Polish counterpart 'to stop Gypsies getting on planes for London'.[33]

The implementation of screening procedures in 2001 represented the culmination of a four-year campaign against the Czech and Slovak Roma which started in the autumn of 1997 and has involved all elements of British society. A small influx of roughly 1500 Roma in 1997 and less than that in the first half of 1998 was 'stemmed in October 1998 when the British government imposed visa restrictions on Slovak citizens'.[34] The few managing to get to Britain were given every 'encouragement' to return. Jan, who was attacked and injured by skinheads in eastern Slovakia, arrived in Dover:

> I was put straight away in Rochester prison and spent nearly two months there. I'd never been in prison before. In Rochester, every Tuesday we had a visit from a Psychological Social Worker. Through an interpreter he told us that we should go home, and that, in this country, there is the same discrimination as in the Czech and Slovak Republics. It wasn't safe for us here ... We asked him why we were in prison – after all, we came here legally. He said it was preventive, so we had the time to think about if we really wanted to stay in this country. If we wanted to go back, we could still do it.

Jan added that he knew what would happen if he returned: 'I'll be killed. After I left, the skinheads told my sister that, if I wanted to stay alive, I should never return. They beat her up and said they would burn her house down. She had to move into an all-Romany street for safety.'[35]

The campaign against asylum seekers in general had developed in Britain throughout the 1990s, encouraged by the Conservatives in government and then in opposition as a populist vote winner, as a way of bolstering their appeal through a crude form of nationalism.[36] In power since 1997, the Labour Party, while maintaining its commitment to anti-racism, especially in relation to the Stephen Lawrence enquiry about the black teenager murdered in 1993 and the subsequent police failures,[37] refused to challenge the rhetoric of anti-alienism or to deal with either asylum seekers at home or potential asylum seekers abroad, any more sympathetically than its political predecessors. Alongside the raising of the political stakes, the press campaign against 'abusive' or 'bogus' asylum seekers became intensive. All the tabloid newspapers (with the exception largely of the independent-minded *Mirror*)[38] and half of the broadsheets joined in although the strongest language and most concentrated coverage has been found in the mass circulation right-wing papers the *Daily Express*, *Mail*, *Sun*, the *Daily Star* and London's *Evening Standard*. It was the last of these that coined the term 'Giro Czechs' to describe the Roma who it claimed were singling out Britain to abuse its social security system, claiming dole, housing, health care and education facilities and becoming rich in the process.[39] According to the *Daily Star* these Roma were 'purely economic refugees' and were dismissed by the *Daily Mail* as 'cynical' and 'bogus'. And utilising the watery metaphors so readily drawn upon by anti-alienists for over a century, the *Sun* warned its readers about 'the flood of Slovakian gypsies'.[40]

This national campaign found a particular local focus – Dover in Kent – a major point of entry for asylum seekers but where in reality less than one thousand asylum seekers were living. In October 1997 the national press reported an 'invasion' of Roma asylum seekers in the town, helping to fuel local xenophobic and racist tendencies. A campaign was orchestrated by the *Dover Express* which in one editorial labelled the asylum seekers 'human sewage'. An accompanying headline stated that 'We want to wash th[is] dross down the drain'.[41] Neo-fascists from outside the region attempted to exploit local tensions further, but in reality the exclusion and violence faced by the Czech and Slovak Roma and other asylum seekers in the Kent coast area has hardly been confined to political extremists. In December 1998 a house in Dover in which an elderly Slovak Roma couple were living was firebombed, there was an arson attack on asylum seekers in Folkestone and 'an assault on a man after he had admitted he was a refugee'.[42]

There were alternative Dover responses, especially support groups set up to help the newcomers in which some local churches and clergy played a prominent role.[43] The testimony of Libuse, who came with her family following extreme racial harassment and an appalling occurrence of gang rape which left huge physical and psychological scars, illustrates, on the one hand, the difficulties involved in Roma gaining refugee status in Britain, and, on the other, the possibility of a more sympathetic welcome on behalf of ordinary people on the Kent coast:

> We came in Summer 1997, and asked for asylum in Dover. We spent three days in a detention centre. Our asylum application was refused at first, but after an appeal we got a year's leave to stay here. We have a flat now, but work very hard to pay the rent. One day, we'd like to own our own business: a bar or restaurant. We both have health problems [her husband was also badly beaten by skinheads] and I worry about my mother and sister a lot back home in Slovakia. But for me, living here is like paradise. People are nice to us. Here, when you are good to people, people are good back to you. Not like in Slovakia.[44]

It remains true, however, that the majority of responses, locally and nationally, to the Czech and Slovak Roma asylum seekers in Kent were negative. In the process of generating such animosity, place identity came to the fore. The symbolic significance of Dover in national mythology, as the principal point of resistance to invasion generally, and specifically in relation to the Second World War, was not lost on contemporaries, and military invasion metaphors were used freely to highlight the dangers facing Britain. Writing in the *Guardian*, one of the few papers to provide an alternative perspective and identify the moral panic about the Roma, Alan Travis and Ian Traynor in an article soberly entitled 'Britain's Little Refugee Problem', that

> You might think, from a perusal of the British papers this week, that thousands of illegal 'scrounging gypsies' – in the populist poetry of Sun-speak, the 'Giro Czechs' – had just swept across the European plains to stage a full-frontal assault on the White Cliffs of Dover.[45]

The port of Dover, according to the *Express*, was 'under siege'.[46] Even the *Independent*, usually liberal-minded on refugee matters, produced the headline 'Gypsies Invade Dover Hoping for a Handout'.[47]

Such paranoia and exaggeration were not to disappear. At the start of 2004, with the prospect of free movement across an extended European Union, the *Express* dedicated the front page to 'The Great Invasion 2004' with the headline subtitled '1.6 million gypsies set to flood in'. It was accompanied on an inside page by a map of Europe with arrows borrowed directly from *Dad's Army*, the most popular post-1945 evocation of Britain during the Second World War.[48] While a comedy, there is a serious message within this television classic which has been shown repeatedly since first being broadcast from 1968 to 1977. To many, *Dad's Army is* Britain during the Second World War. To the cultural historian, Jeffrey Richards, the intense success of *Dad's Army* is due to its celebration of Englishness, tapping into a 'nostalgia not so much for the war as a time of shortage, destruction and loss but as a period of shared effort and sacrifice, common purpose and good neighbourliness and justified struggle against a wicked enemy'. Rather than the Nazis, however, it was now the Gypsies who were set to invade Britain.[49] Yet defeatism had set in: rather than the plucky Home Guard platoon to 'fight them on the beaches', Britain's authorities were in crisis through an 'immigration shambles'.[50] 'We Can't Cope with Huge Gipsy Invasion', was the 'shocking truth' revealed by the *Express*.[51] In 2005, Richard Littlejohn, then of the *Sun*, one of Britain's most popular commentators, and a virulent media campaigner against asylum seekers, re-wrote the signature tune of *Dad's Army*. Rather than the fictional Walmington-on-Sea where the Home Guard will never let the invaders pass, Littlejohn set the scene in an 'Immigration Appeals Tribunal':

> Who do you think you are kidding, Mr Blunkett
> If you think we're going home.
> We are the boys who all know our human rights.
> We'll get legal aid and we're not afraid to fight.

So who do you think you are kidding, Mr Blunkett.
Don't you know old England's done.[52]

Here Littlejohn, along with other columnists in the right-wing tabloid press, provided a form of racist pessimism reminiscent (aside from the use of humour) of right-wing German intellectuals in the late nineteenth century who followed what Fritz Stern described as 'the politics of cultural despair'.[53] Robert Colls, in his study of the construction of Englishness, has highlighted the work of Harold Mackinder and his *Britain and the British Seas* (1902/1930) in which it was emphasised that 'Only in the narrow Dover Straits had she been vulnerable. But England had defeated that channel, and indeed used it to take the best of European culture whilst repelling the worst of continental despotism.'[54] To tabloids such as the *Sun* and the *Express* there was no longer confidence that Dover could, in the twenty-first century, resist 'the worst'.

Returning to the late 1990s, the fear of the 'Gypsy Invasion' of Dover possessed a wider cultural currency. Kent as a whole has a greater resonance in the construction of Englishness beyond its past role in withstanding invasion. Although there are many different strands in the 'idea of England', the countryside has always played a key role in such national imaginings. Within this mythical rural idyll, Kent and the other 'Home Counties' have a particularly important symbolism. Writing for an American audience in 1951 at the time of the Festival of Britain, Ruth McKenney and Richard Bransten were clear: 'Kent, Sussex, and Surrey – these ancient hills saw the beginning of British history. This *is* England.'[55] The vehemence of the reaction to the local presence of the Roma can be partly explained, as Claude Moraes of the Joint Council for the Welfare of Immigrants perceptively noted, by the fear that somehow 'the garden of England, Kent, [was] being violated'.[56]

Through the articulation and encouragement of such fears, local and national hostility towards asylum seekers, and especially the Roma, grew throughout 1998. Aside from those from the Czech Republic and Slovenia, Roma from Romania, fleeing even greater state and public animosity, were the targets of press hatred.[57] In 1999 minor racist riots in Britain against the Roma occurred.[58] The antipathy if not the violence was given official approval in March 2000 when Labour immigration minister Barbara Roche labelled alleged begging by Romanian Gypsy asylum seekers as 'vile'.[59] It was supported by her boss, Home Secretary Jack Straw, who shortly afterwards stated that society had been 'too tolerant' of travellers, and set up procedures to remove the Roma as quickly as possible from the UK.[60] The media campaign against Gypsies intensified with stories of Roma who, it was alleged, were making a fortune in Britain while claiming refugee status in a collective scam.[61]

A month later, in April 1998, and in apparent contrast to what appeared to be open season on asylum seekers, Prime Minister Tony Blair proclaimed that 'This country should always be willing to take in those who are genuinely fleeing persecution. That is a noble tradition of ours and I, for one, would not like to see it disappear'.[62] The historical perspective employed throughout this study has highlighted how attacks on 'abusive' asylum seekers, or what used through much of the twentieth century to be called undesirable aliens, whether by politicians, media or, as we will see, the public, are almost automatically, one might almost suggest, formulaically, preceded by statements such as that by Tony Blair.[63] But why was there such lip service to tolerance and who are those 'genuinely fleeing persecution'? According to the British government, they most clearly were not and are not the Czech Roma. In the UK, over 99 per cent have been *refused* refugee status: 'Of over 3,000 Roma refugees to the UK in 1997 and 1998, only five from Slovakia and one family of three from the Czech republic were successful in gaining asylum'. Such assessment and procedures are clearly subjective – in Canada over 70 per cent of Czech Roma claims had been *accepted* as genuine and approved.[64]

The evidence of the persecution of the Roma in the Czech Republic, Slovakia and elsewhere on the continent is overwhelming and frightening. Discrimination at state as well as at a private level and violence including many murders, often though not exclusively carried out by young skinheads, are an everyday occurrence for the Roma. As Jozef, who came to Britain after intense racial harassment, states, in the Czech Republic 'Roma people don't have any rights. We are not seen as human ... It's not just skinheads who hate the Roma. Skinheads just do the dirty work for everyone else.'[65] Whereas most acts of antisemitism in Europe are monitored, denounced and action taken against them, racism against the Roma is hardly reported, let alone reprimanded.[66] A rare study, carried out by a human rights monitoring group and not an official government body, recorded that, between 1990 and the end of 1997 – the first seven years after the renewal of democracy in the Czech Republic – there were 1,205 racially motivated attacks against the Roma, 15 of which were fatal.[67] In an analysis of the Czech Republic and Slovakia entitled 'razor blades amidst the velvet', Chris Powell argues that 'The police have proved to be reluctant to act where violence has been targeted against Roma. Indeed, such is their anti-Gypsy reputation that Romani victims often decline to report incidents for fear of becoming doubly victimised.'[68]

Many states have been as equally guilty of prejudice as the hostile element of their citizenship. Hoping to reduce their Gypsy population through persecution and resultant refugee movements has been one factor in the discriminatory treatment meted out. A wider issue remains:

why the contrast between the pariah status of antisemitism and the apparent respectability of anti-Gypsy racism in European culture? How is it, as Powell outlines, that a group of young Prague progressives can regard slogans such as 'foreigners out' to be intolerable but simultaneously believe that not liking Gypsies 'doesn't make you a racist'?[69] Furthermore, why is it that there is an 'extraordinary ... depth of hostility towards Gypsies wherever they live'?[70]

In the case of the Jews and antisemitism, it is possible to argue that post-1945 the Holocaust has made such hostility unrespectable. Even so, the impact was far from immediate – awareness of its full enormity did not develop fully until the last quarter of the twentieth century when the murder of six million Jews became symbolic of man's potential for inhumanity and Auschwitz increasingly a religious and secular metaphor for evil.[71] Yet for all its belated recognition, the knowledge of and engagement with the Holocaust stands in stark contrast to the lack of acknowledgment of the genocide committed against Europe's Gypsies during the Second World War. This genocide inevitably still shapes Roma identity today as was marked in the Fifth World Romani Congress held in Prague, July 2000. The Congress produced a 'Declaration of a Nation', the third sentence of which stated

> We, a Nation of which over half a million persons were exterminated in a fergotten Holocaust, a Nation of individuals too often discriminated, marginalised, victim of intollerance and persecutions, we have a dream, and we are engaged in fulfilling it.[72]

At a basic level the knowledge of the Jewish catastrophe compared to the ignorance of the murder of the Gypsies might reflect the greater access to the media of post-war Jewry in contrast to the largely non-literate and marginal Gypsy world. This analysis, however, would be to simplify. There was nothing inevitable about the centrality that the Holocaust now occupies in discussions of modernity and man's capacity for destruction. But once developed, there has been an attraction in focusing on the Holocaust – for all its extreme horror, it is safe territory, and one that gets safer as questions of compensation and prosecution become ones of historical scrutiny rather than implementation. Engaging with the Holocaust is relatively low risk because its very enormity distances us from most everyday questions of 'good' and 'evil'. It is also hazard-free on a very pragmatic level: Jewish refugees either from the Nazi era or thereafter are unlikely now to enter Britain or other western nations, whereas Roma fleeing persecution on the continent, as the tabloids and their scare stories of '1.6 million Gypsies', are. While it is probable that increasing awareness of the Holocaust has not ended many centuries of 'the Jew' being regarded as 'other' to European culture, it has made more blatant manifestations of antisemitism less acceptable. For the Roma themselves, as their 'Declaration of a Nation' made explicit, persecution, past and present, are intimately linked. Such connections between the historical and the contemporary treatment of Roma are rarely made, however, by non-Gypsies. Even when they are made, there is a danger in assuming that recognition of the extermination of Roma in the war would by itself end antagonism to those in contemporary society. Indeed, awareness of the horrors can be cruelly used as yet another weapon to intimidate the Roma population. In the Czech Republic and Slovakia graffiti such as 'Send the Gypsies to the Gas Chambers', is not uncommon.[73] In the older democracy of Britain a train conversation between 'two respectable men' on a train in Scotland recorded by an observer sympathetic to the plight of the Roma showed the dangers of relying on the hope that knowledge of the past will automatically lead to empathy today. It also exposed the power of contemporary anti-Gypsy discourse. One man said to the other 'Gypsies – Ah hate fuckin Gypsies. Hitler killed a lot of gypsies, didn't he? Good.' What is particularly significant is that the conversation illicited no response. 'No-one turned a hair'. As the observer remarked, 'It's impossible to imagine that no one would so much as sniff at similar remarks directed at Jews'.[74]

So, who, if not the Gypsies, are in Prime Minister Blair's words, those 'genuinely fleeing persecution?'. As we have explored at various stages in this study, in terms of political and popular discourse those evoked more often or not in fulfilling the criteria are the refugees of the past and, with particular claim to possess impeccable credentials, Jewish refugees from the Third Reich. Some 80,000 Jewish refugees entered Britain during the 1930s, although just over half were present at the outbreak of war and many fewer than that settled permanently.[75] Whether British refugee policy during the Nazi era was part of a 'noble tradition' is debatable – academic opinion is divided, although on a popular level of heritage representation, as we have seen, the assumption is increasingly one that it was a positive and welcoming policy.[76] In reality responses and attitudes to the plight of the Jews were ambivalent and also far from static – themes that run across chapters 3 and 4 of *Remembering Refugees*.[77] Moreover, some half a million Jews applied to come to Britain and most of those who were let in, essentially on temporary visas, were subject to selection that favoured certain types of entrants according to age, country of origin and skill level – it was a highly racialised and gendered policy. During the Second World War both the chances to escape and the freedom to enter declined drastically – there was, in essence, no British refugee policy towards the Jews of Europe.[78]

But what is often forgotten in contemporary discussions is that at the time only sections of British state and society saw the Jews as deserving asylum: they were not, in today's terminology, always perceived as genuine asylum seekers. Criticised as unwanted aliens who would steal British jobs, the same metaphors of floods and swamping were utilised to ensure that refugee numbers, even at more welcoming moments, would always be strictly controlled.[79] Yet the desire to appear reasonable and tolerant was alive in the 1930s as it is today. A few decades earlier a similar process was at work in responses to East European Jews escaping persecution in the Tsarist empire. Then anti-alienists, as we have explored earlier, inside and outside parliament, contrasted the newcomers to the deserving refugees of the past – the Huguenots fleeing persecution in Catholic France in the seventeenth and eighteenth centuries.[80] Similarly, at the height of the media campaign against the 'Slovak and Czech gipsies in Kent', the *Mail on Sunday* produced an editorial: 'An Abuse of Our Generosity'. Claiming that Britain had become 'the soft touch of Europe', it outlined the facilities that would be offered 'courtesy of the British taxpayer' to these 'gipsies' at a time when Kent County Council was axing 'social services for its own elderly and infirm'. It concluded by stating that

> This country has always offered a safe haven to those genuinely fleeing political persecution. And we have been enriched by the contribution such refugees have made. But our generosity is now being abused. It has gone on for too long. It cannot continue.[81]

The past in the treatment of refugees and asylum seekers is not so much a different as a less dangerous country.

Popular responses

In its penultimate section, this chapter will illustrate how the use of the past to justify exclusion in the present has popular resonance. It will do so through a directive set by the social anthropological organisation Mass-Observation in summer 2000 which was completed by roughly two hundred respondents. As has been noted, Mass-Observation was founded in the 1930s to provide an anthropological exploration of the British by the British, utilising ordinary untrained observers. It faded by the 1950s but was revived in the 1980s and since then several thousand volunteers have kept diaries and responded to specific directives.[82]

The importance of the material collected is not in its potential to be quantified – although numerous, the volunteer writers, as was the case with the earlier Mass-Observers, do not accurately represent the British population as a whole in relation to key factors such as age profile, sex, ethnicity or class. The strength of the project lies in the quality and depth of writing it generated, even though few of its volunteers are professionals in this respect. If they have a major theme in common, it is that they are generally independent-minded and are people able to be reflexive about their own writing, using, and encouraged to use, a life story approach. Writing and the writing process are important to their identity and everyday life. That there is a relative absence of dissonance between official and media representations of asylum seekers and the writings of today's Mass-Observers is testimony to the power of the collaborative process in this area – normally the Observers are sceptical about politicians and what they read, hear and see on the media as is apparent in their war diaries covering conflicts in the Falklands, the Gulf Wars, Kosovo, Afghanistan and most recently Iraq.[83]

Encouraging an autobiographical approach, the summer 2000 directive on refugees asked the observers to write not only about their reactions and experience of asylum seekers today but also their past encounters with refugees. Juxtaposing the two provocatively, the directive asked the observers how they reacted to the remarks of a pro-refugee MP who had stated in parliament that if Anne Frank had tried to get into Britain today as an asylum seeker, she would have been denied entry.[84] The life story approach adopted by many of the Observers enabled them to reflect on how their lives had been touched and even influenced and shaped by refugees in the past. A 36-year-old housewife in County Durham said her first reaction, as an English born person of English born parents, whose husband had similar origins, was 'Oh I don't have any experience of this' but then she remembered involvement with the Vietnamese boat people in the early 1980s.[85] The pattern of initial denial followed by detailed accounts of connections was marked in the responses, revealing the powerful tradition of refugee settlement in twentieth-century Britain but the absence of a national narrative framework in which to place it. Many, indeed, including a surprising number with Huguenot ancestors, acknowledged refugee origins.[86] As one woman, a self-employed clerical worker in East Anglia, put it

> I said at the beginning of this [directive] that I had no experience [of asylum seekers] and that I was English for many generations. However, on my mother's side, my ancestors came to this country as Huguenot refugees fleeing religious persecution in France. So, once upon a time, my family came here as asylum seekers.[87]

Similarly, a retired schoolteacher in Glasgow confronted her own refugee background through the literacy practice encouraged by Mass-Observation: 'As I write [this I] realise that I *am* in a long ago way, an asylum seeker' – one of her ancestors was a Huguenot who helped develop glass blowing in the north-east of England 'to everyone's benefit, both theirs and the area's'.[88]

There were still some, however, such as a middle-aged housewife in Milton Keynes, who totally denied any familial connection to refugees: 'I have none. My family are English through and through. Probably the last foreign blood in our veins was Norman or Viking.' Not surprisingly, she had no time for contemporary asylum seekers:

> I'm appalled by the way people are allowed to come into this country willy-nilly and are given nice places to live and state benefits immediately. It seems to me that an awful lot of people claiming asylum these days regard Britain as a soft touch and have come here purely to get whatever they can out of us. I don't believe a lot of the stories about persecution.[89]

It is this refusal to accept Britain's past diversity that makes it hard for those of immigrant and refugee background to place themselves within a 'local' tradition. In this respect, the testimony of a recruitment consultant in Middlesex is worth quoting at length. She was 'descended from refugees on both sides' – her grandparents on her father's side were Jews coming from Lithuania and the Ukraine who met in London at the turn of the twentieth century. On her mother's side her grandfather's ancestors were French Huguenot silkweavers and her grandmother's 'Scottish peasants driven off the land during the Highland Clearances'. With this background, the Observer was 'sharply aware that if this country had not been at least neutral towards [refugees], if not wholly accepting, then I wouldn't exist at all'. In contrast to the Milton Keynes' respondent, her background made her 'in favour of asylum seekers, refugees, economic migrants and a bit ashamed of the government's response'. Nevertheless, it was tellingly *not* within Britain that she confronted this diverse background, taking us back to the differing fortunes of refugee heritage centres featured in the first chapter of this study:

> The links with the past came home to me when I visited the Museum of Immigration on Ellis Island in New York. I stood there in the entrance hall, which is the building where new immigrants were actually received. There is a big exhibit of a pile of luggage – poor people's luggage – immensely moving. I saw it and thought 'my grandfather was here, totally alone, aged 19, knowing he would never see his family again, speaking only rudimentary English'. I felt moved by the hope and courage of refugees, and appalled at the various events which cause people to uproot themselves from everything they have ever known to go into the unknown, because the unknown with all its uncertainties looks better than the known. I wonder if I would have the courage.[90]

Hardly any of the directive respondents referred to the refugees of the past in negative terms or had anything but positive, though undoubtedly

romanticised memories of them. One whose family hosted Jewish refugees in the 1930s stated that 'Our lives were enriched by meeting so
many strangers'[91] and another who helped the Vietnamese half a century
later wrote that her family 'consider ourselves fortunate to be their friends:
I can't begin to tell you the interest ... they brought to our lives'. Few,
however, connected these positive memories and impressions to the
present. The last mentioned observer was very typical in distancing her
Vietnamese friends with the present asylum seekers who 'seem to be out
to milk us for all we're worth, without putting anything back into the
system'.[92]

The summer 2000 directive responses are notable for the richness of
past refugees referred to – Huguenots, Flemings, East European Jews,
Armenians, refugees from Nazism, Basque refugee children, Poles, Ukrainians during and after the Second World War, Hungarians in the 1950s,
Ugandan Asians, Greek Cypriots, Chileans, Kurds, Vietnamese 'boat
people' and Kosovans. Almost all the memories and representations of
these groups were positive. Indeed, they conformed to a narrative structure of genuine need, a welcome reception, expectation of gratitude on
behalf of those helped and their subsequent contribution to the nation
that had provided them with freedom and safety. Such redemptive narratives were most marked in relation to the Jews, Ugandan Asians and
Vietnamese. A retired radio programme monitor in Suffolk provided a
succinct account of the Vietnamese refugees, contrasting their settlement
with what she identified as the majority of those now coming to Britain
who she was convinced were undeserving. There were two types of asylum seekers, she believed: 'real genuine people fleeing for whatever reason and ungrateful trouble makers, amd more of these than the genuine
ones'. The Observer had only known 'one genuine asylum seeker family'
who were Vietnamese:

> They arrived (husband, wife and 2 children) in a very bad state. They were
> looked after by social services, given western clothes and as soon as they
> recovered with food and rest, set about trying to learn English and helping
> in any way they can. They took on any work they could and again helped
> anyone they could in their community. They are very appreciative of being
> able to stay here.

In contrast, the 'other kind' of asylum seekers were more numerous and
'I feel we are saddled with other countries cast-offs [and] troublemakers
they don't want.'[93]

The pattern of memory as outlined in previous chapters, where some
groups have been valorised and others forgotten, marginalised or
problematised, was replicated in the summer 2000 directive. Those in
the past who were perceived as least fitting the acceptable model of

acceptance–gratitude–contribution were the Hungarians from 1956 and those most conforming to it were the Jewish refugees from Nazism. Turning to the former, it is revealing that few of those recalling the Hungarians could remember when they arrived, querying and crossing out dates in their directive responses, one vaguely suggesting that they came in the 1950s 'I think'.[94] Lacking subsequent memory work from the group itself and more generally an awareness of the specific circumstances in which they fled, the representation of the Hungarians within the Mass-Observation accounts was mixed, with only a handful mentioning them at all. The Hungarians were dismissed summarily by a retired technical writer in Somerset who believed that 'many of them ... caused much trouble and crime'.[95]

Alternatively, reflecting the many who were active in supporting these victims of Soviet oppression, a Birmingham teacher provided a much more positive account, remembering that 'when I was a student I was put in charge of a Hungarian student (1956) who had escaped in London and was given a place at our college. I, and my friends, went out of our way to welcome her'. She added that she never felt any prejudice towards the Hungarians and never doubted that they had a 'right to be here' whereas 'Nowadays it is a different situation' with asylum seekers.[96] The fullest account of a Hungarian refugee was provided by a nurse in Basingstoke. Its non-heroic and slightly tawdry account is markedly different to most of the directive responses on former refugees who tend to be portrayed in a romanticised and idealised way:

> Following the Hungarian uprising in 1956, my father's sister married Steven who came to England as a refugee. I have no knowledge of how he got to England or to East Anglia where my family lived but I do remember him being very tall, very dark and very thin. He always seemed to be hungry and whenever I saw him he was eating something ... My aunt said that 'he'd had a terrible time' – how she knew that I don't know as he spoke very little English ... He ... then got a job as a farm worker and they moved to a tied cottage and subsequently had two children. One day when the boys were both quite small he disappeared with the woman who lived next door and was never seen again by anyone in the family.[97]

Such an account stands in stark contrast to the Mass-Observation narratives constructed in relation to the child refugees.

As we have seen in the previous chapter, it is within the stories of the *Kindertransport* that the 'saving' of refugees coming to Britain is most pronounced. This redemptive theme is reflected in a number of the 2000 Mass-Observation 'Coming to Britain' directive responses. An elderly former teacher recalled how 'in 1939 a number of children were brought over from Germany to this country. A friend of my mothers had a rectory house and offered to give sanctuary to one of the children. He was a Jewish boy, sent by his parents to the safety of Britain.' Soon, the boy had 'settled in happily with the family'. On his thirteenth birthday he was presented with a new bicycle which he drove around the countryside. Alas, a fortnight later he crashed into a delivery van and died of his injuries. Her account ends, in spite of its intense pathos and tragedy, with Britain and the British people as saviours of the boy's freedom:

> My friends had the heartbreaking task of informing his parents that their hope, to be sure of safety from the Nazis, had this traumatic ending ... My sister and I felt the episode so much and never forgot the little boy and his few weeks of happiness.[98]

Some of those who experienced the *Kinder* at school remember them with equal affection and recall the 'thrill' and excitement of their arrival.[99] In a far more businesslike manner, an elderly male Observer, 'retired from the Royal Navy after 40 years and from 10 years in commerce', stated bluntly that his own experience of refugees was 'confined to the arrival at my prep school in the 1930s of several boys of Czech, Austrian and German nationality whose parents had fled from the National Socialist regime, some of them Jewish in religion. They were made welcome though subjected to good-natured teasing, did very well in school once they had mastered English, and subsequently had successful careers.' In contrast, his problem with contemporary asylum seekers was the unsystematic way they were treated which stopped the 'genuine refugees' from finding employment and learning English 'which would help their absorption into the community'.[100]

In such accounts, there was little consideration given to the feelings of the refugees themselves – the emphasis was very much on the help that had been given by Britain and the expectation of gratitude. When the refugees' lives were imagined, the desire for a 'happy ending' was powerful. It was strongly evoked by a middle-aged Observer recalling a family holiday in Margate a few years after the end of the war. On the beach, she was

> fascinated by quite a large group of people (children and adults) sitting nearby. These people were talking in a foreign accent, they were all slightly darker skinned and very dark haired ... and they seemed so very happy and laughing all the time, and my parents told me they were of the Jewish faith and that they had been allowed to come to Britain and work and settle and that they were now so very, very happy as some of them had experienced some very bad times, and I've always remembered them and hoped their lives from then on were more content.[101]

The testimony of a former child refugee within the directive respondents provides a rather different perspective. Gratitude is far from absent in her account, but it runs alongside an acknowledgement that she was initially 'incredibly homesick and cried a great deal and couldn't have been a very rewarding foster child'. She was lucky in that her 'parents had got out of Germany by the very last train'. Even so, as 'refugees [we] had no choice but to accept whatever kindness and help was offered to us, however much of a "come-down" it may have been'.[102]

What emerges most strongly, however, with these accounts of the refugees from Nazism is their undisputable status as 'deserving'. It was rare in this directive for the respondents to consider that it was only with the advantage of hindsight that any refugee group can be considered to have contributed. An intriguing account was provided by a retired physiotherapist who wrestles first with her own origins and then her attitudes towards current asylum seekers. She initially described herself as having 'Anglo-Saxon origins' but then qualified this by acknowledging Huguenot, Irish and Swiss ancestry. The Observer was proud of the contribution made to Britain by her Huguenot forebears, who were silversmiths, and added that similarly 'Jewish refugees from Europe also got safe havens here and greatly enriched our culture and expertise, eg the Amadeus quartet, surgeons, writers etc'. Yet while acknowledging that 'We've all benefited from refugees' she quickly added that 'we are now a small overcrowded island' and that she 'object[ed] to our culture losing its identity'. In turn, this comment was qualified: 'Oh dear – I sound very intolerant and right wing'. Her account continued in similar ambivalent vein – praising the Vietnamese who were absorbed into her Suffolk community and then contrasting their integration with the contemporary issue of asylum seekers (with presumably the Roma in mind): 'it must be very difficult for people in … Dover … where their whole area is swamped – and they can't *all* be political refugees'.[103] Her directive response ended by returning autobiographically and more comfortably to the Jewish refugees from the 1930s. The Mass-Observer's brother had helped bring a Jewish family out of Germany with the help of their local MP, R.A. Butler:

> The family were granted entry [and] have served GB well ever since – and never ceased giving praise and gratitude to the Brits for allowing them in – and saving their lives. During the war we … were asked if we could befriend a girl at my school – who was very Jewish and had got out of Austria. She spent her holidays with us – did well and married a Swede – and somehow her father survived in Austria.

Self-aware to the end, her account ends by acknowledging that it was 'easier to relate to individuals than a plane load of Afghanistans – or a lorry full of Chinese'. These references were revealingly honest if callous – in February 2000 a group of desperate Afghan asylum seekers had hijacked a plane to Stansted Airport and four months later fifty-eight

Chinese migrants had suffocated in a lorry from France and were found dead in Dover.[104] In 1997, the Refugee Council commissioned research to explore why there was limited identification with those seeking asylum in Britain. The debriefing highlighted that ordinary people had little everyday contact with refugees and that their 'invisibility' was intensified by fragmentation through nationality and background.[105] The Mass-Observation directive responses from summer 2000 confirm this earlier analysis – the lack of 'normal' contact, and the absence of a clear narrative of who contemporary asylum seekers actually were, helped the expression of insensitive and hostile comments about the Afghans, Chinese and other asylum seekers attempting to reach Britain.

Mass-Observers push themselves hard to confront some of their own ambivalent thinking, exemplified in the case of another directive respondent, a 48-year-old civil servant, between what one called her 'Guardian' reading on the one side and on the other, a 'Tumbridge Wells' persona. When it came to the Romanian Gypsies, however, she could not tolerate their alleged behaviour in Britain, even if remarking, in the middle of an anti-Roma diatribe, 'Drat, I'm turning into my mother'. But while not liking herself, the Tumbridge Wells persona was winning out: 'it's the contrast between what I feel *should* be a tradition of liberal views embracing other cultures and the sense that some asylum seekers are "taking advantage" and not assimilating'.[106]

Much more often than not, reference to the Second World War and the persecution of the Jews was used not only to bolster Britain's positive image, but to enable criticism of the recent newcomers, especially the Czech, Slovak and Romanian Roma. The strategy of the designers of the Mass-Observation directive was turned in on itself. 'I cannot compare the present surge of *illegal* immigrants with that of the Jews during World War II. They were fleeing persecution by what was then our enemy. Therefore it was only right that we should help them'. The woman writing these comments had the Romanian Gypsies very much in mind, who, she argued, were insisting that they be allowed to beg in Britain because it was their way of life.[107] Only three observers referred to either the persecution of the Gypsies in the past or in the present. One of the three remarked on how in most places in Britain today, public expression of racism is 'now socially unacceptable' but 'when it comes to gypsies, all bets are off'.[108] The Jews, in retrospect, have been proved to be genuine, by what one observer referred to as 'the facts' of the Holocaust.[109] It was fine, remarked one observer, that Britain had a reputation to giving a safe haven to the genuine refugee, but not to 'freeloaders' such as the Romanian Gypsies. 'No way are they refugees'. Denying that the Gypsies were being persecuted he still believed that, quite understandably, the Romanians were glad to see the back of them.[110] Another respondent, an immigration officer, wary of the Official Secrets Act, told the lie of this account. He dealt day after day in Kent with asylum seekers, mainly Gypsies, coming from countries, where, as he put it, the authorities 'have a relaxed attitude to discrimination where gypsies are targetted by skinheads'. Most of the claims for refugee status he and others dealt with were, he stressed, rejected on technical, legal grounds rather than because they were disbelieved.[111]

In 1999, as has been explored in chapter 2, public pressure forced the British government to temporarily and partially open its doors to Kosovan Albanians fleeing ethnic cleansing.[112] An ex-sales assistant in Yorkshire recalled the intense sympathy and work on their behalf around Bradford: 'everyone in the area went out of their way to do all they could to make them very welcome and to feel "at home"'.[113] Simultaneously, the state, supported by most of the media and with apparent public support, were carrying out their own form of removal with the continental Roma. Subsequently, this collaboration has gone further, and all asylum seekers have become demonised in Britain except for those mythic exceptions, 'the genuine refugees'. All major anxieties, especially concerning health care, education, social services, terrorism, employment and pensions are projected onto them. As a retired engineer puts it: 'The situation today cannot be compared to the Second World War ... when the majority of people coming to Britain were genuine asylum seekers and not, as today, trying to get on the social benefits gravy train'.[114] The vision of the future from one Mass-Observer is startling but not that exceptional, taking the responses as a whole: 'Will we find our Englishness so diluted that we are in the minority in our own country? Will we become the slaves, working to provide donations to the gypsies?'[115]

Conclusion

Roy Greenslade has concluded in a study conducted for the Institute for Public Policy Research (IPPR) *Seeking Scapegoats: the Coverage of Asylum in the UK Press* (2005) that

> the term asylum-seeker is, at face value, racially impartial. This means that press and public can speak of asylum-seekers in ways they would never dare to speak of immigrants, say, or black people. It is 'safe' to talk of 'fucking asylum-seekers', though not to use the same description for immigrants or blacks. The press has endorsed and legitimised this abuse.[116]

Has hostility towards contemporary asylum seekers become today's form of respectable racism? While answering affirmatively, the evidence produced in this chapter suggests that asylum-seeker phobia has achieved a form of legitimacy as suggested by Greenslade, and that it has done so by evoking the selective memory of past generosity. Does it then follow that society needs some form of outgroup to collectively hate and thereby create group solidarity – the target moving from, amongst others, Huguenots, to the Irish to the Jews to New Commonwealth migrants to asylum seekers today? Here the answer is negative – as popular resistance to government restrictionism against refugees in the Kosovan war of 1999 or in the many thousands of largely forgotten refugee committees across the twentieth century proved – racism, in contrast to new right rhetoric, is not natural wherever ethnic diversity occurs: there is choice in the matter. Indeed, whilst the majority of the Mass-Observation directive responses in summer 2000 were negative towards contemporary asylum seekers, there were still many who were critical of the policies of the government, hostile reporting in the media, and of the antipathy of those around them.

It is clear from the argument of this chapter that many ordinary people – indeed, the vocal majority at the close of the twentieth century and the start of the twenty-first – cannot be freed from criticism in helping to create what is a corroding atmosphere of asylum-seeker phobia. The dangers of such unrestrained prejudice are beginning to be recognised and research is focusing on its nature: is it, for example, generated from the top down, with governments and/or the media creating hysteria? Alternatively, are its origins coming from the grassroots? Are politicians and newspapers simply (and legitimately) responding to popular pressure from below? The material produced by the Mass-Observation summer directive does not provide a definitive answer, but it does reveal the complexity and interconnected nature of government-media-popular perspectives.

In the 1939 Mass-Observation directive responses on Jews and refugees, the large majority were critical of press reporting, believing the accounts to be exaggerated and hysteria inducing. There were those within the summer 2000 directive who were similarly suspicious and hostile to the media's scare stories about refugees, reflecting the independence of mind that is one of the key characteristics of many Mass-Observers. A young female respondent in Yorkshire believed that

> a lot of hostility has been whipped up in the media towards asylum seekers. Some have been treated very badly – subjected to the kind of verbal and physical abuse and racial hatred which they thought they'd escaped from. If crimes are committed, the finger is pointed towards local asylum seekers ... Asylum seekers become a 'weak' and convenient target.[117]

In relation to the specific subject matter of this chapter, a computer systems administrator in Edinburgh believed that 'prejudice against gypsies is reinforced by the media', adding that it cropped up in 'some of the most unexpected places':

> I remember an 'Independent' banner headline from a year or so back 'GYP-SIES INVADE'. This was one of the more liberal national broad sheets. Even the BBC carried a remarkable piece showing poverty-stricken Gypsies in Rumania celebrating, as we were told in voice over, the fact that they were going to emigrate to Britain and sign on the dole. You have to ask yourself who instigated this party and how did the people thus represented think that they were being shown. Perhaps they thought the cameramen had come to help them.[118]

Similarly an engineer in Nottingham, who had no direct experience of asylum seekers, found his sympathy rising towards them because of the negative press campaign. 'It is difficult not to become annoyed by the small-minded way in which the press stir up hatred towards asylum seekers'. It was, he argued, a form of disguised racism where 'broadly speaking the blacker one's face, the greater the objection'. He pointed particularly towards the campaign of the *Sun* against 'East European gypsies'.[119]

There was a definite view among more liberal-minded Observers that, as a forensic phonetician put it, 'A lot of people [were letting] the tabloids do their thinking for them' – a result of laziness and racism.[120] There was certainly clear evidence within the summer 2000 directive of the influence of the media in a negative direction with several including cuttings from anti-asylum seeker tabloids to reinforce their arguments. A retired administrator in Devon, who was concerned that Britain was being 'swamped by the tide of outsiders entering our country', enclosed an article from the *Daily Mail* entitled 'The centre for refugees is that way. I suggest you go by Tube sir'. He added that it took 'a little believing', but, nevertheless, accepted its contents without question.[121] A former primary school teacher had read in the same paper about 'illegal' asylum seekers being given a furnished house and having the audacity to complain that there was no colour television: 'That sort of thing makes my blood boil.'[122]

It does appear, comparing the 1939 and 2000 Mass-Observation material, that there was proportionally less questioning of the hostile media in the later directive responses. It would be simplistic, however, to conclude that it is the media, and especially the right-wing tabloid press, that is solely to blame for the current moral panic. In his IPPR study, Roy Greenslade comments that 'The influence of the popular press should never be underestimated ... the four popular papers which have run the most critical copy about asylum-seekers are read by more than 22 million people, more than a third of the British population'.[123] Yet even Greenslade, a former tabloid editor himself, acknowledges that the

relationship between the press and public opinion is a complex one –
there is, he argues, a process 'in which the press both reflects and en-
hances public attitudes and thereby sets off a chain reaction in which the
reflection and enhancement go on escalating until reality is buried under
layers of myth and prejudice'.[124] An earlier study carried out by the Information Centre about Asylum and Refugees in the UK (ICAR) in 2004,
while also acknowledging that 'information in the mass media can be
influential', also places emphasis on 'filters', such as 'local experience',
through which ordinary people receive information.[125] They add that

> Direct contact with asylum seekers and refugees, or discussions with those
> who have had direct contact, creates alternatives spirals – urban myths –
> which may correspond to or contradict those expressed in the media but
> are perceived to be independent of them. The extent to which audiences
> are resilient to biases in media signification depends too on how far they
> are sophisticated media consumers or 'critical readers', how reliable and
> relevant they believe the newspapers to be, including how far the papers
> are believed to be in tune with local concerns.[126]

The 2000 Mass-Observation directive responses certainly confirm this
sophisticated approach to the relationship between press and public. They
also add weight to a 2001 survey, 'Profiles of Prejudice', commissioned
by Stonewall's 'Citizenship 21 Project', that other factors aside from the
media were important influences 'on how people feel about minority
groups' (this included ethnic minorities, including refugees/asylum seekers). It suggested that parents were the most important factor, followed,
in order of priority, by television, newspapers, friends, school, religious
beliefs and other family influences.[127] The life story approach of the revived Mass-Observation project reveals in a far more nuanced and multi-
layered way how family and personal experiences and memories com-
bine with political and other ideological perspectives in confronting the
issue of contemporary asylum seekers. The role of the media is clearly
important, and it has intensified since 2000 with an even greater and
more hostile reporting of the issues, but it cannot be taken in isolation.

   The ability of individuals to construct a bogeyman out of asylum seekers *without* the direct influence of the media was shown in the case of an
elderly male respondent in Derby who emphasised his 'five years war
service' fighting fascism. He believed that it was 'only the anonymity
offered by Mass-Observation that enables me to express my views' free
from prosecution under the Race Relations Act. The respondent was
convinced that Englishness was under siege from the newcomers. He had
faith that 'Englishness survives in the hearts of the silenced majority', but
was sure that the damage being done to his country by immigrants and
asylum seekers was *not* being reported in 'our once fearless free press'.

There was, he concluded, 'censorship of this subject … either by omission or silence'.[128]

More common was the view of the female respondent who started out by stating that she had 'great sympathy with genuine refugees who flee their country with little or no alternative. To lose one's home, family and community must be devastating.' She added that she did 'feel that a large number of so-called asylum seekers are merely looking for a better lifestyle and are impinging on our health, welfare and housing systems'. When she read in the press that they came seeking free fertility treatment on the NHS 'I do wonder if this may be taking unfair advantage of our services'. There was, however, a hesitancy in accepting the press reports, wondering 'if [they] can be believed'. Throughout her account a fundamental ambivalence existed – she was deeply sympathetic to the Chinese who had died in the lorry in Dover but suspicious of the motives of economic migrants who came to take advantage 'of all that has been built up by the country's efforts over many years'. Despite her strong feelings, she 'certainly th[ought] it is wrong to abuse [asylum seekers], either verbally or physically'. Finally she ended her directive response by recalling an Austrian friend who had been persecuted by the Nazis. This woman had been given very poor treatment in Britain during the Second World War – 'she was injured in an air raid and neighbours refused to help her in any way' – but was pleased that afterwards that she had lived a long and happy life.[129] The response of most Mass-Observers to refugees and asylum seekers was ambivalent and this was extenuated and complicated further by an ambivalence towards media reporting of the issues.

Taking the 2000 Mass-Observation directive responses as a whole, not surprisingly – given large sections of the media's hostility towards asylum seekers – the impact on ordinary people's attitudes and responses has been negative. In the discussion so far in this section, the focus has been on the press and the public. One crucial element is missing – that of the government, politicians and the state. It would be misleading, by emphasising the complex layers of hostility that run through British society to absolve politicians, and especially the government, from any share of its responsibility for causing this increasingly ugly moral panic. It is, ultimately, the government which is in a position of authority and has the influence to undermine the power of this demeaning collaborationism – demeaning to those at the receiving end but also to those that are manifesting it whether in word, violence or exclusion. Only the government and its state apparatus has the legal authority to allow ordinary people to have ordinary contact with ordinary asylum seekers at home, at work and socially, as in the past, rather than to read about them in sensationalist media accounts or to experience them only in the most degrading

circumstances. Taking together the 'historic' and contemporary autobiographical writing within the Mass-Observation archives, for example, it
is evident that ordinary people in Britain had more intensive interaction
with refugees in the past than they do today. And as recent research by
the IPPR (2005) suggests: 'Meaningful contact with asylum seekers …
generally leads to more tolerant attitudes. Superficial contact can exacer-
bate prejudice and hostility.'[130] It still remains that the public and the
media have choice in the matter of how to respond to asylum seekers and
refugees – they can follow the lead of the activists in the many hundreds
of grassroots organisations who try to confront the dominant negative
climate and provide support for those subjected to it. In freeing ourselves
from this circle of hatred, however, the government is in a uniquely privileged position to do good or cause harm. As it stands, few, whether inside or outside the government have paused to think of what desperation
pushes women, such as the Czech, Slovak and Romanian Roma to beg
with their children in British streets. A retired headmistress in Scotland
criticised Barbara Roche, then Immigration Minister, who had 'said the
ghastliest, uneducated thing about some Roma recently, when the women
were begging on the streets and had their babies with them'. The Observer wondered whether perhaps these women should put their children
in a 'Westminster creche or [an] Oxbridge kindergarten'.[131] Ultimately,
anti-Gypsy sentiment, or what might be termed 'our Roma therapy', heals
none of society's wounds. Underneath its pretence of fragrant reason-
ableness is the stench of racism.

The denial of such racism, in spite of incontrovertible evidence, was
provided in the case of the Home Office's response to the law lords judgment about the screening of Czech Roma in Prague airport in 2001. With
the agreement of the Czech government, British immigration officials
were stationed at the airport and had the clear aim of stopping and dis-
couraging Czech Roma from coming to Britain and claiming asylum.
Some 90 per cent of Roma passengers were stopped compared to 0.2 per
cent of non-Roma – the former were 400 times more likely to be stopped
than the latter. The ruling of the law lords, as we have seen, was unam-
biguous – the operation was 'inherently and systematically discriminatory'. The Home Office argued that it had not meant to discriminate
against anyone – a remarkable claim given that the whole operation was
designed to keep Czech Roma out of Britain and discourage others from
trying to gain entry. Indeed, the Court of Appeal accepted that discrimination in the Prague operation was 'wholly inevitable'.[132] A close parallel
in the convoluted official denial process was provided by the attempt of
the Foreign Office in 1947 to explicitly keep out Jewish displaced persons without discriminating against them on grounds of 'race, nationality,
or residence'.[133] Such discriminatory exclusion of what would later be

termed Holocaust survivors was as successful as the immigration control
procedures aimed at Czech Roma over half a century later.

Competing narratives on refugees and asylum seekers, and how they
have been refracted through the Second World War, have run through
this chapter. The testimony of a Mass-Observer, a female pensioner in
Edinburgh, whose first husband was married to a Jewish refugee from
Nazism, illustrates the tensions between 'now' and 'then' neatly:

> Of course the position then was quite different from the way things have
> been working out in Europe more recently. Then we were at war with
> Germany so the European refugees (not then called asylum seekers) were
> escaping from the enemy with which we were also at war and so we had
> common sympathy with them and largely wanted to help them rather than
> reluctantly feeling we had a moral duty to do so. I think the reference
> made in the directive to people coming from different countries has some
> bearing here. Central Europe from where the war time [sic] refugees came
> was not perceived by us as being so remote as parts of Europe further east
> of which we have less knowledge and familiarity. For this reason the present
> incoming asylum seekers are even more foreign and unknown to us and
> the war in which they have become involved is not, in our perception,
> anything to do with us.[134]

In the case of the Czech, Slovak and Romanian Roma that connection is
even further distanced due to to the stigmatisation of the Gypsies more
generally in European culture.[135] In the Stonewall 2001 survey, Gypsies
and asylum seekers were jointly the groups that people in England felt
least 'positive' towards.[136] In the late 1990s in Britain, when the moral
panic on asylum seekers began to develop, the social acceptability of
anti-Gypsy prejudice played a key role in making asylum-seeker phobia
itself respectable. The distortion was clear in the 1998 figures for asylum
applications. Although much of the hysterical media coverage was on
the Czech and then Romanian Roma, they represented roughly only one-
twentieth of all applications in that year.[137] Writing in 1999, the Refugee
Council suggested that 'Roma provide convenient scapegoats for the hard
example, the populist roar, the tough message: they have no sponsoring
home state to defend them, they are marginalised throughout European
society, they are potent in majority societies only as a symbol of the "outsider"'.[138] In the late 1990s, the pariah status of 'the Gypsy' enabled the
growing campaign in Britain against asylum seekers to gain momentum
and legitimacy.[139] Since then *all* asylum seekers have become stigmatised
and the emphasis, in terms of moral duties, has shifted totally away from
'them' and onto 'us', as will be explored further in the conclusion to this
study.

It is worth closing this chapter by returning to Prague airport, the
place, in 2001, of the blatant discrimination against the Czech Roma

which reflected the culmination of popular and press campaigning and British immigration control procedures over several years. There are, however, other narratives of Prague, or Ruzyne airport, which connect Britain to past world refugee crises. The airport opened officially for commercial travel in 1937. It was from Ruzyne airport that Trevor Chadwick managed to charter a plane and fly a group of Czech Jewish children to safety:

> I took my first air transport rather proudly, on a twenty-seater plane. They were all cheerfully sick, enticed by the little paper bags, except a baby of one who slept peacefully in my lap the whole time. The Customs Officers were a little puzzled and began to open some of the suitcases, which contained the kids' wordly treasures. But when I explained the position they were completely co-operative … I felt depressed as I returned to Prague. Only twenty![140]

How far do we do justice to the memory of those like Trevor Chadwick, who did so much and claimed so little credit, by excluding the descendants of the other major genocidal victims of the Nazis from the very same airport some seventy years later?

Notes

1 Robert Winder, *Bloody Foreigners: The Story of Immigration to Britain* (London: Little, Brown, 2004) pp. 341–2.
2 On 3 June 2004 the Information Centre about Asylum and Refugees in the UK (ICAR), ran a seminar on 'The impact of the media on public attitudes towards refugees and asylum seekers'. Winder's book was regarded as reassuring as it 'identified a cyclical pattern of moral panics whose effect later abated'. Summary of the seminar available on the ICAR website, www.icar.org.uk.
3 'Swan Bake', *Sun*, 4 July 2003; 'Asylum Seekers Ate our Donkeys', *Daily Star*, 21 August 2003. See also 'Donkeys "Eaten by Migrants"', *Express*, 21 August 2003 which, within a paragraph of less than one hundred words, used without differentiation the terms 'migrants', 'asylum seekers' and 'immigrants'. On these and other wild and unfounded allegations, see Roy Greenslade, *Seeking Scapegoats: The Coverage of Asylum in the UK Press* (London: IPPR, 2005), pp. 25–6.
4 The White Queen in Lewis Carroll, *Through the Looking Glass* (Harmondsworth, Middlesex: Puffin Books, 1980 [1872]), pp. 257–8.
5 Miranda Lewis, *Asylum: Understanding Public Attitudes* (London: Institute for Public Policy Research, 2005), p. 40.
6 Brian Fay, 'Historians and Ethics' in special issue of *History and Theory* vol. 43 no. 4 (December 2004), p. 1 devoted to the theme.
7 See, for example, John Sweets, *Choices in Vichy France: The French under Nazi Occupation* (New York: Oxford University Press, 1986).

8 Mark Rawlinson, 'On the Losing Side: Francis Stuart, Henry Williamson and Collaboration', in Silvia Bigliazzi and Sharon Wood (eds), *Collaboration* (Aldershot: Ashgate, forthcoming).

9 Memorandum, November 1945, in National Archives FO 371/45383 E8450, November 1945.

10 The use of the term 'ethnic cleansing' is of relatively recent origin, first used in 1992 in relation to the removal of Muslims from Bosnia. See Tomasz Kamusella, 'Ethnic Cleansing in Silesia 1950–89 and the ennationalizing policies of Poland and Germany', *Patterns of Prejudice* vol. 33 no. 2 (April 1999), p. 52.

11 Alan Travis, 'Asylum Operation Racist, Say Law Lords', *Guardian*, 10 December 2004; details of the case and the judgment of 9 December 2004 can be found in www.parliament.the-stationery-office.co.uk/pa/ld2000405/ljudgment/jd0411209/roma-1-6.htm (accessed 19 July 2005).

12 Paul Langford, *Englishness Identified: Manners and Character 1650–1850* (Oxford: Oxford University Press, 2000), pp. 148–57, 226–7 on decency, fair play and hospitality. See Colin Holmes, *A Tolerant Country? Immigrants, Refugees and Minorities in Britain* (London: Faber & Faber, 1991) for a critique of this mythology.

13 Henry Rousso, *The Vichy Syndrome: History and Memory in France since 1944* (Cambridge, MA: Harvard University Press, 1991); H.R. Kedward and Nancy Wood (eds), *The Liberation of France: Image and Event* (Oxford: Berg, 1995).

14 Phillipe Burrin, *France under the Germans: Collaboration and Compromise* (New York: New Press, 1996), p. 2.

15 See, for example, Julian Jackson, *France: the Dark Years 1940–1944* (Oxford: Oxford University Press, 2001), chapter 20 'Resistance in Society'.

16 Jackson, *France: the Dark Years 1940–1944*, pp. 2–4.

17 Daniel Goldhagen, *Hitler's Willing Executioners: Ordinary Germans and the Holocaust* (Boston: Little, Brown, 1996); Christopher Browning, *Ordinary Men: Reserve Police Battalion 101 and the Final Solution in Poland* (New York: HarperCollins, 1992).

18 Yosefa Loshitzky (ed.), *Spielberg's Holocaust: Critical Perspectives* (Bloomington: Indiana University Press, 1987).

19 *Sunday Express*, 2 September 2001.

20 *News of the World*, 2 September 2001; *Independent on Sunday*, 2 September 2001. In an episode, 'The Germans', of the classic television comedy, 'Fawlty Towers', first broadcast on BBC 2, 24 October 1975 and repeated regularly thereafter, the proprieter of the hotel proves himself pathologically incapable of 'not mentioning the war', driving his German guests to tears and distraction.

21 Jeevan Vasagar, 'History Teaching in UK stokes xenophobia, say German envoy', *Guardian*, 9 December 2002; 'Prisoners of the Past', *Guardian*, 10 December 2002.

22 Jeevan Vasagar, 'Office Made Germans Butt of Hitler Jokes', *Guardian*, 15 November 2002.

23 Mit'a Castle-Kanerova, 'Roma refugees: the EU dimension', in Will Guy
    (ed.), *Between Past and Future: the Roma of Central and Eastern Europe*
    (Hatfield, Herts: University of Hertfordshire Press, 2001), p. 117.
24 Colin Clark and Elaine Campbell, '"Gypsy Invasion": A critical analysis of
    newspaper reaction to Czech and Slovak Romani asylum-seekers in Brit-
    ain, 1997', *Romani Studies* vol. 10 no. 1 (2000), p. 24.
25 Raeka Prasad, 'Airport Colour Bar', *Guardian*, 30 July 2001. See also the
    Guardian, 23 August 2001.
26 *Guardian*, 10 December 2004.
27 See John Solomos, *Race and Racism in Britain* (3rd edition, Basingstoke:
    Palgrave, 2003), pp. 73–4 commenting on Home Office, *Race Relations
    (Amendment) Act 2000* (London: HMSO, 2001), p. 40. Groups to be offi-
    cially discriminated against included Albanians, Afghans, Chinese, Kurds,
    Roma, Somalis and Tamils.
28 Ibid., p. 28.
29 See John Torode, 'Must Britain be Europe's soft touch?', *Daily Mail*, 21
    October 1997 for use of this phrase.
30 Mike Young, *Unwanted Journey: Why Central European Roma are Flee-
    ing to the UK* (London: Refugee Council, 1999), pp. 90–1.
31 Clark and Campbell, '"Gypsy Invasion"', p. 27 utilising the work of Yaron
    Matras.
32 Colin Holmes, 'The German Gypsy question in Britain, 1904–1906' in Ken
    Lunn (ed.), *Hosts, Immigrants and Minorities: Historical Responses to
    Newcomers in British Society 1870–1914* (Folkestone: Dawson, 1980), pp.
    134–59, esp. 148.
33 Donald Kenrick, 'Foreign Gypsies and British immigration law after 1945',
    in Thomas Acton (ed.), *Gypsy Politics and Traveller Identity* (Hatfield,
    Herts: University of Hertfordshire Press, 1997), pp. 100–10 (p. 109 for the
    Polish Gypsies whose numbers were similar to the later Czech and Slovak
    Roma – around one thousand).
34 Will Guy, 'The Czech Lands and Slovakia: another false dawn?', in idem
    (ed.), *Between Past and Future*, pp. 300 and 320 note 58.
35 Young, *Unwanted Journey*, p. 101.
36 Ronald Kaye, 'Defining the Agenda: British Refugee Policy and the Role of
    Parties', *Journal of Refugee Studies* vol. 7 nos 2/3 (1994), pp. 144–59 and
    idem, 'Redefining the Refugee: the UK Media Portrayal of Asylum Seekers'
    in Khalid Koser and Helma Lutz (eds), *The New Migration in Europe:
    Social Constructions and Social Realities* (Basingstoke: Macmillan, 1998),
    pp. 163–82.
37 Brian Cathcart, *The Case of Stephen Lawrence* (London: Penguin, 2000).
38 Arun Kundnani, 'In a Foreign Land: the New Popular Racism', *Race and
    Class* vol. 43 no. 2 (2001), pp. 48–9, deals with the *Mirror*'s position on
    refugees and asylum seekers.
39 *Evening Standard*, 13 and 14 November 1997 for 'Giro Czech' headlines;
    Duncan Campbell and Kate Connolly, 'Gypsy Malady', *Guardian*, 20 No-
    vember 1997 cover the range of headlines in the tabloid and broadsheet

press. Even the *Guardian* was not exempt from using a water invasion metaphor for what was a very small movement. See Alex Bellos, 'Tide of gypsy asylum-seekers ebbs', *Guardian*, 20 October 1997. It was the *Sun*, however, that led the campaign against alleged Gypsy beggars in March 2000. See the *Sun*, 20 March 2000 and for comment Isabel Fonseca, 'The Truth about Gypsies', *Guardian*, 24 March 2000.

40 See Clark and Campbell, '"Gypsy Invasion"', pp. 32, 35.

41 For a review of the press on this subject, see 'Don't Believe the Hype', *iNexile: The Refugee Council Magazine* (February 1999), pp. 12–13.

42 Young, *Unwanted Journey*, p. 69.

43 See Tony Kushner and Katharine Knox, *Refugees in an Age of Genocide: Global, National and Local Perspectives during the Twentieth Century* (London: Frank Cass, 1999), p. 403.

44 Young, *Unwanted Journey*, p. 103.

45 Alan Travis and Ian Traynor, 'Britain's Little Refugee Problem', *Guardian*, 22 October 1997.

46 Maggie Morgan, 'Port Under Siege After Gipsy Bands Head West to Good Life', *Express*, 21 October 1997.

47 *Independent*, 20 October 1998.

48 *Daily Express*, 20 January 2004.

49 *Daily Express*, 20 January 2004 and Greenslade, *Seeking Scapegoats*, p. 22 and Information Centre about Asylum and Refugees in the UK (ICAR), *Media Image, Community Impact* (London: King's College, 2004), pp. 29, 31 for comment on the *Dad's Army* influence; Jeffrey Richards, *Film and British National Identity: From Dickens to Dad's Army* (Manchester: Manchester University Press, 1997), pp. 358–61 on its wider cultural significance.

50 *Express*, 24 February 2004.

51 *Express*, 22 January 2004.

52 Richard Littlejohn, 'I'm Riding Along on the Roof of a Train', *Sun*, 17 June 2005.

53 Fritz Stern, *The Politics of Cultural Despair: A Study in the Rise of the Germanic Ideology* (Berkeley and Los Angeles: University of California Press, 1961).

54 Robert Colls, *Identity of England* (Oxford: Oxford University Press, 2002), p. 239.

55 Ruth McKenney and Richard Bransten, *Here's England* (London: Rupert Hart-Davis, 1951), p. 197. Colls, *Identity of England*, p. 110 argues that in constructions of Englishness, Kent is perceived as being part of the 'real England'.

56 Moraes quoted by Travis and Traynor, 'Britain's Little Refugee Problem'.

57 Young, *Unwanted Journey*, p. 65 provides the figures. In 1997 there were only 60 cases of Romanians (largely Roma) claiming asylum, with the number increasing to 1,015 in 1998. This, however, was out of a total of 46,010 asylum applications that year. The press animosity specifically against the Romanian Roma was especially intensive in December 1998 – see idem, p. 69.

58 See the *Observer*, 15 August 1999.

59 Alan Travis, 'Fast-track Curb on Beggars', *Guardian*, 20 March 2000 and subsequent correspondence, 21 and 22 March 2000 on Roche's comments.

60 For Straw see Mike Diboll and Elane Heffernan, 'Labour's Racism: The Last Straw', *Socialist Review*, June 2000, p. 9. Earlier in August 1999 Straw had referred to travellers as crooks who caused 'all kinds of trouble including defecating in doorways'. Quoted in Vikram Dodd, 'Anger after Straw lets fly at travellers', *Guardian*, 19 August 1999.

61 It was led by the *Sun* and the *Daily Mail*. For a review and analysis see Roy Greenslade, 'We Hate You', *Guardian*, 20 March 2000.

62 Tony Blair, speech of 19 April 2000 quoted in 'A Noble Tradition', *iNexile: The Refugee Council Magazine*, August 2000, p. 6.

63 See the comments of Louise London, 'Whitehall and the refugees: the 1930s and the 1990s', *Patterns of Prejudice* vol. 34 no. 3 (2000), p. 17 who refers to the process as a 'ritual invocation'.

64 'A Noble Tradition', p. 7; Guy, 'Between Past and Future', p. 30 note 59.

65 See part three of Guy (ed.), *Between Past and Future* which does emphasise the variety of responses to and experiences of the Roma across Europe; Zoltan Barany, *The East European Gypsies: Regime Change, Marginality, and Ethnopolitics* (Cambridge: Cambridge University Press, 2002); Young, *Unwanted Journey*, chapter 2 and testimony on p. 99.

66 For exceptions to the reporting, see Isabel Fonseca, 'The truth about Gypsies' and Gary Younge, 'Shame of a Continent', *Guardian*, 8 January 2003.

67 Quoted in Young, *Unwanted Journey*, p. 23.

68 Chris Powell, 'Razor Blades Amidst the Velvet? Changes and Continuities in the Gypsy Experience of the Czech and Slovak Lands', in Acton (ed.), *Gypsy Politics and Traveller Identity*, p. 93.

69 Ibid., p. 93.

70 Angus Fraser, 'Afterword', in Acton (ed.), *Gypsy Politics*, p. 173.

71 See, for example, Rainer Baum, 'Holocaust: Moral Indifference as *the* Form of Modern Evil' in A. Rosenberg and G. Meyers (eds), *Echoes from the Holocaust: Philosophical Reflections on a Dark Time* (Philadelphia: Temple University Press, 1988).

72 Reproduced, with original spelling, in Thomas Acton and Ilona Klimova, 'The International Romani Union', in Guy (ed.), *Between Past and Future*, pp. 216–17.

73 Young, *Unwanted Journey*, p. 102.

74 Mass-Observation Archive, University of Sussex (hereafter M-O: A) Directive 'Coming to Britain', Summer 2000, C2722. The Observer was a 36-year-old computer systems administrator.

75 For the most authoritative figures, see Louise London, *Whitehall and the Jews: British Immigration Policy and the Holocaust* (Cambridge: Cambridge University Press, 2000), introduction.

76 For a review of recent literature and representation see Tony Kushner, 'The Search for Nuance in the Study of Holocaust "Bystanders"' in David Cesarani and Paul Levine (eds), *'Bystanders' to the Holocaust: A Re-*

evaluation (London: Frank Cass, 2002), pp. 57–76.

77 Kushner and Knox, *Refugees in an Age of Genocide*, p. 399.

78 London, *Whitehall and the Jews*.

79 Tony Kushner, *The Holocaust and the Liberal Imagination: A Social and Cultural History* (Oxford: Blackwell, 1994), section 1.

80 See, for example, William Evans Gordon, *The Alien Immigrant* (London: Heinemann, 1903), pp. 6–8 and chapters 1 and 2 of this study.

81 *Mail on Sunday*, 26 October 1997.

82 For an outline of the contemporary project see Dorothy Sheridan, Brian Street and David Bloome, *Writing Ourselves: Mass-Observation and Literacy Practices* (Cresskill, New Jersey: Hampton Press, 2000), chapter 2 and sections 2 and 3.

83 For an analysis of Mass-Observation writing on the Falklands War and 1991 Gulf War see Lucy Noakes, *War and the British: Gender, Memory and National Identity* (London: I.B. Tauris, 1998), chapters 5 and 6 respectively.

84 M-O A: Summer 2000 Directive: Part 1 'Coming to Britain'. The respondents were asked about their direct experience/family connections to asylum seekers, their own views about asylum, and their feelings about governmental and public reactions. Finally they were asked to reflect on links to and debates from the past.

85 M-O A: Summer 2000 Directive, M1201.

86 Robin Gwynn, *Huguenot Heritage: The History and Contribution of the Huguenots in Britain* (London: Routledge, 1985), p. 1 somewhat speculatively suggests that so many French Protestants 'crossed the Channel that it is statistically probable that over three-quarters of all Englishmen alive today have some Huguenot blood in their veins'. The Summer 2000 directive would not support such a high proportion but it would equally suggest that such ancestry was far from rare.

87 M-O: A DR C2053, Summer 2000.

88 M-O A: DR 2224, Summer 2000.

89 M-O A: DR R1025, Summer 2000.

90 M-O A: DR Z2276, Summer 2000.

91 M-O A: DR H1703, Summer 2000.

92 M-O A: DR H1703, Summer 2000.

93 M-O A: DR C1939, Summer 2000.

94 See, for example, M-O A: DR D2589 and W1382, Summer 2000.

95 M-O A: DR W1382, Summer 2000.

96 M-O A: DR R2144, Summer 2000.

97 M-O A: DR R1321, Summer 2000.

98 M-O A: DR T1411, Summer 2000.

99 M-O A: DR M2290, R2136, Summer 2000.

100 M-O A: DR W2117, Summer 2000.

101 M-O A: DR D2585, Summer 2000.

102 M-O A: DR W2267, Summer 2000.

103 M-O A: DR G1416, Summer 2000.

104 Ibid.; *Guardian*, 12 February and 20 June 2000.
105 Rainey Kelly Campbell Roalfe, 'Refugees – From a Small Issue to an Important Cause' (Research debrief for the Refugee Council, October 1997).
106 M-O A: DR G2640, Summer 2000.
107 M-O A: DR G1421, Summer 2000.
108 M-O A: DR C2722, Summer 2000.
109 M-O A: DR J931, Summer 2000.
110 M-O A: DR H276, Summer 2000.
111 M-O A: DR W2174, Summer 2000.
112 Elspeth Guild, 'The United Kingdom: Kosovar Albanian Refugees' in Joanne van Selm (ed.), *Kosovo's Refugees in the European Union* (London: Pinter, 2000), pp. 67–90.
113 M-O A: DR W571, Summer 2000.
114 M-O A: DR B1426, Summer 2000.
115 M-O A: DR G1421, Summer 2000.
116 Greenslade, *Seeking Scapegoats*, p. 8.
117 M-O A: DR A2801, Summmer 2000.
118 M-O A: DR C2722, Summer 2000.
119 M-O A: DR C2717, Summer 2000.
120 M-O A: DR J2830, Summer 2000.
121 M-O A: DR L1504, Summer 2000.
122 M-O A: DR C2834, Summer 2000.
123 Greenslade, *Seeking Scapegoats*, p. 6.
124 Ibid.
125 ICAR, *Media Image, Community Impact*, pp. 7–8.
126 Ibid., p. 12.
127 'Profiles of Prejudice' details available on the Stonewall website; www.stonewall.org.uk. See also Lewis, *Asylum*, p. 26 which suggests that television is the most important source of public information on asylum issues.
128 M-O A: DR R1418, Summer 2000.
129 M-O A: DR1685, Summer 2000.
130 Lewis, *Asylum*, p. 7.
131 M-O A: DR S2230, Summer 2000.
132 *Guardian*, 10 December 2004; www.parliament.the-stationery-office.co.uk/pa/ld200405/ldjudgmt/jd041209/roma-6.htm.
133 National Archives, FO945/5000 W586, 'Recruitment of DPs for Great Britain', 24 March 1947.
134 M-O A: DR S2271, Summer 2000.
135 See David Mayall, *Gypsy Identities 1500–2000: From Egipcyans and Moonmen to the Ethnic Romany* (London: Routledge, 2004), pp. 15–16.
136 Stonewall, 'Profiles of Prejudice'.
137 Young, *Unwanted Journey*, p. 65.
138 Young, *Unwanted Journey*, p. 91.
139 Lewis, *Asylum*, p. 41 highlights how many East European asylum seekers, including Kosovans and Albanians, have become linked with Gypsies 'who

remain one of the most vilified groups in the UK'.

140 Karen Gershon, *We Came As Children* (London: Gollancz, 1966), p. 22. For the importance of this airport in refugee work in 1938 and early 1939 see Doreen Warriner, 'The Winter in Prague', Imperial War Museum Department of Documents.

Conclusion: history, memory and the ethics of asylum

The terrorist attacks on London during July 2005 have provided a fresh impetus to those seeking to restrict the entry to and freedom of asylum seekers in Britain. In particular, that two of the bombers involved with the failed attempts on the capital on 21 July 2005 came to Britain as child refugees has been seized upon by tabloids at the forefront of the anti-asylum seeker campaign to legitimise further their calls for more draconian controls. In a front page banner headline entitled 'GRATI-TUDE!', the *Daily Mail* told its readers that 'Their families came here seeking asylum and were given homes, schooling and all the benefits of British life. How do they repay us? By trying to blow us up'.[1] Such shaping of the life stories of Yasin Hassan Omar, who came to Britain aged eleven from Somalia, and Muktar Seed Ibraham, arriving from Eritrea aged fourteen, both in the early 1990s, could not be further than that increasingly presented of those who came sixty years earlier on the *Kindertransport* as illustrated in chapter 4. On the one hand, in the case of these late twentieth-century refugees, the emphasis is placed on their alleged dubious origins, criminality, benefits fraud and, finally, the ultimate in un-English behaviour – attempted mass murder of innocents.[2] On the other hand, with the *Kinder*, they are increasingly portrayed as a precious 'remnant' rescued from the horrors of the Holocaust and as individuals who became respectable citizens, repaying the debt 'owed' to Britain for saving their lives by their contribution to society. There is, however, aside from the obvious and jarring incongruity of these different narratives of child refugees, something that their representation has in common – in both cases the emphasis is on what they have done to (or for) Britain and a concomitant expectation of, and indeed a demand for, gratitude. Such was the force of anti-asylum seeker hostility after the July bombings that it forced Sandy Buchan, the Chief Executive of Refugee Action, a major charity working on behalf of refugees, to respond defensively, reasserting the expected scenario of those coming to Britain escaping persecution:

Most people of all faiths and nationalities were appalled by the terrorist attacks. But we are dismayed at the shameful way some sections of the press have used the background of the most recent suspects, who arrived in the UK as asylum seekers, to attack the very idea of asylum and to smear refugee communities with accusations of ingratitude. We know from our 24 years of experience that refugees feel a very genuine debt to their host country.

To further undermine the assumption of 'us' being attacked by 'them', Buchan added that it was 'worth noting that the July 7 suicide bombers were British-born, whilst one of their victims, Atique Sharifi, was an Afghan refugee who fled the fundamentalism of the Taliban only to be murdered in the UK'. Sharifi, it has been emphasised, was orphaned by the Taliban, escaping Kabul 'to find refuge in Britain, where he overcame his struggle to learn English and became a model student'.[3] As this study has highlighted throughout, the way refugees are remembered, or forgotten, reveals much about the anxieties and aspirations of the receiving society. Yet alongside the evolution of history and memory, the presence (or absence) of the refugee raises fundamental moral issues for contemporary society.

In January 2003 the veteran black British trade union leader, Bill Morris, argued that it is 'time to accept that asylum is not just a political issue: above all it's a moral one'.[4] Morris, who has campaigned consistently against the Labour government's measures against asylum seekers, is right to point out that contemporary discourse decreasingly focuses on the moral imperatives to help those seeking refuge in Britain. As Matthew Gibney comments in his study of contemporary liberal democracies and their responses to refugees, in twenty-first century Britain what seems lacking is 'a dedication to the principle of asylum that is founded on an *ethical* commitment to alleviating the plight of refugees rather than a *legal* obligation to the minimal requirements of inherited international agreements'.[5] The increasing flirtation of mainstream politicians with removing Britain from such legal agreements is therefore particularly disturbing. Nevertheless, the bulk of the asylum debate at both political and public levels has morality at its very core. The focus, however, is not directed towards the persecuted but on the perceived obligation to protect British people, 'British' values and 'British' culture from the danger of the asylum seeker.

Refugee campaigners and activists place their emphasis on the suffering and persecution that has led individuals to take the drastic step of leaving their homelands. They also stress the need to look after those whose lives have been physically and psychologically damaged. Yet those demanding tightening of entry, and even withdrawal from the 1951 UN Convention Relating to the Status of Refugees, refuse to concede the noral high ground. They claim that a highly selective policy would still allow 'genuine refugees' to gain admittance. More importantly, on ethical grounds, they argue that restriction will protect the ordinary British public from all sorts of harm that the 'asylum lobby' refuses to acknowledge. As Sir Andrew Green, chairman of 'Migration Watch', which has campaigned particularly against the entry of asylum seekers, argued after the July 2005 bombings: 'What about OUR Human Rights?'[6] Finally, any self-doubt about the ethics of advocating a highly restrictive asylum policy has been removed by instrumentalising the past to provide reassurance about the rectitude of current policies: 'Britain has a proud tradition of sheltering the persecuted. But it has no moral or historical duty to be the world's favorite haven for everyone claiming asylum.'[7] Pro-refugee campaigners point to 'history' to highlight what Britain did (and did not do) to help those seeking refuge in the past in order to probe the ethics of why 'asylum has now become such a contentious issue and why the term asylum seeker has become a term of abuse'.[8] Those who are hostile, however, deny any historical parallels. As Melanie Phillips, who believes that 'the Government has lost control of its borders',[9] argues, comparisons between present asylum seekers and those of the 1900s and 1930s were 'denigrating the memory of the genuine refugees of the past'.[10]

Phillips is identified as being part of the 'new right' and as a leading commentator in the campaign to restrict immigrants and asylum seekers. Yet the growing consensus within 'mainstream' politics in believing that the vast majority of contemporary asylum seekers are 'bogus' or 'abusive' was illustrated in May 2002, by the then immigration minister, Lord Rooker, when the Labour government attempted to justify its new restrictive legislation. Refusing to countenance the possibility of escaping persecution as a motive for coming to Britain, Rooker dismissed asylum seekers in as little as ten words: most, he argued, were 'single men who have deserted their families for economic gain'.[11] Not surprisingly, Rooker was reportedly unapologetic in confirming that there were no longer 'any legal avenues by which legitimate refugees might enter the UK'.[12] Moreover, those on the left as well as the right have argued for tight border control in order to save the 'national culture'.[13] In an increasingly hostile atmosphere, relying on international legal protection of refugees alone may not be sufficient to protect the offering of asylum.

The politics of ethics and history, and their interaction, are at the heart of contemporary asylum debates. Ironically, the academic disciplines linked to these issues have largely failed to confront the presence of and response to refugees. The first chapter of *Remembering Refugees* has explored the lacuna of the historical profession in this respect. As a way of quantifying the absence of historical writing on refugees, a survey of papers submitted to the *Journal of Refugee Studies* in 2000, after thirteen years of its publication, was referred to, noting that equal bottom, with just over 4 per cent of the total, was history.[14] In chapter 2, this study analysed, especially through the prism of place identity, how, on a more popular historical level, the heritage industry rarely allows space for the presence of refugees in the distant or recent past. Only a few and carefully selected groups, and especially the help that was given to them, have been recognised and celebrated, especially in relation to those who escaped Nazism. More often are fleeting and sometimes derogatory references to the past presence of refugees as exemplified by the memory work associated with the Hungarians of 1956 and others whose presence was more temporary and/or marginal. Of equal significance is the total absence of attention to those refugees who were excluded or removed and the debunking of those attempting to point out such voids in memory.[15] If those concerned with the past from either a critical or celebratory perspective have at best marginalised and at worst pathologised the refugee, academics involved with the study of ethics have made a similar lack of progress.[16] Returning to the survey carried out by the *Journal of Refugee Studies*, for example, there were no papers classified under the heading 'Philosophy'.[17]

As Peter Singer acknowledges, 'Very few moral philosophers have given any attention to the issue of refugees, even though it is clearly one of the major moral issues of our time and raises significant moral questions about who is a member of our moral community.' Singer points to John Rawls' seminal *Theory of Justice* (1971) which 'deals exclusively with justice *within* a society, thus ignoring all the hard questions about the principles that ought to govern how wealthy societies respond to the claims of poorer nations, or of outsiders in need'.[18] To be fair, the study of ethics and refugee questions extends to a variety of disciplines – law and politics as well as philosophy. Nevertheless, it remains a relatively undeveloped area with only a handful of authors having made a significant contribution. One of the core issues linked to refugees – whether the nation state has a responsibility and obligation to those who are not its citizens – would appear to be an obvious question to be addressed by those concerned with ethics. The reason it has achieved insufficient attention is perhaps to be found in the tendency of much moral philosophy not to go beyond the boundaries of the individual nation. Indeed, even those who have addressed the subject from within law, politics and philosophy (including, ironically, to some extent Singer himself), no matter that most are critical of the paucity of liberal democratic responses, arguing for far more generous policies, ultimately come down on the side of some restraint so as to protect the 'good' of the nation state. A utilitarian approach is often adopted, 'balancing' the needs of refugees/asylum seekers against members of the nation state. If Andrew Shacknove has argued that 'Asylum is a good in itself',[19] other moral philosophers have queried such absolutism. Rather than help clarify the ethical issues underlying asylum, many of those working in moral philosophy have confused matters further by assumptions based on simplistic understandings of history, economics and culture. The most blatant case in this respect, leading to a justification of control, is to be found in Michael Walzer's influential *Spheres of Justice* (1983).

Walzer starts his discussion from the standpoint of existing groups that set up their own terms of membership. Each group is distinctive and has a right to protect itself: 'The distinctiveness of cultures and groups depends upon closure and, without it, cannot be conceived as a stable feature of human life.' The sovereign state, therefore, argues Walzer, has the 'right to control immigration'.[20] Walzer makes a partial exception of refugees but still argues that, as with immigrants, if 'we are forced to choose among the victims, we will look, rightfully, for some more direct connection with our own way of life'. Walzer accepts that 'to take in large numbers of refugees is often morally necessary' but qualifies it by stating that 'if we offered a refuge to everyone in the world who could plausibly say that he needed it, we might be overwhelmed'. He concludes 'I assume that there are in fact limits on our collective liability, but I don't know how to specify them'.[21] In such writings within moral philosophy the analogy of the lifeboat is often given – if, we, well-meaningly, try to help too many the result will be that all will drown.[22] As we have noted, in 1950, the year before the Geneva Convention, the Home Office's official history of refugee movement put this argument forcefully to defend why 'Great Britain cannot be a country of settlement':

> sympathy cannot make room where it does not exist; and Great Britain could no more receive millions of refugees or potential refugees because they were cruelly and unjustly treated on the Continent than the border provinces of the Roman Empire in the 5th Century could admit immigrant German tribes because they were driven on by the invading Hun behind them. When a ship goes down one lifeboat can only take a certain number of survivors, and when it is full, the crew must, however regretfully, refuse to rescue any more.[23]

Singer uses a similarly extreme metaphor – survivors of a nuclear war with only limited spaces available in a fallout shelter.[24] In both cases, however, the lifeboat or shelter analogy is false – it assumes *there is* a fixed number who can be helped without damaging – indeed risking the lives – of all. Rather than assume that the number who can be given refuge through some form of fiercely protected quota system is an absolute given, it is essential to accept that any limitations imposed are socially constructed whether by politicians, economists, cultural commentators, the public or the media. While the scenario of the lifeboat or shelter is, of course, hypothetical, in this particular issue such counter-factual premises are dangerous in assuming the fixity rather than the plasticity of capacity. Following the work of Liza Schuster, which criticises the state and refugee law, it is necessary to recognise 'them as political realities, but as realities to be changed, not accepted'.[25]

Singer, writing ten years after *Spheres of Justice*, is critical of the limitations posed by Michael Walzer which he views as justifying the status quo and especially the typical response of 'moderately liberal governments' to respect the right of asylum 'as long as the numbers are relatively small'. According to Walzer, because refugees unable to reach the border as asylum seekers are not restrained in number they would cause a problem of absorption; there is therefore no obligation to take them in. In contrast, Singer makes the case for supporting those away from the place of asylum as their life chances are seriously diminished otherwise, many rotting away in massive refugee camps. But in arguing for a much more generous refugee policy because of the moral enormity of the situation, Singer still recognises the legitimacy of limiting refugee entry – with large numbers the environment and economy might suffer or 'there might come a point at which tolerance in a multicultural society was breaking down because of a resentment among the resident community'.[26]

Singer not only acknowledges that refugees often offer much economically and culturally, but also accepts that 'Less than generous responses to refugees are usually justified by blaming the victim'. In addition, it must be added, and most dangerously, Walzer accepts uncritically the concept of 'our own way of life' – a homogeneity that immigrants or refugees, unless ethnically or politically similar to 'us' are likely to disturb.[27] The approach of Singer is far more universal and accepting of diversity, yet he still ultimately tempers his approach by what would be 'good' for the nation state. He concludes that

> It would not be difficult for the nations of the developed world to move closer towards fulfilling their moral obligations to refugees. There is no objective evidence to show that doubling their refugee intake would cause them any harm whatsoever. Much present evidence, as well as past experience, points the other way, suggesting that they and their present population would probably benefit.[28]

Once the idea of the refugee as potentially problematic is accepted, there is a grave risk that a less optimistic perspective on history or contemporary economics and ecology than that suggested by Singer could lead to an even less generous intake. While an optimist might argue, say, for a

fourfold increase, those less self-confident might argue for half the existing rate or even less. In short, once pragmatic, utilitarian 'balances' are
employed, the case of unequivocally supporting those seeking refuge according to their need for asylum is fundamentally undermined. There are
moralists, especially but not limited to the the new right, who argue that
the pain threshold should currently be very low. They suggest that even a
small number of additional asylum seekers will destroy the balance of
'race relations', undermine the economy and more generally destroy the
well-being and security of society as a whole. Nevertheless, they still
hope that a few 'genuine' refugees can be supported. At the other extreme, there are those who are disgusted at the moral mean-spiritedness
of the prosperous liberal democracies in the face of huge collective misery of the world's refugee population. Nevertheless, they still accept a
'right ... of extremely limited application' in certain circumstances to
control entry. Such a view has been expressed most recently by Michael
Dummett, Emeritus Professor of Logic at the University of Oxford.[29]

Dummett has been a long-standing campaigner against racial prejudice and for a just immigration and asylum policy. It is significant, returning to the failure of philosophy to engage in questions relating to the
refugee, that Dummett acknowledges it was not his own 'philosophical
views that had impelled [him] into participating in the struggle against
racism'. His *On Immigration and Refugees* (2001) is his first intellectual
foray into the subject and acts as a vigorous moral defence, often blatantly based on Judeo-Christian principles, of a generous interpretation
of the 1951 Geneva Convention. At times Dummett comes close to supporting a world without immigration borders. Yet he makes clear from
the 'outset [a principle] lest it be overlooked among more general considerations. The right is one possessed by groups united by race, religion,
language or culture: such groups have a right not to be submerged.'
Dummett deliberately uses the word 'submerged' in distinction to
'swamped' because of the latter's more 'emotive' appeal and especially
its infamous use by Margaret Thatcher in the build-up to her 1979 general election victory.[30] A deeper knowledge of history, however, would
have prompted Dummett to realise that anti-alien campaigners have long
used a variety of watery (as well as military) metaphors – waves or tides
of undesirables that could swamp or submerge. As W.H. Wilkins put it in
The Alien Invasion (1892), arguing against the entry of 'Russian, Rou-
manian, and Polish Jews' who were 'drawn from the class which goes to
swell the poor-houses and penitentiaries of Eastern Europe', 'something
must be done to divert this stream before it swells into an overwhelming
flood'.[31] In spite of his highly progressive perspective, Dummett still gets
into difficulties by his loose use of concepts such as 'race' or 'culture',
failing to give sufficient weight to their social construction.

It must be emphasised that Dummett does not have in mind the same limited mono cultural vision of 'membership' as does Walzer; he accepts that 'Many people, probably most, have at least a dual identity'. Nevertheless, in answering 'why does a nation have a right not to be submerged', he, like Walzer, accepts the idea of a shared custom and language and that 'cultures are fragile'.[32] It may seem churlish to criticise Dummett, or for that matter, Singer, for accepting the need for some controls when such authors are so clearly in support of a more generous refugee policy than currently is the case in the western democracies. Indeed, Matthew Gibney in the field of politics has criticised theorists such as Singer for their irrelevance to everyday politics because of their alleged idealism:

> Abstraction from what is currently politically possible is essential if widely supported and deeply entrenched practices, such as entrance policy, are to be thoroughly scrutinized. Yet, by choosing to address the current crisis from the perspective of ideal theory, political theorists have deflected attention from the issue of what responsibilities we have good reason to demand that actually existing states accept here and now.[33]

Similarly, Andrew Shacknove has argued for shifting asylum from a human rights to an immigration discourse on grounds of national and international political pragmaticism.[34] When millions experience the misery of refugee camps and worse and the steps taken to achieve asylum become ever more desperate, surely, it would seem, Gibney is right to argue for political realism – of putting forward politically 'realistic' arguments to modify, through an injection of humanitarianism, increasingly hostile western responses?

The ethical case for open borders has been put forward, amongst others, by Joseph Carens. Carens argues that 'the general case for open borders is deeply rooted in the fundamental values of our tradition. No moral argument will seem acceptable to *us*, if it directly challenges the assumption of the equal moral worth of all individuals ... The current restrictions on immigration in Western democracies ... are not justifiable. Like feudal barriers to mobility, they protect unjust privilege.'[35] Matthew Gibney has criticised such idealist perspectives because he believes that, while they 'usually have an element of right on their side ... their prescriptions brush aside the conflicts of value and policy-making'.[36] Moreover, responding to Gil Loescher, who has condemned the international community for its failure to meet its 'ethical obligations to aid and protect refugees', Gibney comments that Loescher 'makes no attempt to explain why Western states have these duties or to outline, within a coherent moral theory, just what these duties might be'. Gibney adds that Loescher is 'far from the only writer on refugee issues to use the language of morality without pausing to examine its implications'.[37] In particular, Gibney emphasises that 'a credible ideal needs to take seriously both the claims of citizens *and* those of refugees', arguing that 'one way of integrating these claims is to require states to accept as many refugees as they can without undermining the civil, political and, importantly, the social rights associated with the liberal democratic state'.[38]

Gibney has provided the most comprehensive treatment of the ethics of asylum. His desire to provide a 'real world' analysis in order to convince 'the governments of liberal democracies [to] take the moral claims of refugees and asylum seekers more seriously' is to be welcomed.[39] Nevertheless, Gibney's lack of historical perspective, and especially the assumptions he makes about the possible impact of the entry of refugees, needs to be seriously queried. All western liberal democracratic nations have experienced traditions of immigration and refugee entry. Britain is no exception although it is a country, as emphasised throughout this study, in strong denial of its past diversity. In the words of the restrictionist, Melanie Phillips, 'Britain is not a country of immigrants. It has had a settled culture for a thousand years, and until recently the number of immigrants was minute.'[40] Moreover, because of its widely-accepted 'myth of fairness' it has failed to accept its powerful tradition of alien control – a part of the past largely ignored by the heritage industry. Rather than undermining the economic and social fabric, including the welfare state, refugees have contributed massively to them. On a cultural level, the mythology of homogeneity and of 'core values' hides the reality of diversity and of different traditions – in the case of Britain, to use one extreme example running counter to another of the 'myths we live by' – that of gentleness – of domestically nurtured political violence and terrorism. Indeed, as Michael Clarke, Professor of Defence Studies at King's College, London, has suggested:

> The more we learn about the two bomb plots in London, the less they fit any of our previous understandings of terrorism. These two jihadi terrorist cells emerge as typically British: full of anomalies, eccentric in their behaviour, gentlemen-amateurs alternating between ruthless homicide and comical incompetence.[41]

Immigrants and refugees, many of whom, ironically, have been at the forefront of constructing 'Englishness' in an idealised form, have added to the fundamental heterogeneity of the United Kingdom. It is a diversity based on many different factors, including – contrary to Phillips' ahistorical perspective – region, class, age, sex, sexuality, religion, politics, as well as, amongst others, traditions of immigration, emigration and internal migration. Finally and most importantly, we need to undermine the political necessity for governments to appease those who are hostile to refugees and asylum seekers by restriction and control. Liza Schuster is thus right to point out that the 'narrowing and polarising of the debate ... to two positions – that is, the human rights of asylum seekers versus the citizenship rights of host populations – overlooks the common ground between these two positions in relation to restrictions on entry'.[42] In contrast, Matthew Gibney believes that such conflict and antagonism between newcomers and receiving society, however unreasonable, is 'in fact real'.[43] Gibney, for example, blames the growth of the far right and violent racism in Germany on the Federal Republic's relatively generous refugee policy. His 'common sense' analysis, however, confuses causality and ends up, as so often is the case with refugees, as Singer puts it, in 'blaming the victim'.[44] In 1950, the Home Office could still justify controls against the 'incautious admission of alien Jews' on the grounds that it 'might give rise to outbursts of Anti-Semitic feeling'.[45] Over fifty years later, such statements are disturbing because of their perverse logic. That unease comes out of the growing awareness of the immensity of the Holocaust and the astonishment that Britain might have kept out its survivors to avoid domestic tension. Yet the growth of the far right in Europe today is no more the fault of asylum seekers and refugees as it was the fault of German Jewry for the success of Nazism. Similarly, the existence of antisemitism in receiving societies such as Britain during the 1930s had domestic roots and was not 'imported' by Jewish refugees. Some contemporaries in Britain, however, blamed German Jews for creating antisemitism at home and abroad.

By close reading of life stories, the complexity and ambiguity of ordinary people's responses to refugees have been emphasised throughout *Remembering Refugees*. Hostility, particularly against contemporary asylum seekers, has not been in any way downplayed or ignored. Indeed, the idea of contemporary asylum-seeker phobia being simply generated from the top down has been criticised in the final chapter. Nevertheless, this study has emphasised how governments have too often ignored the views of those who are sympathetic to the needs of refugees and have been hesitant to take a moral lead and push more positively the ambivalent views of the majority. A detailed historical approach argues strongly that there is much more fluidity in 'public opinion' than might be assumed. Yet one (though not the only) of the key arguments for an ethically-based asylum policy for western liberal democracies rests not on a utilitarian basis that they will do, as shown through historical precedent, more good than harm, but that the needs of an individual to a live a life free of persecution – at a basic level, the right to life – are part of universal human rights. Ironically, liberal democracies often claim their ethical underpinning by stressing the help given to those escaping oppression abroad, pointing out their duty to save the lives of the persecuted. It is a sad reflection on Britain that it tends only to recognise such moral obligations to the needy with the benefit of hindsight. Such self-congratulation has been shown throughout this study with the subsequent memory work associated with the Huguenots, the *Kindertransport* movement and, most recently, the tragedy of the Afghanistani, Atique Sharifi. In the process, those who were not helped, or the ambivalence towards those rescued, have been forgotten.

Remembering Refugees has emphasised that anti-aliens past and present have too often won the battle over the ethics of asylum by focusing on the damage done to 'us', the hosts, rather than the needs of 'them', the refugees whom they denigrate and undermine. As the Reverend G.S. Reaney argued in 1892 in relation to the East European Jews:

> By every moral consideration, bearing alike upon the condition, character, and life of the alien immigrant, as well as upon the state of our own fellow countrymen, whose misfortune it is to be poor, overworked, and underpaid, we, as a nation, are bound to see that, either we shut our ports to the Russian and foreign refugees, or that their settlement in our midst shall not be inimical to their social progress and moral growth, nor dangerous to the health, happiness and ethical betterment of our own people.[46]

Reaney, however, recognised that the persecuted, no matter how unpleasant, had some rights in Britain. At a popular level, as we have seen in chapter 3, during the 1930s the moral imperative to help the persecuted was still a major aspect of public discourse and debate. In contrast, over a hundred years later, those hostile to asylum seekers rarely confront 'both sides' of the ethical debate. As has just been explored, even critics of what Michael Dummett labels the 'morally squalid' – contemporaries who 'incite prejudice' against refugees – still have a tendency to set some limits on the granting of asylum.[47] In Britain, this has led to highly racially discriminatory and selective asylum policies, most notably followed in the late twentieth century and early twenty-first century against the continental Roma.

Yet rather than end this study on a note of pessimism, are there any reasons to be cheerful? How can we move from a vicious circle of mutual reinforcement of prejudice between government, state, media and public to a virtuous one that leads out of the racist maze? A historical perspective provides some grounds for comfort. There have been periods of intense and dominant anti-alienism. Today's situation is not unprecedented – during the 1920s, in spite of the intensity of the continental refugee crisis, Britain took in almost no refugees and deported many who had come before the First World War.[48] It was followed, however, in the late 1930s by a rediscovery of the concept of asylum at a popular level which in turn helped push the government in a more generous direction.[49] More recently, grassroots campaigning pushed the British government into helping Kosovan refugees when it had no intention to do so. As has been noted, post-1999, the British government's treatment of these Kosovan refugees has been immensely shabby, but the press and public sympathy articulated at the time of the conflict is indicative that there is nothing natural or inevitable about anti-alienism.[50] Indeed, opinion polls consistently suggest that three-quarters of the population are in favour of the principle of asylum for those 'genuinely' in need.[51] Sadly, like many temporary refugee movements studied in this book, the experiences of and help given to the Kosovans is fast being forgotten or dismissed at a collective level.

I will end with two clerics – one Christian, one Jewish – and a return to the centrality of an awareness of history and a commitment to refocused ethics, to suggest a way out of the current malaise. James Parkes is now a largely forgotten Church of England minister who worked tirelessly from the 1920s to expose the Christian roots of antisemitism. He campaigned on behalf of European Jewry, helped rescue refugees from Nazism and worked for a genuine dialogue between the Jewish and non-Jewish worlds. In early 1943, when news of the extermination of the Jews reached Britain in great detail, he wrote 'It is said that if we offered unlimited asylum in our own country ... it might lead to a dangerous increase of antisemitism.' There was only one response to such a claim, argued Parkes, from those 'who still believe there is any nobility in the cause for which we are fighting. We will receive them. And if there really be three million of them we will thank God that we have been able to save so many of them from Hitler's clutches'.[52] Parkes' belief in the principle of asylum was absolute: 'It is only in the spirit that we desire to save ALL whom we can reach that we can even undertake action that will save any'.[53] His premise – that if the will to help is there, there is no real reason why unlimited support to refugees cannot be given – rather than qualifying from the start why the granting of asylum might be mitigated, needs to be re-established. Compromising 'their' needs with 'ours' has enabled the moral case for refugees to disappear from view, allowing the free expression of hostility to asylum seekers to reign increasingly unchallenged.

The second cleric is Rabbi Hugo Gryn, an Auschwitz survivor who came to Britain in 1946. The story of his arrival is important in itself and needs analysing away from the redemptive mythology and memory work that is fast developing about its origins.[54] The British government allowed a fixed number of children from the concentration camps to come but on certain terms: they were here to recuperate for a fixed time, they had to be of a certain age and they must not all be Jewish. There were parallels here, on a much smaller scale, with the (forgotten) limitations of the earlier *Kindertransport* scheme. In fact, the major reason that the government agreed to bringing in youngsters from the camps was that it would have been extremely difficult not to – much larger schemes were in operation for children from the western former-occupied countries. So restrictive was the 1945/46 scheme that some of the Jewish child survivors lied about their age to qualify to get in.[55] It is not a very reassuring story, but it has to be added to the narrative of Britain and the Second World War. Unless historians and popularisers of the past in the world of heritage normalise and problematise the responses to and experiences of refugees in Britain, it will continue to be easy to distort that past. Integrating the history of refugees particularly shows the global nature of even the local experience; it also demolishes self-congratulatory myths of tolerance and fair play as being inherent in the national character.[56] The first chapter of *Remembering Refugees* began by quoting Hugo Gryn and his belief that 'future historians will call the twentieth century not only the century of the great wars, but also the century of the refugee'.[57] So far historians have let him down.

Earlier it has been suggested that pragmatic issues – such as the partial invisibility of refugees in surviving documentation – as well as more ideological factors – including the focus on the nation state and the emphasis on permanence over temporariness – go some way to explaining the historical profession's failure to incorporate the 'unwanted' into their narratives. There is another reason, however, why they have not responded to Hugo Gryn's call. The historiographer, Gordon Wright, argued in 1976 that 'The idea of consciously reintroducing the moral dimension into history runs counter to the basic training of most historians, and probably to their professional instinct as well.'[58] Such unease, until recently, has extended into exploring subjects with a clear ethical dimension, including refugee crises that have been a fundamental part of the modern world. In 2004, the extensive and intensive response to a call for papers on 'historians and ethics' in the journal *History and Theory* suggests strongly that a new generation of historians have moved on from Wright's perspective.[59] Moreover, many accept the position of Richard T. Vann that 'Those who accept a recent claim [by Ted Honderich] that we are living in a "dark time of need, a time of attack on moral intelligence" will want to do their part in repelling this attack.'[60] Asylum-seeker phobia has been described by Julia Neuberger, in her plea for a moral reconsideration of the plight of the less fortunate in Britain, as 'ugly, racist, and a cowardly targeting of the vulnerable'.[61] Historians, by focusing on their plight, need to re-connect their profession with an engagement with ethical issues such as asylum, just as those involved with various forms of moral philosophy and refugees need to engage with history.

In 2000, the outgoing editor of the *Journal of Refugee Studies*, Roger Zetter, was pleased that it had been 'successful in opening the field to other disciplines' in a 'field largely dominated by anthropology and law at its inception'.[62] Yet such broadening is still far from complete. As was noted in the first chapter, Zetter, in the first issue of his journal, commented that work on refugees had for the most part 'existed on the periphery' rather than 'the mainstream of academic enterprise'.[63] This is true even within the specific area of migration studies. As Alice Bloch suggests, 'for many refugees the theoretical paradigms of migration do not in fact represent the reality of their experience'.[64] Moreover, if, in recent years, some progress has been made in recognising the significance of refugee studies, the potential contribution that could be made to it by those who study (and represent) the past has been insufficiently recognised.[65] This study has highlighted the importance of memory work in confronting or avoiding the refugee. A new generation of ethically-aware historians, as well as, at a popular level, a form of counter-heritage, is required now to re-present refugees, past and present, who too often have been either demonised or made invisible. An example of how this might, or might not, be put into practice is provided by returning to the representation of the Belgian refugees in Britain.

In the first chapter of this study there was brief discussion of why Agatha Christie chose to make her most famous detective a Belgian refugee. Since her death in 1976, Christie's character, Hercule Poirot, has been celebrated in film and television. The success of such versions of Christie's murder mystery-solving hero prompted Robert Hewison to highlight what he saw as Britain in 'the climate of decline':

> George Orwell is part of heritage now, his reputation safely pinned by a plaque to the wall of a house in Islington. His grimmest prophesies have been duly celebrated for not coming to pass in 1984; his politics have been consigned to 'before the war'. 1937 is half a century away, and if we think of the period at all we are more likely to conjure up an ambience than historical events: the Thirties of Agatha Christie series on television, or the advertisements for the Orient Express. Indeed, we can re-enter the world of Hercule Poirot by taking the train, though it only goes as far as Venice, that classic symbol of sinking European civilization.[66]

Could the heritage industry present Poirot in any other way than the context of Britain as a 'rambling country house'? For Christie, in her last novel before her death: *Curtain: Poirot's Last Case* (1975), there was no place for such rose-tinted nostalgia. Poirot, reflecting on his arrival in Britain recalled it as a 'sad and painful time. I was a refugee, wounded, exiled from home and country, existing by charity in a foreign land. No, it was not gay.'[67] Christie, knowing the Belgian refugees well in wartime Devon, recognised their loss and misery. But when she has Poirot proclaiming, in his last outing as a detective, that he 'did not know then that England would come to be my home and that I should find happiness there', a double fiction is created. The vast majority of Belgians were removed quickly and insensitively after 1918, helping the subsequent collective amnesia about their presence in Britain.[68] Any form of counter-heritage will have to come to terms with the many layers of displacement that is part of the refugee experience, and the recognition, as came with Agatha Christie and the creation of Poirot (a man to the end of his life who was treated as an outsider and 'a foreigner'),[69] of the rupture and privation involved. A start, at least has been made in the form of oral history work amongst refugees and asylum seekers. It includes the Refugee Communities History Project (RCHP), funded by the Heritage Lottery Fund and the Trust for London which 'aims to highlight the economic, cultural and social contribution that refugees have made to London since 1951'. While not without the defensiveness that typified the foundation, and early work, of the Jewish Historical Society of England and the Huguenot Society of London, projects such as the RCHP provide the foundation for later and more critical historiography and counter-heritage work.[70]

But finally, we need to return to Hugo Gryn, a much loved character in late twentieth-century Britain. Born in a town that was under Czechoslovakian, Hungarian, German and Soviet control, he lived and worked in the USA, India and Britain. His life story encapsulates the very artificiality of national borders. He also insisted on the need to accept global responsibilities. In the words of Melanie Phillips 'What was it about him that touched a chord in so many people? At root, it was surely that in an age searching with increasing desperation for moral guidance, he didn't preach moral authority – he embodied it.'[71] Here is part of Hugo Gryn's last speech, delivered to the Refugee Council in 1996:

> it is imperative that we proclaim that asylum issues are an index of our spiritual and moral civilisation. How you are with the one to whom you owe nothing, that is a grave test and not only as an index of our tragic past … I believe that the line our society will take in this matter on how you are to people to whom you owe nothing is a signal. It is the critical signal that we give to our young, and I hope and pray that it is a test we shall not fail.

Here, rather than a human rights discourse, Gryn provided the ultimate humanitarian approach to asylum seekers – they should be given refuge simply because they are in need, even though we owe them nothing. If we fail to, then we risk being labelled as bystanders, 'the real offenders', as

Hugo Gryn argued, 'those people who let things happen because it didn't affect them directly'.[72] And if the virulence of the current campaign continues, which has seen asylum seekers and refugees turned away, murdered, locked out of public sight and deported in Britain and other liberal democracies, the label might be even more damning than Hugo Gryn could have imagined, leaking into that of perpetrator. Throughout 2003 and early 2004, for example, the ugliness of the local campaign in Lee-on-the-Solent against a proposal to create a camp for asylum seekers 'was a wake-up call for anybody who may have deluded themselves into believing that Britain is quite a tolerant, multi-cultural sort of place'.[73] Alternatively, while asylum seekers are today's scapegoats for much of contemporary anxiety, the examples of James Parkes and Hugo Gryn might suggest that helping, rather than denigrating, the victims of persecution may be one way that fear, parochialism and self-centredness – those increasingly blights of the twenty-first century – are minimised and self-confidence, caring and generosity amongst public, government and state can be restored. In the early twenty-first century it is not only asylum seekers who are in urgent need of rescue.

Notes

1 *Daily Mail*, 27 July 2005.
2 See, for example, *Daily Express*, 27 July 2005.
3 Sandy Buchan, letter to the *Guardian*, 29 July 2005. On Atique (or Ateeque) Sharifi see 'The Final Victim', *Independent*, 21 July 2005. More generally, on the 'us/them' dichotomy following the bombings, see Brian Klug, 'Being British and Saying "We"', *Tages-Anzeiger*, 10 August 2005.
4 Quoted in the *Observer*, 23 February 2003.
5 Matthew Gibney, *The Ethics and Politics of Asylum: Liberal Democracy and the Response to Refugees* (Cambridge: Cambridge University Press, 2004), p. 130.
6 *Daily Mail*, 27 July 2005.
7 Editorial, *Daily Mail*, 21 January 2003.
8 Julia Neuberger, *The Moral State We're In: A Manifesto for a 21st Century Society* (London: HarperCollins, 2005), p. 250.
9 *Daily Mail*, 20 January 2003.
10 On the 'Moral Maze', BBC Radio 4, 5 February 2003.
11 Statement made by Lord Rooker, 14 May 2002 reported in the *Guardian*, 15 May 2002. See also Alan Travis, 'Figures, not fairness, behind Blair's new asylum plan', *Guardian*, 24 May 2002 for the wider context of Rooker's remarks.
12 Gibney, *The Ethics and Politics of Asylum*, p. 129.
13 *Prospect* no. 83 (February 2003) and no. 95 (February 2004).
14 Roger Zetter, 'Refugees and Refugee Studies – a Valedictory Editorial', *Jour-*

nal of Refugee Studies vol. 13 no. 4 (2000), p. 352.

15 See, for example, the refusal of the Home Office's 'official' history of refugees in Britain to accept the criticism levelled in the late 1930s by Sir John Hope Simpson. In National Archives, HO 213/1772.

16 I am very grateful to Brian Klug for his helpful critique of the section on moral philosophy that follows.

17 Zetter, 'Refugees and Refugee Studies', p. 352.

18 Peter Singer, *Practical Ethics* (Cambridge: Cambridge University Press 1993, 2nd edition), pp. 252–3. Nevertheless, Joseph Carens, 'Aliens and Citizens: The Case for Open Borders', *The Review of Politics* vol. 49 (1987), pp. 251–73, esp. 255–64 does try to make use of Rawls to support his argument.

19 Andrew Shacknove, 'From Asylum to Containment', *International Journal of Refugee Law* vol. 5 no. 4 (1993), p. 517.

20 Michael Walzer, *Spheres of Justice: A Defence of Pluralism and Equality* (Oxford: Martin Robinson 1983), p. 39.

21 Ibid., p. 51.

22 Joseph Carens, 'Migration and Morality: A Liberal Egalitarian Perspective', in Brian Berry and Robert Goodin (eds), *Free Movement* (New York: Harvester), 1992), p. 30.

23 In National Archives, HO 213/1772.

24 Singer, *Practical Ethics*, pp. 247–9.

25 Liza Schuster, *The Use and Abuse of Political Asylum in Britain and Germany* (London: Frank Cass, 2003), p. 6.

26 Ibid., pp. 253, 261.

27 Walzer, *Spheres of Justice*, p. 49.

28 Singer, *Practical Ethics*, p. 262.

29 Michael Dummett, *On Immigration and Refugees* (London, Routledge 2001), p. 14.

30 Ibid, p. 14. See idem, p. 45 for the emphasis on Judeo-Christian principles.

31 W.H. Wilkins, *The Alien Invasion* (London, Methuen 1892), pp. 37, 52.

32 Dummett, *On Immigration and Refugees*, pp. 17, 19.

33 Matthew Gibney, 'Liberal Democratic States and Responsibilities to Refugees', *American Political Science Review* vol. 93 no. 1 (March 1999), p. 170. See his longer treatment of these issues in idem, *The Ethics and Politics of Asylum*, esp. chapters 1, 2, 7 and 8.

34 Shacknove, 'From Asylum to Containment', pp. 518–19.

35 Carens, 'Aliens and Citizens?', pp. 269–70.

36 Gibney, *The Ethics and Politics of Asylum*, p. 260.

37 Ibid., p. 15 quoting from Gil Loescher, *Beyond Charity: International Cooperation and the Global Refugee Crisis* (New York: Oxford University Press, 1993).

38 Gibney, *The Ethics and Politics of Asylum*, p. 230.

39 Ibid., p. 260.

40 *Daily Mail*, 4 December 2003.

41 Michael Clarke, 'The Contract with Muslims Must Not Be Torn Up', *Guard-*

ian, 26 August 2005.

42 Schuster, *The Use and Abuse of Political Asylum*, pp. 2–3.

43 Gibney, *The Ethics and Politics of Asylum*, p. 79.

44 Gibney, 'Liberal Democratic States', p. 170; Singer, *Practical Ethics*, p. 250.

45 National Archives, HO 213/1772.

46 Rev. G.S. Reaney, 'The Moral Aspect', in Arnold White (ed.), *The Destitute Alien in Great Britain* (London, Swann Sonnenschein 1892), pp. 98–9.

47 Dummett, *On Immigration and Refugees*, p. 44.

48 David Cesarani, 'Anti-Alienism in England after the First World War', *Immigrants & Minorities* vol. 6 no. 1 (March 1987), pp. 5–29.

49 Tony Kushner and Katharine Knox, *Refugees in an Age of Genocide: Global, National and Local Perspectives During the Twentieth Century* (London: Frank Cass, 1999), chapter 5.

50 Guild, 'The United Kingdom: Kosovar Albanian Refugees', in Joanne van Selm (ed.), *Kosovo's Refugees in the European Union* (London: Pinter, 2000), pp. 67–90, Tony Kushner, 'Kosovo and the Refugee Crisis, 1999: The Search for Patterns amidst the Prejudice', *Patterns of Prejudice* vol. 33 no. 3 (1999), pp. 73–86.

51 Miranda Lewis, *Asylum: Understanding Public Attitudes* (London: IPPR, 2005), p. 7.

52 Parkes papers, University of Southampton archive, 60/9/5/1.

53 Ibid.

54 For a redemptive approach, see Martin Gilbert, *The Boys: Triumph over Adversity* (London, Weidenfeld & Nicolson 1996).

55 Kushner and Knox, *Refugees in an Age of Genocide*, pp. 206–14.

56 Paul Langford, *Englishness Identified: Manners and Character 1650–1850* (Oxford, Oxford University Press 2000).

57 Speech published by the Refugee Council as 'A Moral and Spiritual Index' (1996).

58 Gordon Wright, 'History as a Moral Science', *American Historical Review* vol. 81 no. 1 (February 1976), p. 2. For critical comment, see Richard T.Vann, 'Historians and Moral Evaluations', *History and Theory* vol. 43 no. 4 (December 2004), pp. 5–6.

59 See Brian Fay, 'Historians and Ethics: A Short Introduction to the Theme Issue', *History and Theory* vol. 43 no. 4 (December 2004), p. 1.

60 Vann, 'Historians and Moral Evaluations', p. 30.

61 Neuberger, *The Moral State We're In*, p. 309.

62 Zetter, 'Refugees and Refugee Studies – A Valedictory Editorial', pp. 351–2.

63 Roger Zetter, 'Refugees and Refugee Studies – A Label and an Agenda', *Journal of Refugee Studies* vol. 1 no. 1 (1988), p. 2 and initial abstract description of the journal from Oxford University Press.

64 Alice Bloch, *The Migration and Settlement of Refugees in Britain* (Basingstoke: Palgrave Macmillan, 2002), p. 79 and chapter 4 in general.

65 For example, two of the largest humanities funding bodies in 2003 supported with very sizeable awards centres covering forced migration. None of these centres had any interest or expertise in history or ethics.

66 Robert Hewison, *The Heritage Industry: Britain in a Climate of Decline* (London: Methuen, 1987), p. 35.
67 Agatha Christie, *Curtain: Poirot's Last Case* (London: HarperCollins, 2002 [1975]), p. 21.
68 Ibid.
69 Ibid., p. 223.
70 More generally see Lewis, *Asylum*, pp. 57–8 for comment and examples. The RCHP is run by the Evelyn Oldfield Unit, which provides 'professional support & training for refugee organisations', in partnership with 15 Refugee Community Organisations, the Museum of London and London Metropolitan University.
71 Hugo Gryn with Naomi Gryn, *Chasing Shadows* (London and New York: Viking, 2000); Phillips in the *Observer*, 25 August 1996, see also the national British press on 20 August 1996.
72 Hugo Gryn, 'A Moral and Spiritual Index' (London: Refugee Council, 1996).
73 Kathryn Flett, 'Little Britain', *Observer*, 9 May 2004 in response to the Dispatches' documentary, *Keep them Out*, Channel 4, 6 May 2004.

Bibliography

Primary sources

Unpublished materials

British Library
'Living Memory of the Jewish Community' interviews, National Sound Archive

Cheadle Library
Barnes Hospital files
Historic buildings files

Imperial War Museum
'Britain and the Refugee crisis' oral history collection
Doreen Warriner papers

London Metropolitan Archives
Board of Deputies of British Jews archive
Central British Fund archives

Manchester Central Reference Library (Local Studies)
City of Manchester Council Minutes
Jenazian, B., 'The Armenian Merchants and the Armenian Community in Manchester'

Manchester Jewish Museum
Harris House Diary
Refugee oral history collection

Museum of London
'The Peopling of London' files

National Archives
Colonial Office papers
Foreign Office papers
Home Office papers
Ministry of Labour papers

National Labour Museum
Labour Party archives

Refugee Council
Hungarian refugee files
Rainey Kelly Campbell Roalfe, 'Refugees – From a Small Issue to an Important
   Cause' (Research debrief, October 1997)

Rothschild Archive
Anthony de Rothschild papers

University of Southampton
Parkes papers
Schonfeld papers

University of Sussex
Mass-Observation archive:
   Diaries, 1939–51
   File reports, 1937–51
   March 1939 directive: 'Jews'
   Summer 2000 directive: 'Coming to Britain'

Printed primary materials

Autobiographical

Agate, James, *Ego: The Autobiography of James Agate* (London: Hamish
   Hamilton, 1935)
Alibhai-Brown, Yasmin, *No Place Like Home* (London: Virago, 1995)
Blend, Martha, *A Child Alone* (London: Vallentine Mitchell, 1995)
Christie, Agatha, *An Autobiography* (London: Collins, 1977)
Cole, G.D.H., and Margaret (eds), *Rural Rides ... by William Cobbett* vol. 1
   (London: Peter Davies, 1930)
Feuchtwanger, Edgar, 'Recovering from Culture Shock', in Peter Alter (ed.), *Out
   of the Third Reich: Refugee Historians in Post-war Britain* (London: I.B.
   Tauris, 1998)
Gershon, Karen, *A Lesser Child* (London: Peter Owen, 1994)
Gershon, Karen (ed.), *We Came as Children: A Collective Autobiography of
   Refugees* (London: Gollancz, 1966)
Gissing, Vera, *Pearls of Childhood* (London: Robson Books, 1988)
Gryn, Hugo, with Naomi Gryn, *Chasing Shadows* (London and New York:
   Viking, 2000)
Jacoby, I., *My Darling Diary* (Cornwall, no place: United Writers, 1998)
Josephs, Jeremy, *Rosa's Child: the True Story of One Woman's Quest for a Lost
   Mother and a Vanished Past* (London: I.B. Tauris, 1996)
Kranzler, David, and Gertrude Hirschler (eds), *Solomon Schonfeld: His Place in
   History* (New York: Judaica Press, 1982)
Leverton, Bertha, and Shmuel Lowensohn (eds), *I Came Alone: The Stories of
   the Kindertransports* (Lewes: Book Guild, 1990)

Mehran, Alfred, *The Terminal Man* (London: Corgi, 2004)

Mikes, George, *How to be an Alien* (London: Andre Deutsch, 1946)

Mikes, George, *How to be a Brit* (Harmondsworth: Penguin, 1987)

Oppenheimer, Deborah, and Mark Jonathan Harris (eds), *Into the Arms of Strangers: Stories of the Kindertransport* (London: Bloomsbury, 2000)

Priestley, J.B., *English Journey* (London: Victor Gollancz, 1934)

Rice, Alan, 'Exploring Inside the Invisible: An Interview with Lubaina Himid', *Wasafari* no. 40 (Winter 2003)

Rosemarine, Barney, *Haimishe Laffs and Chaffs* (Altrincham: John Sherratt & Sons, 1962)

Roth, Joseph, *The Wandering Jews* (London: Granta, 2001)

Saville, Annette, *Only a Kindertransportee* (London: New Millennium, 2002)

Sheridan, Dorothy (ed.), *Among You Taking Notes ... The Wartime Diary of Naomi Mitchison* (London: Gollancz, 1985)

Stanhope-Brown, James, *A Styal of Its Own (1894–1964)* (Manchester [?]: Christine Pothecary, 1989)

Steele, Dora, *Cheadle Remembered* (Manchester: Neil Richardson, 1983)

Zurndorfer, Hannele, *The Ninth of November* (London: Quartet, 1983)

Books, articles, reports, museum catalogues and pamphlets

Angell, Norman, and Dorothy Buxton, *You and the Refugee* (Harmondsworth: Penguin, 1939)

Audit Commission, *Another Country: Implementing Dispersal under the Immigration and Asylum Act 1999* (London: Audit Commission, 2000)

Baldwin, Stanley, *The Plight of the Refugees* (Ottowa: Canadian National Committee on Refugees, 1939)

Batey, Mavis, David Lambert and Kim Wilkie, *Indignation! The campaign for conservation* (London: Kit-Cat Books, 2000)

Bloomsbury House, *Whilst You are in Britain* (London: Bloomsbury House, 1939)

Blunkett, David, 'Integration with Diversity: Globalisation and the Renewal of Democracy and Civil Society', in Phoebe Griffith and Mark Leonard (eds), *Reclaiming Britishness* (London: Foreign Policy Centre, 2002)

Brindley, W.H. (ed.), *The Soul of Manchester* (Manchester: Manchester University Press, 1929)

Buxton, Dorothy, *The Economics of the Refugee Problem* (London: Focus Publishing, 1939)

Chiat, Sheila, *Journeys to Freedom* (London: Leo Baeck College, 2000)

Cresswell, Yvonne (ed.), *Living with the Wire: Civilian Internment in the Isle of Man During the Two World Wars* (Douglas, Isle of Man: Manx National Heritage, 1994)

English Heritage, *Power of Place: The Future of the Historic Environment* (London: English Heritage, 2000)

Golding, Louis, *The Jewish Problem* (Harmondsworth: Penguin, 1938)

Gordon, William Evans, *The Alien Immigrant* (London: Heinemann, 1903)

Greenslade, Roy, *Seeking Scapegoats: the Coverage of Asylum in the UK Press*

(London: IPPR, 2005)

Grenville, Anthony, *Continental Britons: Jewish Refugees from Nazi Europe* (London: Jewish Museum, 2002)

Gryn, Hugo, *A Moral and Spiritual Index* (London: Refugee Council, 1996)

Heritage Lottery Fund, *Who Do We Think We Are?* (London: Heritage Lottery Fund, 2005)

Holder, John, *Royal Victoria Country Park: The Story of a Great Military Hospital & Royal Victoria Park* (Winchester[?]: Hampshire County Council, no date)

Hyde, Matthew, Aiden O'Rourke and Peter Portland, *Around the M60: Manchester's Orbital Motorway* (Altrincham: AMCD Publishers, 2004)

Information Centre about Asylum and Refugees in the UK, *Media Image, Community Impact* (London: King's College, 2004)

Krausz, Ernest, *Leeds Jewry: Its History and Social Structure* (Cambridge: Jewish Historical Society of England, W. Heffer, 1964)

Lawson, Alan, *'It Happened in Manchester: The True Story of Manchester's Music 1958–1965'* (Bury: Multimedia, no date)

Lewis, Miranda, *Asylum: Understanding Public Attitudes* (London: IPPR, 2005)

London Committee of Deputies of British Jews, *Objections to the Aliens Bill* (London: London Committee of Deputies of British Jews, 1904)

London Museum of Jewish Life, *The Last Goodbye: The Rescue of Children from Nazi Europe. An Educational Resource about the Kindertransport* (London: London Museum of Jewish Life, 1996)

McKenney, Ruth, and Richard Bransten, *Here's England* (London: Rupert Hart-Davis, 1951)

Makepeace, Charles, *Cheadle and Gatley in Old Picture Postcards* (Zaltbommel, Netherlands: European Library, 1988)

Movement for the Care of Children from Germany, *First Annual Report: November 1938–December 1939* (London: MCCG, 1940)

Movement for the Care of Children from Germany, *Instructions for the Guidance of Regional and Local Committees* (London: Bloomsbury House, 1940)

Museum of Science & Technology in Manchester, *Souvenir Guide* (Manchester: Museum of Science & Industry, no date)

National Museum of Labour History, *The Pump House: People's History Museum, A Guide* (Manchester: National Museum of Labour History, 1998)

Portal, William, *The Manors and Churches of Laverstoke and Freefolk in Hampshire* (no place of publication: Hampshire Field Club, 1908)

Presland, John [Gladys Bendit], *A Great Adventure: The Story of the Refugee Children's Movement* (London: Bloomsbury House, 1944)

Reaney, G.S., 'The Moral Aspect', in Arnold White (ed.), *The Destitute Alien in Great Britain* (London: Swann Sonnenschein, 1892)

Reunion of Kindertransport, *Kindertransport 60th Anniversary* (London: Reunion of Kindertransport, 1999)

Sandell, Elsie, *Southampton Cavalcade* (Southampton: G.F. Wilson, 1953)

Sandell, Elsie, *Southampton Through the Ages* (Southampton: G.F. Wilson, 1960)

Smiles, Samuel, *The Huguenots* (London: John Murray, 1868)

Smith, Stephen (ed.), *Our Lonely Journey* (Newark: Beth Shalom, 1999)

Union of Orthodox Hebrew Congregations, *The Child Estranging Movement* (London: Union of Orthodox Hebrew Congregations, 1944)

Whitchurch Silk Mill, *Whitchurch Silk Mill* (Basingstoke: Whitchurch Silk Mill, no date)

Wilkins, W.H., *The Alien Invasion* (London: Methuen, 1892)

Wolf, Lucien, 'A Plea for Anglo-Jewish History', *Transactions of the Jewish Historical Society of England* vol. 1 (1893–94)

Young, Mike, *Unwanted Journey: Why Central European Roma are Fleeing to the UK* (London: Refugee Council, 1999)

Document collections

Cantril, Hadley (ed.), *Public Opinion 1935–1946* (Princeton: Princeton University Press, 1951)

Hyslop, Donald, Alastair Forsyth and Sheila Jemima (eds), *Titanic Voices* (Southampton: Southampton City Council, 1994)

Kampe, Norbert (ed.), *Jewish Emigrants of the Nazi Period in the USA* (Munich: K.G. Saur, 1992)

Langer, Jennifer (ed.), *The Bend in the Road: Refugees Writing* (Nottingham: Five Leaves, 1997)

Smithies, Bill and Peter Fiddick, *Enoch Powell on Immigration* (London: Sphere Books, 1969)

Literature

Ambrose, Kenneth, *The Story of Peter Cronheim* (London: Constable, 1962)

Carroll, Lewis, *Through the Looking Glass* (Harmondsworth: Puffin Books, 1980)

Christie, Agatha, *Curtain: Poirot's Last Case* (London: HarperCollins, 2002)

Christie, Agatha, *The Mysterious Affair at Styles* (London: HarperCollins, 2001)

Christie, Agatha, *The Mystery of the Blue Train* (Glasgow: Collins, 1989)

Cooper Clarke, John, *(I Married a) Monster from Outer Space* (1979)

Koralek, Jenny, *War Games* (London: Egmont Books, 2002)

Kramer, Lotte, *The Phantom Lane* (Ware: Rockingham Press, 2000)

Naipaul, V.S., *The Enigma of Arrival* (London: Penguin, 1987)

Roston, Leo, *The Return of Hyman Kaplan* (London: Penguin, 1979)

Samuels, Diane, *Kindertransport* (London: Nick Hern Books, 2004)

Sebald, W.G., *Austerlitz* (London: Hamish Hamilton, 2001)

Sebald, W.G., *The Emigrants* (London: Vintage, 2002)

Sebald, W.G., *The Rings of Saturn* (London: Harvill Press, 1998)

Szirtes, George, *The Budapest File* (Newcastle: Bloodaxe Books, 2000)

Newspapers and journals

AJR Information
Daily Express
Daily Mail

Daily Mirror
Daily Star
Daily Telegraph
Evening Standard
Financial Times
Guardian
The Independent
iNexile: The Refugee Council Magazine
Jewish Chronicle
Jewish Gazette
Jewish Quarterly
Jewish Telegraph
Mail on Sunday
Manchester Metro News
New Pioneer
News Chronicle
New Statesman
Observer
Picture Post
Prospect
Publications of the Huguenot Society of London
Southampton Times
Southern Daily Echo
Southampton Times
The Spectator
Star
Stockport Express
Stockport Messenger
Stockport Times
Sun
Sunday Express
The Times
This England
This is Hampshire
Times Literary Supplement
Transactions of the Jewish Historical Society of England

Official publications

Aliens Act, 1905 (11 August 1905), 5 EDW.7
Department for Culture, Media and Sport, *Libraries, Museums, Galleries and
    Archives for All* (London: Department for Culture, Media and Sport, 2001)
Hansard
Home Office, *Fairer, Faster and Firmer. A Modern Approach to Immigration
    and Asylum* (Cmd 4018, London: HMSO, 1998)
Home Office, *Race Relations (Amendment) Act 2000* (London: HMSO, 2001)
Home Office, *Secure Borders, Safe Haven: Integration with Diversity in Modern*

Britain (Cmd 5387, London: HMSO, 2002)

Papers Concerning the Treatment of German Nationals in Germany 1938–9 (Cmd 6120, HMSO: London, 1939)

Royal Commission on Alien Immigration: Minutes of Evidence (Cmd 1742, London: HMSO, 1903)

Royal Commission on The Press 1947–1949: Report (Cmd 7700, London: HMSO, 1949)

Films and documentaries

Anne Frank Remembered (1995)
His Majesty's Most Loyal Enemy Aliens (1993)
In This World (2003)
Into the Arms of Strangers (2000)
Keep Them Out (Channel 4, 6 May 2004)
Life is Beautiful (1998)
Rescued: A Sixty Year Journey (2000)
Schindler's List (1993)
The Terminal Man (2004)

Museums, exhibitions and site visits

Bury Art Gallery & Museum
Heritage Centre, Spitalfields, *Suitcases and Sanctuary* (2000)
Davies, Howard, *Home and Away* and *Images of Exile* touring photographic exhibitions
Huguenot Garden, Southampton
Jewish Museum, *Closing the Door* (2005)
Jewish Museum, *Continental Britons* (2002)
Jewish Museum, *The Last Goodbye* (1996)
Jewish Museum, permanent exhibitions (Finchley and Camden Town sites)
Kindertransport memorial, Liverpool Street Station
Klevansky, Rhonda, *Fragments of Another Life* (photographic exhibition, St Mary's Church, Southampton)
Macclesfield Heritage Centre
Manchester Jewish Museum, *Before the Holocaust* (1986)
Manchester Jewish Museum, permanent exhibition
The Museum of London, *The Peopling of London* (2003)
Museum of Science & Industry in Manchester
Pump House Museum, Manchester
Quarry Bank Mill, Styal
Royal Victoria Country Park, Netley
Southampton International Airport
Southampton Maritime Museum
Urbis Museum, Manchester
Whitchurch Silk Mill, Hampshire

Websites

Association of Jewish Refugees www.ajr.org.uk
Hampshire County Council www.hants.gov.uk
Hampshire Record Office hants.gov.uk/record-office
Houses of Parliament www.parliament.the-stationery-office.co.uk
Information Centre about Asylum and Refugees in the UK (ICAR) www.icar.org.uk
Kindertransport Association www.kindertransport.org
National Trust www.quarrybankmill.org.uk
Refugee Council www.refugeecouncil.org.uk
Stonewall www.stonewall.org.uk
UNHCR www.unhcr.ch

Other primary sources

Property development publicity material for Spitalfields, London; Southampton
and Manchester in author's possession

Secondary sources

Acton, Thomas (ed.), *Gypsy Politics and Traveller Identity* (Hatfield: University
of Hertfordshire Press, 1997)
Ager, Alastair (ed.), *Refugees: Perspectives on the Experience of Forced Migra-
tion* (London: Continuum, 1999)
Alaimo, Kathleen and Brian Klug (eds), *Children as Equals: Exploring the Rights
of the Child* (Lanham: University Press of America, 2002)
Angell, Norman, and Dorothy Buxton, *You and the Refugee* (Harmondsworth:
Penguin, 1939)
Arendt, Hannah, *The Origins of Totalitarianism* (London: George Allen &
Unwin, 1958)
Barany, Zoltan, *The East European Gypsies: Regime Change, Marginality, and
Ethnopolitics* (Cambridge: Cambridge University Press, 2002)
Barkan, Elazar, *The Retreat of Scientific Racism: Changing Concepts of Race in
Britain and the United States between the World Wars* (Cambridge: Cam-
bridge University Press, 1986)
Barnett, Ruth, 'The Acculturation of the Kindertransport Children:
Intergenerational Dialogue on the Kindertransport Experience', *Shofar* vol.23
no.1 (Fall 2004)
Baucom, Ian, *Out of Place: Englishness, Empire, and the Locations of Identity*
(Princeton: Princeton University Press, 1999)
Baum, Rainer, 'Holocaust: Moral Indifference as *the* Form of Modern Evil', in
A. Rosenberg and G. Meyers (eds), *Echoes From the Holocaust* (Philadel-
phia: Temple University Press, 1988)
Baumel, Judith Tydor, *Unfulfilled Promise: Rescue and Resettlement of Jewish
Refugee Children in the United Stated 1934–1945* (Juneau: Denali Press,
1990)

Benjamin, Walter, *The Arcades Project*, trans. Kevin Eiland and Kevin McLaughlin (Cambridge, MA: Harvard University Press, 1999)

Berger, John, *Keeping a Rendezvous* (London: Granta Books, 1992)

Berghahn, Marion, *Continental Britons: German-Jewish Refugees from Nazi Germany* (Oxford: Berg, 1988)

Bermant, Chaim, *Point of Arrival: A Study of London's East End* (London: Eyre Methuen, 1975)

Bettelheim, Bruno, 'The Ignored Lesson of Anne Frank', in idem, *Surviving and Other Essays* (New York: Knopf, 1979)

Black, Jeremy, *Modern British History since 1900* (Basingstoke: Macmillan, 2000)

Bloch, Alice, *The Migration and Settlement of Refugees in Britain* (Basingstoke: Palgrave Macmillan, 2002)

Bloxham, Donald, and Tony Kushner, *The Holocaust: Critical Historical Approaches* (Manchester: Manchester University Press, 2005)

Bouquet, Tim, and David Moller, 'Are We a Tolerant Nation?', *Reader's Digest*, November 2000

Boyarin, Jonathan, *Storm from Paradise: The Politics of Jewish Memory* (Minneapolis: University of Minnesota Press, 1992)

Bramwell, Anna (ed.), *Refugees in an Age of Total War* (London: Unwin, Hyman, 1988)

Breitman, Richard, and Alan Kraut, *American Refugee Policy and European Jewry, 1933–1945* (Bloomington: Indiana University Press, 1987)

Brenner, Michael, Rainer Liedtke, and David Rechter (eds), *Two Nations: British and German Jews in Comparative Perspective* (Tubingen: J.C.B. Mohr, 1999)

Browning, Christopher, *Ordinary Men: Reserve Police Battalion 101 and the Final Solution in Poland* (New York: HarperCollins 1992)

Burrin, Phillippe, *France Under the Germans: Collaboration and Promise* (New York: New Press, 1996)

Buruma, Ian, *The Wages of Guilt: Memories of War in Germany and Japan* (London: Jonathan Cape, 1994)

Cahalan, Peter, *Belgian Refugee Relief in England during the Great War* (New York: Garland, 1982)

Carens, Joseph, 'Aliens and Citizens: the Case for Open Borders', *The Review of Politics* vol. 49 (1987)

Carens, Joseph, 'Migration and Morality: A Liberal Egalitarian Perspective', in Brian Berry and Robert Goodin (eds), *Free Movement* (New York: Harvester, 1992)

Cesarani, David, 'Anti-Alienism in England after the First World War', *Immigrants & Minorities* vol. 6 no. 1 (1997)

Cesarani, David, 'Dual Heritage or Duel of Heritages? Englishness and Jewishness in the Heritage Industry', in Tony Kushner (ed.), *The Jewish Heritage in English History* (London: Frank Cass, 1992)

Cesarani, David, and Tony Kushner (eds), *The Internment of Aliens in Twentieth Century Britain* (London: Frank Cass, 1993)

Cesarani, David, and Paul Levine (eds), *'Bystanders' to the Holocaust: A Re-*

evaluation (London: Frank Cass, 2002)

Chamberlain, Mary, and Paul Thompson (eds), *Narrative and Genre* (London: Routledge, 1998)

Channing, Ronald, 'Kinder's Lifetime Odyssey', *AJR Information*, July 2000

Cheyette, Bryan, *Constructions of 'the Jew' in English Literature and Society: Racial Representations, 1875–1945* (Cambridge: Cambridge University Press, 1993)

Clark, Colin, and Elaine Campbell, '"Gypsy Invasion": A Critical Analysis of Newspaper Reaction to Czech and Slovak Romani Asylum-seekers in Britain, 1997', *Romani Studies* vol. 10 no. 1 (2000)

Cohen, Phil, 'Rethinking the Diasporama', *Patterns of Prejudice* vol. 33 no. 1 (1999)

Cohen, Robin, *Frontiers of Identity: The British and Others* (London: Longman, 1994)

Cohen, Stanley, *Folk Devils and Moral Panics* (London: Routledge, 2002, 3rd edition)

Colijn, G. Jan, 'Anne Frank Remembered', *Holocaust and Genocide Studies* vol. 10 no. 1 (Spring 1996)

Colls, Robert, *Identity of England* (Oxford: Oxford University Press, 2002)

Cunningham, Hugh, *Children and Childhood in Western Society since 1500* (London: Longman, 1995)

Curio, Claudio, '"Invisible" Children: The Selection and Integration Strategies of Relief Organizations', *Shofar* vol. 23 no. 1 (Fall 2004)

Davies, C. Stella, *A History of Macclesfield* (Manchester: Manchester University Press, 1961)

Diboll, Mike, and Elane Heffernan, 'Labour's Racism: the Last Straw', *Socialist Review*, June 2000

Diner, Hasia, Jeffrey Shandler and Beth Shindler (eds), *Remembering the Lower East Side* (Bloomington: Indiana University Press, 2000)

Dubrovsky, Gertrude, *Six from Leipzig* (London: Vallentine Mitchell, 2004)

Dummett, Michael, *On Immigration and Refugees* (London: Routledge, 2001)

Dwork, Deborah, *Children with a Star: Jewish Youth in Nazi Europe* (New Haven: Yale University Press, 1991)

Eaglestone, Robert, *The Holocaust and the Postmodern* (Oxford: Oxford University Press, 2004)

Eskin, Blake, *A Life in Pieces* (London: Aurum Press, 2002)

Fay, Brian, 'Historians and Ethics', *History and Theory* vol. 43 no. 4 (special issue) (December 2004)

Feingold, Henry, *The Politics of Rescue: The Roosevelt Administration and the Holocaust, 1938–1945* (New Brunswick: Rutgers University Press, 1970)

Feldman, David, *Englishmen and Jews: Social Relations and Political Culture 1840–1914* (New Haven: Yale University Press, 1994)

Feminist Praxis nos. 37 and 38 (special issue) 1993

Fishman, Bill, *The Streets of East London* (London: Duckworth, 1979)

Foster, Paul (ed.), *Bell of Chichester (1883–1958)* (Chichester: University College Chichester, 2004)

Frangopulo, N.J. (ed.), *Rich Inheritance: A Guide to the History of Manchester* (Wakefield: S.R.Publishcrs, 1969)

Friedlander, Saul, *Nazi Germany & the Jews: The Years of Persecution 1933–39* (London: Weidenfeld & Nicolson, 1997)

Fryer, Peter, *Staying Power: The History of Black People in Britain* (London: Pluto Press, 1984)

Fulbrook, Mary, *German National Identity After the Holocaust* (Cambridge: Policy Press, 1999)

Gainer, Bernard, *The Alien Invasion: The Origins of the Aliens Act of 1905* (London: Heinemann, 1972)

Garrard, John, *The English and Immigration: A Comparative Study of the Jewish Influx 1880–1910* (London: Oxford University Press, 1971)

Gartner, Lloyd, 'Notes on the Statistics of Jewish Immigration to England, 1870–1914', *Jewish Social Studies* vol. 22 no. 2 (1960)

Gedi, Noa and Yigal Elam, 'Collective Memory – what is it?', *History & Memory* vol.8 no.1 (spring/summer 1996)

Geertz, Clifford, *Local Knowledge* (London: Fontana, 1983)

Gilbert, Martin, *The Boys: Triumph over Adversity* (London: Weidenfeld & Nicolson, 1996)

Gibney, Matthew, *The Ethics and Politics of Asylum: Liberal Democracy and the Response to Refugees* (Cambridge: Cambridge University Press, 2004)

Gibney, Michael, 'Liberal Democratic States and Responsibilities to Refugees', *American Political Science Review* vol. 93 no. 1 (1999)

Gilkes, Michael, 'The Dark Strangers', in Lesley Smith (ed.), *The Making of Britain* (Basingstoke: Macmillan, 1988)

Goldhagen, Daniel, *Hitler's Willing Executioners: Ordinary Germans and the Holocaust* (Boston: Little, Brown, 1996)

Gopfert, Rebekka, *Der Judische Kindertransport von Deutschland nach England, 1938/39: Geschichte und Erinnerung* (Frankfurt: Campus Verlag, 1999)

Gottlieb, Amy, *Men of Vision: Anglo-Jewry's Aid to Victims of the Nazi Regime* (London: Weidenfeld & Nicolson, 1998)

Graham, Brian, G.J. Ashworth, and J.E. Tunbridge, *A Geography of Heritage: Power, Culture & Economy* (London: Arnold, 2000)

Gregory, Derek, *Geographical Imaginations* (Oxford: Blackwell, 1994)

Guild, Elspeth, 'The United Kingdom: Kosovar Albanian Refugees', in Joanne van Selm (ed.), *Kosovo's Refugees in the European Union* (London: Pinter, 2000)

Guy, Will (ed.), *Between Past and Future: The Roma of Central and Eastern Europe* (Hatfield: University of Hertfordshire Press, 2001)

Gwynn, Robin, *Huguenot Heritage: The History and Contribution of the Huguenots in Britain* (London: Routledge, 1985)

Gwynn, Robin, 'Huguenots and Walloons in Dorset, Hampshire and Wiltshire', *Hatcher Review* vol. 2 (1984)

Halbwachs, Maurice, *On Collective Memory* (Chicago: University of Chicago Press, 1992)

Hammel, Andrea, 'Representations of Family in Autobiographical Texts of Child Refugees', *Shofar* vol. 23 no. 1 (Fall 2004)

Haslam, Dave, *Manchester, England: The Story of the Pop Cult City* (London: Fourth Estate, 1999)

Hathaway, James, 'A Reconsideration of the Underlying Premise of Refugee Law', *Harvard International Law Journal* vol. 31 no. 1 (1990)

Hewison, Robert, *The Heritage Industry: Britain in a Climate of Decline* (London: Methuen, 1987)

Hewison, Robert, 'The Heritage Industry Revisited', *Museums Journal* vol. 91 no. 4 (April 1991)

History and Theory vol. 43 no. 4 (2004) special issue 'Historians and Ethics'

Hoare, Philip, *Spike Island: The Memory of a Military Hospital* (London: Fourth Estate, 2002)

Hobsbawm, Eric, and Terence Ranger (eds), *The Invention of Tradition* (Cambridge: Cambridge University Press, 1983)

Hoffnung, Annetta, *Gerard Hoffnung: His Biography* (London: Gordon Fraser, 1988)

Holmes, Colin, *John Bull's Island: Immigration & British Society, 1871–1971* (Basingstoke: Macmillan, 1988)

Holmes, Colin, *A Tolerant Country? Immigrants, Refugees and Minorities in Britain* (London: Faber & Faber, 1991)

Holmes, Colin, 'The German Gypsy question in Britain, 1904–1906', in Ken Lunn (ed.), *Hosts, Immigrants and Minorities: Responses to Newcomers in British Society 1870–1914* (Folkestone: Dawson, 1980)

Holmes, Colin, and Sean Kelly, '"A Question of Ways and Means": Hungarian Immigrants to Britain 1956–7', paper at 'Immigration, History and Memory in Britain', conference, De Montford University, September 2003

hooks, bell, 'Representing Whiteness', in Lawrence Grossberg, Cary Nelson and Paula Treicher (eds), *Cultural Studies* (New York: Routledge, 1992)

Inman, Ken, and Michael Helm, *Bury and the Second World War* (Warrington/Formby: Inman and Helm, 1995)

Irwin, Zachary, review of *Refugees in an Age of Genocide*, *Library Journal*, 15 September 1999

Jackson, Anthony (ed.), *Anthropology at Home* (London: Tavistock Publications, 1987)

Jackson, Julian, *France: the Dark Years 1940–1944* (Oxford: Oxford University Press, 2001)

Kahn, David, 'Diversity and the Museum of London', *Curator: The Museum Journal* vol. 37 no. 4 (1994)

Kaye, Ronald, 'Defining the Agenda: British Refugee Policy and the Role of Parties', *Journal of Refugee Studies* vol. 7 nos 2/3 (1994)

Kaye, Ronald, 'Redefining the Refugee: the UK Media Portrayal of Asylum Seekers', in Khalid Koser and Helma Lutz (eds), *The New Migration in Europe: Social Constructions and Social Realities* (Basingstoke: Macmillan, 1998)

Kedward, H.R., and Nancy Wood (eds), *The Liberation of France: Image and Event* (Oxford: Berg, 1995)

Kennedy, Robert (ed.), *A Nation of Immigrants* (New York: Harper and Row, 1964)

Kershen, Anne, *Strangers, Aliens and Asians: Huguenots, Jews and Bangladeshis in Spitalfields 1660–2000* (London: Routledge, 2005)

Kertesz, Margaret, 'To Speak for Themselves? Mass-Observation's Women's Wartime Diaries', *Feminist Praxis* nos 37 and 38 (1993)

Kidd, Alan (ed.), *Manchester* (Keele: Keele University Press, 1993)

Klug, Brian, 'Being British and Saying "We"', *Tages-Anzeiger*, 10 August 2005

Korte, Mona, 'Bracelet, Hand Towel, Pocket Watch: Objects of the Last Moment in Memory and Narration', *Shofar* vol. 23 no. 1 (Fall 2004)

Kundnani, Arun, 'In a Foreign Land: the New Popular Racism', *Race and Class* vol. 43 no. 2 (2001)

Kushner, Tony, *The Holocaust and the Liberal Imagination: A Social and Cultural History* (Oxford: Blackwell, 1994)

Kushner, Tony, *We Europeans? Mass-Observation, 'Race' and British Identity in the Twentieth Century* (Aldershot: Ashgate, 2004)

Kushner, Tony, 'An Alien Occupation – Jewish Refugees and Domestic Service in Britain, 1933–1948', in Werner Mosse (ed.), *Second Chance: Two Centuries of German-speaking Jews in the United Kingdom* (Tubingen: J.C.B. Mohr, 1991)

Kushner, Tony, 'Great Britons: Immigration, History and Memory', in Kathy Burrell and Panikos Panayi (eds), *Histories and Memories* (London: I.B. Tauris, forthcoming, 2006)

Kushner, Tony, 'The Holocaust and the Museum World in Britain: A Study of Ethnography', in Sue Vice (ed.) *Representing the Holocaust* (London: Frank Cass, 2003)

Kushner, Tony, 'Kosovo and the Refugee Crisis, 1999: The Search for Patterns Amidst the Prejudice', *Patterns of Prejudice* vol. 33 no. 3.

Kushner, Tony, 'Local Heroes: Belgian refugees in Britain during the First World War', *Immigrants & Minorities* vol. 18 no. 1 (March 1999)

Kushner, Tony, 'Looking Back with Nostalgia? The Jewish Museums of England', *Immigrants & Minorities* vol. 6 no. 2 (1987)

Kushner, Tony, 'Meaning Nothing But Good: Ethics, History and Asylum-seeker Phobia in Britain', *Patterns of Prejudice* vol. 37 no. 3 (2003)

Kushner, Tony, 'New Labour Old Racism', *Jewish Socialist* no. 46 (Spring 2002)

Kushner, Tony, and Katharine Knox, *Refugees in an Age of Genocide: Global, National and Local Perspectives during the Twentieth Century* (London: Frank Cass, 1999)

Langford, Paul, *Englishness Identified: Manners and Character 1650–1850* (Oxford: Oxford University Press, 2000)

Lanzmann, Claude, *Shoah: An Oral History of the Holocaust* (New York: Pantheon Books, 1985)

Lappin, Elena, 'The Man With Two Heads', *Granta* no. 66 (Summer 1990)

Larsen, Egon, 'What Every Child Should Know', *AJR Information*, June 1962

Lashitzky, Yosefa, *Spielberg's Holocaust: Critical Perspectives on* Schindler's List (Bloomington: Indiana University Press, 1997)

Lawson, Peter, 'Three Kindertransport Poets: Karen Gershon, Gerda Mayer and Lotte Kramer', in Ulrike Behlau and Bernhard Reitz (eds), *Jewish Women's Writing of the 1990s and Beyond in Great Britain and the United States* (Trier: Wissenschaftlicher Verlag Trier, 2004)

Layton-Henry, Zig, *The Politics of Immigration: Immigration, 'Race' and 'Race' Relations in Post-War Britain* (Oxford: Blackwell, 1992)

Loescher, Gil and Laila Monahan (eds), *Refugees and International Relations* (Oxford: Oxford University Press, 1989)

London, Louise, *Whitehall and the Jews 1933–1948: British Immigration Policy and the Holocaust* (Cambridge: Cambridge University Press, 2000)

London, Louise, 'Whitehall and the Refugees: the 1930s and the 1990s', *Patterns of Prejudice* vol. 34 no. 3 (2000)

Loshitzky, Yosefa, *Spielberg's Holocaust: Critical Perspective on Schindler's List* (Bloomington, IN: Indiana University Press, 1997)

Lowenthal, David, *The Heritage Crusade and the Spoils of History* (Cambridge: Cambridge University Press, 1998)

Macklin, Graham, '"A quite natural and moderate defensive feeling?" The 1945 Hampstead "anti-alien" petition', *Patterns of Prejudice* vol. 37 no. 3 (2003)

Malet, Marian and Anthony Grenville (eds), *Changing Countries: The Experience and Achievement of German-speaking Exiles from Hitler in Britain from 1933 to Today* (London: Libris, 2002)

Malkki, Liisa, 'National Geographic: The Rooting of Peoples and the Territorialization of National Identity among Scholars and Refugees', *Cultural Anthropology* vol. 7 no. 1 (February 1992)

Malkki, Liisa, 'Speechless Emissaries: Refugees, Humanitarianism, and Dehistoricization', *Cultural Anthropology* vol. 11 no. 3 (August 1996)

Malmgreen, Gail, *Silk Town: Industry and Culture in Macclesfield 1750–1835* (Hull: Hull University Press, 1985)

Mandler, Peter, *History and National Life* (London: Profile Books, 2002)

Marks, Jane, *The Hidden Children: The Secret Survivors of the Holocaust* (London: Bantam Books, 1995)

Marrus, Michael, *The Unwanted: European Refugees in the Twentieth Century* (Oxford: Oxford University Press, 1985)

Massey, Doreen, 'Double Articulation: A Place in the World', in A.Baumer (ed.), *Displacements: Cultural Identities in Question* (Indiana: Indiana University Press, 1994)

Massey, Doreen, 'Places and Their Pasts', *History Workshop Journal* no. 39 (spring 1995)

Mason, Peter, *Hampshire: A Sense of Place* (Crediton: Hampshire Books, 1994)

Mayall, David, *Gypsy Identities 1500–2000: From Egipcyans and Moon-men to the Ethnic Romany* (London: Routledge, 2004)

Merriman, Nick (ed.), *The Peopling of London: Fifteen Thousand Years of Settlement from Overseas* (London: Museum of London, 1993)

Neuberger, Julia, *The Moral State We're In: A Manifesto for a 21st Century Society* (London: HarperCollins, 2005)

Neumeier, Beate, 'Kindertransport: Childhood Trauma and Diaspora Experience', in Ulrike Behlau and Bernhard Reitz (eds), *Jewish Women's Writing of the 1930s and Beyond in Great Britain and the United States* (Trier: Wissenschaftlicher Verlag Trier, 2004)

Nevin, William, *Facing the Nazi Past: United Germany and the Legacy of the Third Reich* (London: Routledge, 2001)

Nicolson, Colin, *Strangers to England: Immigration to England 1100–1945* (London: Wayland, 1964)

Noakes, Lucy, *War and the British: Gender, Memory and National Identity* (London: I.B. Tauris, 1998)

Noiriel, Gerard, *La Tyrannie du national: le droit d'asile en Europe 1793–1993* (Paris: Calmann-Levy, 1991)

Nussbaum, Felicity, 'Toward Conceptualizing the Diary', in James Olney (ed.), *Studies in Autobiography* (New York: Oxford University Press, 1988)

Offer, Dalia, and Lenore Weitzmann (eds), *Women in the Holocaust* (New Haven: Yale University Press, 1998)

Oldfield, Sybil, '"It is Usually She": The Role of British Women in the Rescue and Care of the Kindertransport Kinder', *Shofar* vol. 23 no. 1 (Fall 2004)

Patterns of Prejudice vol. 37 no. 3 (2003) special issue on 'Racism and Asylum in Europe'

Page, William (ed.), *The Victoria History of the Counties of England: Hampshire and the Isle of Wight* vol.5 (London: Constable, 1912)

Pellew, Jill, 'The Home Office and the Aliens Act, 1905', *Historical Journal* vol. 32 no. 32 (1989)

Perks, Rob, 'The Ellis Island Immigration Museum, New York', *Oral History* vol. 19 no. 1 (spring 1991)

Pevsner, Nikolaus, and Edward Hubbard, *The Buildings of England: Cheshire* (London: Penguin, 1990 [1971])

Pitcher, Anne, *Whitchurch* (Basingstoke: Bird Brothers, 1984)

Portal, William, *Some Account of the Settlement of Refugees (L'Eglisse Wallonne) at Southampton* (Winchester: Jacob and Johnson, 1982 [1902])

Porter, Bernard, *The Refugee Question in Mid-Victorian Politics* (Cambridge: Cambridge University Press, 1979)

Proudfoot, Malcolm, *European Refugees: 1939–52. A Study in Forced Population Movement* (London: Faber & Faber, 1957)

Pym, John (ed.), *Time Out Film Guide* (London: Time Out, 2000, 8th edition)

Rawlinson, Mark, 'On the Losing Side: Francis Stuart, Henry Williamson and Collaboration', in Silvia Bigliazzi and Sharon Wood (eds), *Collaboration* (Aldershot: Ashgate, forthcoming)

Relph, Edward, *Place and Placelessness* (London: Pion, 1976)

Ria, Antonia, *Italians in Manchester* (Aosta: Musumeci Editore, 1990)

Richards, Jeffrey, *Film and British National Identity: From Dickens to Dad's Army* (Manchester: Manchester University Press, 1997)

Richmond, Colin, *Campaigner Against Antisemitism: The Reverend James Parkes 1896–1981* (London: Vallentine Mitchell, 2005)

Roche, T.W.E., *The Key in the Lock: Immigration Control in England from 1066 to the Present Day* (London: John Murray, 1969)

Rose, Peter, *The Subject is Race: Traditional Ideologies and the Teaching of Race Relations* (New York: Oxford University Press, 1968)

Rosenberg, A., and G. Meyers (eds), *Echoes From the Holocaust: Philosophical Reflections on a Dark Time* (Philadelphia: Temple University Press, 1988)

Rowbotham, Sheila, *Hidden from History: 300 Years of Women's Oppression and the Fight Against It* (London: Pluto Press, 1973)

Rousso, Henry, *The Vichy Syndrome: History and Memory in France Since 1944* (Cambridge, MA: Harvard University Press, 1991)

Rubinstein, W.D., *The Myth of Rescue: Why the Democracies Could Not Have Saved More Jews from the Nazis* (London: Routledge, 1997)

Russell, David, *Looking North: Northern England and the National Imagination* (Manchester: Manchester University Press, 2004)

Samuel, Raphael, *Theatres of Memory* vol.1 *Past and Present in Contemporary Culture* (London: Verso, 1994)

Samuel, Raphael and Paul Thompson (eds), *The Myths We Live By* (London: Routledge, 1990)

Schachne, Lucie, 'It Takes More Than the Generation', *AJR Information*, July 1966

Schama, Simon, *A History of Britain* vol. 3 *The Fate of Empire 1776–2000* (London: BBC Worldwide, 2002)

Schuster, Liza, *The Use and Abuse of Political Asylum in Britain and Germany* (London: Frank Cass, 2003)

Schuster, Liza, 'Common Sense or Racism? The Treatment of Asylum-seekers in Europe', *Patterns of Prejudice* vol. 37 no. 3 (2003)

Scouloudi, Irene (ed.), *Huguenots in Britain and their French Background* (Basingstoke: Macmillan, 1987)

Shacknove, Andrew, 'From Asylum to Containment', *International Journal of Refugee Law* vol. 5 no. 4 (1993)

Sharf, Andrew, *The British Press & Jews under Nazi Rule* (London: Oxford University Press, 1964)

Shatzkes, Pam, *Holocaust and Rescue: Impotent or Indifferent? Anglo-Jewry 1938–1945* (Basingstoke: Palgrave, 2002)

Sheridan, Dorothy, Brian Street and David Bloome, *Writing Ourselves: Mass-Observation and Literacy Practices* (Cresskill: Hampton Press, 2000)

Sherman, A.J., *Island Refuge: Britain and Refugees from the Third Reich 1933–1939* (Berkeley: University of California Press, 1973)

Sieburth, Richard, 'Benjamin the Scrivener', in Gary Smith (ed.), *Benjamin: Philosophy, Aesthetics, History* (Chicago: University of Chicago Press, 1989)

Simpson, John Hope, *The Refugee Problem: Report of a Survey* (London: Oxford University Press, 1939)

Singer, Peter, *Practical Ethics* (Cambridge: Cambridge University Press, 1993)

Skinner, Patricia, 'Confronting the "Medieval" in Medieval History: The Jewish Example', *Past & Present* no. 181 (November 2003)

Snowman, Daniel, *The Hitler Emigres: The Cultural Impact on Britain of Refugees from Nazism* (London: Chatto & Windus, 2002)

Solomos, John, *Race and Racism in Britain* (Basingstoke: Palgrave, 2003)

Stacey, Tom, *Immigration & Enoch Powell* (London: Tom Stacey Ltd, 1970)

Stamp, Gavin, 'A Culture in Crisis', *The Spectator*, 12 October 1985

Stepan, Nancy, *The Idea of Race in Science: Great Britain 1860–1960* (Basingstoke: Macmillan, 1982)

Stern, Fritz, *The Politics of Cultural Despair: A Study in the Rise of the Germanic Ideology* (Berkeley and Los Angeles: University of California Press, 1961)

Stone, Dan, *Responses to Nazism in Britain, 1933–1939* (Berkeley: University of California Press, 1973)

Sweets, John, *Choices in Vichy France: The French Under Nazi Occupation* (New York: Oxford University Press, 1986)

Taylor, A.J.P., *English History 1914–1945* (Oxford: Oxford University Press, 1965)

Tuan, Yi-Fu, *Space and Place: The Perspective of Experience* (London: Arnold, 1977)

Tuitt, Patricia, *False Images: The Law's Construction of the Refugee* (London: Pluto Press, 1996)

Turner, Barbara Carpenter, *A History of Hampshire* (London: Darwen Finlayson, 1963)

Turner, Barry, *… And the Policeman Smiled: 10,000 Children Escape from Nazi Europe* (London: Bloomsbury, 1990)

Turner, Barry, *The Long Horizon: 60 Years of CBF World Jewish Relief* (London: CBF, 1993)

Urry, John, *Consuming Places* (London: Routledge, 1995)

Vergo, Peter (ed.), *The New Museology* (London: Reaktion Books, 1993)

Vernant, Jacques, *The Refugee in the Post-War World* (London: George Allen Unwin, 1953)

Vice, Sue, *Children Writing the Holocaust* (Basingstoke: Palgrave, 2004)

Walker, Greg, *The Private Life of Henry VIII* (London: I.B. Tauris, 2003)

Walker, Greg, 'The Roots of Alexander Korda: Myths of Identity and the International Film', *Patterns of Prejudice* vol. 37 no. 1 (2003)

Walzer, Michael, *Spheres of Justice: A Defence of Pluralism and Equality* (Oxford: Martin Robinson, 1983)

Wasserstein, Bernard, *Vanishing Diaspora: the Jews in Europe since 1945* (London: Hamish Hamilton, 1996)

Wilkins, W.H., *The Alien Invasion* (London: Methuen, 1892)

Wilkomirski, Benjamin, *Fragments* (Basingstoke: Picador, 1996)

Williams, Bill, 'The Anti-Semitism of Tolerance: Middle-Class Manchester and the Jews', in A.J. Kidd and K.W. Roberts (eds), *City, Class and Culture* (Manchester: Manchester University Press, 1985)

Williams, Bill, 'Heritage and Community: The Rescue of Manchester's Jewish Past', in Tony Kushner (ed.), *The Jewish Heritage in British History: Englishness and Jewishness* (London: Frank Cass, 1992)

Winder, Robert, *Bloody Foreigners: The Story of Immigration to Britain* (London: Little, Brown, 2004)

Wood, Marcus, *Blind Memory: Visual Representations of Slavery in England*

and America, 1780–1865 (Manchester: Manchester University Press, 2000)

Worcester, Robert, *British Public Opinion: A Guide to the History and Methodology of Political Opinion Polling* (Oxford: Blackwell, 1991)

Wright, Gordon, 'History as a Moral Science', *American Historical Review* vol. 81 no. 1 (1976)

Wright, Melanie, 'Don't Touch My Holocaust: Responding to *Life is Beautiful*', *Journal of Holocaust Education* vol. 9 no. 1 (Summer 2000)

Wright, Patrick, *A Journey Through the Ruins: The Last Days of London* (London: Radius, 1991)

Wright, Patrick, *On Living in an Old Country: The National Past in Contemporary Britain* (London: Verso, 1985)

Zetter, Roger, 'Refugees and Refugee Studies – A Label and an Agenda', *Journal of Refugee Studies* vol. 1 no. 1 (1988)

Zetter, Roger, 'Refugees and Refugee Studies – A Valedictory Editorial', *Journal of Refugee Studies* vol. 13 no. 4 (2000)

Unpublished

Gemeiner Bihler, Lori, 'German-Jewish Refugees in London and New York, 1935–1945: A Comparative Study of Adaptation and Acculturation' (PhD thesis, University of Sussex, 2004)

Hill, Paula 'Anglo-Jewry and the Refugee Children 1938–1945' (PhD thesis, University of London, 2001)

Kopell, Anne, 'Citizenship None' (Leo Baeck Institute, New York, AP5791, A281n)

O'Brien, R., 'The Establishment of the Jewish Minority in Leeds' (PhD thesis, Bristol University, 1975)

Sharples, Caroline, 'Reconstructing the Past: Refugee Writing on the Kindertransport' (MA dissertation, University of Southampton, 2002)

Stanley, N.S., '"The Extra Dimension": A Study and Assessment of the Methods Employed by Mass-Observation in its First Period, 1937–40' (PhD thesis, Birmingham Polytechnic, 1981)

Index